Sick Little Monkeys

THE UNAUTHORIZED REN & STIMPY STORY

BY THAD KOMOROWSKI

FOREWORD BY BILLY WEST

BearManor Media

Albany, Georgia

Sick Little Monkeys: The Unauthorized Ren & Stimpy Story

Copyright © 2017 Thad Komorowski. All Rights Reserved.

No part of this book may be reproduced in any form or by any means, electronic, mechanical, digital, photocopying or recording, except for the inclusion in a review, without permission in writing from the the publisher.

Published in the USA by
BearManor Media
P.O. Box 71426
Albany, GA 31708
www.BearManorMedia.com

Edited by Frank M. Young and David Gerstein

Cover Drawn by Stephen DeStefano

Cover Painting by Bill Wray

Cover Design by Shawn Wolfe

Softcover Edition
ISBN-10: 1-62933-182-1
ISBN-13: 978-1-62933-182-9

Printed in the United States of America

To Mom: Stimpy is a cat.

To Dad: No, I still don't know who this show is aimed at.

*And to sweet Grandma:
See what buying me all of those Looney Tunes and Tom & Jerry videos has caused?*

Foreword

Wow!

The Ren and Stimpy Show.

Back then I lived in the ass-end of Chinatown in New York City, and my wife and I would take a Sunday morning walk. There was a bar restaurant called Telephone and it was mobbed inside all the way out to the street.

We squeezed into the place to find out it was a *Ren & Stimpy*-watching party (lots of Bloody Marys)! This show was three weeks old and it was already a cultural phenomenon.

It evoked such feelings in the audience and the animation industry! It has been the template for voice performances, artistry, and style for animated shows to this day.

Sick Little Monkeys: The Unauthorized Ren & Stimpy Story is beautifully written and a pretty accurate behind-the-scenes story about the manic ups and downs of one of the greatest cartoons ever made.

I'm glad Thad wrote it, because now you can figure out who the good guys were and who the bad guys were.

Joy....

—*Billy West*

Preface to the Revised Edition

It *is* a little ironic that a book about the history of *Ren & Stimpy* demands eternal refinement from its author.

I plead you loyal readers not to be too upset with me. The first edition of *Sick Little Monkeys* was a kind of unpolished final draft, despite a dedicated staff of proofreaders working on it. Typos, clumsy grammar, a few outright factual errors, and some awkward typesetting prevent me from looking at that edition with pride today. This is still my first book, and it has been a profound education in what to do and what not to do in the world of publishing.

Maybe my experience parallels the show I have written about. *Ren & Stimpy* was rather ropey but engaging in its first few episodes, and by the second season it really was *the* cartoon we were all searching for.

The generous and positive reception to *Sick Little Monkeys* has been gratifying for not one serious negative review exists. Hearing from friends at Cartoon Network and DreamWorks that copies of the book have been passed between offices—the subject of excited gossip—was certainly flattering. But nothing beats accolades from those you have written about.

Shortly after the book's February 2013 release, animation writer Paul Dini wrote to me to say how much he enjoyed it. "Though I never worked on *Ren & Stimpy*, I knew just about all the key players and it was amazing how vividly you captured the incidents and personalities of that time." Paul had no reason to butter me up—he is only quoted a handful of times in the book—and his message pinpointed my aim: to present *Ren & Stimpy*'s cast of characters as real people.

But Paul's kind words were nothing compared to a face-to-face meeting in September 2013 with Billy West, backstage at the 92nd Street Y in New York. There he relayed a message from himself and the underrated writer and cartoonist Jim Gomez: "Your writing blew everyone away."

My meeting with West took place at a launch party for Mathew Klickstein's book, *Slimed! An Oral History of Nickelodeon's Golden Age*, a book that has received far more attention—if not praise—than my own. Klickstein touched briefly upon the *Ren & Stimpy* history, and did so with the blessing of John Kricfalusi and others whom I did not interview. It was further vindication for me that the history as relayed with their input—by Klickstein—did not contradict the version relayed without it by myself. Aside from a few juicy quotes, Klickstein's version reads as the same saga of artistic vanity, corporate self-satisfaction, and heroic fantasy that I had to untangle in my own book.

I am rather disappointed that Kricfalusi himself has not directly responded to *Sick Little Monkeys*. I did not clarify exactly why Kricfalusi was uninvolved in the first edition, so I will take the opportunity to share the evidence that he had full knowledge of my project. As per this e-mail reprinted below:

> **From** spumko@aol.com   Wed Sep 30 23:01:59 2009
> **To:** thadkomorowski@yahoo.com
> **Subject:** you need to get help
>
> It's not healthy for you to be so obsessed over someone you have never even met. Or to harass girls who have never done anything to you. You're gonna end up in a mental hospital or worse if you don't see a shrink.
>
> All your crazy deeds are on record and are adding up. I'm sure people like Bob are not going to like it when they find out you are using them to stir up your own trouble.[1]

When I received that dark threat (carbon-copied to his worthless attorney), I knew then that I would not make any further attempts to contact John Kricfalusi—and that my book would suffer considerably. I came to learn that he actively told people to not talk to me, further casting aspersions on my sanity. What a pity. I would have loved to have spoken with all of those people and include their fresh voices, even Kricfalusi's. (And all these years later, I still do not know what the hell this "harass girls" business is about. I'd *like* some girls to harass, but…)

This is not a perfect book, but anyone buying it for a second time should be rewarded. Therefore, in this new edition: illustrations are anything but sparse, information in the episode guide has been expanded, elaboration added where it was needed, and fresh anecdotes

---

1   The "Bob" referenced is the animator Bob Jaques, ex-bosom buddy of Kricfalusi.

are woven into the existing narrative. The rollercoaster ride has been repaired and is just as riveting and cautionary as ever.

You have been warned.

Thad Komorowski
New York
July 2016

Preface to the Original Edition

Why devote so much time and energy to writing a book about *The Ren & Stimpy Show*? I am sometimes kept awake at night pondering that very question. The short answer is that dead men made almost all of the cartoons I like best. There are still books waiting to be written about those cartoon makers and studios, and I may possibly get to them someday. But if one is going to expend a gargantuan amount of time writing about something, perhaps it is wisest to write about one's own time first.

I was part of the generation that grew up on the original Nickelodeon broadcasts of *Ren & Stimpy*. Sadly, I did not recognize its exceeding brilliance in those days. I was actually far more critical as a child than I am now; if it was anything but *Looney Tunes*, it was garbage. As I began my serious animation studies in my early teens, however, I realized—upon revisiting *Ren & Stimpy*—that it was an anomaly: the only television cartoon I could actually take seriously. Elitist though it may be to say so, no other television show—animated or otherwise—combined everything I loved about the arts and sciences as did *Ren & Stimpy*. I had to know everything possible about this strange creature, and immediately discovered that the backstory was just as exciting and insane as the show itself. Unfortunately, most of the existing histories of the show, online or in print, were conspicuously incomplete, biased, and littered with misinformation. "You know," I thought, "maybe someone should write a book about this show."

It was around then that I came into contact with Bob Jaques. In his spare time, when he is not busy being one of the world's greatest living animators, Bob is an animation historian and expert on all things Popeye. After hearing some of his absolutely bonkers stories about working on *Ren & Stimpy*—most of which have remained untold until this book—he suggested that I harvest my youthful energy into researching the show and writing about it. That pretty much clinched it. I had to be the first one to seriously write about this show the *right* way. Bob's constant assistance, knowledge, and moral support throughout this project were essential to its completion. I can never thank him enough.

Sound knowledge of *Ren & Stimpy* and the art and history of the animation industry is not a prerequisite to reading this tale, although it would be highly advisable not to pick up this book as a complete novice. I have tried to do everything in my power to make this as accurate, entertaining, and readable a book as possible. Time will tell if I was successful. Regardless, in spite of its many imperfections, *Sick Little Monkeys* aims to be the "go-to" book for anyone looking for

Preface to the Original Edition

Ren & Stimpy information. Going by my own tremulous experience assembling it, it will probably remain the only book on the subject.

Before you go any further, you should know upfront that animation legend John Kricfalusi—beyond being the central character in this story—had nothing to do with the making of this book. I am afraid I have only myself to blame, for he and I waged Internet battles typical of many that he has had with former friends, fans, and colleagues. He called me a stupid kid for disagreeing with him. I called him an asshole. Wash, rinse, (hwarf?) repeat. Smart move, eh? The lesson learned is maturity—a lesson I have had the privilege of learning again and again. Then again, if maturity and handling things the "right" way were guiding principles in the lives of the artists discussed in this book, *Ren & Stimpy* would not exist.

Fortunately, John K. has been so generous with making his words and knowledge public that it became unnecessary to get his voice firsthand; getting others' recollections was far more important, simply because no one else had taken the trouble to do so. As reception to this book will undoubtedly prove, memory can be fleeting and should be taken with a grain of salt.

Thankfully, through thorough research, I was able to effectively utilize the information within my dozens of interviews. Not only was there an overwhelming pattern to the interviewees' answers, there was steady corroboration that told a clear story. Combined with a sizable library of earlier interviews by other writers, press clippings, and studio documentation, what you are reading is a first in cartoon history: a colorful, diverse, and highly accurate account of one of the most fascinating stories in 20th century animation.

Thad Komorowski
Niagara Falls
August 2012

Ackowledgments

Frank Young is largely responsible for this book's existence. I had been putting off actually getting down to writing this book for ages; interviews were being conducted and new documentation was coming in all of the time, but I stupidly chose to focus on completing college instead. It was only when I enlisted Frank as an editor that the writing process sped up considerably. His appreciation of all the art forms and sound mastery of the written word made him the ideal collaborator.

David Gerstein, one of the most important animation historians and Disney comic book editors, took the original book and polished the text for the revised edition. Simply as a favor, I might add. Given his passionate thoroughness and accuracy, I can say without reservation that if David's name is not in the acknowledgements of a book on American animation that you probably should not bother reading the book.

Over the years that I researched and wrote this book, more than sixty people consented to interviews regarding their involvement with the shows and films I have written about. Many later recanted their commitment to an interview. Others simply stopped responding once they saw—from my questions—that this book was not going to be light reading.

I regret that not every person listed here has been equally represented in the book. Some are not even quoted at all. If they have been omitted in the text, it is due to my own narrative and journalistic shortcomings, not because of anything they had to say. Regardless, each of the following people has my gratitude for allowing me to conduct an interview with them—either through e-mail, over the phone, or in person—and for contributing to my understanding of this very critical time in animation history.

Nathan Affolter, Kelly Armstrong, Howard Baker, Craig Bartlett, Jerry Beck, Ed Bell, Elinor Blake, Wil Branca, Kent Butterworth, Bob Camp, Cheryl Chase, Vanessa Coffey, Sherm Cohen, Mark Colangelo, Robertryan Cory, Nick Cross, Chris Danzo, Stephen DeStefano, Paul Dini, Arthur Filloy.

Colin Giles, Jim Gomez, Steven Gordon, Mary Harrington, Tom Hay, Ron Hughart, Bob Jaques, Dan Jeup, Michael Kerr, Mike Kim, Tom Klein, David Koenigsberg, Mitchell Kriegman, Doug Lawrence, Steve Loter, the late Carl Macek, Scott Mansz, Jamie Mason, Will McRobb, Brian Mendelsohn, Helder Mendonca, Bob Miller.

Joe Orrantia, Shawn Patterson, David Pietila, Chris Reccardi, Jordan Reichek, Chris Ross, Chris Sauve, Don Shank, Linda Simensky, Libby Simon, Roy Allen Smith, Greg Stainton, Steve Stefanelli, Byron Vaughns, John Vincent, Teale Wang, Billy West, Scott Wills, Bill Wray, and Ron Zorman.

Acknowledgments

In addition, Jim Ballantine, Charlie Bean, Ken Davis, the late John Dorman, Greg Duffell, Reg Hartt, Mark Kausler, Mike Kazaleh, Warren Leonhardt, Tom Minton, Jamie Oliff, Marc Perry, Richard Pursel, Katie Rice, Jim Smith, and Carey Yost all provided helpful information through correspondence.

Interviews and recollections, of course, cannot provide a completely accurate account of what happened, but studio documentation can sure help. I profusely thank Jim Ballantine, Jerry Beck, Chris Danzo, Norman Hathaway, Bob Jaques, Mark Kausler, and David Koenigsberg for their generosity in sharing various pieces of archival paraphernalia. Daniel Persons graciously allowed me to extensively quote his pieces on the show in *Cinefantastique*; they are the only texts, prior to this book, that gave a sense of what really happened. Conversations with Mathew Klickstein, and his book *Slimed! An Oral History of Nickelodeon's Golden Age*, were also exceptionally useful.

One cannot write about films properly without actually seeing them. Assembling a full collection of a television show barely twenty years old in its complete, undamaged form is a harrowing feat if the rightsholders—when issuing the shows to home video—choose to not do them justice. Greg Method and Mike Russo deserve accolades for their fandom, which compelled them to preserve every single original airing of *Ren & Stimpy* and then some. Should a legitimate box set of the show ever surface, we owe it to their diligence to know what to look for in it—and what to whine about.

Michael Barrier, Jerry Beck, Rodney Bowcock, Chris Boyle, Charles Brubaker, Craig Dauterive, Kurtis Findlay, David Gerstein, Guillermo Gomez, Bob Jaques, Charlie Judkins, and Jack Theakston read all or parts of the manuscript and offered many helpful suggestions. Familial support may seem obligatory, but I owe my parents, Thad and Victoria Komorowski, a tremendous debt of thanks, as well as my sister, Genna Komorowski, and my grandmother, the late Genevieve

Komorowski. All proved eternally supportive of my egregious lifestyle as an "animation historian."

I would also like to thank the following people for their support and encouragement throughout this project. However small they feel it was, I appreciate all they have done for me: Barbara Audet, Christian Bajusz, Adam Blake, David Gemmill, Samantha Glasser, Allen Jankowics, Ryan Khatam, Owen Kline, Mark Mayerson, Trevour Meyer, Kylie Pierce, Shaun Poust, Brian Rank, Emilie Ross, Michael J. Ruocco, Steve Stanchfield, Tommy Stathes, Lea Tsamardinos, and Ryan Undercoffer.

Finally, I give thanks to Ben Ohmart, who had the foresight to contractually commit me to writing this book—and to publish it.

Introduction
Animated Reality

Which art form became the most corrupted in the second half of 20th-century America? This topic could be heatedly debated. The case for animation being the most violated is perhaps strongest.

Passionate, meaningful cultural movements have come in and out of play in music and live-action film for centuries. Yet animation only receives such attention in rare spurts, otherwise falling into wastelands that span decades. While the independent animation scene worldwide will always be stimulating and vivacious, those films are not what the masses perceive as "animation," any more than independent live-action films are recognized as "movies." It was commercial theatrical and television animation's highly visible decline—into literal hell—over a quarter-century that damaged the art form's reputation beyond repair.

There are many factors to consider when analyzing how this happened. The most obvious and widely professed explanations lay outside the creators' control. Cited as the beginning of the end was the Supreme Court case *United States v. Paramount Pictures* (334 US 131), also known as the *Hollywood Antitrust Case of 1948*. The Court decided that the movie studios held a monopoly over film distribution with the practice of block-booking. This system distributed cartoons as part of a theatrical program package; box-office returns were divided over the entire package, thus helping to subsidize cartoon production.

In the presence of block-booking, the art of animation largely flourished. The medium rose to a peak (any arbitrary year in the latter half of the 1940s) and was able to linger there for a time. The subjective components that contributed to the kind of character animation at which the Disney, Warner Bros., and MGM cartoons excelled are too numerous to list here. What remains incontrovertible is that the money was actually available to *allow* the mid-century animation studios to thrive the way they did.

With the demise of block-booking, however, shorts no longer shared the wealth of the features. The animation studios' respective distributors were not willing to throw their own money at the productions. Within a few years, what was known as the Golden Age of animation came to an end. Most animation studios had survived on a mere technicality: each major distributor only had animated cartoons because everyone else had them. With theaters unwilling to pick up the dime, budgets dwindled and doors closed.

Still-breathing operations had to cut corners. Walter Lantz was not a producer recognized for artistic elegance, and his cartoons were among the first to exemplify animation stripped to its barest essentials when he reopened—after a brief shutdown—in 1950. The later Lantz cartoons' stiff movement, fewer drawings, and increasing number of held poses made for a stark contrast to the near-Disney quality that the studio had been turning out as late as 1948. As it did at Lantz, this frugality infected most of the Hollywood and New York studios in the early 1950s (with the exception of Paul Terry's studio, whose cartoons were instantly retrograde as soon as they were made). Even Walt Disney knew the fun was over and soon set the tide for the industry in another way, just as he had throughout the medium's history: he was the first major animation player to stop regularly producing shorts.

Bill Hanna and Joe Barbera, directors and producers of the MGM *Tom & Jerry* series, lovingly embraced the increasingly rigid production mentality more than any of their peers. In their final MGM cartoons of 1958, the animation is so deliberately wooden and mechanical that it is barely any different from what the duo would produce for television, that other often cited nail in the coffin for animation's artistic livelihood. Pre-production for their first independent television series, *Ruff & Reddy*, began while their staff was still on the MGM payroll. Their step forward into the television arena was not just a natural fit—it was craftily planned.

The budget and time restrictions of television are self-evident. The need for material on a weekly basis makes production values slim, and causes story material to dwindle quickly. Live-action television at least had the benefit of experience; the half-hour, low-budget comedy had long been perfected by theatrical two-reelers, making the transition to the television sitcom format more natural.

Animation could not make that leap. Its lush movement was replaced by "limited animation," the idea of using fewer drawings and getting the acting and action across with strong poses. Certain animation directors had used this technique for decades in theatrical shorts; the effect was bastardized after the leap to television. Single animators were required to animate not just entire six-minute cartoon shorts, but full half-hours on a regular basis. The animation could no longer carry the pictures. Strong voices, design, and writing would now carry the heaviest workload.

Most of the early television cartoons produced under these limitations have not aged well. They have stood the test of time only because they retain a charm that evokes nostalgia. In actuality, series like Hanna-Barbera's *Yogi Bear* and *The Flintstones* are glacially sluggish, tepidly written, and almost entirely dependent on the charismatic voice work of Daws Butler. The work of Mel Blanc, the Warner Bros. cartoon voice legend and Butler's theatrical equal, was getting tired by the time television arrived, yet that was after some twenty years of voicing the same characters. In the harsher and fast-paced television climate, Butler ran out of steam in just five years.

The Hanna-Barbera model became the standard for all animation produced in this period. Bob Clampett—a far superior, more individualistic director than Hanna and Barbera had ever been in the theatrical era—may have gotten "fuller" animation out of his crew on *Beany & Cecil*, but the lack of substance is identical. Jay Ward's *Rocky and His Friends* and *Dudley Do-Right*, on the other hand, had practically zero animation or art direction and compensated for that shortcoming with exceptionally strong comedic writing.

Television would eventually introduce the practice of outsourcing animation production to other countries in order to exploit cheap labor. As the 1970s arrived, more and more work was sent overseas. It was not enough to farm out the actual animation. Soon even the layouts (the drawings that plan and stage a scene, giving cues to the animators) and backgrounds were being done outside of North America. The process cynically industrialized the animation medium in a way that could never be applied to music or live-action film. It reduced animation's most important aspects to mere paper pushing.

Yet outsourcing ultimately had little true impact on the artistic merit of television animation of the time. Lou Scheimer, whose Filmation studio emerged in 1963, took pride in the fact that he kept all of the work stateside. In reality, anything produced at Filmation ended up looking as good or as bad as the outsourced shows from other studios.

By the late '60s and early '70s, when censorship codes and executive interference truly began to interfere with the cartoons' creative content, artlessness in television animation was a steady practice. When Peggy Charren began making noise with her misguided Action for Children's Television, the network and studio heads welcomed further restrictions with open arms.

What is most interesting is not that the television animation system was clearly reflected in contemporary theatrical shorts (so much so that theatrical Warner, Lantz, and Paramount shorts could be broadcast on the small screen mere months after their theatrical debuts, and blend in seamlessly with made-for-television work), but that the sins of the television animation system had pre-television origins.

There will always be debate over the theatrical cartoons' individual subjective merit. Indeed, some classic studios have filmographies as crass as the worst television product. Yet the theatrical cartoon, like all media of the period, lacked permanence.

There was no expectation that theatrical cartoons would be seen beyond their original run in theaters (save a possible reissue seven years later). Thus, lapses in creativity are understandable. On the other hand, makers of television cartoons had a sense of permanence from day one. They knew their work would be rerun and syndicated. Their inventive failings are also understandable due to the insatiable demand of television, but still less forgivable. Television cartoon makers had the foresight that the theatrical animators did not.

Much more controversial is the theatrical animation artist's role in establishing the television formula. Before Hanna and Barbera's experiments with cutting corners in their final MGM cartoons, there was United Productions of America. UPA, as it was better known, was founded on the basis of going against the grain—and out of their way—to make cartoons that did not fall into the funny animal genre so dominant in the 1940s. The UPA brain trust consisted of artists who were more typically designers than animators. All other elements of their films became subservient to design.

There is great validity to the design-first method, as exemplified by UPA's best work: the films made during John Hubley's reign as supervising producer and director at the studio, a period when the virtues of incorporating modern art into animation were plainest. Once Hubley was ousted, however, for tenuous ties to the Communist Party at the height of the Red Scare, UPA failed—the rest of its top brass were nowhere near as visionary as he. These artists were not interested in the cinematic potentials of design-driven character animation. There is no character animation in the majority of their films, only design. The drawing got cruder; the stories became blandly childish; and the design was there for design's sake. UPA cartoons became, essentially, a prototype for standard television animation.

UPA's lasting influence went beyond forcing the other studios to modernize the look of their pictures to garner critical reception. At the time that the major theatrical studios adopted limited animation techniques, the work was still in the hands of people classically trained in knowing the role every drawing played once it left their desks. By contrast, UPA's system—in which the designer rules all, regardless of training—undermined the animator's role. This made television's overseas production system possible, in which the foreign studio (where the animation is done) is compliant to the demands of the domestic studio (where pre-production is done). Layouts began to be drawn less by animators than by merely proficient draftsmen, for there was no longer any real *animation* to be done in the Hollywood studios; the concept of general animation knowledge became largely extinct. It is a disturbing case in which artistic innovation became the germ for corruption.

Suffice to say, by the 1980s, it was highly improbable that an artistic voice could be heard from within the bowels of the barbaric television cartoon. Modern animation "auteurs" had risen and fallen from power through the years (all stories worthy of their own books), though their works were confined to the theatrical animated feature. Ironically, or maybe appropriately, it was a theatrical animation "auteur" who made it feasible for a TV animation "auteur" to even exist.

Chapter 1
Ralph's Benefit Plan

In the dark ages of animation's history, Ralph Bakshi was one of a handful of directors to emerge with something to say. But he often had a great deal of trouble saying it. Bakshi was one who viewed restrictions as opportunities. When he was directing shorts at Terrytoons and Paramount in the 1960s, he embraced and exploited financial and technical limitations for artistic gain. In Bakshi's 1967 short *Marvin Digs*—one of the final Paramount cartoon releases—the cheapened movement enhances the gruff charm of its artwork and story about a literal ball-of-hair hippie and his braggart father. Bakshi's 1960s theatrical shorts, more than any other shorts at the time, suggested a potential for highly personal and consistent achievements in animation.

Bakshi did graduate to highly personal animated features in the 1970s, yet the needed consistency never really came. The patchwork of Bakshi's earliest features ideally suits their subject matter. The chaos of *Fritz the Cat* and, especially, *Heavy Traffic* helps Bakshi bring a gritty earnestness to the screen in a way unequalled in animation before or since. Bakshi's contemporaries, particularly Disney, went out of their way to ignore what was going on in the world; by contrast, Bakshi pulled no punches in presenting the mire and filth of Vietnam-era America. Any perceived crudeness in the drawing and animation was necessary. Had *Heavy Traffic* been drawn and directed in the "accepted" pseudo-Disney feature animation style, the results would have been insincere, working against Bakshi's goal. "I want people to believe my characters are real, and it's hard to believe they're real if they start walking down the street singing," he said.[1]

An overwhelmingly compelling self-promoter, Bakshi was able to get financial backing and distribution for ten years in spite (or because) of his eccentricities, which included randomly firing and rehiring people and locking employees out of his building. Each successive film after *Coonskin*—Bakshi's last feature of any merit—illustrated a further descent into a kind of artistic chaos. Whereas the earlier work exhibited an embraceable unevenness, the intentions behind Bakshi's later work began to make sense to no one but himself.

Many up-and-coming animators mentored under Bakshi during this period; the most remembered and cited protégé, in more ways than one, was John Kricfalusi. Kricfalusi grew up in Ontario, Canada, moving to Hollywood months after being expelled from Sheridan College's animation program. At school, he made a name for himself as something of an anarchist "more concerned with partying and stuff" than in completing assignments.[2] "He had been kicked out, as his teachers thought he had no talent and told him he was a bad influence," film scholar Reg Hartt recalled.[3]

It was not a great loss, by any account. "No animation skills do you learn in animation school," Kricfalusi said.[4] His fellow classmates largely agreed. Artist Jim Gomez said he still had not learned how to do a "fargin' walk cycle" before he dropped out to join Kricfalusi and his girlfriend and fellow animator Lynne Naylor in Hollywood.[5]

The television animation business was in wretched shape when Kricfalusi reached Hollywood in 1979. The industry-wide practice of gross inbreeding made the product of various studios into indistinguishable junk. New shows were only marketable to the networks if they were based on (or ripped off from) existing properties or had strong toy-selling potential. Most efficiently, studios settled on producing shows actually based on toys.

The departmentalization of television animation production had reached new lows by the 1980s. A cartoon's directorial duties were divided among six or seven people who would often never speak to each other. Artists were removed from the writing process, while hired-gun scriptwriters were more than happy to fulfill the networks' demands for banality.

Most horrifying of all was not the fresh young talent being underutilized, but the old. Veterans of the Warner, MGM, Disney, and Paramount studios—well past retirement age—toiled away in droves in the various television factories. The studios helped the veterans make a living in their twilight years, but their vitality was completely burned out. Tex Avery died while making *Kwicky Koala*, an insipid derivation of his earlier Droopy character, at Hanna-Barbera. If one of American animation's greatest, most important directors was allowed to meet such a gruesome end in the modern television system, it did not bode well for anyone else.

"When I first came down, I was naïve," Kricfalusi told Harry McCracken. "I thought, 'Well, they're going to welcome me with open arms, because there's nobody with any talent down there.' And it turns out there's tons of people with talent; it's the system that's all screwed up."[6] Fans will see the names of countless modern day animation superstars in the credits of Filmation and Hanna-Barbera shows. It would be foolish to try and find any signs of their individuality; a vision as singular as John K.'s, naturally, could not exist in this era of television animation.

In the early 1980s, however, John K.'s singular vision was still in gestation. Bill Wray termed John K.'s work of the period as "a retarded Basil Wolverton meets Hanna-Barbera, but [with] something cool

From *Ted Bakes One* (1981), the first cartoon directed by John Kricfalusi (with Bill Wray). Courtesy of Norman Hathaway.

about it."[7] Kricfalusi made an animated television bumper with Wray, as well as Naylor and Gomez, for the cable network Channel Zero in 1981. Titled *Ted Bakes One*, it revolved around a chicken trying to expel an egg from his anus. It was little more than the student film Kricfalusi might have made had he completed his education at Sheridan; the lack of animation experience by the crew was overwhelmingly obvious.

John K. spent his early professional career fighting for individuality. In doing so, he built a rapport with a subset of animation people also dismayed by the hollow kiddie television ghetto of the 1980s. Animator Bob Jaques, who was at Sheridan with Kricfalusi (and expelled shortly after him), remembered that John K.'s rebellious nature attracted people as much as his talent. "He would say things to get people fired up and excited. 'We're gonna be animation rock stars, we're gonna make Clampett look like a piker!'"[8]

The closest thing to a directorial voice Kricfalusi could find in the television studios was a gig supervising layouts in Taiwan for a 1985 revival of Hanna-Barbera's *The Jetsons*. There he employed the earliest version of his character layout theory. He strove to make the acting and actions as precise as possible in the pre-production stage while also instilling life into the work. Ergo, something special might actually survive in the overseas pipeline. "Animation needed to become lively again, and I didn't care where it would happen, as long as someone was doing it," he once wrote.[9]

Whereas the original *Jetsons* in 1962 had merely been insufferable, the new version completely annihilated any sheen that the characters or concept may have had. The show's abominable quality had nothing to do with the work of Kricfalusi, nor that of Lynne Naylor and David Feiss, who worked with him in Taiwan. The Hanna-Barbera system was designed to produce garbage. No noble effort could change that. If someone wanted to do important work, it would have to be done outside that system.

Lynne Naylor, when she was working with John K. in Taiwan on Hanna-Barbera's *The Jetsons* at Cuckoo's Nest, 1985. Courtesy of Norman Hathaway.

John K.'s artistic aims often sabotaged his chances of being rehired at the cartoon factories. During *The Jetsons*, he infuriated upper management by redrawing already-finished scenes. At other studios, he just stopped showing up for work altogether. He dreamed of having his own studio and producing cartoons to his taste, a desire that no existing outfit could satisfy. Kricfalusi's crusade against the Hollywood television shops resulted in the formation of Popular Animation, a three-way partnership with fellow Filmation veterans Tom Minton and Jeff Johns. Despite its name, the new enterprise folded almost as soon as it opened. Never one to be disillusioned, Kricfalusi spent countless hours assembling presentation art and series proposals. His forte was the creation of characters radically different from the conventional 1980s stereotypes. John K. himself doubted that anyone would actually give him money to bring them to life.

When asked why he did not pursue the independent route and bypass the suits altogether, John K. replied that he saw himself as a working man with schedules to make cartoons. Alone and with others' help (particularly that of Lynne Naylor), he hoped to find a large-bankrolled investor who might see the self-professed genius in his art.

§

John K.'s association with Ralph Bakshi goes back further than most histories recount. Historian Jerry Beck recalled that Kricfalusi looked to seriously work with the heavyweight champion of adult animation almost as soon as he arrived in Hollywood. "He'd write these long letters [to me] and say, 'Can you hook me up with Ralph Bakshi?'"[10]

Bakshi said he hired Kricfalusi and others during the production of his feature film *Fire and Ice* in 1982, though they began working for him as early as 1981. "John and Tom Minton walk into my studio as young kids and say they want me to do shorts," Bakshi said to Jason Anders. "I gave them a room in the back to do storyboards to show me what they're talking about. So they started to draw storyboards and I just said, 'I don't know what I'm going to do with these boards, but go ahead and make me laugh.'"[11]

Some of the projects Kricfalusi—but not necessarily Minton—were involved with had titles like *Spectre of the Bugger Boys*, *A Big Negro for the Little Lady*, and *Wayne Newton: Naked and Slippery*. A later script for a proposed live-action feature was entitled *The Zany Chinaman*. Suffice to say, the only way such ideas could have been created on the clock in the 1980s animation scene was if the letterhead read "Bakshi Productions, Inc."[12]

None of John K.'s early ideas made it past the development stage, but a kinship developed between Bakshi and Kricfalusi. The mentor always promised his pupil: "We'll be partners—fifty-fifty!" In time, Kricfalusi began to see Bakshi as "the most important figure in my career"[13] and as a representative of all good things that had been beaten out of the business—in short, a man's man.

After *Fire and Ice* tanked in 1983, Bakshi briefly retired from animation and returned to New York to pursue an ill-fated live-action career. In 1986, Bakshi landed a gig doing a music video for the Rolling Stones' song *The Harlem Shuffle*. The idea for the project was to have Bakshi direct the live-action portion in New York while a handpicked crew did animation for the video in Los Angeles. John K. was hired as the director of the animated scenes; he in turn enlisted Bob Jaques as the animation director. Lynne Naylor was heavily involved with both design and key animation. Others along for the ride included animator Pat Ventura, background artist Vicky Jenson, and layout artist Jim Smith.

The Harlem Shuffle is the earliest filmed instance of something recognizable as the work of John Kricfalusi and his cohorts. Described accurately as "Warner Bros. meets Hanna-Barbera meets acid,"[14] its character design and layout is mostly cribbed from Bob Clampett's two black caricature-centric shorts, *Coal Black and De Sebben Dwarfs* and *Tin Pan Alley Cats* (both 1943). The story of an animated cat pursuing a buxom girl juxtaposes awkwardly with Bakshi's footage of the band. It was different, though, with exceptional hints of brilliance in John K.'s design and Lynne Naylor's animation of the girl. The first true collaboration between a core group of artists unsullied by a joyless, assembly-line industry, *The Harlem Shuffle* suggested the same questions as had Bakshi's own earliest work: what could these people do under fewer constraints?

Attached to a top *Billboard* single, the music video was a hit. It rekindled Bakshi's interest in animation and his desire to work further with that group of young talent. He and producer Tom Klein

Scenes from *The Harlem Shuffle*, the Rolling Stones music video directed by Ralph Bakshi and John K. Courtesy of Bob Jaques. © CBS.

moved to Los Angeles after scoring a development deal with Tri-Star Pictures for *Bobby's Girl*, an animated feature in the vein of the nostalgic sex comedy formula so popular in the 1980s. Working with a development team consisting of Kricfalusi, Naylor, Smith, and others, Bakshi found himself consistently at odds with Tri-Star over the vision for the project.

"It wasn't really heavy, adult-oriented, but it wasn't for young kids," Klein said of the movie. "And the studio told us, rather than develop the artwork [and] storyboard more, they [wanted us to focus] on the screenplay." By fall 1986, *Bobby's Girl* had been rewritten numerous times, and there was the strong likelihood that Tri-Star would bring in outside writers. The project was left to die once the initial money ran out.[15]

During and after the *Bobby's Girl* debacle, Bakshi worked with his team to pitch other shows at various television networks. The team clung to the notion that getting a break or two would result in a studio that produced nothing but great animation, year-round. In early spring 1987, Bakshi, partnered with John Hyde (an executive producer on *Fire and Ice*), made the rounds unsuccessfully pitching original series concepts to the major networks.

As John K. tells it, by the time Bakshi met CBS's Judy Price, his legendary volatility could no longer be contained. In his desperation, he pulled the Terrytoon favorite Mighty Mouse out of his memory bank and pitched it to Price as a series. Somebody drew a pose or two of the character to show as a presentation. Price loved it and closed the deal. Immediately after, Bakshi got on the phone with Hyde and said, "Find out who the fuck owns Mighty Mouse—I just sold it to CBS." (In reality, a Mighty Mouse revival *was* one of the shows Bakshi had planned to pitch *because* he knew CBS and Viacom owned the character.)

Bakshi bestowed upon John K. the esteemed title of supervising

Ralph's Benefit Plan

The mentor and the mentee: Ralph Bakshi and John Kricfalusi.
Courtesy of Norman Hathaway.

director on the show, giving him an authority he never had in the industry before. Kricfalusi, in turn, "raided the studios" for other artists who hated the '80s animation climate and "couldn't wait to work on a cartoon that might be fun."[16] The staff at Bakshi's was a multifaceted mixture of folks: Kricfalusi's old cohorts from Canada, other co-workers from various studios, youngsters on break from CalArts, and "a few of [Bakshi's] elder folk that nobody worked around with."[17]

Mighty Mouse: The New Adventures (originally *The Extraordinary Adventures of Mighty Mouse*) was the first show in years where artists and creative types were involved in every step of the process. Character layout was done completely in-house; scripts avoided hackneyed verbiage. The Bakshi studio also reinstated the old unit system, wherein a single director was involved with nearly aspect of the production. The show ultimately achieved what no other revival did—it further developed the source material. Unlike the attempted reboots of the Warner characters ("Which they try to do forever and fail always, they're just sacrilege," commented Jim Gomez[18]), *Mighty Mouse: The New Adventures* had no classic reputation to live up to. Mighty Mouse was given a backstory and "secret" identity, his original nonentity personality at Terrytoons now a thing of the past. Mundane, creaky melodrama and violence were replaced with a self-awareness foreign to the original article.

Some old-time clichés stuck around with a twist. In the 1940s, a Mighty Mouse cartoon could reach its climax before Mighty belatedly showed up to "save the day." Bakshi's crew carried on that tradition—but did so to mock the formula and ruffle feathers at the network. To meet CBS' request to see more of the titular character, Bakshi would playfully suggest that his artists "have him stop a train." It was comedy writing worthy of Jay Ward, a comparison made by many that always bothered John K. "It's just a different style of humor," he said. "It's a compliment to me, though, because what they really mean is it's one of the few funny TV shows."[19]

The *Mighty Mouse* scripts were mostly written by CalArts recruits like Jim Reardon, Rich Moore, and Andrew Stanton, with seasoned veteran Tom Minton as the head visionary. Minton was, *Mighty Mouse* producer Tom Klein described, "a writer who really got the idea you can write a script while focusing on the animation content of the short."[20] Minton's scripts were blueprints that conveyed plenty of the cartoon's content while still allowing for the artists' input. This mindset worked against the network's edict that the final picture must reflect the writer's script verbatim, successfully eradicating the stumbling block that Minton and other writers had encountered at Filmation and elsewhere.

Kricfalusi in particular constantly tried to improve the scripts, asking for frequent changes. "This wasn't really a bad thing, because some of the stories really needed the extra steps of refinement and thought," storyboard artist Byron Vaughns said. "Frankly, John's idea of heaven was making drastic changes in the layout phase."[21] Adherence to character layout never played as vital a role in theatrical animation as it did in television. Its purpose was to serve as a guide from which animators could draw inspiration, and to ensure that the director's intentions came through. Layouts were not the strict mandates they became when this process was abused in later television animation. Because animation was too expensive to do in-house, layout was considered the next best way to make the characters come alive on screen. As Kricfalusi said: "The cartoons had no chance of working without [layouts]."[22]

The high level of quality and expectations were critical factors in the grueling conditions at the Bakshi-Hyde studio. Bakshi sold *Mighty Mouse* to CBS in April 1987 and episodes needed to be on the air in September. A $250,000 per episode budget was locked with no chance of getting additional money. Housed in a North Hollywood building, employees found sixteen-hour workdays to be the norm in the first month of the production. Each layout artist's quota was six scenes per day—approximately sixty workable drawings. "It's going to be very tough around here for awhile," Bakshi wrote in a memorandum to his employees. "Then it's going to get to be a lot of fun."[23]

Dealing with the man himself could be a pleasure or drawback, depending on the person speaking. Director Kent Butterworth, lovingly described as "Ralph's bitch" by a few contemporaries, described daily interaction with Bakshi as "the Genius-Asshole Rollercoaster.

One minute you're a genius, the next thing you're hopeless!"[24] There was never a sense of certainty as to what Bakshi wanted as a hands-on producer. "What he believes in changes from minute to minute, and you can see that in all his pictures," Kricfalusi said shortly after the first season wrapped.[25] Indeed, it would be odd if screaming did not emanate from wherever Bakshi was in the studio. Sometimes he would call four-hour meetings to explain why it was important to meet deadlines.

Nevertheless, the pros of working at Bakshi's far outweighed the cons. For most of the crew, it was the first time they ever experienced any kind of creative freedom and could interact with other parts of the studio to improve their work. "That show would've never been possible [if it weren't for Bakshi]," Jim Gomez said. "Not just the fact that he sold the show, but to create an environment to do what we wanted, without interference. That was just unheard of, to let cartoonists create content."[26]

Observed Tom Minton: "To me those days may as well have happened yesterday because my generation spent a decade or so working on absolute garbage and Bakshi's *Mighty Mouse* series marked our deliverance to something better. That series wasn't perfect by any means but it kicked open the door. I don't think the younger people in our crew, for whom *Mighty Mouse* was their first gig, fully realized what a chance it represented at that time. How could they?"[27]

§

The concept of "director's vision" was nonexistent in television animation at the time. Its establishment was probably the greatest achievement of Bakshi's *Mighty Mouse*. Bakshi's leadership made it possible not only to identify an artist by his or her drawing style, but also to gain something of a sense of overall tone and vision.

The key phrase is "something of," as, for the most part, the *Mighty Mouse* cartoons are equally chaotic and blaring regardless of who directed them. Their appalling animation, done at James Wang's Cuckoo's Nest Studio in Taiwan (a studio used at John K.'s insistence because he had trained artists there on *The Jetsons*), is largely responsible for the cartoons' failings. *Mighty Mouse* may be a recordholder for the greatest number of animation and shooting errors in television history; smears are arbitrary and lip-sync is nonexistent.

Nevertheless, the long hours spent—by key timer Bob Jaques and the layout crew—in making sure everything was explicitly laid out in the exposure sheets were not entirely in vain. The artists' distinctive styles are still recognizable in the finished cartoons, even if a lack of precision—caused by brutal deadlines—largely massacred the cartoons' intentions. Before this system of layout could actually work, the artists would need to bring the animation process under their direct and total control.

Bob Jaques himself was an essential part of the artistic atmosphere in the studio; an atmosphere that allowed Bakshi to ensure that "people supported other people's weaknesses."[28] Whereas Kent Butterworth, Steve Gordon, and Bruce Woodside could actually time their own cartoons, directors John K. and Eddie Fitzgerald did not know how to time, and left the job to Jaques and Butterworth.

Gordon and Woodside, both of whom had worked for Bakshi in the past, were certainly the two Kricfalusi referred to as the "lame" directors on *Mighty Mouse*: the "safe directors that were hired because Ralph was worried that the crazy directors would be irresponsible."[29] By the time Gordon and Woodside were brought in, the majority of the artists had been hired and all the creative decisions made. Indeed, Gordon felt that he and Woodside were there solely because Bakshi needed "a couple of people he could depend on to get some of the shows out without any drama."[30]

Gordon's and Woodside's episodes are examples of "standard" cartoon direction at its finest. If the script was solid, they were fine; if the script was weak, nothing was done to improve them. Woodside's "Scrap Happy" is almost Filmation-like in its direction; writer Minton's idea—that the orphan character Scrappy is a parody of Saturday morning clichés—is handled in a straightforward manner and sapped of any satirical value.

The arrangements at the studio were not ideal for either director. Along with being branded as Bakshi's "responsible" people—an uneasy position—they were also given minimal access to the studio's top draftsmen; Gordon boarded and laid out his two episodes entirely alone. If there is no zest in these cartoons, it is because it was not going to be there in the first place. "It was just a job for me—no better and no worse," reflected Gordon.[31] It was by no means an opinion shared by other "senior" employees. Kent Butterworth, who called the series "the best creative environment" he ever worked in and probably his favorite job, period, was enthusiastic and it was reflected in the cartoons he directed.[32]

That creative environment worked well for some, but not as well for others. "Chaos for chaos's sake" is an apt description of Eddie Fitzgerald's "Witch Tricks", the only cartoon he fully directed. In it, orphan Scrappy takes over the duties of an ailing tooth fairy and manages to stir the ire of a witch. Though well drawn, the short is almost incoherent, going off the rails when Scrappy inexplicably sports a talking hat and pair of pants. Obviously meant as a tribute to the beautifully surrealistic work of Bob Clampett and the Fleischers, "Witch Tricks" takes the most superficial elements of those cartoons and piles them on unsparingly.

Ironically, it was paying tribute to Clampett that helped do Fitzgerald in at Bakshi's. Most of the layouts for "Witch Tricks" were littered with Fitzgerald's notes, asking the animators to reference

Eddie Fitzgerald, a regular artist for Bakshi and Kricfalusi, seen in front of a storyboard for *Christmas in Tattertown* in 1988. Courtesy of Jerry Beck.

Clampett-directed Warner cartoons like *Kitty Kornered* (1946); a completely unrealistic expectation of animators in an Asian sweatshop. Weekly shipping deadlines were compromised to get the layouts back to a functional state. Fitzgerald would later recall that he let his second cartoon, "Catastrophe Cat", go through completely undirected—giving him time to focus on extensive preliminary work for his third, "This Island Mouseville", which ended up unceremoniously turned over to Bruce Woodside.[33]

This kind of "auteur" behavior did not sit well with Bakshi, who ended up exploding at Fitzgerald ("I told you—no more of this crazy shit!") and firing him twice in one day. After the first firing, Fitzgerald's wife called Bakshi and told them that they couldn't afford for this to happen. Bakshi agreed to take him back. When Fitzgerald returned to the studio later, Bakshi screamed, "I thought I fired you! Go home!"

§

As the supervising director, John K. felt the most production pressure. He had no track record of success at any job in Hollywood; nevertheless, Bakshi revered and believed in him enough to give him what Steve Gordon called "his first chance at pushing his point of view and his first attempt at career suicide, all rolled into one."[34]

Kricfalusi was good at studio politicking. He was notorious for regarding the younger artists with jealousy; he was said to hold Gordon and Woodside in equal contempt; yet he was regularly given near-exclusive access to the studio's best artists, giving his episodes a significant visual edge over the other directors'. Lynne Naylor, whom he called "the backbone of the studio," was inseparable from his unit.[35] Her role in providing his episodes' vigor, clear acting, and staging was one matched by few others at Bakshi's. The same could be said for Jim Smith or Bruce Timm, the latter hired against Kricfalusi's opposition. Timm came at the recommendation of Jim Gomez and subsequently faced layout tests and lessons at the hands of John K., as did many others.

"He can tear you down and kind of inspire you at the same time," Timm said. "He would take your drawing, lay a sheet of paper over it, and fix your drawing and show you what it should look like. His other technique was to ridicule your drawing."[36] Ridicule came mostly behind Timm's back, with Kricfalusi dismissively calling his drawings of the character "Mighty Man." Artistic vanity could not be justified for very long, however. Work needed to be done—fast.

Having fun while urgently trying to get work done was not exclusive to anyone. A sense of honor was at stake when it came to getting John K.'s cartoons finished on schedule. Jim Gomez and Bob Jaques remember Kricfalusi saying, "We can't miss any airdates, or I'll get fired," then disappearing midweek with zero explanation to consume alcohol. "Lynne, Bruce, Bob, and myself worked all day and night to get it done, only taking breaks for cereal," Gomez said. "It's not that we begrudge that, but it was a lot of work. But we were kids then, and it was easier to work fourteen, sixteen, eighteen hours a day."[37]

The method of character layout that Kricfalusi had developed at Cuckoo's Nest, and further refined at Bakshi's, called for more drawings, passion, and originality than a typical animation layout did. Merely blowing up storyboards was not enough. You needed to capture every whim Kricfalusi wanted in your drawing and push the scene to its limit—and then some. Said Timm: "There was no stock, so you had to draw every scene from scratch."[38] Kricfalusi could not afford to play god too often, however. There was definitely work by the artists and himself that he would have done over on *Mighty Mouse*—had he been fully in charge, rather than subservient to Bakshi. "That created some animosity, [but] at the end of the day we simply had to deliver the show," Tom Klein said.[39]

In spite of the incapacitations, it is only in John K.'s *Mighty Mouse* cartoons where the position of "cartoon director" is noticeably elevated to a facsimile of "filmmaker." His early efforts, like "Me-Yowwww!" and "Scrappy's Field Day", are sloppy and nearly indistinguishable from the other directors' work. They also are infected with series-wide issues of artless bedlam and non-sequiturs that make sense to no one. Yet Kricfalusi was remarkably fast in bringing his ambitious nature to the screen. He was heavily involved in the writing process and also did numerous layouts for important acting scenes himself. If it was going to bear the stamp of a John Kricfalusi cartoon, then it *had* to be a John Kricfalusi cartoon.

"Night of the Bat-Bat" and "The League of Super-Rodents" introduced the first wholly John K. creation to television: the Cow, a comedic villain voiced to perfection by character actor Mike Pataki. According to Kricfalusi, however, Bakshi misdirected Pataki in the recording session. "Mike read every line completely backwards and upside down and put the stress on all the wrong parts of the gags," he said. "I went back and took all the layouts and redrew them all to make the Cow react as if he didn't understand the lines he was reading in the script."[40] Since the drawings still matched all the inflections in the voice, the udder-sporting male Cow looks funny and *moves* funny.

The first season of *Mighty Mouse* featured many pop culture parodies—none more brutal than "Mighty's Benefit Plan". The idea to parody Ross Bagdasarian's *Alvin and the Chipmunks* was born from Bob Jaques' frustration of being denied a screen credit for his work on *The Chipmunk Adventure* movie. "I wanted to get back at Ross [Bagdasarian Jr.] for denying me credit, so I proposed that John pitch an idea for a Chipmunk parody—a rise to fame story like that of the Beatles, using material from the Chipmunk feature," Jaques said. Jaques also insisted that the Bagdasarians' dead dog Tiger Lily be a part of the story as talking roadkill.[41]

Kricfalusi loved the idea and shared Jaques' enthusiasm for poking fun at the eccentricities of the Chipmunks, having worked in the same building as the Bagdasarians during the production of *The Harlem Shuffle* video. He boosted the irony meter by enlisting former Chipmunk artists, like Byron Vaughns (storyboard) and Ken Boyer (layout), to do work on the picture. The savagery behind it enhances its hilarity and gives the plot direction. All of the jokes work, however, even if the viewer does not know their origins, making "Mighty's Benefit Plan" possibly the series' most wholly satisfying episode.

"Night on Bald Pate" and "The Littlest Tramp" both feature the human drama as a centerpiece. Glimmers of real character development arise not from Mighty Mouse, but villains Petey Pate and Big Murray (a Kirk Douglas caricature in looks, if not voice). They are not the generic goons or moustache-twirlers synonymous with Terrytoons and Saturday morning, but truly disturbed sadists. "The Ice Goose

Cometh" successfully wrings comedic homoerotic tones out of old Terrytoon favorite Gandy Goose, here seen trying to adjust to life in the '80s without his long-lost buddy Sourpuss the cat. The implications of their relationship are never more obvious than in a scene, laid out by Kricfalusi himself, in which Mighty Mouse embraces Gandy, cooing, "We'll make it work!"

With such racy content, *Mighty Mouse* proved itself a breeding ground for material that stone-faced corporate suits had successfully obliterated from television animation since the 1960s. Veterans of the show are still uncertain how they managed to do it, but it all came down to the presence of Bakshi. The sheer volume of Bakshi's work is a unique case in animation. That such a singular animation visionary has authored so many completed, released works is an indisputable anomaly. Bakshi described himself on *Mighty Mouse* as having "dropped back to a producer's role, with all the knowledge and experience that I have gained. My job is to take all the knowledge I have, pointing to new young talent, and standing behind them not only in fights with CBS, but also creatively at meetings."[42] He was not a self-promoter on the show, but a highly successful talent agent for others.

Beyond advocating for his artists' interests, Bakshi shielded them from spite. His employees never saw a single note from CBS or Standards and Practices. Bakshi kept them all; some suspect he burned them. Others claim they saw him hang up the phone upon getting a censor to admit he had no legal authority over the production. Bakshi's dynamic with the network, combined with the dedication of the studio's artists, resulted in the greatest animated television show possible for the time period under the harshest production schedule imaginable. Even if it was, in retrospect, largely unwatchable.

Examples of John K.'s own layouts for *Mighty Mouse: The New Adventures*. From "Mighty's Benefit Plan", "The Ice Goose Cometh", and "The Littlest Tramp." Courtesy of Bob Jaques. All © Viacom.

RALPH'S BENEFIT PLAN

23

SICK LITTLE MONKEYS

Regardless of the studio's earnest intentions, *Mighty Mouse: The New Adventures* was not a phenomenal success. It did only decent in the ratings. "It was the reviews that kept us alive," Bakshi said.[43] Called "not just subversive, downright seditious,"[44] the show was indeed something of a godsend to animation students, professionals, and general audiences alike: a Saturday morning cartoon with actual humor and art direction. Animation critic Charles Solomon gave an apt summation: "Not all the gags work, but it's refreshing to see people trying something new on Saturday morning."[45] By the time the show began airing, CBS had still not ordered a second season and the entirety of Bakshi's staff had disbanded. As late as January 1988, continuation was still uncertain.

Even if a new season was ordered, it was highly unlikely that John K. would come back for it. "Ralph and I are having one of our yearly fights, and I think it's gotten really bad this time," he told Harry McCracken. "And if he does it himself, it'll be just another thing worthy of the name 'Ralph Bakshi.' It'll make no sense at all. So that'll be the end of it."[46] The master and pupil bickered, via two 1988 issues of the animation magazine *Animato*, over who was more responsible for the series' success. They never delved into the exact reason why they parted ways; in later years, Bakshi ridiculously claimed to have fired Kricfalusi well after he actually left the studio. It seems obvious that raging egos were the real cause of the split, not that any further evidence is needed.

During the *Mighty Mouse* period, John K.'s first taste of a real directorial role had an overwhelming effect on his view of what an animated production should be. Kricfalusi made no qualms about voicing his opinion that the best episodes were the ones he spearheaded; he openly resented decisions Bakshi made throughout the series. He disliked the fact that he could not supervise post-production. He also believed—incorrectly—that the "cheater" episodes, incorporating footage from both earlier episodes and older Terrytoons, were a waste of money.[47] In reality, according to Bakshi, there was no way *Mighty Mouse* could have been laid out in-house had these episodes not kept costs under control.[48]

Tom Klein tried to bring Kricfalusi back for the second season. In so doing, Klein observed that a main bone of contention was Kricfalusi's desire to have a say in who was hired—and to disband the unit system. "He wasn't as keen to have all those other directing units working side by side," Klein said. "He preferred to have it all just one vision. John felt he was running the ship and wanted to get credit for it, and Ralph very much saw it as his company and his project."[49] In the downtime between *Mighty Mouse* seasons, Kricfalusi made a deal with ABC to helm a revival of Bob Clampett's *Beany & Cecil* at the studio DIC. Now his own man, Kricfalusi had no intention of rejoining forces with Bakshi, and he took most of the *Mighty Mouse* crew with him.

Sans both Kricfalusi and John Hyde, Bakshi would produce one more truncated season of *Mighty Mouse* in an abandoned Van Nuys school building. Though Bakshi and his crew had delivered every single episode on time and on budget, the first season had not brought in much money for CBS. Thus, the network only ordered six new episodes. It was just as well, seeing as most of the crew had jumped ship. Reasoned Kent Butterworth: "It's the same money to do six shows with half the payroll."[50]

Butterworth took over as supervising director, while Bakshi himself sat in the director's chair on two cartoons. The leaner crew was able to turn out a more solid show in the second season than the larger crew had in the first. "There was a standard that we all kind of internalized [on the first season]," layout artist Ed Bell said. "We kind of rallied in the second season, 'Let's just do the best thing we can do with the resources that we have. The lady who runs the network doesn't like any of us.'"[51]

While the show's Taiwanese animation was as bad as ever, the second season gained a general coherency that the first season had lacked. John K.'s theatrical inflections and workmanlike mentality were abandoned. The show was now a strict animated farce and more Jay Ward-like than ever before, with Mighty Mouse's romp through Saturday morning animation in Butterworth's "Don't Touch That Dial" being, inarguably, the best cartoon of the second season. It amps up the brutality of "Mighty's Benefit Plan" and pairs it with a worthier subject: the abysmal state of television animation, a subject all of the artists could relate to. In this eleven-minute segment, writers Tom Minton and Jim Reardon set a self-awareness standard that many later television shows would try and fail to match. Mike Kazaleh's layout supervision, nailing the looks of the abhorrent *Scooby-Doo* and *Real Ghostbusters*, makes the satire's sting even sweeter.

The wheels came off *Mighty Mouse* during its prime. Reverend Donald Wildmon started a media firestorm when he accused the star character of snorting cocaine in an episode and claimed that Ralph Bakshi was promoting drugs to children. The scene in question came in John K.'s "The Littlest Tramp," in which Mighty Mouse sentimentally sniffs a crushed flower given to him earlier in the cartoon. Of course, the joke always *was* that the pose of Mighty exaggeratingly inhaling the flower up his nose looked like he was snorting cocaine; nobody thought, however, that it would be caught.

The studio actually got the jump on Wildmon, as Tom Klein's brother had a job opening mail for senators in Washington. He discovered Wildmon's accusation and immediately notified the *Mighty Mouse* crew. Bakshi acted on his own accord and blasted Wildmon for his "lunacy," much to CBS's chagrin. They would have preferred Bakshi respond through CBS's attorney from the start, Klein said.[52] The irony of the controversy is that there had been plenty of content throughout the series that groups might justifiably have condemned, but chose not to. "At the end of the episode ["The Littlest Tramp"], Kirk Douglas marries a tiny little female mouse and gives her a soulful kiss, and they get in a convertible and it drives away and explodes in a mushroom cloud, and nobody says a word about that," quipped writer Jim Reardon.[53]

Wildmon demanded the resignation of Bakshi and Judy Price, to which the network curtly replied, "CBS categorically denies that Mighty Mouse or any other character was shown sniffing cocaine."[54] By July, however, Bakshi had conceded to have the footage taken out of the cartoon for reruns.[55] The damage was done. Those who mattered came down correspondingly harder on the show. McDonald's threatened to pull its sponsorship if the superhero Bat-Bat's line, "Just say 'no' to canned laughter," was not removed from "Bat with a Golden Tongue"; several endings had to be proposed for "Mighty's Wedlock Whimsy" before CBS would sign off on it. Once Bakshi's crew delivered the last episode, *Mighty Mouse* was cancelled. Bakshi tried to keep his studio going with the specials *Christmas in Tattertown*, *Dr. Seuss' Butter Battle Book*, and *Hound Town*, but closed shortly afterwards.

In hindsight, Ralph Bakshi's foray into television animation may be a more significant legacy than his work as a movie director. After Bakshi's first pictures in the 1970s, people waited in vain for a renaissance that never came; by the end of the decade, it became clear that Bakshi himself was the only one taking his progressive (and self-destructive) path. By contrast, the artistic integrity and energy of his *Mighty Mouse* had an almost instantaneous effect on the industry, opening doors for all animation people.

Said Ed Bell: "To see him have balls, the kind of balls that Ralph has. Ever since that job, I think none of us have been able to not think, 'Why can't we say no to something, why can't we be that much more stronger or bold?'"[56] If *Mighty Mouse: The New Adventures* does not hold up as a whole, the series is still significant due to what it enabled its artists to do afterward.

§

The Hollywood animation product of the late 1980s increasingly began to reflect the influx of new talent. New movies and television shows made it ever more apparent to young artists like Doug Lawrence that, "Hey, shit, there might be something happening in California, maybe this is gonna elevate animation a little bit."[57]

Ralph Bakshi's *Mighty Mouse* was one of the earliest examples of a newfound appreciation for the commercial animated cartoon, though not the first. Before it came "Family Dog", an animated episode of Steven Spielberg's *Amazing Stories* anthology television show written and directed by Brad Bird. Broadcast in February 1987, Bird's show is the comedic story of a dog who is cruelly unappreciated by his owners. Their neglectful attitude escalates into dire consequences for the whole town. The show is a strikingly nuanced and satirical view of suburban family life, illustrated by stylized design from Tim Burton and animation with coherent direction. Unlike Bakshi's *Mighty Mouse* in every way possible, "Family Dog" is not risqué material in the guise of a children's program, but a primetime animated cartoon aimed at adults. It served as a template for all the half-hour animated sitcoms that would follow in the '90s, even if most largely disregarded the foundation Bird had set.

Director Don Bluth had dominated the Hollywood animated feature in the first half of the 1980s. His *The Secret of NIMH* (1982) and *An American Tail* (1986) did not say anything that animated features had not said before. Rather, they merely emphasized how standards had slackened so abominably in Disney feature films that an imitator could produce a reasonable facsimile, even without the Mouse's resources. Directors Ron Clements and John Musker's *The Great Mouse Detective* (1986) for Disney would help reclaim some of the studio's former glory on a miniscule budget. Future stalwart animators Glen Keane and Andreas Deja's work in *Mouse Detective* carries a vivacity unseen in Disney's films for decades. It was only a hint of what would come in later features, eventually exposing how shallow Bluth's artistic endeavors to out-Disney Disney really were.

There was never a sense that John Kricfalusi was trying to establish himself as an imitation of anyone. He was always his own man and his own talent. He has, however, always passionately revered the work of Bob Clampett at the Warner studio in the Golden Age. Appreciation became worship to a point where, according to the Kricfalusi gospel, Clampett did everything "better than me and better than everyone else."[58] Kricfalusi, like many other young animators, got to know Bob Clampett in person near the end of his life, becoming friends with the famous director and his kin. Being an apprentice to Clampett was a sort of part-time job for Kricfalusi, which involved doing drawings of Bugs Bunny, Daffy Duck, and Tweety for Clampett's fans and illustrating the family's Christmas cards.

Bob Clampett and John Kricfalusi at the Fox Venice Theater in Los Angeles for a retrospective of Clampett's work, 1981. Courtesy of Norman Hathaway.

Like his Warner peers, Clampett had no financial claim to the characters created on the studio's dime (Tweety in Clampett's case). Clampett was also broke from the deal he made with ABC to turn his sensational *Beany & Cecil* puppet show into an animated cartoon. Clampett agreed to let ABC keep all synchronization rights (picture and sound) and certain merchandising for ten years, after which all rights would revert back to Clampett. The show was renewed until 1968, and Clampett faced a whole decade of hard times when unable to sell another series. Byron Vaughns once asked Clampett when he would bring *Beany & Cecil* back so Vaughns could work on it. Clampett replied: "[It's] up to you new guys in animation to do your own thing."[59]

After Clampett's death in 1984, John K. remained close to the Clampett family. Four years later, Clampett's widow Sody and son Rob wrangled a deal with ABC to revive *Beany & Cecil* for modern television. One of the stipulations set before the family signed off was that Kricfalusi would direct the new show. He was, after all, "carrier of the Clampett torch" in their eyes, and they would not have it any other way.[60]

The failure of the new *Beany & Cecil* was inevitable from the beginning. It was obvious to everyone who came over with John K. from *Mighty Mouse* that this was not going to be the same kind of hard-but-fun experience. It was instead, like Kricfalusi's stint on *The Jetsons*, another futile attempt to harvest creativity from a business model designed to produce junk. The episodes that were actually finished and broadcast are a testament to this.

At the time, John K. was on the outs with Ralph Bakshi. He did not seem to fully appreciate the role his mentor had served on *Mighty Mouse*, nor did he realize how essential that role was to the series' success. Under Bakshi, Kricfalusi and the other artists had had zero interaction with CBS—and no jurisdiction over the budget and schedule. Though John K. had a title with some sheen at Bakshi's, his job there was really the same as everyone else's: to be creative and finish the work on time. By the time the offer came to do *Beany & Cecil*, Kricfalusi had unwisely convinced himself that he was the real captain of the Bakshi ship—both artistically and administratively—and that he could do it again.

"What he didn't fully recognize is the degree to which Ralph and I shielded him on *Mighty Mouse* from the network's demands," Tom Klein said. "Ralph was the one who shouldered the constant complaints from the network. I think on *Beany & Cecil*, John didn't want to be boxed in by production limitations, that everyone should see the wisdom of simply putting all the work into making the show great and that somehow the studios should recognize that and allow the time and the money to do it."[61]

Jennie Trias and Jeff Holder, the executives at ABC Children's Programming, were no Ralph Bakshis. They were the stereotypical, restrictive network executives Kricfalusi and many others have frothed about over the years. They had no intention of making *Beany & Cecil* a continuation of "that *Mighty Mouse* crap." Trias also had little interest in new series concepts. Any new show must be based on something old. "It was really difficult to try and find properties that kids were really interested in, so we got into the habit of finding pre-sold names," she once said of ABC's lineup. "These shows were based on what kids knew."[62]

Bob Clampett's *Beany & Cecil* did not exactly fit that bill, as one would be hard-pressed to find a child in the 1980s familiar with the brand. Originating as a puppet show and television's earliest sensation in 1949, the characters—a young boy and his "Sea-Sick Sea Serpent" pal—went on to live a long life in a series of syndicated animated cartoons. Produced in the early 1960s, the cartoons had a quirky charm and visual sheen; certainly the Clampetts squeezed more animation quality out of every dime than Hanna-Barbera did. The writing, though, consisted entirely of flaccid puns and weirdness for weirdness' sake. By the 1980s, any notoriety the characters had was strictly nostalgic. A series of VHS tapes (of which John K. illustrated several covers), representing the entirety of the animated series, sold fairly well at the time. Perhaps a revival of the show could prove viable and trigger a new franchise, ABC and the Clampetts hoped.

Richard Raynis, a producer at DIC, was instrumental in installing John K. as the producer and director of *Beany & Cecil*. He was of the opinion that Kricfalusi was the man for the job because he understood Clampett and his style better than anyone else. Kricfalusi also had an ensemble of like-minded artists that would follow him to any job and weave anything into gold. If the aspirations were so high, however, the show should never have been given to DIC in the first place. It was, as Jim Gomez said, a place not exactly known for "producing the best stuff."[63] DIC was one of the many animation shops that sprang up solely to serve the networks' needs for quick, crass product when Hanna-Barbera and Filmation could not fit it into their schedules. The concept of in-house layout—which Raynis convinced ABC to allow at Kricfalusi's insistence—was not part of the regular DIC process. Pre-production at DIC usually ended at the storyboard and design stage, with shows coming back from various corners of the earth completely finished. The *Beany & Cecil* crew therefore had to bring in makeshift animation desks to do the layout in-house.

But DIC was at least a studio with a track record for completing projects, something both the Clampett family and John K. lacked. ABC needed a guarantee that *Beany & Cecil* would be delivered. Given the events that transpired, DIC CEO Andy Heyward obviously shielded his company in the contract from any problems caused by the principals. His long-term interest was pumping out more junk with ABC, after all. Even if it meant letting the Clampetts and John K. hang themselves.

§

For the staff, studio furniture was a minor inconvenience compared to the fiasco of actually writing the show's stories. Kricfalusi wanted to eliminate the script process altogether and do the writing at the storyboard stage. Trias and Holder rejected that scenario without hesitation, as did Sody Clampett; they felt only a non-drawing writer should script the cartoons. When Kricfalusi asked widow Clampett if her late husband—obviously, an artist—had written the original *Beany & Cecil* cartoons, she responded, "Well, yes, but that's different. He's Bob!"[64]

In contrast to the use of artist-written scripts at Bakshi's, ABC insisted on the use of a story editor: the standard way for a network to control what goes into a television cartoon's scripts and keep artist input to a minimum. The role of story editor was traditionally filled by "writers who don't know how to write for animation,"[65] a bone of contention for Kricfalusi and many other artists working in the television industry. In the late 1980s, the average scriptwriters for television animation had zero interest in the medium. They were merely using gigs in children's programming as a stepping-stone to live-action careers. Chuck Lorre, ABC's first choice as *Beany & Cecil*'s story editor, unquestionably fit this description. Lorre had written for a number of cookie-cutter animated shows in the 1980s and had since moved up the ladder to a story editor position in live-action sitcoms. He originally declined the *Beany & Cecil* gig because "the idea of working on some insipid Saturday morning cartoon was laughable." Lorre later reconsidered, however, when the Writer's Guild strike of 1988 temporarily put him out of work.[66]

Conflict arose as soon as Lorre entered the production. Kricfalusi said Lorre was also contracted to compose stock music for the series—a task of more concern to Lorre than the quality of the stories. "[Lorre] had no loyalty to us, no loyalty to the Clampetts, no loyalty to the history of animation, didn't like the artists, and proceeded to write the worst scripts in history," Kricfalusi said.[67] Countering this, Lorre said Kricfalusi's status as "the Walt Disney of toilet, onanism, and vomit jokes" was a poor match for the original show's style and claimed that he was trying to protect the show from Kricfalusi's supposed lapses in taste. Wrote Lorre: "Try as I might, I could not stand by and let good ol' Ceec puke up his own eyeballs, or step inside a giant conch shell to (wink, wink) 'pleasure himself.'"[68] Lorre originally had the network's backing, just as Kricfalusi had the Clampetts'. The latter team won out after they convinced ABC that Lorre was causing the problems. Lorre's stock music was not used; his scripts were rewritten without his consent.

Whether Lorre was fired or quit the production is uncertain. The parties involved cannot agree on one story. Lorre described at length his boardroom altercation with Sody and Rob Clampett and being fired the following morning[69], while many crewmembers (including Kricfalusi) said that he quit of his own free will. The new story editor, writer Paul Dini, said that when he arrived on the production, there were already conflicting stories regarding Lorre's departure. All Dini knew for sure was that Lorre was leaving—and that he had "all but hit the silk at that point, just saying, 'Take it over, good luck with it all.'"[70]

Dini was someone who actually liked the original *Beany & Cecil* show and admired what Kricfalusi and his crew had been doing elsewhere, "[bringing] back the old Warner Bros. style of animation, which nobody seemed to be doing at that time."[71] Likewise, Kricfalusi appreciated having a supporter in a high-ranking place. But only one cartoon that Dini wrote ever aired ("The Courtship of Cecilia"), and it is indistinguishable from Lorre's in quality; anything resembling a joke was completely sanitized by the ABC executives. "As bland as the gags were in the storyboards, they still hated them," Bruce Timm said. "They thought they were off-color, they were too violent, they were too this, too that."[72] Trias later accused the staff of "not delivering the show that we bought," and said how the shows didn't "address" children. Sody Clampett contested that Trias wanted something that *Beany & Cecil* never was. "The *Beany & Cecil* cartoons were adventures," Clampett said. "Jennie Trias wanted stories about Beany cleaning his room."[73]

According to Dini, pitching an idea to ABC with Kricfalusi was akin to "sitting in a room of Easter Island faces. It wasn't that they didn't think the cartoon was funny. They had a way of doing things and it was, 'We control the process, we do the approvals, nothing gets by us.' And I got to the point where I'm just saying, 'Why did you buy this show? Why did you want this crew working on it?'" What ABC was really looking for was a way to appear to be cutting edge, sans the risks that status entails. They wanted a "silly show," as Dini said, with no further aspirations than that.[74]

Hanna-Barbera's *A Pup Named Scooby-Doo* premiered on ABC the same day as *Beany & Cecil*. Like DIC's show, it was very much in the mold of Bakshi's *Mighty Mouse*. Hanna-Barbera's show was full of self-referential humor, took jabs at the inanity of the original *Scooby-Doo*, and was even drawn and animated similarly to Bakshi's show. It was the first original show Hanna-Barbera had done in decades (Bill Hanna directed the first episode himself), and it ironically built upon the foundation laid by *Mighty Mouse* better than *Beany & Cecil* did, if only superficially. Given that Hanna-Barbera's show was allowed to exist on the network for three whole years, it is apparent that ABC was not against making *Beany & Cecil* a humorous show. They were just against *who* was making it humorous.

§

Beany & Cecil was Kricfalusi's second great artistic assembly in the 1980s, and the one during which most of his main collaborators became friends. More students from CalArts, artists freshly relocated from New York City, and chance arrivals from the comics industry joined Kricfalusi's ranks. Combined with the majority of the former *Mighty Mouse* crew, this represented a strong and passionate team—of which ABC was unworthy and unappreciative.

While Kricfalusi may have had his first real directing job at Bakshi's, the DIC show gave him his first taste of authoritarian control over the drawing end of a production. Insofar as he was almost completely left out of the writing process, Kricfalusi pleaded with the network, "You've got to at least *draw* these funny."[75] His idea of drawing a "funny" show was far more defined than ABC's concept of a "silly" show.

Whereas at Bakshi's Kricfalusi was merely one of several strong, individualistic talents, on *Beany & Cecil* he was the guiding light—and experimented with filtering his personal skill through others' hands, as his use of the unit system indicates. Eddie Fitzgerald, Jim Smith, and Bruce Timm were graciously afforded director credits and assigned pseudo-units, yet they had far less control than a director on *Mighty Mouse*. The *Beany* directors were merely layout supervisors on episodes they had boarded, handing off scenes to arbitrarily assigned layout artists. In other words, as Timm recalled, the directors were "John's wrists, following orders."[76]

This methodology was born from Kricfalusi's ongoing insistence that few people—on any of his productions—are capable of maintaining the intent of his artistic vision, and that it is his duty as a director "to retrain everyone, to get them to not tone down whatever we sent them to work from."[77] There was no chance to implement this educational strategy on *Mighty Mouse*, and opportunities were just as slim on *Beany & Cecil*, but he was determined to try regardless. Working under Kricfalusi as an artist in any capacity has been consistently described as "boot camp," where one is stripped down and rebuilt to the director's standards. He and the other head artists would be "very candid about they wanted," layout artist Bob Miller said, "but justifiably so. It was our job to give them what they wanted." Kricfalusi would routinely go over an artist's work, breaking down exactly what was wrong with their layouts and how they could improve upon them in their second attempts. As a guideline, he provided his own sketches, always signed, "Your pal, John." "That last part made the criticism easier to swallow, believe me," Miller said.[78]

This school-like environment, however admirable it may be for bettering the artists' skills and the production's value, proved unworkable within the network television animation system. Certainly it was unrealistic when the quota per layout artist was twenty scenes per week, with artists already working late into the night to meet deadlines. The educational value of certain exercises—like having artists spend days at a time tracing old Dell issues of the *Beany & Cecil* comic book—was also questionable. "He does these weird fucking things, where we're living in this insane world," Jim Gomez said. "It's like, 'What are you doing?'"[79]

After an exhausting week, Kricfalusi would invite all of the crew to his and Lynne Naylor's apartment for an open house dubbed "Theory Night" on Fridays. These gatherings began during *Mighty Mouse* as a way for the crew to get to know each other better and philosophize about what makes entertainment work. "But mostly an excuse to drink heavily while bitching about animation and stuff," the artist Chris Reccardi said.[80]

In retrospect, it is startling that *Beany & Cecil* came after *Mighty Mouse*, rather than before. Instead of serving as a means for John K. and the others to further hone their skills as cartoon-makers, the production process was regressive. Due to the story editor conflict, stories were not approved in a timely fashion, greatly impacting the show's production schedule. The crew still had to make *Beany & Cecil*'s September 1988 airdates, despite the fact that layout did not begin until well into June. Such a production timeline was not uncommon at DIC, but only because their productions more typically bypassed the layout stage altogether.

As a result, Kricfalusi's rigid standards fall apart in the finished cartoons; his attempts at cartooning-coaching were evidently in vain. There is scant visual evidence that masters like Jim Smith, Lynne Naylor, or Bruce Timm were even involved with the catastrophic results—even though they were. Good drawings carelessly mutate into crude scrawls, even more often than they did in *Mighty Mouse*. The animators at Wang Animation (formerly Cuckoo's Nest) appear not to have used mouth charts at all. The absence of Bob Jaques—who refused to work on the show—is also painfully clear. Gone is the snappier timing found in *Mighty Mouse*, with episodes of the traditional six-minute length feeling as bloated and glacial as those clocking in at a ridiculous fourteen minutes.

Lynne Naylor at work on DIC's *Beany & Cecil*. Courtesy of Jerry Beck.

Brilliant, funny artwork had been expected to support lame writing—and now this artwork was scarcely in evidence, leaving *Beany & Cecil* with little chance of success. To be fair, Kricfalusi, Dini, and even Lorre obviously knew the show's characters and concepts. Mercifully absent from the show are the repugnant lessons about sharing and respect so common in Saturday morning television. Beany and Cecil are still allowed to sail on the Leakin' Lena while Dishonest John tries to put one over—but only in the most mundane, committee-cleansed way imaginable. The original 1960s *Beany & Cecil* could be rude while retaining a sense of innocence. The 1988 cartoon was juvenilely patronizing; its lapses into humor were few and jarring.

Kricfalusi tried to exploit ABC's ignorance of the animation process by adding jokes in the layout stage that had not been in the scripts or storyboards. These jokes were often innocent background actions: the sort of arbitrary, nonsensical gags common in *Mighty Mouse* that no one cared about or gave second thought to—except for ABC, as it turned out. Eddie Fitzgerald quickly became a sort of scapegoat for these additional, unapproved jokes when the cartoons he was supervising played for ABC's tyrannical executives in rough-cut form on the moviola. The network was livid; less by the additional content itself than by the fact that that it was unsanctioned by ABC. Said Dini: "It wasn't a question if it was funny or not, it came down to a struggle for power."[81]

Kricfalusi fired Fitzgerald, and his cartoons subsequently went through layout unsupervised. The conflicts with the network continued. Every joke added after the storyboard stage was accounted for and argued over. Further writing came to a standstill. Consequently, the workload for the crew became correspondingly scarce—to the point that Jim Smith was able to work as a layout supervisor on both *Beany & Cecil* and Bakshi's second season of *Mighty Mouse*. Some artists, like Bruce Timm and Jim Gomez, left the production to avoid the

Examples of Bruce Timm's storyboards for the ill-fated *Beany & Cecil* revival. © Bob Clampett Productions. Courtesy of Norman Hathaway.

imminent crash. Timm recalled that ABC's regular interference stoked John K. to move beyond the commendable stance of "let's make this the best cartoon we can" to a position of "let's make this the most shocking, offensive cartoon we can."[82] If the castrated finished episodes are any indication, Kricfalusi absolutely failed at this aim. An unaired cartoon that got as far as the rough cut stage, "D.J. Goes Ape", highlights Dishonest John getting impregnated by Ping-Pong the giant ape; at times, ABC seems to have enabled Kricfalusi's efforts.

What likely killed *Beany & Cecil* was the act of Kricfalusi writing a public letter to Jennie Trias and Jeff Holder. Most of DIC's top people were recipients, as were Peggy Charren of Action for Children's Television and *Time*'s movie critic Richard Corliss (though his name is misspelled in the correspondence). "I have come to the conclusion that it is long past the time for diplomacy," Kricfalusi wrote, going on to blame their interference as the sole cause of all the production's problems. Their insistence on having approval over every last drawing and gag, Kricfalusi scolded, was stifling creativity of which Trias and Holder should be more appreciative. "It defies all rational comprehension that you should worry so much about it. You should thank us for it. This is your chance to redeem Saturday morning's abysmal reputation. In five years, you'll be copying this style anyway."[83]

Kricfalusi was absolutely correct. Whether his condescension was justified or not, he perfectly summed up the average artist's frustrations with the status quo. His argument was valid: it would be foolish for ABC to interfere with the increasing likelihood that Saturday morning might be fun again. That said, a wise argument could not fully absolve John K. of blame for the show's failure. *Beany and Cecil* had more than a few of the hallmarks of what storyboard artist Bob Camp called "a pretty typical John Kricfalusi production, with everyone just doing whatever the hell they wanted."[84] With his intense direction style unleashed for the first time, anything that was not bogged down considerably by the network was bogged down by Kricfalusi himself.

By including Charren and Corliss as recipients of the letter, Kricfalusi was obviously making a bid for outside attention and support—a factor that could only have added more friction to his daily routine with the network. But when a show is as bad as his *Beany & Cecil* was, the general public does not care why it was bad. They only know that they dislike it and immediately seek entertainment elsewhere. Barely five half-hours had been completed on *Beany & Cecil* when the hammer came down. It was a striking contrast with *Mighty Mouse*, where—without Kricfalusi in charge—an entire thirteen-episode season had been completed on time with a near identical-staff, despite the same ridiculously short production schedule.

As October rolled along, all of the finished *Beany* episodes had aired and Kricfalusi was spending increasingly more time secluded in his office, away from the crew. With no notice, the suits came around DIC to tell everybody that the show was canceled and to get off the premises. Without Ralph Bakshi acting as his shield, Kricfalusi found it impossible to get his work onto network television in an unblemished state. Most of the crew was able to find work fairly quickly after *Beany*

& Cecil was cancelled, but Kricfalusi—as the main offender in this fiasco—had burned one bridge too many. If he wanted to get his work seen by the general public again, he would need to pursue a path less beaten.

Chapter 2
Nickelodeon's Foist Material Possessions

The animation landscape underwent a radical makeover in 1989. By this time, well-crafted work from Hollywood was no longer confined to sporadic spurts. Animated cartooning was discovered to be a wildly profitable venture, if one just made the effort to give the public something of redeeming value. This was a gravy train that many were eager to board.

The stimulus of this movement was, inarguably, the release of *Who Framed Roger Rabbit* in June 1988. Taking place in 1947 Hollywood, the story entangled "toon"-hating live-action detective Eddie Valiant (played by Bob Hoskins) in the world of the obnoxious animated Roger Rabbit and a case involving murder, estate fraud, and the Technicolorsoaked Toon Town. The film had three creative visionaries: executive producer Steven Spielberg, director Robert Zemeckis, and animation director Richard Williams. Viewing the film today, one can see the creative commotion playing out onscreen. The light comedy/murder mystery mixes awkwardly with a ridiculous seriousness, manifesting itself in blatant metaphors for racial discrimination. Williams has since admitted to an open disdain for the wacky type of animation that the movie was supposed to be celebrating; that disdain taints the film. The actions are played too fast to read, and the acting is foppish. Reams of characters from classic Disney and Warner cartoons serve as window dressing in their gratuitous cameos. In its cynical, stereotypical portrayal of what the 1947 Hollywood cartoon represented, *Roger Rabbit* could be read as self-aware—were Spielberg and Zemeckis's unctuous love for the 1940s not so obvious. Accordingly, the film is a creative free-for-all with little focus, clumsily trapped between adulation and disdain.

Yet *Roger Rabbit*'s enthusiastic reception was unanimous in 1988. In addition to garnering accolades from the Academy for its perfect special effects, *Roger* was the first animated film of any kind since Ralph Bakshi's heyday to deal directly with adult subject matter—and get praised for doing so. *Roger Rabbit* was also a top box office contender and the second-highest grossing film of 1988, something unheard of for an animated cartoon. Its success taught an important lesson to the Hollywood film industry, Chris Reccardi said: "You can make real money off of the shit."[1]

1989 saw the release of *The Little Mermaid*, the Disney studio's first animated hit in nearly twenty years. Originally seen as a fluke by skeptics, it overhauled and updated the studio's public image. "Disney" no longer meant a studio that, in the distant past, once made colorful musicals with charismatic animation; it was now a studio back in action.

In the world of television, thanks largely to the backing of writer and producer James L. Brooks, cartoonist Matt Groening struck a deal with the FOX Network to do a half-hour primetime series centered on characters he had created for short *Tracey Ullman Show* interstitials. The resulting show, *The Simpsons*, made FOX a serious competitor with the other major networks. It was a weekly reminder that the animated cartoon could successfully showcase smart, adult humor—even if kids still wanted Bart Simpson t-shirts and video games.

The Hollywood animation scene still lacked strong, individual voices, even as standards steadily improved industry-wide. Disney feature artists only did as Disney wanted and innovated within those boundaries. The company's foray into (or surrender to) television animation—with shows like the popular *DuckTales* in 1987—merely put higher budgets and a wholesome Disney veneer on typical Saturday morning concepts, even if it meant bastardizing a prime source like the work of cartoonist Carl Barks in the process.

Drawing hands on *The Simpsons* were kept on a leash. They were expected merely to illustrate the scripts and take zero artistic license of their own, as director Kent Butterworth found out when he was fired and blamed for the earliest episodes' "cartooniness problems."[2] Though decision-makers clearly wanted to have the writers and voice actors do the heaviest lifting, artists like David Silverman and Brad Bird instilled the kind of visual acting necessary to make *The Simpsons* a worthy contender in the world of sitcoms. Groening never appreciated or recognized this aspect of the series' success, however, and the show ultimately grew stiffer (in every respect) each season.

While Groening was animation's first "celebrity," of sorts, in the modern era, he was not an animation artist. Nor was he a dominant creative force; there is an overabundance of evidence that others' contributions in *Simpsons* writing sessions were stronger than his. Nevertheless, Groening's popularity showed that the public was receptive to the idea of an animated visionary, even if the studios and networks were not offering opportunities for one to rise to power. Warner Bros. certainly did not when it built a television animation department from scratch in 1989. Its first venture, *Tiny Toon Adventures*, used the classic *Looney Tunes* and *Merrie Melodies* as a springboard. The show was centered on wacky teenage characters that looked upon Bugs Bunny, Daffy Duck, and others as mentors while remaining separate entities; young Buster Bunny, Plucky Duck, and so forth literally took lessons from the older characters. Many artists joined the project thinking they might be able to recapture the spirit of classic cartoon making. Steven Spielberg, bitten by the animation bug after *Roger Rabbit*, was attached to *Tiny Toons*, which meant high budgets and supposed artistic freedom.

As it turned out, certain parties received more freedom than others. Producers Jean MacCurdy and Tom Ruegger hired a smorgasbord of people for *Tiny Toons*: artists associated with John Kricfalusi from *Mighty Mouse* or *Beany & Cecil*, non-drawing writers who had worked with Ruegger in the past, and improv comedians with a vague association to cartoons. Each group had its own ideology of how to make a cartoon, and the groups clashed fiercely.

Whereas artists like Bob Camp thought *Tiny Toons* would be an opportunity to do "real, real Warner Bros. cartoons" rather than "the usual crap," the non-drawing writers sought to do something more topical with animation.[3] The more spirited directors often rewrote scripts without the writers' consent; writers retaliated furiously. Director Eddie Fitzgerald, fresh from another stint at Bakshi's, was originally allowed to skip the script process all together; that privilege was revoked when he was six weeks behind schedule after boarding and re-boarding a single six-minute cartoon.

The finished cartoons are endearingly uneven in light of this conflict of interests. Satire is drowned amid nonsensical gags and traditional Bugs Bunny plot ideas are stretched out to obscene lengths.

What one sees play out through the first 65-episode season of *Tiny Toons* is the incompatibility of two different ideals that stemmed from *Mighty Mouse*: the regeneration of the classic cartoon style versus an effort to make cartoons humorously trendy. The writers' philosophy eventually won out over the artists', and the written script became law. Future Warner series would have more in common with *The Simpsons* than with *Looney Tunes*, anthropomorphic animals notwithstanding.

Another positive effect of *Who Framed Roger Rabbit* was that it had revived an active interest in classic animation. Its success made studios and networks seek to recapture the power animated cartoons once had. Yet it seemed the studios and networks were reluctant to showcase any new kind of individuality. The new films and shows succeeded at meeting past standards rather than surpassing them. Transcendence was sorely missing from what many called an "animation renaissance," and it was not going to come from the establishment. There was the sense in the industry that a new visionary from outside was needed.

John Kricfalusi, therefore, could not have timed his ouster from DIC and *Beany & Cecil* any better. Mere months after *Roger Rabbit*, it was no longer idealism to imagine a new production model: one no longer reliant on hack executives and factories. After a short period of freelancing for Bill Kroyer and Hanna-Barbera, Kricfalusi "had had it," Jerry Beck remembered. "It was time to do his own thing, it was almost like he felt, 'That's it, I can't work for other people anymore, I'm gonna do cartoons my own way.' Even though he had no job to do it."[4]

Kricfalusi had no revenue to start a studio, either. But this did not stop him from co-founding one with fellow artists Lynne Naylor, Jim Smith, and Bob Camp—the three other artists most responsible for forging what would be known as the "John K. style." Naylor and Smith had already been crucial to many of Kricfalusi's earlier artistic successes. Camp was new to Kricfalusi's inner circle. He was an established and versatile artist in the comic book world and had worked in New York for Rankin-Bass before moving to Los Angeles to work at DIC. Camp's draftsmanship and rich sense of humor became the crux of his friendship with Kricfalusi. The joint venture, Spumco (named after the fictional entity Raymond Spum, the "true" creator of animation), came together in 1989. Its original focus was illustration, as Kricfalusi had soured on the animation business altogether. Naylor worked at various freelance layout jobs, while Smith and Camp still held down desks at *Tiny Toon Adventures*.

During the late 1980s, Kricfalusi enjoyed the fortune of having a strong connection with animation producer Carl Macek, better known as one of the people (along with Fred Ladd) responsible for the popularity of Japanese anime in North America. It was a role Macek continued to uphold in 1989, when he and Jerry Beck formed Streamline Pictures as a means of distributing the work of filmmaker Hayao Miyazaki in the United States. Macek had known Kricfalusi for many years and became reacquainted with him in 1988, while both were working at DIC.

Shortly after, Macek entered into what he described as a "frenetic" period of his life: trying to found Streamline while also functioning as Kricfalusi's *de-facto* talent agent, providing studio space for Spumco and becoming a full-time partner. Attempts at pitching and finding potential animation work proved more entertaining than profitable. "One trip to Florida didn't pan out in terms of us getting any business, but it was hilarious because of just the shenanigans that you have to put up with trying to intrigue people with the idea of the kind of material that John was going for," Macek said. "He had shows called *G.I. Babies, Ripping Friends*. All these, on the surface, interesting, traditional shows; but once you got into it, there was always some subversive element from John's point of view that would radically change the perception people had of him."[5]

Most of the work Spumco did in its earliest days is largely forgotten, ranging from defunct toy lines to a poster for a Bob Clampett art exhibit. The studio's first job, described by Camp as "an absolute failure," was designing and illustrating an anti-drug board game for Play to Win, Inc.! entitled "Captain Quantum Vs. the Ugly Druggies."[6] The game was never available for retail; supposedly because it was made strictly for educational purposes, though it was more likely too comical and insincere to be of genuine academic value. Kricfalusi would have to bring Spumco into the world of animation if he wanted to be noticed again.

§

In the midst of the renewed industry-wide interest in producing quality animation in the late 1980s, the children's cable network Nickelodeon began producing original animated programming. Owned by MTV Networks—a subsidiary of Viacom—Nickelodeon was not the place one would think of to look for product on the cutting edge. It was primarily a rerun depot, and its original children's programming could be summed up as what Jim Gomez called "this low-budget thing where they throw green shit at each other."[7]

The network's first animated productions were two holiday specials produced and aired in 1988-89. The first, *Christmas in Tattertown*, produced with Ralph Bakshi and intended as a pilot for a "Tattertown" series, was poorly received. Their second special, a package entitled *Nickelodeon's Thanksgiving Fest*, fared better. It made a strong case for Nickelodeon president Gerry Laybourne's desire to produce animation that went against the assembly-line formula of network television.

Laybourne—clearly influenced by her husband, independent animator Kit Laybourne—desired a lineup of shows that were "creator-driven" with star artists at the helm. Vanessa Coffey, an independent producer working with Nickelodeon at the time, said it was Laybourne's mission to uphold the network's philosophy of "respecting kids" by not doing "half-hour toy commercials. [Laybourne] purposely went after animators, and not big production companies, to do the shows."[8]

Coffey, serving as a consultant, was flown out to Los Angeles by Nickelodeon in the summer of 1989. The network put out the word that Coffey was scheduling meetings with independent animators; wherein they would pitch ideas for children's animated series to be aired on Nickelodeon, but made at their own studios. When John K. heard about this, he was beside himself. "They wanted something inspired by the animators themselves," Kricfalusi said to Wheeler Dixon in 1992. "They wanted to get the animators' vision onto the screen. I didn't believe it for a second."[9]

Spumco was not the kind of studio Nickelodeon had in mind to produce a show. Other animation people and studios that met with Coffey, like Klasky-Csupo, had the advantage of having actually produced animation before. "We weren't really an animation studio," Macek said. "[It was] just a bunch of artists that hung out in my office. I had to beg [Coffey]. I convinced her that she couldn't leave without seeing John's work. Reluctantly, she gave us a slot, the last slot that she had before she left to go back to New York."[10]

Spumco went all-out to prepare for Kricfalusi's meeting with Coffey at the Sheraton Universal Hotel, going as far as making foam-core and cardboard cutouts of the characters in addition to traditional artwork. A plethora of series was pitched to Coffey. Among them were *He-Hog the Atomic Pig*, *The Predator*, *Jimmy's Clubhouse* featuring Jimmy the Retarded Boy (later rechristened Idiot Boy), and *Your Gang*, an all-star show in the vein of Hal Roach's classic *Our Gang* live-action shorts.[11]

Kricfalusi completely cut loose during his pitch in Coffey's humid hotel room, giving a performance "so charismatic and so outrageous" that it convinced Coffey, without a doubt, that she had to get this artist's work on television.[12] "I did the same thing I'd done for the majors," Kricfalusi said. "I jumped all over, screamed, sweated all over, flailed myself against the wall, and instead of phoning the police, she rushed me to New York."[13]

Along with Kricfalusi's pitch, other potential series that Coffey "really fell in love with" included animators Gabor Csupo and Arlene Klasky's *Rugrats* and cartoonist Jim Jinkins' *Doug*.[14] In all, Nickelodeon would greenlight eight pilots in 1989. Only John K., Klasky-Csupo, and Jinkins would get a chance at a series.

Shortly after their original meeting, Kricfalusi and Macek were flown out to New York City to feverishly—and captivatingly—pitch Spumco material to Nickelodeon executives in person. The response was fairly unanimous, culminating in Laybourne shouting, "Buy something from this man!" Macek commented that as much as Kricfalusi's energy impressed Nickelodeon, his "aesthetic perceptions with what he wanted to do with animation" impressed them just as much. "His approach was totally unique because he was most interested in giving the cartoonist the upper hand in designing and powering the show. I'm more like a businessman, so I was there to be the voice of sanity, to form the crust, and then John and his artists were like the icing on top of the cake. That was how we positioned our business."[15]

Of the various Spumco series that were pitched, Nickelodeon loved *Jimmy's Clubhouse* and had a lukewarm reaction to the others. *Your Gang* was not particularly desirable, given that Nickelodeon was already buying the kid-centric *Rugrats*. Coffey did, however, like the two pets of the *Your Gang* cast, Ren Höek and Stimpy, and asked if Kricfalusi could do a show centered on them. "He had said he had actually had those characters for a lot of years, but didn't think that anybody would ever buy them, so he put them into that show, because he wanted them to be somewhere," Coffey said.[16]

John K.'s conception of the dog and cat characters came almost in a stream of consciousness. Stimpy, the cat, was influenced in personality and design by a dopey cat in the Bob Clampett Tweety cartoons *Birdy and the Beast* (1944) and *A Gruesome Twosome* (1945). Kricfalusi's interpretation of the cat would get progressively weirder over time. Ren, the dog, was inspired by a 1946 Elliot Erwitt photo featuring a sweater-wearing Chihuahua, something Kricfalusi found absolutely hysterical. "Here's this psychotic-looking monster in a cute sweater, and that just right away was a concept in my head that I thought was hilarious," he said.[17]

The name "Stimpy" originated on a *National Lampoon* record and was a nickname given to Harold Duckett, a roommate of Kricfalusi's in Oakville, Ontario. (Lynne Naylor had also named one of her stray cats Stimpy.) Ren Höek was the actual name of the landlord whose building Kricfalusi lived in when he first arrived in California; he branded his Chihuahua character with the moniker at the suggestion of one-time co-worker Joel Fajnor.

The exact time and location of the characters' genesis is uncertain, as Kricfalusi has offered several stories. One story holds that they came to be while he was sketching on a barf bag on his flight to Los Angeles in 1979.[18] In another story, he claimed to have come up with them while working at Calico Creations in Northridge.[19] This is in contrast to the recollections of others, who remember cat and Chihuahua drawings alongside other Kricfalusi creations in his Sheridan College days; at any rate, the Erwitt Chihuahua photo was being made fun of there.

Originally, Ren was envisioned as a psychotic Peter Lorre-esque character that would call people up, threatening to kidnap their babies. Stimpy was barely defined at all; his only trait—which stuck with the character—was that "[he] has no idea what's going on. He only has one nerve ending and it reacts slowly to sensation."[20] While Kricfalusi

One of John K.'s earliest drawings with Ren and Stimpy identified by name. Courtesy of Bob Jaques. © Viacom.

was living in Van Nuys with Lynne Naylor and fellow former Sheridan students Jim Gomez and Felix Forte, many story bibles for possible series and feature ideas were helmed, like *Mildman*, the world's first gay superhero. Ren and Stimpy were among many former doodles developed into actual characters in a concept called *Cartoon Cavalcade* (later renamed *Your Gang*).

"One of the defining ideas that developed [then] that really summed up Stimpy's personality was this idea that Stimpy actually loved his litter box so much he had to hug it," Gomez said. "I thought Stimpy should pull his litter box around on wheels like a wagon not only because it made him appear childlike, but also in case he needed to take a dump. Lynne was the one who took it a step further and said, 'No, he really loves his box. Not only does it mean everything to him, but it's the only thing he owns.' This idea that he would love and cherish and hug his litter box really stuck, and that was the thing that formulated and summed up Stimpy's character on many levels."[21]

Kricfalusi had tried to bring Ren and Stimpy to life previously when he and Eddie Fitzgerald penned *Spectre of the Bugger Boys*, a fairly pornographic cartoon short script for Ralph Bakshi. Such a short never got past the proposal stage. Later, Ren and Stimpy were among the many characters Bakshi originally tried selling to CBS in 1987. Rather than retaining the characters—as he was entitled to—Bakshi let Kricfalusi take them with him when they parted ways.[22] Such a complex history only indicates that the characters held a special place in Kricfalusi's heart. At the time of his meeting with Coffey, he was obviously just dying for a chance at his own show (even, potentially, two); so he agreed with Coffey to axe the *Your Gang* concept and focus on Ren and Stimpy.

Nickelodeon offered to buy both *Jimmy's Clubhouse* and a show centered on his cat and dog characters. But at Nickelodeon, getting a pilot meant that if the show went to series, Kricfausi would be obligated to sell Nickelodeon most related rights; a point for which Kricfalusi was unprepared. The regulations that protected studios and creators from having to sell their properties wholesale to the broadcast networks did not apply to cable television. Major broadcast networks were seen as having an advantage over smaller entities like Nickelodeon. Thus, cable networks were allowed to buy ideas and concepts in toto, to help build their libraries and meet the competition.

"We walked through Central Park and discussed the pros and cons of that deal," Macek said. "Eventually, we came to the conclusion that [Kricfalusi] had more invested in Jimmy the Idiot Boy. It had more potential than Ren and Stimpy, in his point of view. John is such a mercurial person and can create characters just walking down the street."[23] Kricfalusi said he still fought to keep ownership of his characters, but Nickelodeon would not relent. "So when I knew I had to give up the rights, I said, 'All right, well, take my second-best characters,' and I kept Jimmy."[24]

The pilot for *Ren Höek & Stimpy* went into production in the final months of 1989. Before work started, Carl Macek and John Kricfalusi parted ways. Macek felt that he would not fit into what Kricfalusi was planning for the studio. "He wanted me to play a particular role in Spumco, and I chose not to want to do that."[25]

Streamline Pictures subsequently moved out of the building on Melrose Avenue, but not before a slightly messy divorce, given that Macek was a legal partner in Spumco. The split was probably worth it to Kricfalusi, who was glad to see Macek go. Said Jerry Beck: "From what I observed, Carl was John's worst nightmare. John equated Carl to a 'network executive:' a non-artist who thinks of himself as a creative, and John couldn't have that."[26]

In the end, it was decided that should the pilot make it to series, Macek would receive $1,000 from Kricfalusi for every episode produced, marking the first personnel break-up in the history of *Ren & Stimpy*. It was to be one of many.

§

The production of *Big House Blues* (as the pilot came to be known) was as artistically pure as possible for television in 1989. Kricfalusi, Naylor, Smith, and Camp began work on a storyboard in December 1989 and completed it, with network revisions, a month later. In what Camp called a "nonsense story" at best, Ren and Stimpy are imprisoned at a dog pound and face "the big sleep" at the hands of a cruel, burly dogcatcher—if Ren does not lose his mind first.[27] It was intended as a six-minute short; once the team timed it, they found it could only work at eight minutes. Coffey approved not just the extra length of the short, but all of its content.

Layout from *Big House Blues*, drawn by John K. Courtesy of Bob Jaques. © Viacom.

The four Spumco "Big Shots," as they came to be known, represented a different dynamic than when the studio would employ a small battalion of artists. The Big Shots' proximity allowed each to play off the others' strengths, with everything passing under "ringleader" John K.'s vigilant eye.[28] As director, he could cast scenes at layout according to each artist's specialty. The four made up a stylistic quartet, each focused on one of Spumco's earmarks: Kricfalusi on the wild acting (Ren's freak-outs), Naylor on the cute scenes (much of Stimpy), Smith on the "manly," solidly drawn pieces (almost all of the dogcatcher), and Camp on high comedy.

Half of *Big House Blues*' animation was done at Spumco, calling for the production to bring in outside help from Hollywood. Three scenes were freelanced to David Feiss, an old cohort of Kricfalusi's; several

CalArts students who met the director's demanding standards were hired as assistant animators.

Said Jordan Reichek, an assistant animator on the pilot: "All I knew of this 'Kricfalusi' person was that many fellow students came back from their interviews with him in either emotional shock or tears. However, when someone showed me some hijacked model sheets for this pilot, I was hooked. I was blown away at this absolute departure from the status quo and I knew I had to be a part of it. [Kricfalusi] struck me as someone with a passionate resolve to not take the same path as the herd."[29]

To help offset the cost of doing so much work in Hollywood, Kricfalusi called on Bob Jaques to animate half of the pilot. Jaques and his wife Kelly Armstrong had just set up a small studio, Carbunkle Cartoons, in Vancouver. Even though the two of them made up the entirety of their staff, they jumped at the chance to animate Spumco's crazy drawings.

It was Jaques who pushed Kricfalusi to give the show a more exaggerated animation style. Had it originally gone as planned—as some surviving pencil tests indicate—*Big House Blues* would have been animated in the style of an Ed Benedict-designed cartoon done at Hanna-Barbera in the 1950s. "Real easy and simple like Huckleberry Hound," prospective artists like Don Shank were originally told by Kricfalusi.[30]

Such a limited approach would have undermined the kind of acting that John K. was trying to achieve with his works. A character was never truly alive in a Hanna-Barbera cartoon, and certainly not in Kricfalusi's sense of the word. "There was no way we could do that with the material on *Ren & Stimpy*," Jaques said. "You couldn't just throw a timing chart on the layouts and have them in-betweened. Extreme or expressive movement and acting require extreme action."[31]

From *Big House Blues*, animated by David Feiss. Courtesy of Bob Jaques. © Viacom.

What animation there is in *Big House Blues* is disorderly at best. It is better than Bakshi's *Mighty Mouse*, yet no one animator draws—or even animates—the same way in the picture (a result likely intended by Kricfalusi). This sort of chaos, traditionally left to chance by animators in Asia, was controlled by key creative figures on *Big House Blues*. This provides a clear indication that, as of early 1990, nobody was exactly sure how to make these characters move—particularly in the scenes animated at Spumco. Many scenes were animated well enough, but others were profoundly sloppy. Scenes like John K.'s shot of Ren at the toilet bowl read poorly. His intention was to have Ren exhibit his characteristic trait of being in a state of "lucidity and emotion," then "revert to insect instinct as he ventured dutifully to his next emotion";[32]

but Ren is completely weightless and moves as if he is underwater. The scene is a complete technical disaster; it works in neither acting or action.

Carbunkle's scenes on the pilot fared marginally better, if only because Jaques and Armstrong knew the technicalities of the animation process better than the Spumco artists did. Rather than ensuring that the layouts made it to and from overseas intact in the finished cartoon, Jaques's responsibility now was making sure that the Spumco drawings actually worked when animated.

"Oftentimes they would look like aliens from different worlds as one drawing flipped to the next," Jaques said. "It was a strict rule of John's to follow the layouts exactly as drawn without deviation, so we had to devise ways to mask the extreme changes, different volumes, and weird expressions, to prevent the character poses [from] melting and morphing as they moved into one another."[33]

Spumco's origin as an illustration studio underlies this issue. Unlike Bob Jaques, the vast majority of the Spumco artists did not know the nuts and bolts of actually animating. They were, mostly, cartoonists at heart, trying to instill an animated cartoon with the kind of liveliness found in the illustrations of a prime issue of *MAD* magazine. Rather than aping designs and approaches that had proven suitable for animation, Spumco sought to animate the kind of style that most would not even dare to try. Of the four "Big Shots," only Naylor had ever seriously worked before in the industry in the role of animator, whereas *Big House Blues* may have been the first time Smith ever animated. John K. had animated on obscure commercials in his early days; otherwise, he only animated for himself, and even then took the title of "animator" out of necessity. Camp was out of the picture on animation, busy doing all of *Big House Blues'* backgrounds "because nobody else could paint."[34]

Animating the show in Canada exposed many problems still

inherent in Kricfalusi's layout system. These flaws would not have come to light had the layouts been shipped solely to Asian animation studios. There, the layouts would pass from desk to desk as with any other production. At a studio like Carbunkle, the animators conscientiously set out to enhance the acting and motion and preserve what the layout artist had personally invested in each scene. If this called for extra work on the part of the animator—adding new drawings to scene folders or disregarding some drawings completely—so be it. Jaques was a skilled enough animator that Carbunkle could enable Spumco and make any drawing work. "We had been on so many productions that emphasized the technical side rather than good art or funny stories that [the extra work] was well worth it," Armstrong said. "I would pick animating from outstanding but technically challenged layouts any day over crappy, stiff layouts that were posed perfectly for animation."[35]

Some decent, well-articulated acting does come through in *Big House Blues*, particularly in an Armstrong-animated sequence of Ren dreaming he is making love to a beautiful woman, who turns out to be Stimpy. Here, Armstrong is not just exaggerating beyond what was common in animation at the time, as Kricfalusi once pointed out; but the drawings work to "drive the point of the scene home, right down to the minutest details."[36] As shaky as this early work is, Carbunkle's footage still lays a visible foundation for improving television animation, one they would build upon and eventually perfect.

§

Bucking the status quo even further, Kricfalusi was averse to hiring established voice actors for the pilot. Roles were filled by those already associated in some way with Spumco. The studio's all-around sound master Henry Porch did a voice, as did Cheryl Chase, who had heard of the pilot while working for Streamline Pictures. Every "Big Shot" provided a voice for *Big House Blues*, John K. playing Ren. It was only

Stimpy that was voiced by someone outside the closely-knit group.

Billy West was a well-established radio personality and musician before meeting John K. in 1988. West's take on the role of Cecil the Sea-Sick Sea Serpent was his first voice for animation, and one of the few saving graces of the abominable *Beany & Cecil* revival; his performance, as well as his grasp of comedy, greatly impressed Kricfalusi. But what really made an impact on Kricfalusi was the fact that West could do a perfect imitation of Larry Fine from the Three Stooges comedy team.

West had originally recorded a Fine voice for the "Looney Lemur" character in a *Beany & Cecil* episode that was never produced. The idea for a Larry Fine voice did not die when the project did. Said West: "He had already got an assload of me during the *Beany & Cecil* days, and he was, 'I want that Larry Fine!' It wasn't like he just dreamt it up."

West has claimed that he was originally asked to voice both Ren and Stimpy, going as far as to say that in Kricfalusi's earliest meetings with Nickelodeon, it was West's original audition tape that helped sell the show. West was living in New York at the time; Kricfalusi brought him over to the MTV building to record samples of both characters' voices, to help solidify the characters beyond the actual drawings for the Nickelodeon brass.

"We go in there, and he brought some scripts with him, [saying], 'I want you to read both parts,'" West said. "And we were in a closet at MTV in a hallway. This is him being Bob Clampett: 'We'll just use somebody's car who's parked in the lot, nobody'll care.' There was a broomstick and one of those janitor pails that had the wringer, and someone came in and helped him out and put a mike on it. And I was there reading, we did it a couple of times. He said, 'Alright, I'll be back.'

"He called me up later, 'Well, congratulations, we've got a show. What you did sold the show.' He said those exact words to me. It sounds very romanticized, but this is exactly what happened." Before long, though, Kricfalusi would end up voicing Ren, and West only Stimpy. "I'm sure it was his original plan that he was gonna do the Ren voice, and I was the useful idiot that was willing to do anything."[37]

The role of Stimpy was not one to be slighted. West's performance as Stimpy throughout the character's history was unlike anything typically heard in animated cartoons. Not merely an imitation of Larry Fine, Stimpy's voice was an energized, dopey, childish amalgam that gave the character an inimitable distinction. Stimpy's voice was also as far removed as possible from the voice that all dimwitted cartoon characters seemed to have possessed for decades: a caricature of Lon Chaney Jr.'s performance as Lennie in the movie *Of Mice and Men* (1939). That kind of individuality was a breakthrough in itself.

Big House Blues was in production for most of 1990. Understandably so, given that Spumco had to produce an eight-minute short entirely in North America for the low figure of $80,000. There was no incentive to get it done in a timely fashion. Now directing his first film in his own studio, Kricfalusi felt obligated to make it his in every way, even if this meant redrawing layouts that other artists had already finished, or adding more poses to the layouts for scenes already in animation at Carbunkle.

Such directorial control was not a great fit for television animation, given that scheduled airdates depend on shipping dates being met. Production on the cartoon started late because, Kricfalusi said, everyone at Spumco had the flu. None of the pilot's materials were delivered to Carbunkle or Bardel Studios (the Vancouver ink-and-paint house used on the pilot) in a single shipment. Work left Spumco as it met Kricfalusi's approval. Given that a potential series was at stake, no one seemed to mind the pilot taking its time—not even the network.

Nickelodeon also did not openly object to the kind of content it was getting from Kricfalusi. *Big House Blues* is the first mainstream animated short in history to feature a cat vomiting a hairball and clinging to his litter box. The foreboding theme of euthanasia at a dog pound might also have been deemed extreme for children's television, yet Nickelodeon most certainly did not give that a second thought.

Nevertheless, there emerged during the pilot a sense that Nickelodeon could be continually unclear on what was pushing the limit—and what was not. In particular, Vanessa Coffey was not sold on the cruelty inflicted upon Phil the Dog. She requested—while the cartoon was still in pencil test—that the dogcatcher not jab Phil in the back as he marches him to the gas chamber. On the other hand, Coffey also axed a tacked-on ending in which Phil would rise from his grave, telling the kids that he is alive after all. "I put that ending into the cartoon to sell killing him in the first place," Kricfalusi said. "Later, Vanessa called me up and said, 'Listen, don't tell anybody, but let's just not do that ending.' So she was my partner-in-crime on that one."[38]

Glen Daum, the music composer for Bakshi's *Mighty Mouse*, was not quite as forgiving of the pilot's content, as he rescinded his offer to score it at the last minute. After seeing a rough cut of *Big House Blues*, Daum supposedly said he could not be involved with such a "distasteful" project. Fortunately for the production, Henry Porch unearthed the Associated Production Music library and worked with Kricfalusi to create a suitable soundtrack.

This soundtrack was not the typical marriage of jarring stock music to inappropriate visuals so common in television animation. Good aesthetic sense allowed the Big Shots to juxtapose prerecorded, pre-1970s music tracks to the animation perfectly, as if the soundtrack had not been planned well after the fact. As Chris Reccardi remembers, this exemplified Kricfalusi's understanding of how the soundtrack deserves as much attention as the other elements of an animated cartoon. "It's not that [music] is more important than the other stuff, [because] an inappropriate score can distract and wreck the story pretty easily. It's another important tool needed to build a successful cartoon."[39]

As musicians, Reccardi, Jim Smith, and Reccardi's friend Scott Huml embraced Kricfalusi's enthusiasm for the significance of the soundtrack. The music of the trio's band, Der Screamin' Lederhosen (a band that existed, Reccardi quipped, as an excuse for them to smoke pot at Smith's house), did not match the style of the surrounding stock music at all. Yet the cribbing of Howlin' Wolf blends in almost organically, akin to the drawings in motion. "[Kricfalusi] wanted some crazy Chaino-style music for the dog pound sequence," Reccardi said. "He also wanted some gutsy blues stuff for the title card and end credits. When the show went to series, John convinced Nick to use those two pieces for the beginning and end titles, mainly as an alternative to what might have been really dumb theme songs."[40]

Upon seeing the completed *Big House Blues*, Nickelodeon began its schizophrenic relationship with *Ren & Stimpy* in earnest. The short was indeed bought and marketed as the pilot for a children's television series. The disorienting fact, however, was that it could be viewed as anything but childlike. "My dream was that [Spumco] would pitch to *Saturday Night Live* and get a regular short cartoon," recalled Jerry Beck. "I thought what these guys were doing was perfect for that. But they ended up always pitching children's things, and I felt like they were aiming in the wrong direction."[41]

Apart from introducing the concepts of gross-out and bodily function humor to children's programming, John K. reinvented the idea of truly psychotic characters in animation. These were not the stock "goofball" type that had long plagued the medium, but characters with full-blown mental problems. Ren's psychoses in particular are clearly evident. One second he is calmly speaking to his partner, then screaming and slapping him the next. The dogcatcher seems almost sexually stimulated by sending animals to "the big sleep," perversely leering the entire time. These adult elements mix pleasantly with the stock plot devices of children's fare. A lesson in the value of friendship

From a scene, animated by Kelly Armstrong, in *Big House Blues*. Courtesy of Bob Jaques. © Viacom.

is emphasized when Ren tells a girl that he will only let her bail him out of the pound if she will take Stimpy, too.

Linda Simensky, who worked with Coffey in development at Nickelodeon, said the network knew that Spumco's show was not a perfect fit with their other creator-driven properties. Whereas the *Doug* and *Rugrats* pilots were whimsies clearly directed at kids, *Ren & Stimpy*'s whimsy was subversive—aimed solely at animation geeks and its own creators. "Everybody knew there was something very unusual about it," Simensky said. "There were a lot of women network executives who didn't quite know what to make of it all, and had a little bit of the realization that it might be kind of an odd property."[42]

While *Big House Blues* only did fairly well in focus testing, Nickelodeon wanted to work with John K. regardless of how well the pilot scored. As Coffey told Kricfalusi, "The kids laughed a lot more at your cartoon than the others."

A six-episode first season of *Ren Höek & Stimpy* was officially ordered in September 1990. In December, the pilot started to make the rounds in the film festival circuit, baffling and entertaining children and adults alike. "It was pretty risky; everybody at Nickelodeon was kind of nervous about it," Coffey said. "I told Gerry if she would do the show, if it didn't work, she could fire me. So she said she would give me six half-hours. That's why *Doug* and *Rugrats* had thirteen initial [episodes] at the time, because Nickelodeon was concerned. [*Ren & Stimpy*] was sort of above the line of what they wanted to do for kids."[43]

Thus, Nickelodeon's relationship with John Kricfalusi and Spumco expanded. The network bought a show that they simultaneously wanted and did not want, apparently thinking they could tame the creator once real money began changing hands. *Ren & Stimpy* would make Nickelodeon a key player in changing the face of mainstream animation—and become a thorn in its side.

Animation ID: Big House Blues

What follows is a scene-by-scene breakdown of the pilot episode, *Big House Blues*. Identifications are provided by studio documentation, by John Kricfalusi's blog, and by correspondence with the various animators.

Sc. #	Animator	Sc. Description
Sc. 1	No Animation	"Now believe it or not, I've been known to lie..."
Sc. 2	Jim Smith	First shot of Ren and Stimpy.

Sc. 3	No Animation	BG of prehistoric cat and Chihuahuas
Sc. 4	No Animation	BG of R&S "united in the face of adversity."
Sc. 5	John "Moose" Pagan	Close-up of R&S's eyes.
Sc. 6	Kelly Armstrong	Old Man Hunger gnawing Ren's belly.
Sc. 7	Armstrong	Old Man Hunger gnawing Stimpy's belly.
Sc. 8	Armstrong	R&S eat bread in the park.
Sc. 9	Armstrong	R&S chewing, get tapped on shoulder.
Sc. 10	Armstrong	Pigeon with blackjack.
Sc. 11	Armstrong	R&S stick out tongues.
Sc. 12	Armstrong	Pigeon eats chewed bread off tongues.
Sc. 13	Smith	Pan down on R&S in rainstorm.
Sc. 14	Smith	Close-up of two shivering.
Sc. 15	No Animation	BG of sun shining.
Sc. 16	Smith	R&S's eyes widen.
Sc. 17	Bob Jaques	R&S are run over by truck.
Sc. 18	Jaques	Truck stops, out comes dogcatcher.
Sc. 19	Smith	"Hot diggety dog!"
Sc. 20	Lynne Naylor	R&S are scraped off pavement.
Sc. 21	Andy Bartlett	R&S are scraped off pavement. Truck drives off.
No Sc. 22		
Sc. 23	No Animation	BG of dog pound.

Sc. 24	No Animation	BG of R&S with dogcatcher.
Sc. 25	Smith	"You boys like to have fun don't you?!"
Sc. 26	Bartlett	"Yeah, sure, fun!"
Sc. 27	David Feiss	"Go ahead, have fun!" Dogcatcher shakes ass.
Sc. 28	Jaques	R&S shrug.
Sc. 29	Jaques	Entire party scene in pound cell.
Sc. 30	Feiss	Phil the dog: "Whatdaya think, boys?!"
Sc. 30A	Bartlett	R&S nod in agreement.
Sc. 30B	Feiss	Phil gets yanked off-screen.
Sc. 31	Bartlett	Phil is marched by leering dogcatcher.
Sc. 32	Armstrong	Ren talks to Jasper. "He's goin' to SLEEP!"
Sc. 33		John K./Naylor Ren grabs Stimpy.
Sc. 34	John K./Naylor	Ren fluffs Stimpy like pillow and dives into him.
Sc. 35	Armstrong	Ren wooing Stimpy in his sleep.
Sc. 35A	No Animation	Stimpy's sleep-encrusted eyes of morn.
Sc. 35B	Armstrong	Ren kisses Stimpy and realizes what he's done.
Sc. 36	Jaques	Ren takes, "I've been poisoned!" Runs off-screen.
Sc. 36A	John K.	Ren drinking out of toilet.
Sc. 36B	John K.	"Have you no sense of hygiene?" Ren walks away.
Sc. 37	John K.	Ren greets Jasper.
Sc. 38	Jaques	"You don't wake up, from the BIG sleep."

Sc. 39	John K.	Realization hits Ren.
Sc. 40	John K.	"The big sleep?!"
Sc. 41	John K.	Ren grabs Stimpy: "The big sleep?!"
Sc. 42	John K.	Ren's heart hammers, pants.
Sc. 43	John K.	Stimpy turns directly at camera in confusion.
Sc. 44	John K.	"What's the big sleep, Ren?"
Sc. 45	John K.	Ren pulls Stimpy in: "He's...."
Sc. 46	John K.	"DEAD!"
Sc. 47	John K.	"Dead you idiot!"
Sc. 48	Feiss	Ren piles on top of Stimpy & breaks down crying.
Sc. 49	John K./Naylor	Ren and Stimpy alone in cell.
Sc. 50	John K./Naylor	Stimpy hwarfing hairball onto Ren, smacking.
No Sc. 51		
Sc. 52	Jaques	Dogcatcher leans in; girl darts through his legs.
Sc. 53	Jaques	Ren plays poodle, dogcatcher grabs him.
No Sc. 54		
Sc. 55	Ron Zorman	Girl clutches Ren and takes him away.
Sc. 56	Jaques	Iron bars close on Stimpy.
Sc. 57	Jaques	"I'm alive! I'm alive!"
Sc. 58	Pagan	Stimpy's eyes fill with tears.
Sc. 59	Armstrong	"I'm out of here, JACK!"
Sc. 60	Jaques	Stimpy waves goodbye.
Sc. 61	Armstrong	Ren can't stand his good impulses.
Sc. 62	Armstrong	Ren bargains with girl, kicks ladybug.

Sc. 63	Jaques	Stimpy shakes head uncontrollably.
Sc. 64	Armstrong	Girl makes up mind: "Okay."
Sc. 65	Armstrong	Stimpy crushes Ren in joy.
Sc. 66	No Animation	BG of R&S's new home.
Sc. 67	No ID	Door opens.
Sc. 68	Naylor	R&S at front door, in awe of new home.
Sc. 69	No Animation	BG of living room interior.
Sc. 70	John K.	R&S skip through house, come to halt.
Sc. 70A	John K.	R&S cowering at mom's feet.
Sc. 71	Armstrong	Mom pulls out sweater for Ren.
Sc. 72	Armstrong	Mom puts Ren in sweater.
Sc. 73	Armstrong	Stimpy's gift is presented—the litterbox.
Sc. 74	Jaques	"My foist material possession!"

Chapter 3
Taming an Untamed World

Production began on the six-episode order of *Ren Höek & Stimpy* (later rechristened *The Ren & Stimpy Show*) in October 1990. The series is a landmark in television animation, a show in which there was a concerted effort to bring almost every aspect of the production under the artists' control—an anomaly for television production, both creatively and monetarily. Nickelodeon paid for everything, with the money going directly to John Kricfalusi.

As producer and studio head, he was responsible—for the first time in his career—for the welfare of his employees and contractors. He also felt it his duty to exert as much control over the production at Spumco as possible. Before production started, he asked Vanessa Coffey to have the show's layout done Stateside and—most significantly—to do away with the scripting process altogether, conducting the real writing on storyboards. Coffey "agreed to this system," and it appeared to be perfect for television animation in 1990.[1]

Kricfalusi hired Christine Danzo as series producer, to fill the dearth of production savvy at Spumco after Carl Macek's departure. John K. found Danzo willing and intelligent enough to accept his altered production system and to trust the artists. He considered her a better fit than others due to her mastery of "working with the 'bad boys' of animation," which included a number of years as a producer for Ralph Bakshi.[2]

Word of Spumco spread around Hollywood, and finding artists who wanted to work on the show was easy. Finding those *capable* of working on it was an entirely different matter. In its earliest months, *Ren & Stimpy* had a skeleton crew that did not expand far beyond the Spumco "Big Shots." Joining the studio as writers and board artists were Chris Reccardi, Jim Gomez, and Vincent Waller: a newcomer who entered the Spumco circle through Bob Camp, whom Waller had known since high school.

Spumco did not require any more artists at that time. The biggest sticking point at the beginning of production was getting stories approved by Nickelodeon. The rejection of an entire storyboard for an epic entitled "The Wilderness Adventure" proved the submission process would not be as idealistic as Kricfalusi had expected. Most of the show's eleven-minute cartoons spent an average of two months in preliminary outline stages before being cleared to move to the storyboard phase. Each board also required full approval by Nickelodeon. As a result, the first season was not completely written and boarded until well into March 1991.

Complications between Spumco and any network were inevitable. Camp summarized the prevailing attitude at Spumco as "if you couldn't draw, you didn't count or matter."[3] It was a reactionary stance against the non-artists regularly found in most animation productions, one that flourished in their absence and dominated the Spumco-Nickelodeon dynamic. When it came to writing *Ren & Stimpy*, Kricfalusi claimed his edict of "if you can't draw, you don't write" did not come about because cartoonists made better writers. Rather, he felt cartoonists were the only ones who truly understood what could realistically be achieved in animation. "We know what you can and can't do. The writing is actually the easiest part. We can write a story in an afternoon, but the hard part is to make the stories work."[4]

The story process Kricfalusi used for *Ren & Stimpy* was designed, as was everything in his studio, to give the edge to the artist. Writing began once Kricfalusi had a story premise approved by the network; premises were "not much of anything" beyond "notions or jump-off points," Jim Gomez said.[5] The next step was to flesh out the story in a textual outline; only roughly and briefly, in theory. Long gone were what Waller called the "ponderous forty-six to sixty-page scripts" that the Big Shots were forced to work from on previous jobs. In their place were "truly funny outlines that were written by artists for artists to riff on."[6]

The storyboard was where the dialogue, acting, and life were created in a Spumco cartoon. No longer did Kricfalusi and the others depend on "unwieldy" scripts that got "lost in random details."[7] The artists went back to how cartoons had largely been written in the theatrical animation era: on the storyboard, relying on pure visual storytelling. "We took it back, tried doing it the old way, which is why the cartoons have more personality and more visual humor," Jim Smith told Dan Persons. "Everybody on the crew is invited to come in and look at the storyboard and throw in ideas. This is what gives [a cartoon] all of its depth."[8]

As one producer said, John K. expected everything that "flew off his fingertips" to be the way things should be from start to finish. Nickelodeon, however, insisted on having complete editorial approval of both the outlines and the storyboards, as Nickelodeon was well aware of the changes that could occur between those stages. Consequently, those wearing the "non-artist" hat at Nickelodeon were greeted with open animosity by the Spumco artists—with Kricfalusi's voice the loudest and most prevalent. It did not matter that Nickelodeon's supervising producer, Mary Harrington, had been an active John K. fan long before *Ren & Stimpy* started. She was still telling him what to do, and that arrangement did not suit him.

Mitchell Kriegman was the network's overall story editor on the premiere *Nicktoons* line-up, having previously created the live-action series *Clarissa Explains It All*. Kriegman had long relationships with *Doug* and particularly *Rugrats*; but he was only story editor on *Ren & Stimpy* for its initial six episodes (and possibly even fewer). "When I met John, I [thought he was] potentially like Tim Burton or something," Kriegman said. "He just has a visual storytelling genius and a language that is unique and great. I immediately recognized it, but it didn't matter because I was the enemy."[9]

Kricfalusi and Bob Camp, who took on the role of the show's head writer, both recalled their interactions with Kriegman disdainfully, thinking him to have a very patronizing view of children's comprehension. They tried to explain to him that the show's format was in the vein of *Rocky & Bullwinkle*: full-length cartoons mixed with short, unrelated interstitials, in which the characters lived and acted in a variety of environments. Kriegman supposedly responded, "It won't work. Kids won't be able to understand that. Kids won't be able to follow that. I think it will be more of a challenge to write stories within a restricted environment, than to open the possibilities up." Kricfalusi was stymied by this reaction, whereas Camp more or less flipped out. "Who do you think you're talking to?" Camp asked. "I'm not eight. It's

John Kricfalusi in the "Space Room" at Spumco, reenacting a typical Nickelodeon conference call. Courtesy of Norman Hathaway.

more of a challenge to push your head through a concrete wall, but I'm not going to do it."[10]

Meetings between Spumco and Nickelodeon people typically played out in this manner. More often, however, Kricfalusi in person proved more effective at explaining his ideas than any text outline could be. Premises on paper typically yielded what Chris Danzo called a "Whaaat?" response from Nickelodeon. "We finally realized that [if] John would go on a plane, go to New York, pitch everything verbally, all of a sudden they would get it. That was what they loved. But then they'd go back and draw it, and then it'd be like, 'Oh there's some objectionable stuff put in there that was never really discussed in the first place.'"[11]

New York's supervision over the writing proved counterproductive before long. "Nurse Stimpy" underwent five rewrites before finally proceeding to storyboard.[12] Kricfalusi felt Nickelodeon's genuine misunderstanding of animation's fundamentals caused the constant back-and-forths: "Story editors tend to think of everything as if it's really happening. My theory is that, 'No, it's not happening—it's a fucking lie.' Whoever is the best liar is going to be the most successful."[13] He often singled Kriegman out with Nickelodeon as a target for his resentment. For Kricfalusi, Kriegman typified the sort who wanted cartoonists to go out of their way to be uncreative and unfunny. Kriegman found the whole debacle humorous because he was in fact merely acting as a mercenary: voicing general concerns to Nickelodeon and Kricfalusi that he may not have necessarily felt himself. "The irony to me, of [John K.'s] attitude towards me in the writing, is that I agreed with him. I just had a job."[14]

One exchange over a storyboard between Kricfalusi and Kriegman regarded a graphic close-up of one character as the punch line of a scene. It was akin to the kind of abrupt cutting that Bob Clampett did in his 1940s cartoons, married with a Basil Wolverton edge and an inclination towards gross imagery. A single drawing as a punch line, however, proved too foreign a concept for production hands brought up in the insipid television system. Kricfalusi remembered that his recurring response of "that's the joke" rarely went over well with Nickelodeon. "We don't want to hear, 'that's the joke,'" he said they replied. "We want an explanation for why this is amusing." "When we'd say, 'But it's a cartoon,' they'd really go crazy," Kricfalusi explained. "They hated that explanation even more than, 'That's the joke.'"[15] Yet many of these time-consuming exchanges were born out of naiveté, not willful oppression. "Certainly not wanting to sabotage the way John said, keeping it from being funny," Danzo said. "Everyone's goal was to make it funny and acceptable."[16]

Several exhaustive disputes indeed focused on the show's unfamiliar style. When producer Roy Smith helped Nickelodeon give comments on Spumco's storyboards, he was unfamiliar with Kricfalusi's penchant for awkward jump cuts. Smith noted on the board, "This is a jump cut." To which John K. retorted: "This is supposed to be a jump cut, goddammit."[17]

Far more disturbing to the Nickelodeon executives than pseudo-auteur theories was Spumco's passion for innuendo, bodily functions, and what Linda Simensky called "all sorts of in-jokes and obscure references that staff at Nickelodeon didn't feel were funny or understandable by anyone."[18] The network was not enthralled with the many uses of used Gritty Kitty Litter, Stimpy's "Magic Nose Goblins," or the latent gay overtones they found in the storyboards. When Kricfalusi was told to cut such material, then production assistant Richard Pursel said he would try to emotionally strong-arm Vanessa Coffey and other executives by accusing the network of "taking Christmas gifts away from the kids!"[19] Nickelodeon, for its part, also established unrealistic attitudes from the beginning, with Vanessa Coffey telling artists, "You are God—create."

"I told John when we started the series that I didn't want him to hold back, that it was my job to pull him back," Coffey said. "I wanted him to go for it, and the deal was I would tell him when he went too far. And I'd go to my company and go through it, and they would tell what was too far and what we should do with the show."[20] Kriegman criticized this kind of arrangement as being partly responsible for Spumco's hostile reactions to rejections. It was far too naïve for a network to even suggest that creators have no restrictions, given the kind of personalities they had hired.

"[John K.] was just given an unrealistic idea of how much latitude he really had," Kriegman said. "When reality set in, the network finally [said], 'No restrictions is great as long as you're not doing something that's so offensive that the network's not going to be able to run it.' And John is somebody who naturally pushes limits."[21]

Though John K. often states that *Ren & Stimpy* was strictly a children's show and that he wrote the cartoons for that audience, most of his colleagues would disagree. Only a small fraction of material written for the show ever made it to air; it was very much a "put in twenty things so we can get in two" scenario. Kricfalusi's style, as a rule, is notorious for being "offensive to the max," Camp said. "That's his whole thing, to try and shock and offend people. He likes to play the victim, but that's the name of the game. Of course if you put cartoons like that in the public eye, shit's gonna get cut out!"[22]

Camp could get just as heated as anyone, calling himself Kricfalusi's "right-hand asshole" at the studio and "someone even more volatile than I am" by Kricfalusi himself.[23] Camp supposedly threatened to strangle executives during their very first meeting over the show's content (he denied this ever happened, though admitted he was "really mean" to Kriegman specifically). Fellow Spumco writers eventually had to stop showing Camp network notes altogether because of his hostile reactions.[24]

What is most intriguing about the first months of *Ren & Stimpy* is that Nickelodeon did almost nothing to address the artistic vanities permeating from Spumco during the writing process, or as Camp more bluntly termed them, "our shitty fuck you attitudes."[25] Nor was Nickelodeon quick to rectify their own mismanagement. Soon a power struggle began to emerge—but at this early stage of production, both the network and the studio were too guileless to recognize it.

Kricfalusi's excellent sense of showmanship was one factor that kept Nickelodeon from seeing any danger signs. Like his mentor Bakshi, John K. was an ardent salesman of his ideas and someone who "really got off with going further than what people were comfortable with," writer and story editor Will McRobb said. "He was sort of a bully that way, but at the same time a genius. He'd get in these small rooms with these nervous executives and he would just be foaming at the mouth, doing voices, sweating, waving his hands around, and when it was over, you'd seen an amazing show. You knew you were dealing with a legend, that's for sure."[26]

McRobb began to receive the show's premises and outlines and succeeded Kriegman as story editor before Spumco's writing on the first season was completed.[27] Kriegman left with no hard feelings towards Kricfalusi, only with a deeper admiration for him. He strongly felt Nickelodeon should have appreciated Kricfalusi for the behavior they were instead quarreling about. "The bottom line about the cartoon is, if everybody knew what they were getting into, they may not have done it to begin with."[28]

§

As endlessly passionate and fascinating as the Spumco-Nickelodeon relationship was, a far more interesting, intensive dynamic occurred within Spumco itself. The artists working on *Ren & Stimpy* were few in number, but tightly knit. They quickly became more involved with each other beyond the work on their desks. "There was the same type of pleasures and pain one would find in a family," layout artist Jordan Reichek said. "Rivalries, shared joy at the latest screening, fallings out. The atmosphere at Spumco was one that felt like a big part of your life, not just a job."[29]

Working at the studio has also been compared to "being in a garage band"; certainly, the prevailing "critical loud-mouthed assholes" attitude played a role in that perception.[30] The fridge in the layout room was always filled with beer. Artists would break out their instruments immediately after work when they were not drinking further at the Smalls bar across the street. Said Richard Pursel: "John loved to bring execs in to show us [Pursel, Camp, and Waller] off and say, 'Of course you have to have long, flowing blond hair to write at Spumco!'"[31]

For Spumco, establishing a studio that could make Golden Age-style cartoons in the modern, brutal animation industry did not just require a revised production system and a rebellious nature. It involved making the studio itself a resurrection of Termite Terrace (where the Warner cartoons of the 1930s and early 1940s were made), right down to the brick and mortar; hence Spumco's decision to stay in the same aging, musty-smelling building Carl Macek had chosen out of his frugality. Rumors circulated that the building had once been a private bathhouse for Paramount executives across the street from the studio's main lot. "It had that sweaty, naked old man vibe, [but] was more conductive to creativity," Gomez said.[32]

The hiring of new staffers at Spumco was a very discriminating process, so the studio never filled up with people overnight. Many Warner Bros. layout artists who had worked previously with Kricfalusi would have bolted the second they were offered work at Spumco, but very few were deemed worthy and capable—even those, like Kricfalusi's longtime flunky Eddie Fitzgerald, who actively begged to work on *Ren & Stimpy*. As Camp said in 1992, "There's a lot of people that want to do this stuff, but there's very few people that can actually draw it."[33]

John K. had already assembled his core crew of draftsmen. It included his studio co-owners along with Chris Reccardi and Vincent Waller, the two non-owners who had the most input in the studio's house style. Save for a handful of people, *Ren & Stimpy*'s layout team consisted of people Kricfalusi had either met or worked with on *Beany & Cecil* and afterward. Clearly he chose those whom he perceived as most valuable. The challenge was not so much scouring Hollywood for "budding Harvey Kurtzmans," or finding people willing to work below union scale, as background artist Bill Wray once explained.[34] It was finding people compatible with the studio's environment: one completely centered on Kricfalusi's temperament, and on meeting its demands. Said Reichek: "They cannot just simply be great artists in of themselves. Rather, ones that have skills and tastes similar to John."[35]

Kricfalusi's combative streak ultimately proved too alarming for many. Some embraced it, almost convinced by his bullying that the show was too good or too difficult for them to work on. This trait—Kricfalusi's ability to entrance—made him both successful at singling out talent and at establishing a highly eclectic studio. Color key supervisor Teale Wang described Kricfalusi as being able to find out what makes someone tick in an instant. "John offered me a full-time job, [but] I told him I was going back to *The Simpsons*. He looked at me and said, 'Oh, I get it. You like it safe. You don't like to take chances. I understand.' I got so pissed off, I told him to fuck off and that I'd take his job! I was actually shaking. He knew exactly what he was doing. I only knew him two weeks, but he figured me out in two minutes."[36]

Hiring at Spumco began in earnest in early 1991. There was a lean crew before that, given the short episode order and how long it took to get the writing and storyboards approved by Nickelodeon. A full team of artists was not required immediately. The studio was a mom-and-pop shop in the earliest months of the production, with John K. and Lynne Naylor as the key artists and the others following in their wake.

Though credited as a "Big Shot" through the entire first season, Naylor spent an exceptionally brief time on the *Ren & Stimpy* series. She worked on the first episode, "Stimpy's Big Day", then was gone from the production before March 1991. Nevertheless, her impact and influence on the series and studio was at least equal to Kricfalusi's. Naylor had been Kricfalusi's girlfriend since Sheridan College and was easily his strongest collaborator during that thirteen-year period. Having already co-created the characters and their identities, Naylor had also worked with Kricfalusi on transforming his initial designs of the characters.

The simplification of the character designs was to the series' detriment, Kricfalusi said. The pilot episode used only "the best people," and the stylistic modifications were for the weaker draftsmen's benefit. "When we had to produce multiple episodes at once, I had less time to spend on each one, and we had to hire twenty times as many people and train them all to do this completely foreign style and approach to cartooning."[37]

If Kricfalusi's own "full" animation of the characters in *Big House Blues* is an accurate yardstick, modifications were needed to make these characters survive the rigid television animation pipeline. Extraneous details (notably Ren's tail) were lost, as was much of the "underground" look to the characters. They began to look more commercially viable and traditional—a remarkable feat, given the singular vision behind them. Through Kricfalusi and Naylor's collaboration, Ren and Stimpy were molded into something more streamlined, appealing, and easier to animate—or at least as easy as anything on the show could be.

Naylor's early work became something of a guideline for the rest of the studio's artists. Although Spumco had many artists capable of handling acting scenes and complicated movements, Naylor's relative facility was unmatched. She quickly became the Stimpy expert, just as Kricfalusi gained notoriety for being the only one who truly mastered drawing Ren. (Many have said that Kricfalusi's and Naylor's own relationship was the template for Ren and Stimpy's.) When artists would have trouble drawing Stimpy, John K. would tell them to look at Naylor's scenes in "Stimpy's Big Day" for reference and inspiration. She was also unquestionably responsible for establishing Spumco's trademark "sexy" girls: the kind that exhibited an understanding of the female form and an ability to "exude pure sensuality and innocence at the same time," Chris Reccardi noted.[38]

Naylor was often remembered—in spite of her unbelievable talent and helpfulness—as someone who seemed to have taken a beating long before *Ren & Stimpy* began. As she and John K. came up through the ranks and progressed artistically, their relationship decayed. "She was building up with all this tension because she felt the deadlines much more oppressively than John did," said David Koenigsberg, the studio's technical director. Spumco boys would be making wisecracks, but Naylor "was like the uptight librarian reminding everyone, 'We have to go back to work now.' She was serious, it was not a joke. I remember talking to her one day about how we should laugh at this, and she really couldn't."[39]

Naylor was finishing layouts for "Stimpy's Big Day" when she finally broke up with Kricfalusi and left the studio. "When John told me to sit down, he had something important to say, I thought he was gonna fire me," Richard Pursel recalled. "I must've looked like a beaten puppy. Instead he said, 'I love you!' Then added, 'No I'm just joking. Lynne and I are breaking up and I need you to find me a new place to stay.' It fell to me to find new apartments for both of them."[40]

Naylor was unable to immediately find a position after her departure from Spumco. Kricfalusi had wasted no time denouncing her to the Hollywood animation scene at large, spreading tales that "she was just the girlfriend," hanging around contributing nothing. Bruce Timm—whose dream project *Batman: The Animated Series* was starting at Warner Bros. around the same time—knew the truth, however. Timm hired Naylor, who, by Timm's own admission, radically overhauled his show's female character designs.[41]

In a stroke of good fortune, the raw drama buzzing around Spumco did not impact the tone of the first *Ren & Stimpy* episode. Any unrelated devastation was kept away from the cartoon; quite necessarily, as "Stimpy's Big Day" was the cartoon that established the Ren and Stimpy dynamic and fleshed out their personalities. The opening scene, laid out by Naylor, crystallizes the flavor of the series. Ren chastises Stimpy for being three years old and still sitting on his litter box watching cartoons. Ren asks Stimpy: "Don't you know cartoons will ruin your mind?" He pops open Stimpy's head to reveal a peanut-sized brain—the side effect of watching too much animation—and promptly flushes it back down into his skull like a toilet.

Stimpy says more than the few words and sound effects he uttered in *Big House Blues*. He wants to believe that his cartoon idol, Muddy Mudskipper, is real, and that he stands a chance of winning $47 million and an appearance on the show; but he also wants to appear respectable in Ren's eyes. Ren's personality has no similar compass. Just like the show's drawing style, his nature changes from scene to scene. He feels guilt for chiding Stimpy, but is quickly overcome by greed and obsession when he finds out that the show and contest is not a scam: Stimpy really has become an overnight celebrity. Ren is driven to a state of manic depression by his longing for his feline companion, seeing Stimpy's face in everything from his pillow to a bag of Gritty Kitty Litter.

There is no disputing that "Stimpy's Big Day" had depth that other television cartoons lacked. No longer forced to reinvent the mediocre creations of their long-deceased heroes, the artists were able to channel their energy into giving life to wholly original characters. The story's expanded, half-hour length (the second half of the show was branded "The Big Shot") emphasizes the ambition to truly bring the characters into being. "There was so much we wanted to do with the story, we had trouble packing it into one eleven-minute cartoon," Camp said. "It was actually easier to stretch it than to compress it."[42]

Much like the *Tiny Toon Adventures* cartoons that the Spumco crew reviled, "Stimpy's Big Day" is littered with references to 1950s pop culture. Stimpy and Muddy Mudskipper may reenact a *Yogi Bear* episode, but rather than using the reference as mere window dressing, the writers celebrate the past as they mock it. Stimpy is too stupid to remember his lines, and quotes other Hanna-Barbera shows—as well as cartoon characters that Hanna-Barbera did not even make, like Popeye the Sailor and Elmer Fudd.

"Stimpy's Big Day" offers up a world in which it feels entirely natural to superimpose Kirk Douglas' face over the Hollywood hill; whereas the effect would stick out and fall flat in another studio's cartoon. Everything going on in the Spumco picture is so absurd that a little more absurdity is not going to hurt.

Adding to the cartoon's ridiculousness is a gross-out factor—an element confined solely to John K.'s independent pitches, and completely foreign to his previous work on *Mighty Mouse* and *Beany & Cecil*. The whole plot revolves around Gritty Kitty Litter and does nothing to hide the product's primary purpose. The lack of subtlety is emphasized by a scene in which the character Mr. Horse relieves himself behind curtains to test the brand's "absorbency."

Underneath the subversive attention to psychoses, nostalgia, and bodily functions, "Stimpy's Big Day" and all subsequent *Ren & Stimpy* shows do have the intricacies of a true children's cartoon, as Vanessa Coffey repeatedly reminded the public when the show was accused of being vapid. "There's no profanity or truly sadistic and deviant behavior in this show. It's harmless fun, [and not] at all empty for kids. There's this positive role model of two guys whose relationship is based on true friendship. That's important and meaningful to kids."[43]

When approached about the adult nature of the series, Kricfalusi made similar remarks. "It's absolutely, completely a kids' show," he said. "That's why it's got kids' stuff in it. That's why it's got boogers in it."[44] He later added, "We haven't done our adult show yet. You haven't seen adult entertainment until that one comes out."[45]

To say *Ren & Stimpy* is aimed squarely at a single demographic—be it children or adults—is, of course, a lie. The sole audience in mind, and the arbiters of what worked and what did not, were always the cartoonists at Spumco and John Kricfalusi especially. Many at

Nickelodeon did not think that sensibility would coincide with that of the general population. They were soon proven wrong—and by a larger margin than they ever expected.

§

Despite the success of "Stimpy's Big Day" in creating a winning thematic blueprint for the series, the cartoon is a technical travesty. The drawing is occasionally poor, the animation mostly rigid, and the cleanup and ink-and-paint work is absolutely atrocious. In effect, John K.'s eye for detail turned blind during the first season of *Ren & Stimpy*.

Animation for several of the first season's cartoons, including "Stimpy's Big Day", was done at the Lacewood studio in Ottawa under the direction of Jamie Oliff. Given Lacewood's murky history—involving several changes in name and management—Oliff admitted that his studio "was not the perfect place to do a show like *Ren & Stimpy*."[46] The careless manner in which the animation was handled by Lacewood is startling. Characters melt and pop from pose to pose just as they had in *Mighty Mouse* and *Beany & Cecil*. Layouts may not have been technically perfect; but the mercenary workers that dominated Lacewood made no attempt to transcend the layouts or to preserve the draftsmanship. Spumco simultaneously used the studio Bon-Art in South Korea. In many instances, the Korean animation was actually better than that of Ottawa.

Said Oliff: "I remember having to call a meeting of all the animators and give them a really good going over, because so many of them had such a lousy attitude. They were really lucky to get to work on a project like this, and most of them didn't know what the hell they were doing. A few of the animators really surprised me and recognized what a great opportunity it was. But after years of working on low-quality junk, most were unprepared for a show of the quality of *Ren & Stimpy*."⁴⁷

By the time of "A Cartoon" (better known as "Untamed World"), the last episode to pass through Lacewood, the quality had at least reached the same level as Korean factory animation. Oliff called Kricfalusi and begged him to not send any more shows due to Oliff's own displeasure with the results. This confused Kricfalusi and the other artists, for they thought Lacewood was doing fine—the drawings in all of the Lacewood pictures were still funny, and the jokes came through clear enough, even if no real character animation was involved.

Far more disturbing and noticeable to Spumco was the hatchet camera and ink-and-paint work being done overseas at Fil-Cartoons in the Philippines. A Hanna-Barbera servicer that Bob Jaques once called "the cheapest shithole studio I've ever had the displeasure to work at," Fil-Cartoons was the textbook example of a sweatshop in animation.⁴⁸ Employees were often seen sleeping outside the building because their wages did not cover rent. Toilet paper was not supplied in the bathrooms for fear that the impoverished employees would steal it. On top of all that inhumanity, Spumco had gotten a cheap rate on the ink-and-paint services. So while an episode of *Tiny Toon Adventures* might pass through with no scars, Fil-Cartoons was predisposed to hate *Ren & Stimpy*.

The animator Howard Baker was hired by Spumco as an overseas supervisor after he finished directing on *Rugrats*. By the time Baker arrived at Fil-Cartoons, "Stimpy's Big Day" had gone through camera and ink-and-paint completely unsupervised—a fitting explanation for why the finish on that episode is particularly ungodly. "The very first *Ren & Stimpy*, where Ren's eyelids are black, that's a painting mistake," layout artist Chris Savino said in 1992. The question of whether the outlines of Ren's eyelids, or the eyelids themselves, were black was obviously lost in translation when the Filipino studio consulted Kricfalusi. "John's like, 'Of course they're supposed to be black, what do you want?' So they painted [his eyelids] black. And every time he blinks, they go black."[49]

Overhauling Fil-Cartoons to accommodate a show like *Ren & Stimpy* was not going to happen overnight—even if it meant Baker had to find missing scenes and animate them himself. He described Fil-Cartoons' method of organization as "ingenious. You could go to any department and ask the manager when [was] the last time they had the scene, and then follow the trail until you found it."[50] Baker's perseverance was not strong enough, however, and others at Fil-Cartoons made no attempt to rectify the problems. The later first-season episodes bear fewer mistakes, but the results still made Spumco's more discerning figures livid, Jaques in particular. *Ren & Stimpy* was undoubtedly a thankless chore for Fil-Cartoons, so why bother keeping off the blemishes? Spumco had only provided them with very early drawings of the characters as a guide (some predating even *Big House Blues*), and the need to stay on schedule was neglected, as at all of Spumco's satellite studios. "When I said I needed it by Friday, it always fell on deaf ears," Baker said. "The scenes wouldn't come and then I couldn't get it done on time."[51]

Fil-Cartoons' failures were inevitable, said Koenigsberg, who maintained that the studio followed most of the instructions he gave them. "When you use [overseas studios] for animation, you're gonna to get problems. And you're surprised by what? You have to know that going in. You can't be, 'Oh, I'm shocked that they screwed that up!' Come on."[52] No one at Hanna-Barbera would have cared had their cartoons come back with painting and camera errors. They belonged, after all, to a long tradition of faceless hackwork. The Spumco staff, on the other hand, made their cartoons with far more passion and originality. Their indignation with overseas technical blunders was a given.

§

As *Ren & Stimpy* developed, other elements of animation commanded John K.'s attention. Color and backgrounds became a particular new fixation for him. Though Kricfalusi had battled for authority over voice direction and music in previous productions, he had been indifferent to decisions on backgrounds. He gave little input, for instance, to the work of artists like Vicky Jenson and Ted Blackman in the 1980s. Bruce Timm recalled that Kricfalusi was disinterested in backgrounds during *Mighty Mouse* and *Beany & Cecil*: "He really only cared about the character drawings, so it was like, 'Ah, somebody's got to draw the backgrounds, it might as well be [Blackman.]'"[53]

But Kricfalusi became aware of the importance of good background work on *Ren & Stimpy*. In 2007, he stated "background styles can and should vary wildly" while making sure "they compose around the characters, give mood to the stories, and tickle the eyeballs."[54] Most of the background design on the show's first season was wisely entrusted to Jim Smith, the studio's master of perspective. Cheri Pederson and Caren Scarpulla were the first two background artists hired. The background art director, Bill Wray, had returned to Hollywood after a long hiatus from animation. He made good on his promise to Kricfalusi that he would come back "if we could do a cartoon our way."[55]

The backgrounds quickly became the most unambiguously successful aspect of the first season of *Ren & Stimpy*. Spumco made every shot of a cartoon into an experimental event without smothering the acting or actions, evoking the stylization of 1950s Hanna-Barbera cartoons while verging on pure abstraction.

It was not an overnight success, of course. Kricfalusi and Wray were unrelenting in their critiques of their two background artists' work. In particular, a moon in the "Yak Shaving Day" segment came under savage scrutiny—Kricfalusi had it painted over and over again and nothing pleased him. Despite the fact that Pederson and Scarpulla had gotten much better at their jobs as the season progressed, they were let go anyway. It came down to Wray to finish the bulk of the first season's background color, though Bob Camp has joked "he won't take responsibility for [them]."[56]

The show's most celebrated background technique came into its own fairly early: the use of still paintings for extreme character close-ups, exaggerated to achieve an emotional effect—typically disgusting shock. It was a fitting technique for limited animation. In "Fire Dogs", Ren is given mouth-to-mouth resuscitation by the appropriately named Fat Lady. Ren's horror is captured by a graphic close-up of the Fat Lady that emphasizes every single one of her facial flaws, a far more compelling effect than any take of Ren screaming could be.

Occasionally, the backgrounds are a cartoon's only redeeming quality, as in "Robin Höek" and "The Littlest Giant", two cartoons made under the "Stimpy's Storybook Land" banner. Smith's take on the style of illustrator N.C. Wyeth gives the cartoons an appropriate storybook look and feel—but covers for the worst kind of predictable cartoon writing: the type where, Camp said, "you have to wait for the guy to say what's going to happen before it happens."[57] Not even *Ren & Stimpy* could avoid an overemphasis on certain elements to disguise the lack of character animation.

As the first-season artists developed a feel for what the series was about, attempts at economization were sometimes more blatant than was necessary. "Nurse Stimpy" illustrates how far off the rails a cartoon can go without attentive, strong direction. Chris Reccardi storyboarded the cartoon; his boards were enlarged by Camp and shipped to animation, unchanged, as layouts. Not a single bit of acting or humor comes off remotely well in the result: its story of Stimpy trying to cure an ailing Ren is merely an exhibition of toilet humor. John K.'s indifference to the cartoon while it was being made—the story was rewritten four times—explains its clumsy execution. "It's a really ugly cartoon," Kricfalusi told Dan Persons, without the benefit of the kind of acting he normally embraced.[58] He declined to take directorial credit for the short, hence the "Raymond Spum" pseudonym.

The only saving grace of "Nurse Stimpy" is Bill Wray's repulsively engaging background work, which may be solely responsible for establishing the show's reputation for gross-out humor. But no one on the inside was fooled by this attempt at style over substance. At the cartoon's premiere party, Camp—who co-wrote it—said to Kricfalusi, "Well, John, you finally directed a Hanna-Barbera cartoon."[59] The failure emphasized how vital an element strong character layout was to the series's success. Its importance in *Ren & Stimpy* cannot be overstated. Layout was where "the real shit happened," as Reccardi said, and where John K. exercised the most control as director.[60]

By working with others' characters, and by making a concerted effort at conveying character acting through drawings, Kricfalusi had learned how much power one has over a cartoon. Kricfalusi wanted to push this method of control even further with his own creations, Ren and Stimpy. "If you want to have any detailed and specific control over the finished acting and performances of the characters, you can use layouts to do it. We always did this at Spumco, and our characters' performances are what many fans remember about the shows."[61]

The already rigorous process, barely achievable at Bakshi's, only became more complicated at Spumco. John K. was a studio owner and his own boss. He answered to no one in the building; no piece of artwork, layout or otherwise, could leave the building without his approval. Layout artists at Spumco typically received a section of the cartoon's storyboard from Kricfalusi, who explained what he wanted and expected out of each scene, doing additional drawings on the spot for guidance. These straightaway drawings, layout artist Don Shank said, were "more often than not amazing and could just be resized on the Xerox and used in your actual layout."[62] After the artist had completed his first-draft layouts, Kricfalusi would then go over them, almost always calling for changes and sending the work back for corrections. Once finished, the layout (and artist) would return to Kricfalusi for final approval, starting the cycle anew. An artist would often have to revise a scene three or four times before Kricfalusi finally approved the layouts and they were shipped to the animation house.

Kricfalusi's direction style was always incredibly didactic, almost "aggressive to the point of being combative," the artist Stephen DeStefano said.[63] Spumco quickly became as much a school as a studio, where artists doubled as pupils and employees. "You learn a lot, but then you learn how bad you are," layout artist Mike Kim said. "I think a lot of us were petrified of him, but you could never learn as much in such a short period of time."[64]

This method of browbeating artists with constant revisions was really less a method of education than a means of control—a passion for which Kricfalusi had spent decades nurturing. Jim Gomez recalled that Kricfalusi started a "coloring book club" when he was much younger, in which all members had to color Hanna-Barbera coloring books exactly as their club leader did. Kricfalusi's widely acknowledged practice of living vicariously through the layout artist—"making him redraw it fifty times until he couldn't stand it anymore and have to do it himself"—can only be seen as the culmination of a long-standing pattern.[65]

The top layout artists usually drew the storyboards, and each one had extensive input from John K. himself, guaranteeing his stylistic presence before layout even began. No artist was exempt from the accusation that "you didn't follow the board." Even Jim Smith fought with Kricfalusi over the fact that Smith's layouts for the "Sci-Fi Intro" (which precedes "Space Madness") did not follow Bob Camp's boards perfectly. This "follow the board" mandate was soon hammered into everyone's heads. Shank and many others soon became "painfully aware of when layout poses lost the spark of the original board," engendering a general feeling of inadequacy throughout the studio.[66] Drawing Ren and Stimpy, producer Roy Smith said, was not just "based on whim," but based on John K.'s whim. "If the guy captured John's whim, then fine, it was good. But if you didn't, John would want to do it his way."[67]

Consequently, Kricfalusi's own claim that "the real John K./Spumco style is the combination of whichever artists worked on which cartoon and what we were thinking about at the time" is not entirely accurate.[68] John K. was the center of the *Ren & Stimpy* universe for a reason: the show was the product of the artists channeling whatever Kricfalusi was thinking at the time.

On average, a single scene of animation consisted of ten layout drawings; during the first season of *Ren & Stimpy*, the quota for layout artists was fifteen scenes per week.[69] This meant that, on top of all other duties that came with being a studio head, Kricfalusi had to review and correct thousands of drawings every week. Most industry professionals would have found this practice—even in theory—to be insane. To John K., it was perfectly attainable. Every cartoon, whether it works as a whole or not, shows the benefit of his attentiveness. Though peppered with instances of weak timing, writing, drawing, or animation, the cartoons' overall vitality carries them a long way. When Kricfalusi and his cohorts were wholly successful, as with "The Boy Who Cried Rat!" or "A Cartoon" (Bob Camp insisted "Untamed World" is a misnomer), they managed to bring to the screen the sheer joy and pure anarchy that came with working at Spumco.

The season's best cartoons were the products of strong collaboration between Kricfalusi and his top artists, which proved to be the series' formula for success. Vincent Waller worked closely with John K. on the look and story of the crude but charming "Rat"; Mike Fontanelli, well-acknowledged as a top layout artist at the original Spumco, laid out a prolonged sequence involving Ren getting chewed up by Stimpy.

Jim Smith in his office at Spumco during the first season. Courtesy of Jerry Beck.

Spot-gag cartoons are a potential kiss of death for just about any animated series. "A Cartoon" overcomes these limitations with a resoundingly even pace, funny non-sequiturs, and hauntingly atmospheric layout work. As the picture's key artist, Jim Smith had a hand in almost every scene, a striking example of what Eddie Fitzgerald called Smith's ability to "do things nobody else in the studio could do."[70]

In contrast to the more outspoken and volatile personalities of Kricfalusi and Camp, Smith chose to let his output show his stature in the studio hierarchy. As Jordan Reichek said, "Jim spoke softly, but shit, that man's stick is HUGE!"[71] In "A Cartoon", Smith's reinterpretations of Ren and Stimpy as various other creatures perfectly capture the downright eeriness of ugly animals in their natural habitats. Smith caricatures nature to great humorous effect, where even the blank stares of the Needle-Billed Chihuahua or Crocostimpy are brilliant sight gags in themselves.

The miniseries "Commander Höek and Cadet Stimpy"—a concept Kricfalusi claims Nickelodeon originally hated—offers a curious yet perfect illustration of the first season's varying levels of success. Born from one of John K. and Jim Smith's writing sessions at a bar, the outer space format gave the artists license for drawing and writing increasingly weirder material.

The worst entry is "Marooned", the victim of an alleged freelance timer's attempt to slow down every gag to help pad the running time. (Old Bakshi cohort Kent Butterworth was blamed at the time, but he claimed innocence and said he never touched the episode.) What started as a funny storyboard by Reccardi became a cartoon in which every gag is ineptly telegraphed. When Ren gets his head bitten by a "space cabbage" that Stimpy serves him, the attack should happen quickly enough to elicit surprise as well as laughs; as it plays out in the cartoon, we know the carnage is going to happen long before it actually does.

"Black Hole" is marginally better. Camp dubbed it "a cartoon without a director," and it plays like one.[72] Ren and Stimpy journey through an uncharted galaxy and transform into various mutated beings until they literally implode at the cartoon's finish. "Black Hole" at least attempts to build up genuine suspense to an ironic ending, but it is still a foreboding predecessor to many future *Ren & Stimpy* cartoons that lack coherent gag structure, substitute silliness for substance, and suffer from non-direction.

The origins of "Black Hole" have been heavily disputed. Camp claimed more than once to have *de facto* co-directed it with John K., describing it as the picture on which he got his "feet wet as a director." Kricfalusi fervently denied this on principle, claiming that since neither he nor Camp supervised the production from start to finish, the lack of a director credit is appropriate. "A director is somebody who, right from the story stage, follows it all the way through to the end, and it's his idea and vision," Kricfalusi told Dan Persons.[73]

Kricfalusi also refuted the idea that Will McRobb contributed anything to the story,[74] though McRobb himself cited it as his one real writing job on the series.[75] Two important points emerge from this quarrel. First, John K. is thoroughly convinced that a non-drawing writer could not contribute anything meaningful to one of his pictures; and second, Spumco staffers could fiercely desire proper credit, even for Spumco's failures.

At the opposite end of the spectrum from "Black Hole" is the debut "space" cartoon, "Space Madness": *Ren & Stimpy's* first genuine masterpiece and the one that made Kelly Armstrong—among others—think: "Now I understand what this series is going to be."[76] During their thirty-six year journey in space, Ren succumbs to the dreaded Space Madness disease from isolation. While not Ren's first nervous breakdown of the series, this was the first truly effective one. As the Chihuahua becomes more irritable and psychotic by the second, quoting Kirk Douglas in *Champion* (1949), we witness something more than random insanity. Strong pacing, drawing, animation, and deft voice work believably emphasize the performance.

Billy West claimed that Kricfalusi probably intended to do the voice of Ren himself from the beginning, though such an impression was not apparent immediately.[77] To relieve himself of at least one duty, Kricfalusi spent months searching for another Ren Höek voice. Auditions were held as late as April 1991, well into the production of the series. Trying out were voice artists Joe Alaskey, Frank Welker, Carlos Alazraqui, and *Mighty Mouse*'s Patrick Pinney.[78] Ultimately, after counseling with others, Kricfalusi chose to continue voicing his own creation. "Nobody could do it to the degree he wanted it, and to me, there were ten people who could have done it," Chris Danzo said.

"Most people couldn't get that edge. Even Billy couldn't even do it to the degree that John wanted."[79]

Kricfalusi's decision was justified by his performance on the voice track for "Space Madness". His best reads are truly demented, channeling the most skin-crawling and shocking of Peter Lorre's mannerisms. Ren's raving about his "beloved ice cream bar" contrasts well with Billy West's work. An aggressive narrator character, later dubbed the Salesman, makes his first appearance; West's intimidating voicework in the role drives Stimpy to unusually extreme behavior: not just physical abuse or anguish, but sealing his own doom. West's masterful variation in vocal technique, from subtle to booming, had been quite absent in most animated cartoons, television or otherwise.

Shallow is the cartoon that depends solely on strong voicework, rather than balancing the voices with equally compelling animation. "Space Madness" is blessedly not one of them. Nor is it discernibly harmed by non-Spumco hands, like many other cartoons of the first season; Bill Wray called it "the only one that was close to what we wanted."[80] "Space Madness" was another strong collaboration between Jim Smith and John K., along with Chris Reccardi. The cartoon embodied spirited acting in its layout work. Smith composed very complicated, organic shots of the spaceship interior, upon which Ren and Stimpy—and their states of mind—read pitch-perfectly. The eye is drawn to the characters rather than the backgrounds, an excruciatingly difficult effect to achieve in a highly stylized environment. Smith pulled this sort of flair off regularly and, as his colleagues said, rather effortlessly.

Bob Jaques' studio, Carbunkle Cartoons, had not done much work on the series since the pilot, though he and Armstrong were brought to Spumco to help kickstart the season's production. (Jaques did storyboard slugging and sheet timing and Armstrong drew character layouts on various interstitials and "The Boy Who Cried Rat!") By

June 1991, scenes for *Space Madness* were being delivered to Carbunkle in Vancouver and handed out to animators.[81]

Carbunkle's first job, on the interstitial "Stimpy's Breakfast Tips", was completely ravaged by Fil-Cartoons in ink-and-paint. Bad exposure and painting ran rampant and several pieces of animation were dropped entirely. The Filipino studio, in what Jaques termed "a retarded move," added animation when they were not supposed to. One shot of a Muddy Mudskipper cereal-bowl caddy, for instance, originated as a still painting by Bill Wray. Fil-Cartoons assumed Carbunkle had made a mistake in leaving motion out of the scene, and proceeded to animate Stimpy's hand coming in to place the caddy—as well as the inanimate Muddy's eyes.[82]

There was no way to differentiate Carbunkle's work on "Breakfast Tips" from that of other animation houses, but the studio's exalted status on the series was plainly apparent in "Space Madness". The Spumco-Carbunkle dynamic illustrated the way the animation system ideally works—in which an animator transcends the layouts given to him or her. "His animation made our acting way better, because he animated it beautifully," Kricfalusi said of Jaques' direction. "He adds subtle nuances to make the acting more rich."[83]

The animator's role in enhancing the level of acting in the Spumco cartoons makes it curious that only individual layout artists—not animators—ever tend to be mentioned in press pieces and oral histories on *Ren & Stimpy*. It is understandable, and lamentable, that those who toil away in the Korean sweatshops are never fully recognized for their work on American productions. The manner in which cartoons reach Asian animators' desks is pure assembly-line, regardless of what American directors may profess. Such was not the case at Carbunkle. As Mike Kim said, "These guys *here* [in Hollywood] can't draw them."[84] Actually animating Ren and Stimpy was correspondingly harder. John K.'s edict—that artists could not tone down or change even one line in his drawings—naturally extended to the animation houses. Kricfalusi apparently resigned himself to accept subpar work in many instances; a plethora of scenes in non-Carbunkle episodes look as though the original layout was not followed at all.

At Carbunkle, animator Ron Zorman described how he and others learned the importance—and complications—of sticking to Kricfalusi's layouts and making sure they were not weakened. The crew shared Jaques' opinion that the task called for a fair amount of resourcefulness. "*Ren & Stimpy* animation is tricky because it involves the animator sticking to layout drawings that don't always flip well," Zorman said. "They're funny to look at but they don't always make sense for animation purposes. Your job as the animator is to find creative ways to get them to work because John will notice if they've been altered."[85]

At Carbunkle, the animators took their roles seriously when it came to instilling life into characters. "I think that each of us approached our scenes in roughly the same way—by acting [them] out ourselves," said the animator Scott Mansz, who joined Carbunkle in the show's second season. Interaction at the Vancouver studio was encouraged because "each scene was really a sort of evolution. There was always someone gesturing emphatically or mumbling the dialogue to themselves at their desk. Sometimes we had to use the hallway when more space was needed to avoid knocking things (or people) over!"[86]

It is no mere coincidence that the animation in "Space Madness" is more effectively intense than in other shorts. Spumco sent its most passionate stories to Carbunkle because Jaques, like Kricfalusi, was a director who pushed his crew past their self-perceived limits—but in a far more productive and decisive way. "Bob would come in with the exposure sheet saying, 'I'm trying to do something here,' and [he] would explain what [he's] trying to get," the animator Chris Sauve said. "And we'd just try it and do it, pull out a frame, or push this farther.

In 'Space Madness', where he goes, 'Do you have to keep tapping like that?!' I just drew it. I had done this drawing and went to lunch and when I came back there was a drawing of Bob's on top of it that was really nice and it said, 'More intense.'"[87]

The Carbunkle couple was insistent that their product still qualified as limited television animation; just done with more finesse than the norm, as Armstrong explained:

> "We did use lots of 'cheats' for various problems, but eventually the animation style came down to moving the characters fully when they were in action, then holding them when we could. Rather than limited, the style we developed was more pose-to-pose animation, like modified Chuck Jones style. We developed an extended limited lip-sync style too and usually kept the bodies still when the mouth was moving so there would just be one set of paint-backs with each mouth shape instead of a million variations. Bob was getting really good at acting theory and he separated action in the animation too, so we could use less line mileage but keep the illusion of fuller animation but for a television budget and schedule. We used lots of overshoots, pops, shrink takes, staggers and canny displacement—none of which had been incorporated into television animation for some time."[88]

Jaques was unrelenting in his opinion that Fil-Cartoons ruined most of the animation in "Space Madness". Bad camera errors and dropped animation were present—not at the level of other first-season cartoons, but enough for Jaques' own discriminating eye to notice. Laypeople—and even John K.—were not aware of these problems. But Kricfalusi could still find flaws, even in Carbunkle's work. Before camerawork began, John K. had an artist redraw and animate the effects for the floating bathwater scenes because Carbunkle's work was not to his liking. "The design of the water varied from layout to layout, so, as per the rules, we followed the layouts," Jaques said. "He could have sent the footage back for changes, but it was that growing OCD in him that made him want to touch stuff that was beyond his skill level."[89]

Jaques' brand of follow-through was the push and commitment that the cartoons needed to gain their prestigious status. While thanks to John K. and his in-house crew, most viewers loved *Ren and Stimpy* as a whole, the episodes in which Spumco collaborated with Carbunkle are those that elevate *Ren & Stimpy* from mere television show to something resembling film—and give Kricfalusi true bragging rights as as one of the medium's most important directors. Hence Bob Camp's comment: "All of John's greatest animation, that he holds up as the basis of his genius, is all Bob Jaques' animation."[90]

This is not to say that Carbunkle "made" Spumco, as cartoons lacking Carbunkle's touch are often tremendously entertaining. Rather, Carbunkle was a vitally important element in what David Koenigsberg called "pulling off" *Ren & Stimpy* as a whole. "The first time I saw the board for 'Space Madness', I looked at it and I said, 'Oh my god, we have to do everything right for this to work.' That was the turning point where, I can't say everything was working, but it showed what we were capable of doing."[91]

Indeed, "Space Madness" was the first *Ren & Stimpy* cartoon to show the method to John K.'s own perceived madness. Just about everything clicked for an important and gratifying moment in television history, exemplifying the virtues of the animated cartoon as a means of artistic vision and collaboration. "A cartoon like 'Space Madness' could never be made as an independent film— or even at another studio with all the same people," Kricfalusi said.

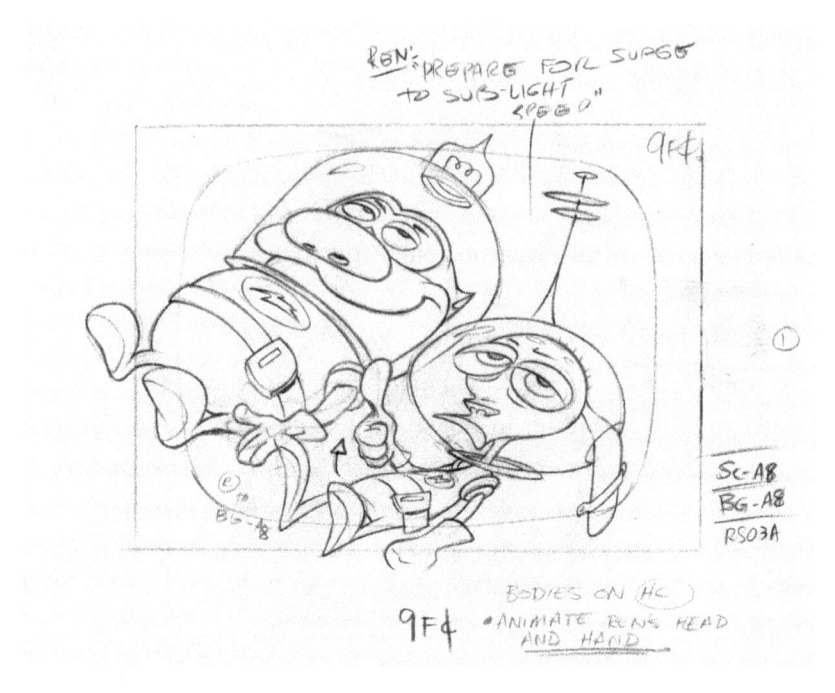

Layout drawn by Bob Camp for the "Sci-Fi" introduction that precedes "Space Madness". Courtesy of Bob Jaques. © Viacom.

"It took a lot of top talent, a production system designed for talent, and a sympathetic creative director who urged the best from everyone. And a network executive who allowed it to happen. More than what we all thought we were capable of, I'm sure."[92]

§

The fact that "Space Madness" exists might have been part of *Ren & Stimpy*'s undoing. It proved that the capabilities of a television cartoon could indeed be redefined—but not on a typical animated series budget and schedule. It was against most of the crew's natural instincts to make a cartoon without being exceedingly particular.

A cartoon with less attention to direction and detail than "Space Madness" often risked missing its scheduled airdate.

Only rarely did a Spumco cartoon have visible signs of haste, as was the case with "Fire Dogs". It was, by Kricfalusi's own admission, "written in an afternoon"[93] and what Camp called "a regular cartoon; lots of mayhem and running around and physical humor. It's not the usual bizarre fare."[94] Rushed through Spumco without anyone slugging the storyboard, "Fire Dogs" was among the few cartoons that came in critically under-length, at less than eight minutes. There was no hope of sending more "Fire Dogs" footage through Carbunkle and Lacewood; the cartoon's rushed production had already divided animation duties between the two. Instead, Fil-Cartoons was given the job of animating a previously cut sequence that was reinstated, involving Mr. Horse being interviewed about his crippling fall to the pavement.[95] The amateurish drawing and animation of this section are a testament to its frenzied conception.

Layout drawn by Kelly Armstrong for the original "Powdered Toast Man" interstitial. Courtesy of Bob Jaques. © Viacom.

Lengths of the Spumco cartoons varied wildly in the first season; most were actually shorter than the typical Saturday morning cartoon's eleven minutes. The reasoning behind this was to accommodate a proposed format that filled the remaining time with *Ren & Stimpy*'s celebrated bumpers and fake commercials. In the spirit of Jay Ward's *Rocky & Bullwinkle*, these one-to-two-minute jaunts were usually just as memorable and varied as the longer cartoons.

Ren and Stimpy taught kids about Yak Shaving Day, and showed how to open new boxes of cereal (to get the prize inside) without their parents knowing. Stimpy's alter ego, Dr. Stupid, enlightened children with fascinating tidbits about bean slabs and camels' humps. The world was also introduced to intriguing breakfast products like Powdered Toast—and its superhero spokesman Powdered Toast Man. At the finish of each show, Ren consoled a downcast Stimpy and suggested something he could do until the next show; it typically involved one of Stimpy's orifices.

The fake commercial for the kids' toy "Log" appropriates nostalgia (its boy lead, animated by Kelly Armstrong, is obviously derived from breakfast mascot Marky Maypo) and crystallizes the series' knack for making absurdity commonplace while satirizing the fact that advertisors can sell you anything.

These bumpers were created with the intention of allowing more time to be spent working on the actual cartoons. But they were a disaster in practice. Originally, there was high ambition regarding these short pieces; outside designers were hired for them. But as Spumco awaited Nickelodeon's full approval on each one, Kricfalusi realized that "each of these short pieces has to be treated like a whole new cartoon in conception, storyboard, layout, [etc.]," as he wrote to Chris Danzo.[96]

Accordingly, just to have something finished, these short pieces were gracelessly rammed through the system. Some were not even used in the first season's original broadcasts. At least one "Goodbye" bumper never aired at all.

It is easy to blame John K. for much of the series' lateness. His all-consuming desire for control over the entire product did cause most of the delays. The reward during this period was that the show had zero equals in the world of animation. Reality often hit the studio hard, though, when it became painfully clear that almost all of the holdups were coming from the director's chair.

"In a production line, you can only go as fast as the smallest department, and John was the smallest department," Chris Danzo said. "Everything had to funnel through him, so he had things backed up all over the place. John had to be [in charge down] to the minutest detail of every production, of running the studio. *He* had this vision, and *you* can't do it; he tried too hard. There was [always] a parade of artists coming into my office in total frustration, even the ones who were close to him."[97]

When confronted with the consequences of his painstaking direction, Kricfalusi countered that producing more footage faster (i.e. getting footage done on time) would mean "poorer quality overall" and "less good footage." Comparing *Ren & Stimpy* to *Doug* in terms of proper cartoon management was illogical in Kricfalusi's mind. Despite sharing the same network and program block, *Ren* and *Doug* were neither artistically nor monetarily on the same level. "*Doug* has thirteen half hours," Kricfalusi wrote in a memo to Danzo. "Our show is much harder to draw and animate. Our story format is much more complex. We have the best cartoonists and writers in the industry. We have to pay competitive rates in L.A."[98]

But Kricfalusi could not blame Nickelodeon's interference for how long the *Ren & Stimpy* cartoons were taking to draw. Not once does he mention network changes in his studio-wide "Big Layout Memo." Rather, Kricfalusi outlines how the layout artists should be doing fewer drawings to "get back on schedule."

"We are doing 'limited animation,'" he wrote to his artists. "A layout should just have enough clear information for the animator to understand the scene." Among what he described as "lies" were not to add animation breakdowns to layouts; to use more holds and reuse more poses; and not to add actions that are not in the storyboard.[99] These were all rules that the artists broke time and time again, with Kricfalusi himself the biggest offender. What is *Ren & Stimpy*, after all, if you do not break every rule, including your own?

Spumco's reputation for such skylarking was precisely why Nickelodeon became intensely overprotective of the show. The network feared that John K. would not be able to deliver if they did not step in. Nickelodeon's goal was to be just as involved as Kricfalusi in every aspect of the production. Beyond scrutinizing every aspect of the budget and schedule, the network insisted on being privy to the creativity at Spumco—exposing their own ignorance in the process. Kricfalusi said that a secretary (most likely him disparaging Mary Harrington) of Vanessa Coffey's sent a thirty-page list of requested changes "a month after we had shipped the first couple of episodes to be animated! And what were the changes about? Ninety percent of them were to tell us that the scenes on the storyboards didn't 'hook up.'"[100]

The network also tried getting around Kricfalusi whenever they could, in the hopes that other people at Spumco might temper what Nickelodeon pereceived as John K.'s erratic behavior. Nickelodeon attempted—behind Kricfalusi's back—to make critical comments directly to the artists and try to have someone keep track of every change made from storyboard to layout. This was naïiveté on Nickelodeon's part, Danzo insisted, but it was still frustrating. Nickelodeon felt they were teaching Spumco, while the studio was adamant that the network was in need of education. "I had to write to them and say, 'You can't go directly to the artists, because it's counterproductive, it's very confusing to the artists, and for certain John has to know what's going on.' Everyone wanted the show to succeed; they didn't want it to go down. They were just protective."[101]

The network initially lacked the foresight to see that *Ren & Stimpy* would be part of their library and on the air forever—an ironic stance, given that Nickelodeon was born as a rerun repository. Their overprotective behavior grew largely out of fear of failure. This was their first foray into full-scale animation production; one bomb in that debut could put an end to future endeavors. Yet Nickelodeon's nervousness seemed like unjustified caution to the crew of *Ren & Stimpy*. Everyone involved at Spumco knew the show was "this really great secret that was going to be premiered to the world," voice artist Cheryl Chase said.[102] David Koenigsberg, the poor soul enlisted by Nickelodeon to keep track of post-storyboard changes (giving up after barely a week), realized that Spumco had captured lightning in a bottle. Koenigsberg, like everyone else at the studio, implored Nickelodeon to exploit it. "You have to convince the network that this is in their best interest in the long run. Let us spin gold for you, stop trying to make us stop spinning gold for you. I'm there, and I know the long-term interest in everyone that it's better to make these shows good while we're all here."[103]

The network interference caused by Nickelodeon's lack of worldliness was not the root of all the series' foibles, as many Spumco people claim. Nickelodeon was relatively toothless compared to the truly meddlesome people in broadcast television; suits at focus groups and competing networks, who often relished abusing animation artists. Rather, Nickelodeon's naïveté proved most fatal to *Ren & Stimpy* because it entailed their acceptance of the Spumco lifestyle, which was never made clearer than during the first season.

Nickelodeon planned to launch its *Nicktoons* lineup on 11 August 1991 and wanted a new episode of each series each week. The only show of the three that did not meet that commitment was *Ren &*

Stimpy. When new episodes of *Doug* and *Rugrats* aired on August 18th, a repeat of "Stimpy's Big Day" was run. "From public record, it was fucked from the beginning," Bob Camp stated. "The stupid show didn't deliver. The second cartoon wasn't delivered and they had to rerun the first cartoon."[104]

Spumco was originally contracted to deliver one episode per week over a six-week period, approximately two to three weeks before the episode was slated to air. As overtime became more and more frequent at the studio in the summer of 1991, it became obvious that Spumco would not fulfill its agreement with Nickelodeon. Well into August 1991, half of the episodes had not been animated. Why did Nickelodeon not object more loudly? The network staff may have been silently aware of their own involvement in delaying the series' production. They certainly understood that *Ren & Stimpy* was vastly superior to the other *Nicktoons* and, as a result, would simply take longer to make—though no one at the network would dare say so in plain terms.

"The show was just harder than we thought it was going to be to make," Vanessa Coffey said. "It was very full animation, it was trying out a lot of new things, and John is a perfectionist. The others [*Doug* and *Rugrats*] were obviously hard too, but it was very full animation. The layouts were being done here, and the other shows were shipping that sort of stuff overseas. John had never delivered a show on that kind of schedule before, so I think he promised more than he could deliver, and we just accepted that."[105]

Nickelodeon's acquiescence to accommodating Spumco proved costly. The two parties agreed to change the terms of the original agreement, allowing the delivery of a new half-hour of *Ren & Stimpy* every other week over a twelve-week period. As a result of this decision, Nickelodeon had to calm down (and pay off) disgruntled advertisers while saying—just as Spumco had said to them—"We can't deliver what we promised over six weeks, but we can do it in twelve." "It was tough on every level: Viacom, ad sales, viewers, and me," Coffey explained. "Obviously, when launching a new series you would like to have new episodes each week but that was not the case with *Ren & Stimpy*. It was stressful every episode because I never knew if I would actually get the episode on time!"[106]

Even with the extended deadlines, Spumco still did not deliver in a timely fashion. The haphazard "Fire Dogs" was late, so a cutdown version of *Big House Blues* was run in its place, much to John K.'s chagrin. The premieres of "Marooned" and "A Cartoon" turned up with reruns of "Robin Höek" and "Space Madness" respectively. By December 1991, the highly ambitious, costly episode "Stimpy's Invention" had still not aired and gained notoriety as "the lost episode of Ren & Stimpy."

For original viewers, watching *Ren & Stimpy* on Nickelodeon was a frustrating experience given the lack of new content. Its ratings reflected that. Though the show was part of the historic 2.9 rating when the Nicktoons block launched, its ratings were almost always behind those of *Doug* and *Rugrats*.[107] Shortly after New Year 1992, in the final first-season cartoon, Spumco's emphasis on quality over quantity—and timeliness—would pay off with a vengeance.

Chapter 4
Stimpy's Invention

During the writing sessions for *Ren & Stimpy*, Bob Camp came up with an idea for a short entitled "Stimpy's Inventions," in which Stimpy makes Ren the guinea pig for his useless creations. What might have ended up as an inconsequential gag picture quickly evolved into something considerably more elaborate. Camp said that John K. "fell so in love with [the idea] that he constantly re-refined everything in it to the point of ridiculousness, until everything was perfect."[1] The title became singular and it developed into one of the funniest—and most delightfully odious—animated character studies ever produced.

During a car ride home after the idea was born, Kricfalusi

suggested to Camp: "Look, why don't we have him have a real fit and go insane at one point, and then Stimpy decides he's going to make the invention that's going to cure Ren."[2] The focus of the picture was the Happy Helmet, a device that forces Ren to be happy at all times and to "do wonderful things for my best friend Stimpy." Against his will, he serves Stimpy's many repulsive needs, all with a smile on his face. The biggest insult to Ren's integrity—during the cartoon's climax—is a forced dance with Stimpy to the cat's favorite song, "Happy Happy Joy Joy." Perhaps the artists knew they were onto something with the story. Yet no one at the studio or network could have predicted the full year that "Stimpy's Invention" would take to make.

The dispute over who was responsible for the cartoon's prolonged production and extreme tardiness can be whittled down to two sides: John K. versus almost everyone else involved. "It took longer because it took forever for them to approve it," Kricfalusi said to Dan Persons. "They wanted me to throw it out completely when they saw the storyboard—they just did not get it. Finally, I had to throw myself on my knees and just beg [Vanessa Coffey] to let me do it."[3]

John K.'s drawings of Ren wearing the Happy Helmet. © Viacom. Courtesy of Norman Hathaway.

There is credence to the director's story. As written and boarded, it was obviously less a children's television show than a live-action-style "psychodrama," with plenty of material Nickelodeon objected to or eliminated. "The main note I remember was the reaction to Ren smiling so wide that the top of his head separated from his lower jaw, and bounced around like a happy cork," Vincent Waller wrote. "That was just too horrible and jarring to air."[4]

That scene did indeed make it into the picture, along with many other elements Nickelodeon was wary of, specifically many Camp drawings of Ren getting psychotically happier (some were cut, most remained). Waller also recalled the network's nervousness over what they considered a child-abuse subtext: Ren rolling his newspaper to beat Stimpy. Waller and Kricfalusi spoke of a ridiculous back-and-forth over the scene in which Stimpy uses a duck as a soldering gun. "They thought it looked too painful for a duck, because it might hurt a duck to have his head do things to hard metal like this," Waller remembered. "We could change it to a woodpecker because woodpeckers are used to having their beaks do things like this." Kricfalusi responded most diplomatically to this request: "I just sent them back a note saying, 'No.'"[5]

No Nickelodeon staffer of the period denies that arguments like this occurred. But neither Vanessa Coffey, Mitchell Kriegman, nor Will McRobb remember the clashes escalating to a point at which they wanted to completely abandon the cartoon, as Kricfalusi has frequently claimed. The cartoon was in outline form for a period of nearly six weeks and was fully written and boarded by Camp at the end of February 1991.[6] If Nickelodeon had such serious problems with the storyboards for the cartoon, it was unknown at the time to many at both the studio and the network.

"We were not going to bag, ever, 'Stimpy's Invention', the whole show," said Coffey. "There were just pieces of it that [Nickelodeon] didn't want to air. That particular episode was not about fighting over content—it was more about the perfectionist part of it. John didn't want to send certain things over until it was perfect."[7]

Most Spumco staffers of 1991 share Coffey's view. Chris Danzo, who had been acutely aware of material being completely thrown out in the first season, remembers nothing of the kind happening with "Stimpy's Invention". "I don't think anything would have gotten made if Nickelodeon didn't like it. If they hated something, it would have never gotten made. I think he had to push to suggest certain things, but everyone had the show's best interests in mind."[8]

Even if Nickelodeon had wanted to throw out "Stimpy's Invention" in its entirety, the resulting delays would have occurred very early in the production. Instead—according to Camp, one of the cartoon's chief architects—most of the delays sprang not from Nickelodeon, but from Kricfalusi's micromanaging directorial style. "We killed ourselves on [it]. That's why we never finished it. We kept fucking with it and fine-tuning it. That show was a magic combination. It was my drawings coupled with John being fanatical about this cartoon and not letting up on any point, beating everybody to death to get perfection."[9]

Camp's boards mirror the final cartoon almost perfectly, and Kricfalusi was exactly right about not watering down the originals; it would have killed the picture, as Camp's boards are practically character layouts themselves. "I was in the room when Bob was boarding, and he basically wrote and directed that cartoon in the storyboard stage," Jim Gomez said. "So what you saw in the end result was right off the board, only in color; kind of like [Hayao] Miyazaki."[10]

The drive to make "Stimpy's Invention" the hit of the season forced the megalomaniac Kricfalusi to shatter the production schedule entirely. Rescheduled for broadcast in October 1991, the short was still not even completely animated at that point. Nothing mattered to John K. except that the cartoon be the best Nickelodeon would ever air. "He

Stimpy's Invention

One of Bob Camp's storyboard drawings of Ren's transition considered too extreme by Nickelodeon. © Viacom.

just took back everything that the artists have done and said, 'I want to do it this way, it's even more funny if we try it this way,'" Chris Savino told Jon Drukman in 1992. "It didn't matter about the budget, it didn't matter about the deadline. As long as it was as funny as he wanted it and he made the audience laugh, then that's the way it's gonna be."[11]

The layouts done by Jordan Reichek for the sequence with Stimpy's first attempt at building the Happy Helmet—and the result farting in his face—apparently strayed so far from Kricfalusi's rough drawings that they had to be redone ad infinitum until they met the director's approval. Said Reichek: "Those scenes were nightmares. A lot of footage for one stationary set-up. [It was] integral to the story and John was very hands on. The action that was on camera was so important: Stimpy's acting. Watching Larry Fine in full-screen operate on someone's open chest cavity is not nearly as effective as a close-up on his demented face while you hear the wood sawing and jack hammering off screen."[12] The accepted truth, that John K. would eventually redraw everything himself in layout, is hardly an exaggeration here; the main reason for the cartoon's lateness *was* that he was redrawing more and more layouts.

Areas of production that rarely posed extensive problems became muddled on "Stimpy's Invention". One of the cartoon's most infamous delays involved neither acting nor drawing. A single gift box, the one containing Stimpy's "Sta-Put Socks," held up production for an extraordinary length. Said Teale Wang: "John told me to 'make it girlie.' I started mixing paint, [and] gave him about four or five versions to choose from. This went on for about a month!"[13] Wang's accumulated work on the scene became "like something out of *The Shining*," Jerry Beck said, who saw "four walls filled with cels of one thing—but all different colors—the box that Stimpy gives Ren," on one of his regular visits to Spumco.[14] "There must have been at least fifty versions of the present," Wang added. "He ended up choosing the very first one I ever did, but I don't think he was ever really happy with it."[15]

Had the box incident been an isolated case, there might be little truth to the charge of Kricfalusi being an indecisive director. But as production moved along it became impossible to predict what his next move would be, and he would become irate if one tried to second-guess his decisions. David Koenigsberg found this out upon accurately guessing which color Kricfalusi would pick for the Happy Helmet: "He comes storming into our workspace, and yells at me in front of everyone, 'You're wrong!!' and storms out. He wasn't kidding around, he was really fucking angry. And I remember looking at Chris Reccardi,

'I don't know what that was for.' And Chris says, 'Welcome to the club.'"[16]

Kricfalusi's direction at Spumco also severely bottlenecked the animation process in Canada, as scenes trickled into Carbunkle throughout August and September 1991. The Vancouver crew was forced into a temporary three-week layoff—there was not enough footage coming in to keep the animators busy.[17]

Though most of the cartoon went to Vancouver, "Stimpy's Invention" had the distinction of being the only first season *Ren & Stimpy* cartoon with extensive footage animated in Los Angeles. Julian Chaney animated the scene with Ren going through the kitchen drawer; the "Happy Happy Joy Joy" dance was by Steve Markowski. Animation veteran Mark Kausler animated two key scenes with a kind of passion: Ren smashing his head (and the Happy Helmet) with the hammer, and Stimpy dancing with his ass.

Kausler described Kricfalusi as "not an easy director to please" and that "he didn't always know what he was looking for." Kausler animated both of his scenes at least five times each. One of Kausler's takes of the ass dance "was so exaggerated that Stimpy's cheeks were like a giant waving flag. John at first rejected that version as too extreme for him. Several weeks later, John called me and wondered if I still had the drawings from the 'extreme' version of the scene. I told him I did, and he decided to use them after all. That job paid $35 a foot, and that was for the 'approved' foot, so I think he got a good deal."[18]

These directorial decisions could not be blamed on Nickelodeon; and the network, ultimately responsible for indulging the director, could not deny responsibility for having done so. "Stimpy's Invention" was still in production in October 1991, well after most of the Spumco artists were dismissed for the break between seasons. Despite Kricfalusi's proclamations to the contrary, the costly revisions were caused by the excessive fine-tuning he demanded as a filmmaker, not by the mandates of an editorial board of non-artists. Danzo recalls Kricfalusi locking the door of his office and refusing to "let it out until he had gone through the entire show and had it the way he wanted."[19]

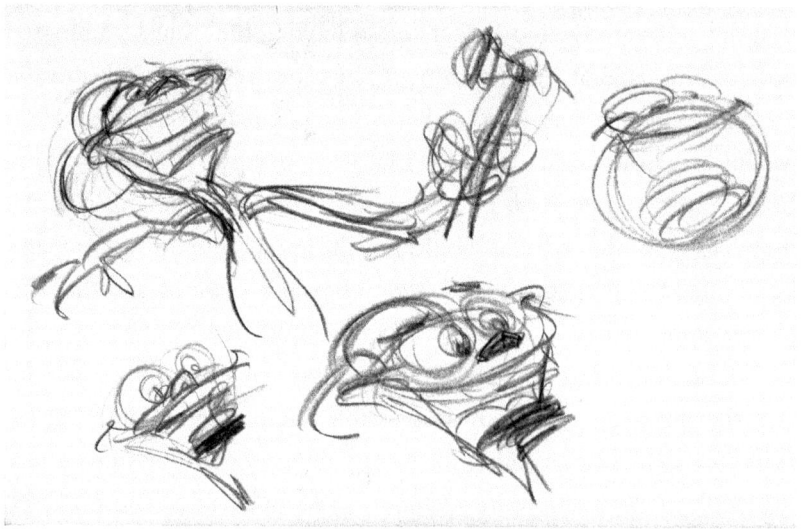

TOP: John K.'s rough for the hammer scene that was animated by Mark Kausler in "Stimpy's Invention".
BOTTOM: Kausler's own roughs.
Both courtesy of Mark Kausler. © Viacom.

At one point, due to Kricfalusi going—in Koenigsberg's words—"a little bit nuts," all production on the cartoon came to a standstill for an entire month. He began redrawing scenes that were either already being animated at Carbunkle or already completed in Hollywood, bringing the show "to a complete halt."[20] The scenario is all too familiar to scholars of commercial Hollywood's more fanatical directors. Such stories almost always have the same ending—artistic overindulgence, failure, and takeover. John K. did not face that sort of grisly climax on "Stimpy's Invention". He was supported by a credulous financial backer and had a studio full of artists who acted as positive reinforcement. Kricfalusi could make the cartoon the way he wanted not only because he was permitted to—but because he had true creative support. "That's why it's such a good cartoon," Camp said. "But any sane or rational person would've said, 'Ah, it's good enough, as long as it's on time.'"[21]

By the time "Stimpy's Invention" (along with "Black Hole", which had been held up for weeks after its completion by Bon Art in Korea) was ready to be shipped to Fil-Cartoons for ink-and-paint, Howard Baker had quit the production and Spumco was left without an overseas supervisor. Bob Jaques was Kricfalusi's first choice to take over, but Jaques had had enough of working in Asia for a lifetime. Shortly after turning down Kricfalusi's request, Jaques saw a workprint of "Fire Dogs" and discovered how Fil-Cartoons had vandalized Carbunkle's footage. He had a change of heart, deciding it best for the survival of "Stimpy's Invention" if he took the job of overseeing it in the Philippines.

When Jaques arrived at Fil-Cartoons in November 1991, most of the work done so far on "Stimpy's Invention" was unsalvageable. So much of the animation had been dropped out to save time and money that Jaques had to utilize the original raw pencil test to save the picture. "There was one instance when I was checking an exposure sheet and noticed that the camera move had been rubbed out and changed from a three-frame move to an eleven-frame move," Jaques explained. "I asked the checker [at Fil-Cartoons] why he changed the exposure. He told me you couldn't do a three-frame camera move. It was almost like a dogma to him, and clearly the result of faulty training that impacted our animation. If you know what you're doing you can do pretty much anything in animation. The fact is, you completely control everything in the frame."[22]

In barely a month, Bob Jaques had done what everyone else was afraid to do at Fil-Cartoons: overhaul the system to allow artistry's survival. Some of the cartoon could not be saved due to its gargantuan production time. The workprint, rather than the negative, was used to fix the sparkling effects on Stimpy's underwear after he sticks them on. The scene has unintended dirt lines in the broadcast copy as a result; but it still works as a sort of fatuous special effect, designed to echo a 1950s commercial.

Jaques also reshot the scene he had animated of Stimpy's epiphany ("I must use my gift of invention to save Ren!") on Koenigsberg's personal camera in Hollywood, because "Fil-Cartoons had done what I told them not to do—tamper with the animation. (I assume it was a final 'fuck you' to me for shaking up their system.)" A shadow Kricfalusi had demanded be added to Stimpy's face, but "looked awful" in execution, was also removed while saving the animation. "I re-shot it and cobbled together as many mouths as I could, which is why the lip-sync isn't perfect."[23]

As Jaques rescued "Stimpy's Invention" from incompetence in the Philippines, the first four half-hours had already aired in their entirety, with the fifth still held over. Amazingly, Nickelodeon's next decision demonstrated absolute blind faith in Kricfalusi: they picked up the show for a second season of twenty episodes, even though the first season of six still had not been fully delivered. Such a grand and willful display of naïveté raised eyebrows, enough to make producer Chris

Technical director David Koenigsberg (sitting) using his personal camera to shoot a scene animated by Bob Jaques (leaning). Courtesy of Jerry Beck.

Danzo leave the series. "We had finished negotiations, it was signed, the deal was made, and I was like, 'Okay, I'm clean.' I left because I couldn't get the show out of his office and I was like the intermediary. I was really the one who tempered both [John K. and the network]. Because Vanessa and Mary [Harrington] would fluster me, and John semi-flustered me."[24]

When the sixth episode finally arrived, Nickelodeon billed it in advertising as the "lost episode" of Ren & Stimpy, to the Spumco staff's bewilderment. "We thought it was lost forever," Coffey said. "I kept saying, 'John, where is it?'"[25] Its critical acclaim as the hit of the season, just as Kricfalusi predicted, justified Nickelodeon's decision in signing Spumco up for a second round. The ramifications of this tolerance—allowing the cartoon's creator to spend a full year making one cartoon— would soon come back to haunt Nickelodeon.

With "Stimpy's Invention", Kricfalusi delved further into his characters' psychoses than any director of animated comedy shorts had done before. It is easy to see why Nickelodeon was afraid to air a cartoon of this nature. Ren is truly being tortured, mentally and physically. He hates every minute of being under the Happy Helmet's control, and there is no mistaking the pain behind every single one of his Ed Roth-inspired grimaces. Meanwhile, Stimpy is completely oblivious to his pal's suffering—he is in his own state of brainless ecstasy. He believes that the more he torments Ren, the more he is helping him. It is a completely innocent form of torture; the idea that he is hurting Ren never occurs to Stimpy. When he asks Ren if he is angry after Ren frees himself from the Happy Helmet, Ren's anger is a genuine shock to him.

The Ren and Stimpy chemistry reaches perfection during the short's climax when Stimpy plays his "Happy Happy Joy Joy" record. While Stinky Whizzleteats (Kricfalusi doing a Burl Ives impression) screams quotes from the movie *The Big Country* (1958) in the background, Ren tries to end his suffering. He strikes blows to his own head to help free himself from the mind control—and enjoys it. Stimpy thinks his pal is merely having a good time and joins in by doing just about the most asinine thing imaginable: making his ass cheeks bounce to the music.

An ideal balance of genuine turmoil with uproarious comedy, "Stimpy's Invention" is the crowning example of Kricfalusi's collaborations with Bob Camp. Camp's gift for funny drawing is not merely illustrating an amusing idea, but as Jim Gomez described it, "[creating a] drawing that has some inherent charm, life, attitude or gesture that makes it funny unto itself." Kricfalusi's drawings, by contrast, are "more intense, full of dramatic or extreme acting."[26] Kricfalusi's forceful approach demanded that he focus on one individual scene at a time, just to get the richest possible acting out of it. Camp's approach, by comparison, is far more relaxed, allowing him to take a few steps back and see the scene, sequence, or cartoon as a whole.

The scene of Ren's psychotic distortions when he tries to free himself from the Sta-Put Socks, laid out by Jim Smith and animated by Kelly Armstrong, may be read as horrifying from the anger Ren exhibits; but it is still funny, because Ren pathetically tries to escape as a real chihuahua would. It is a fine example of what Smith described as the prevailing theory at Spumco: "Every drawing is custom-made for that particular scene or emotion."[27] There is no stock or on-model method to get this brand of acting across; only pure ingenuity makes it possible.

This ambitious brand of acting required animation just as powerful, so effective in its outcome that even Kricfalusi was surprised. "I didn't think they'd ever figure out how to animate [those] scenes. I posed it all out thinking, 'No way they'll ever get this right,' or I was going to get notes back from Bob saying, 'John, you're crazy, this won't work.' But they did it perfect."[28]

Kricfalusi's sanity was certainly on Jaques' mind when the layouts came in. In the past, Jaques had typically taken only inconsequential scenes for himself; this time, however, he animated what he described as the "ball-buster" sequence of Ren screaming that he is happy and "must go do nice things," because he did not want to burden anyone else with the work. Kelly Armstrong, meanwhile, was used to taking the series' hardest scenes—simply by virtue of being the team's most gifted animator and quickest problem-solver. When she tackled the beginning of Ren's transformation ("No... got to... fight it!") in "Stimpy's Invention", the complicated sequence was just par for the course.

"Ren was staggering and in a transition between two poses, and he was delivering dialogue," Armstrong explained. "Since Ren was talking, acting, and transitioning all at once, the mouths had to be animated in one order, but 'pinned' onto his head in a radical stagger order, and all had to work with the staggering, acting body. It doesn't look like much on screen, and it wasn't difficult to animate, but it was quite a mental puzzle to figure and dope it out."[29]

By this time, the other animators were expected to know what they were doing and to find similar solutions themselves. Recalled Ron Zorman of his scene with Ren's head-splitting laugh: "The layout definitely had his head split in two, but it was really up to me to figure out how the laugh would play. I also added the tongue flopping around like a worm during the laugh."[30]

John K.'s obsessive direction in Hollywood was ably matched by Bob Jaques' own discerning eye, and what the world received—regardless of whether Spumco shipped everything in a box to Asia or not—was a perfectly animated and acted cartoon: the kind previously thought impossible in television animation. "When Ren does these wild expressions, the drawings are very scary and weird and odd," Kricfalusi told Persons. "Yet [Carbunkle] animate[s] them with such fluidity, with such grace, that to me, when they do it, it turns the stuff into art."[31]

This fusion regularly resulted in the series' golden moments, the art of a collaborative medium at its zenith. "Stimpy's Invention" is packed with such pure spirit and insanity that the cartoon not only reaches the ceiling, it literally destroys it. The climactic crisis continues building to a point where a resolution becomes unimaginable. So the story just stops with Ren's epiphany that he *loves* being angry, as he gives thanks to the bewildered Stimpy. "I figured that I wanted to pack as much pure entertainment into the cartoon and not waste time with formula structure that usually includes formula filler," Kricfalusi said. "I figured "Stimpy's Invention" was over after the song; there was a big climax with Ren exploding so let's just *stop* and leave everyone with their mouths hangin' open. I didn't want the audience to settle down to calmness. I wanted them to crave more."[32]

"Stimpy's Invention" did, indeed, make the world crave more. It was the hit of the series when it finally premiered in February 1992, throttling its viewers just as Ren does Stimpy. Unbeknownst to its eager audience was the fate that hung over the series—a fate of which people at Spumco were very much aware, and at which they consciously scoffed. "[John K.] doesn't care about money, he doesn't care about the Nickelodeon people, he just wants it the way he wants it," Savino said at the time. "Although he does kinda have to go on their guidelines, or they're going to kick him out."[33]

With "Stimpy's Invention", Kricfalusi proved that cartoons offering a Golden Age level of originality and entertainment could be produced in Hollywood television animation. What was never made clear was that the time and monetary restrictions that come with that peculiar outlet for animated filmmaking would have to be completely bulldozed. That demolition was one that the television industry was not inclined—and never will be inclined—to put forward. Considering this, it is astonishing that *Ren & Stimpy* even went on to a second season. Nickelodeon's insatiable need for quality product prevailed over common sense.

The day Bob Jaques left for Fil-Cartoons, Chris Danzo left Spumco. Libby Simon immediately replaced her; Kricfalusi offered her the position of series producer while they were seeing Jaques off at the airport. Danzo bid farewell with no hard feelings, knowing full well that the Spumco-Nickelodeon relationship would founder. "It was the direction being made, it was really out there. But totally ignored, as if, 'Oh, they wouldn't do that.'"[34]

Animation ID: Stimpy's Invention

What follows is a scene-by-scene animator breakdown of the episode *Stimpy's Invention*. Identifications are provided by studio documentation and correspondence with the various animators.

Sc. #	Animator	Sc. Description
Sc. 1	Kelly Armstrong	Opening pan, "Will you help me try out..?"
Sc. 2	Armstrong	"Go away, I'm busy!"
Sc. 3	Bob Jaques	"OH, PLEASE!"

No Scs. 4-5		
Sc. 6	Armstrong	"Alright, alright, sure."
Sc. 7	Chris Ross	Stimpy is elated.
Sc. 8	Chris Sauve	"I'm losing my patience!"
No Scs. 9-10		
Sc. 11	Chris Sauve	"Ladies and gentlemen..."
Sc. 12	Ross	"The Cheese O' Phone!"
Sc. 12A	Ross	"Now we can talk to cheese..."
Sc. 12B	Ross	Close-up of Ren.
Sc. 13	Ross	"...regardless of their foreign tongues!"
Sc. 14	Ross	Stimpy sprayed with limburger.
Sc. 15	Ross	Stimpy digging, pan to infuriated Ren.
Sc. 16	Ross	Stimpy finds remote-control shaver and uses it.
Sc. 17	Sauve	Ren gets fur shaved off.
Sc. 18	Sauve	Stimpy presents gift: "...FOR YOU."
Sc. 19	Ross	Ren ponders what gift is.
Sc. 20	Ross	Ren opens box and finds Sta-Put Socks.
Sc. 21	Ross	Ren puts on socks & finds out they're full of glue.
Sc. 21A	Armstrong	Ren snaps and tries to free himself.
Sc. 21B	Jaques	Stimpy has his epiphany—he must save Ren.
Sc. 22A	Sauve	Effects: shot of Stimpy's laboratory door.
Sc. 23	Andy Bartlett	Stimpy working at table.
Sc. 23A	Ron Zorman	Stimpy takes off goggles; lightning strikes.

No Scs. 24-25
Sc. 26	Sauve	Effects: Stimpy in front of glowing equipment.
Sc. 27	John "Moose" Pagan	Stimpy at dial.
Sc. 28	Sauve	Eye-blink footage: Stimpy.
Sc. 29	Sauve	Effects: Stimpy's door.
Sc. 30	Armstrong	Stimpy using duck and beaver, first failure.

No Sc. 31 (third shot of door added post-storyboard)
| Sc. 32 | Sauve | Effects: Stimpy in front of glowing equipment. |

No Sc. 33
Sc. 34	Zorman	Stimpy throws switch.
Sc. 34A	Bob Bennett	Effects: Rods light up.
Sc. 24	reused	
Sc. 34B	Zorman	Stimpy sweating, drinks sweat out of goggle.
Sc. 35	Bennett	Stimpy at table again.
Sc. 35A	Zorman	Stimpy's got it: "EUREKA!"
Sc. 36	Jaques	Back upstairs: "Are you feeling any BETTER?"
Sc. 37	Ross	"What are you up to?"
Sc. 38	Ross	"Oh, nothing…"
Sc. 39	Sauve	"What do you have behind your back?"
Sc. 40	Ross	Ren gets up, rolling newspaper.
Sc. 41	Ross	Ren walking forward, whapping newspaper.
Sc. 42	Sauve	Stimpy slams on Happy Helmet.

Sc. 43	Sauve	"Hey, what ees this thing?!"
Sc. 43A	Sauve	"Get it off me!"
Sc. 44	Sauve	"...Now you'll always be happy!"
Sc. 45	Sauve	"And this..."
Sc. 46	Sauve	Shot of hand with remote control.
Sc. 47	Ross	"You sick little monkey!"
Sc. 48	Sauve	Happy Helmet starts to kick in.
No Sc. 49		
Sc. 50	Zorman	"Hey, it works!"
Sc. 51	Armstrong	"No... got to fight it!"
Sc. 52	Zorman	Stimpy laughs, hits button again.
Sc. 53	Sauve	Ren's face cracks.
Sc. 54	Zorman	Stimpy hits button again.
Sc. 55	Ross	"Can't... lose... control..."
Sc. 55A	Ross	"Will... strong..."
Sc. 55B	Ross	"Body... weak!"
Sc. 56	Zorman	Final laugh and button hit.
Sc. 57	Ross	Ren loses control.
Scs. 58-61	Cut	
Sc. 62	Jaques	STIMPY! I'M SO—HAPPY!"
Sc. 63	Jaques	"I-MUST-GO... DO... NICE... THINGS!"
Sc. 63A	Ross	Ren walks off to do nice things against his will.
Sc. 64	Zorman	Ren happily ironing Stimpy's BVDs.
Sc. 65	Jaques	Stimpy slaps on BVDs.
Sc. 66	Zorman	Ren prances into room, spots litterbox.
Sc. 67	Zorman	Ren brings litterbox to trash.
Sc. 68	Ross	Ren insanely dumping out Stimpy's

Animation ID: Stimpy's Invention

		feces.
Scs. 69-72	Cut	
Sc. 73	Armstrong	Ren in bed.
Sc. 74	Armstrong	Stimpy pulls into driveway.
Sc. 75	Ross	Ren wakes up.
Sc. 76	Zorman	Stimpy opens door.
Sc. 77	Ross	Stimpy calling for Ren.
Sc. 78	Ross	Close-up of Ren's face.
Sc. 79	Zorman	"I will make him happy again!"
Sc. 80	Ross	Ren gets up.
Sc. 81	Zorman	Stimpy spots Ren.
Sc. 82	Sauve	Ren on stairs, staggering in bathrobe.
Sc. 83	Ross	"If you think you're happy now...!"
Sc. 84	No Animation	BG of record album.
Sc. 85	Ross	Stimpy dashes off.
Sc. 86	Zorman	Stimpy puts on record.
Sc. 87	Steve Markowski	Entire "Happy, Happy, Joy, Joy" dance.
Sc. 88	Jaques	Ren hops into kitchen.
Sc. 89	Julian Chaney	Ren at kitchen drawer, gets hammer.
Sc. 90	(out of order) Jaques	Stimpy dancing.
Sc. 91	Mark Kausler	Ren hits self with hammer.
No Sc. #	Kausler	Stimpy dancing with his ass.
Sc. 92	Armstrong	Ren strangles Stimpy.
Sc. 93	Armstrong	"Wait a minute! I LOVE being angry!"
Sc. 94	Ross	"Happy to be of service...?"
Sc. 95	Zorman	Ren's final shot before iris out.

Chapter 5
Animation Rockstars

Nickelodeon picked up *The Ren & Stimpy Show* for a second season as part of what Geraldine Laybourne called a $40 million "surefire investment" in November 1991.[1] It was undoubtedly inadvisable to order twenty more episodes from a studio that still had not delivered six episodes on time, but Nickelodeon continued their deal with John Kricfalusi regardless. It seemed foolish *not* to pick the show up, for it was becoming increasingly popular in the world of cable television.

Through most of 1991, *Ren & Stimpy* had to share the glory with *Doug* and *Rugrats*. As the new year rolled in, however, it became obvious that one thing was not like the others. The first five episodes of Spumco's series were shown in a seemingly endless barrage of

Nickelodeon reruns on Sunday mornings. Word quickly spread about this subversive hybrid of Bob Clampett and *MAD* magazine, masquerading as a children's program. In response, December 1991 saw the show picked up secondhand for a six-week Saturday night MTV engagement.[2] It was on this music station that—it is widely accepted—*Ren & Stimpy* gained its status as a staple of '90s pop culture. "Nobody watched Nickelodeon," Bob Camp said. "It was out there, the kids saw it, but as soon as it started running on MTV, we got lots of calls from people who didn't even know it existed."[3]

Ren & Stimpy represented a fusion that animation had not achieved successfully for decades: modernity reinforced by nostalgia. Certainly nostalgia can go too far and denigrate aspects of pop culture. The best American animation usually embodied the aura of its era without disregarding the preeminent traits of years past.

In California, the Disney studio of the 1930s captured America's desire for escapism. On the East Coast, the Fleischer Studio encapsulated the gritty way of life during the Great Depression. Disney's flights of fancy provided a world into which audiences could submerge to avoid the looming global conflict; the Fleischer cartoons mirrored a more ignorant, indifferent public, with star characters interested in little more than their next meal. Both studios strengthened these American views with character acting of varying success levels. The strongest Disney and Fleischer characters were hardly comparable to the cream of sound or silent live-action personalities; most, save Popeye the Sailor, barely surpassed the stature of silent cartoon star Felix the Cat.

In the 1940s, as the artform of theatrical animation reached its zenith, the Warner Bros. and MGM cartoon departments depicted an America forced into conflict and losing its innocence. This zeitgeist crystallized in the form of Bugs Bunny and Daffy Duck, entities as compelling as any other fictional creation in the 20th century. Director

Tex Avery scorned such rounded personalities in his MGM films (ironically, considering he created both Warner characters) and chose to make his animated characters into one-dimensional representatives of specific human traits (lust, greed, and so forth), all in the name of comedy.

In the 1950s, the United Productions of America (UPA) studio had high ambition and ultimately succeeded at its goal: infusing pretentious art into animation. Every other studio followed suit, resulting in a cheapened artform that welcomed the harsh climate of television with open arms. The decline creepily mirrored the collapse of the movie studio system in the 1950s and '60s, in which live-action American film aped European cinema without understanding the first thing about it—and ended up floundering noisily to find an identity.

Television and theatrical studio animation were absent from most of the movements in American culture from the 1960s to the 1980s. The Disney studio and Hanna-Barbera still existed, but remained in a bubble and at a wasteful standstill. Certainly no other visual medium suffered as harshly. It was about time for animation to get out of the mid-century and catch up with the times. *Ren & Stimpy* accomplished this with a vengeance. John Kricfalusi, Jordan Reichek said, "did what other great creators of pop culture have done: combine the favorite cultural ingestions of their youth into something that comments on and then expresses new thoughts of that art."[4]

Unlike *The Simpsons*—the *other* most influential animated television show of all time—the makers of *Ren & Stimpy* relished the fact that their characters were drawings. The production offered an exciting hybrid of the energy of Bob Clampett, the appealing stylization of the otherwise abysmal Hanna-Barbera cartoons, the demeanor of the best print cartoonists (Harvey Kurtzman and Milt Gross specifically), and the most psychotic acting of mid-century live-action film. The show's flagrant individuality made it impossible to ignore. In the absence of any equivalent, *Ren & Stimpy* managed to almost effortlessly establish itself as a mainstay of American pop culture. Spumco's self-assured artists were not surprised by the show's success. "Most people at the studio were ready to do cartoons like this when we were fifteen, and we had to wait until we were thirty-five," Bill Wray said. "And spent fifteen years working in shit houses thinking, 'There's no hope left. It's just never gonna happen.' And then it happened."[5]

Of course, no one could have predicted the degree of this phenomenon. Tom Hay, a radio personality and longtime friend of Kricfalusi, was not fazed when John K. called him to brag about the show's success, thinking at first that it was another of Kricfalusi's ego trips. "Yeah right, John's makin' it big, he's probably working on *Mighty Mouse* or something. Then I go in this comic book store in Vancouver, there's this frickin' display of *Ren & Stimpy* stuff. That's when I realized, 'Holy crap, he *is* making it big.'"[6]

The universal popularity of *Ren & Stimpy* made it the first show its staffers had ever worked on that was all the rage while they were actually drawing it. Many claimed that the hype surrounding the series made you feel like an "animation rockstar" or "like being in the fucking Beatles," Camp said.[7] Driving this point home to the show's crew was a signing at Golden Apple Comics in Los Angeles. Three thousand people turned out for the seven-hour event, with t-shirts running out early.[8]

"We started getting closer to the store and there were thousands of people, lined around the block," Bob Jaques said. "It started at two and was supposed to go until 5:30. It ended at 9:30."[9] Added Teale Wang: "People were lined up around the block to meet us, see us, get a drawing, and of course meet John. It was the first time we all realized *Ren & Stimpy* was a huge hit."[10]

The line at the infamous Golden Apple Comics signing, 2 March 1992. All photos courtesy of Jerry Beck.

Display window at Golden Apple Comics.

Animation's Rockstars

John K. surrounded by fervent admirers, and layout artist Charlie Bean.

Layout artist Mike Fontanelli, animator Kelly Armstrong, and layout artist Don Shank.

Animation director Bob Jaques, layout artist Mike Kim, director/writer Bob Camp, and background supervisor Bill Wray.

John K., in a rare secluded moment that day.

Reminders of the show's popularity invaded Spumco itself; offers to do voices and to collaborate came pouring in. Celebrities who asked to do voices on *The Simpsons* may have gotten a gracious, obligatory response from that show's producers, but they would have to pass Kricfalusi's acid test to be deemed worthy of *Ren & Stimpy*.

Kricfalusi visited a dying Frank Zappa at his home to record his voice for the Pope in "Powdered Toast Man"; other crew members were, understandably, not allowed to come, but Kricfalusi had the rock legend sign everybody's albums anyway. Artist Elinor Blake spoke of an unproduced episode entitled "Cellulettes", "which was Stimpy joining a girl group, and Phil Spector had agreed to do the voice for the producer character; his name was Ernie Vulva."[11] One memorable incident occurred when Robin Williams' agent called to ask if his client could do a voice on the show. The agent was asked, undoubtedly on Kricfalusi's orders, to tell Williams "he's a fucking fag."

"People would come in from Red Hot Chili Peppers and Fishbone in the middle of a work day, go visit with John, look at his stuff, and take off," said layout artist Ed Bell. "We were kind of right in the middle of Hollyweird."[12] John K. lamented that he might become one of "those people I see on the cover of *People* magazine[,] the ones whose eyes I want to gouge out."[13] Still, he was proud that he and his cohorts were fulfilling his lifelong ambition of "destroying the minds of America."[14]

Ren & Stimpy was a key player in what many considered a renaissance in animation during the early 1990s, one that many "pray[ed] for without realizing [they were] part of it," Billy West said.[15] But Kricfalusi always vehemently disagreed with the idea of putting such a label on the era. "People forget what renaissance means. Renaissance means a flowering of creativity. It doesn't mean a garbage dump of creativity. That's what we have right now."[16]

The director was astute in his irritation, but still incorrect. A renaissance is defined as a revival or renewed interest in an art under the influence of classic models, which could indeed be applied to animation in the early 1990s. *Ren & Stimpy* differs from its contemporaries, however, in regard to how its classic models were applied—and exactly which ones were influential. *The Simpsons*, for instance, took more influence from live-action sitcoms than from any cartoon. The new Warner Bros. Animation television division used the 1940s and '50s *Looney Tunes* as window dressing rather than inspiration in their series *Tiny Toon Adventures* and *Animaniacs*. In the feature film realm, Disney had redeemed itself with audiences via *The Little Mermaid* and *Beauty and the Beast*—movies that generated the same excitement *Snow White and the Seven Dwarfs* and *Dumbo* once had. Unfortunately, the fact of "Disney" being a brand name limited the studio's artistic potential, keeping their work trapped within moviegoers' expectations of what a trademarked Disney film should be.

Ren & Stimpy at its best evokes the same aesthetic response as some of the Golden Age's best and brightest because it was not merely an inbred knockoff; it was made with the same guiding principles. It took influence not only from Bob Clampett and other animators, but from other art forms such as print cartooning and live-action film. Kricfalusi's artistry reflected more than just his influences—and his artistic power to emulate them. He actually had something *new* to say in using his influences, and surrounded himself with likeminded and equally talented people. Had there never been the chance for a second season of *Ren & Stimpy*, the opportunity to fully realize this potential would have never come.

Like *The Simpsons*, *Ren & Stimpy* was one of the first cartoons to triumphantly pull animation up from the ghetto of "kiddie entertainment." Rather than handling potentially rude material with ambivalence, *The Simpsons* and *Ren & Stimpy* embraced their characters' humanity like few shows had before. The shows' casts went beyond the average drawn characters by making their audiences fully aware of themselves as individuals: individuals who experienced bodily functions and were capable of indulging in the more deviant facets of human behavior.

The Simpsons bridged a gap between young and old viewers; but it was essentially a primetime show, marketed towards adults, that kids also wanted to watch. It was a forbidden fruit for the twelve-and-under crowd. *Ren & Stimpy*, by contrast, was always marketed as children's television—even if some parents forbade their kids from viewing it. Its rude content made adults want to watch it, and the show became an immediate rave in college campus circuits.

In time, *Ren & Stimpy* reruns on Nickelodeon would average ratings of 2.1 million households weekly[17] (sometimes reaching as high as 5.8[18]), with thirty-five percent of viewers over the age of eighteen.[19] Future polls would show that the viewers of *Ren & Stimpy* were mostly over the age of thirteen. Vanessa Coffey remained adamant that "you have to play to your demographic,"[20] yet the *Nicktoons* demographic—slated age three to eleven at the time—was missed almost entirely by *Ren & Stimpy*. Even John K. expressed shock that adults were watching the show, and that frat boys were synchronizing their binges with it. He maintained that the show was being made for kids—going as far as jokingly telling Dick Van Dyke that Van Dyke should be ashamed for being a fan of *Ren & Stimpy*.[21]

"It's great that adults watch it, but I program for a kids' network," Nickelodeon's vice president of programming Herb Scannell said to the press. "In terms of advertising, nobody buys time from us to reach adults."[22] *Ren & Stimpy*'s older audience consequently required MTV Networks' sales department to go after specific advertisers and agencies—in a special effort to profit from the show's unique demographic of viewers in their teens and older. "It's terribly inefficient to have a sales department geared towards [one] demographic, and then to have this one half-hour that suddenly skewers into this whole other demographic," David Koenigsberg said. "[Nickelodeon] hated the show [for that]; they won't admit that, but they did."[23]

Moving *Ren & Stimpy* to MTV might have been prudent. Such a move would have eliminated the marketing problem and, theoretically, most of the battles over content between Spumco and Nickelodeon. Whether Nickelodeon hated *Ren & Stimpy* or not, though, they still wanted to keep the show—and its viewers—all to themselves, rather than sharing the wealth with a sister company. "Just because Viacom owns all the networks doesn't mean we don't still compete with each other," Coffey told Mathew Klickstein. "We were getting good ad sales off the show. And kids loved *Ren & Stimpy*."[24]

The show's youth quotient was made plain in June 1992, when deals were made to license *Ren & Stimpy* to Nintendo and Mattel for children's products.[25] A comic book by Marvel was announced for a September launch. Much to Kricfalusi's resentment, Bakshi alumnus Mike Kazaleh handled most of the comic's art duties. John K. felt that he alone—as the series' creator—should be doing the comic, and forbade his staff from contributing to it.[26] Dan Slott wrote most of the best issues, with early input from story editor Will McRobb, and both Slott and Kazaleh kept out of the show's politics. While the art was far removed from that of the Spumco staff, the show's spirit was easily emulated and the comic lasted nearly four years.

Laybourne stated that the network's "philosophy has evolved over the years." Rather than trying to "improve kids" with education and "perfect role models," they would give kids something fun to watch.[27] Elaborated Linda Simensky: "[Nickelodeon still] wanted to be responsible for kids, but also wanted to push the envelope."[28] This ideology allowed John Kricfalusi to progress like nobody before him in television animation—and nobody since. Nickelodeon's sense of responsibility towards children, however, would soon cause utmost tension. Now the network knew what *Ren & Stimpy* was about, the network had promised to make things easier for Spumco. But if anything, day-to-day relations during the second season got worse.

Will McRobb replaced Mitchell Kriegman near the end of the approval process on the first season. He seemed a more natural fit as the show's story editor. McRobb's own live-action creation for Nickelodeon, *The Adventures of Pete and Pete*, was—in its day and way—as delightfully subversive a children's show as *Ren & Stimpy*. Correspondingly, McRobb claimed to have "some sense of what might be too out there, and what would work fine."[29]

John K. would later accuse McRobb of tyranny—but no tyranny is revealed by a perusal of McRobb's own notes on the second season. These are not the notes of a clueless secretary, but observations from a man with sound knowledge of television writing. Bob Camp and Jim Gomez went as far as describing McRobb as an actual writer for the show: "doing good work and putting up with our bullshit and get[ting] little or no credit."[30] There is an air of excitement in McRobb's notes on Spumco-written outlines, accurately predicting that "Man's Best Friend," "Svën Höek", and "A Visit to Anthony" were destined to be "classic" and "genius" episodes.[31]

Nevertheless, McRobb retained the kind of editorial voice that creative minds like Kricfalusi find offensive. In McRobb's own words, it was his duty to "wield the logic club."[32] His questions could range from "If Stimpy invents rubber nipples, how could the husband be short on nipples?"[33] Or, "Why does Dad's question about how they move make Stimpy puke?"[34]

Just as in the last season, the main goal of these notes was to stamp out what Simensky called "all the bits of innuendo [John K.] would pretend weren't innuendo" in the outline stage.[35] Many were caught; the most memorable instance came during the writing of "Rubber Nipple Salesmen", when McRobb told Kricfalusi and co-writer

Vincent Waller that "You can't use the word 'nipple' without having it preceded by the word 'rubber.'"[36]

A fart-lighting climax from "Lair of the Lummox" was excised in its entirety. An outline written by Waller entitled "Onward and Upward" was rejected immediately upon receipt; McRobb and the rest of the Nickelodeon brass thought its story of Ren and Stimpy living in a spittoon was not only repulsive, but incapable of sustaining itself for eleven minutes. Kricfalusi also discovered that meta-humor was forbidden if it made fun of the Nickelodeon brass. When the outline for "Stimpy's Cartoon Show" portrayed Ren as an animation executive who couldn't draw, McRobb and Vanessa Coffey became livid over the lambasting. McRobb tersely wrote, "Maybe you thought we had a sense of humor about ourselves—we don't." Kricfalusi was able to deceive them, saying that the untalented non-artist Ren was a parody of *himself*—not Coffey or anyone else at the network. The cartoon was subsequently approved for production.[37]

Kricfalusi complained that he had "to go through this obstacle course just to get one dumb idea on the screen."[38] Most of the time, however, many of the artists, including Kricfalusi himself, were consistently amazed at what actually *did* get through. Camp commented in retrospect that they "got away with murder" on the show.[39] A lack of alertness might allow certain jokes to get by, such as the word "dingleberry" in "Stimpy's First Fart"; but if something particularly raunchy made it through, the Nickelodeon people were aware of it. "If things got on the air, it was because we allowed them to get on the air," said Coffey. "We had the pope holding onto Powdered Toast Man's buttocks. That's pretty risqué."[40]

McRobb was also surprised at how "shockingly lenient" the network could be, considering the kind of material the cartoonists were providing. It was obvious that Kricfalusi and the others simply did not like being told what they could and could not do. When Kricfalusi was asked to change something, McRobb recalls his exasperating reply: "Really? It's not like they're fucking, or anything."[41]

The most serious delays in the approval process often occurred after McRobb gave Spumco the "green light" to proceed with a story. Reportedly, another executive at Nickelodeon would often demand changes well *after* a storyboard had been approved. Coffey never denied that this happened. Indeed, she remembered having allowed the network to reject stories and gags that she, herself, had cleared, only adding to the confusion.[42] Kricfalusi once remarked to the press that it could take as long as thirty-six days to get full approval on a story.[43] Spumco was often well into the layout process when demands for changes were belatedly made.

"One person would approve of something, and then a whole group of people didn't approve of it," producer Libby Simon said. "Meanwhile, we were already moving on and getting the work done. They had people in place that really didn't know about writing and animation, and they just made it difficult for the artists and John to move forward on things."[44]

No one from Spumco has ever been specific about when these late changes were demanded—or which cartoons they affected, apart from Camp's statement that "Out West" had gags "cut out for one reason or another and we had to make last-minute substitutions, so it wasn't quite as funny."[45] There is no doubt that these incidents occurred regularly. Camp also commented that Nickelodeon had three 'r's' in their approval process: "resistance, reluctance, and resentment."[46] Much later in the show's lifetime, producer Jim Ballantine would warn the network that to renege on storyboard approval was cost-"prohibitive," and that it was "demoralizing to the staff to have what has been labored over changed or thrown out at the last minute."[47] Ballantine's philosophy was gained from observation of production at Spumco, but it was not a philosophy actively embraced by anyone at Nickelodeon while he was there.

These battles over content were routine, given the show's popularity and the attention that its subversiveness was receiving. Most news and magazine articles expressed delight over the content *Ren & Stimpy* was getting away with on children's television. "It was really praising John for pushing so hard, and Nick felt a little more in the hot seat at that point," Simensky said. Unlike the first season, during which Nickelodeon's panic was due to inexperience at producing an animated show, Nickelodeon was now worried for a different reason: "People are looking at these things very critically; we better be careful, because otherwise we're gonna get in trouble."[48]

Coffey found that Kricfalusi, too, had drastically changed attitudes from the first season, at which time he was happy just to have some amount of control over his own show. When others demanded ideas thrown out, he would express outrage and disappointment—but get over it. After the show became popular, on the other hand, it was either his way or the highway. "It became a very difficult struggle, one that you normally shouldn't have to have. I don't mind a good fight, but it started feeling like hell."[49]

Kricfalusi said network intrusion in the first season was minimal compared to the second season, "when a lot of people began interfering with it."[50] Aside from the battles over content, he was likely referring to the decision to hire Roy Smith in December 1991, a decision that Chris Danzo cited as having been "forced upon" Spumco by Nickelodeon.[51] It was the network's hollow attempt to place their own sheriff in the Hollywood studio. Smith's job was to make sure the show stuck to its budget and schedule in the second season. Smith was also responsible for bringing in the show's new production manager, Jim Ballantine.

Smith said he was viewed by Kricfalusi as "the Nickelodeon spy sitting in on the show," because he was not an employee of Spumco—and therefore did not have to jump when John K. said jump, like everyone else in the building. "I didn't want to be [a spy], but that's what he turned me into. I'm sitting around like an idiot most of the time, feeling [like] exactly what I was, the Nickelodeon spy. I helped wherever I could, whenever he'd let me. But frankly, he didn't want my hands touching anything. He didn't want me to see anything."[52] The instatement of Libby Simon as Spumco's producer was not helping things either. While it may have been possible to conspire with Chris Danzo to get tasks finished, there was no such leeway with Simon: to stoke John K.'s ego was stoking her own.

By way of his own talent and Nickelodeon's wallet, Kricfalusi had been given a genuine taste of power and stardom. Like all similar pop culture superstars, he had a preference for breaking the rules. *Ren & Stimpy*'s popularity gave him a newfound, irrevocable license to disregard any authority in order to achieve artistic nirvana. And like anyone who has ever dared to defy a corporate giant, he became even angrier and more rebellious when the giant began acting the part.

§

Spumco was determined to make this new set of shows better than the first. Irrespective of *Ren & Stimpy*'s great popularity, it remained an anomaly in Kricfalusi's career simply for having survived beyond one season. Aware of that season's imperfections, Kricfalusi sought to vanquish any future defects and produce as wholly perfect a television cartoon as possible.

Kricfalusi could not achieve this alone. He continued to rely on his crew to help fulfill his dream of collective artistic vision. He showed immense pride and faith in them and kept many employed between seasons—even when there was no *Ren & Stimpy* work, paying them largely out of his own pocket.

In early 1992, part of that downtime was devoted to a very different Nicktoons project: laying out an episode of *Doug* to keep money rolling into the studio. Working on such atypical material gave the Spumco artists a taste of the "schizophrenic life" that Will McRobb says he long experienced, story editing both Nickelodeon shows—and receiving John K.'s "brutally honest" opinion of *Doug*.[53] It was a joyless job; Kricfalusi "didn't give a shit" otherwise, Jerry Beck said.[54] The specific episode of *Doug* on which Spumco worked cannot be determined today, but David Koenigsberg noted that the Spumco crew could not resist defacing the backgrounds with hidden Rens and Stimpys.[55]

While waiting for Nickelodeon to fully approve *Ren & Stimpy* cartoons for production, Kricfalusi set up cartooning classes. These classes, taught by him and his other top artists, were intended not only to improve an artist's drawing abilities, but to change their entire outlook on animation. The classes moved from writing to painting to even sculpting—making even more obvious the fact that Spumco was both a studio and a school. Here, artists were strictly paid to learn.

"When we first started Spumco, John would make me watch cartoons and write thesis papers on 'em," Camp said. "If you can imagine watching a Tex Avery cartoon, *Deputy Droopy*, and writing a paper on it. But it taught me a lot about writing and cartoon form as a film form."[56]

The intensity of the Spumco art classes "could be cut with a knife," animator Dan Jeup observed. "All the artists, experienced and apprentices, were hungry to learn animation and improve their drawing skills. I couldn't believe what I was seeing. It didn't take me long to discover that this wasn't your typical television animation production."[57]

Many Spumco artists have called Kricfalusi's directing style didactic. This perhaps explains why these "drawing boot camps" came to him so naturally; why a lot of depression and anxiety filled the studio's atmosphere; and in spite of it all, exactly why so many of these jaded artists continued to stay. "I was so depressed and insecure all the time, afraid of failing, that I had trouble working," Chris Reccardi said. "When I got my first storyboard done on time that was reasonably clear and well done, John added a lot of stuff and embellished it, but then he gave me an extra check in my envelope. It was a bonus for good work. He did have the ability to reward as well as to punish."[58]

Most of the principal first-season *Ren & Stimpy* staff was recalled for the second. With twenty shows slated for production, it became essential that Spumco recruit more artists. Ad space in *Comic Buyer's Guide* was bought for the purpose of tantalizing prospective employees. "Can't sleep at night? Tired of working on crummy cartoons? Your troubles may be solved!!!" Applicants were invited to apply by faxing their drawings of Ren and Stimpy to Spumco, but only if they could draw "really well."[59]

Few applicants were given layout tests; fewer were hired. Spumco was extremely selective and did not embrace many of the personalities prevalent in Hollywood animation. Camp quipped that too many of the *Ren & Stimpy* hopefuls were used to the "established" model in typical animation studios: "a $1,000-a-week job, sitting on their ass fucking off."[60]

Many new hires, like background painter Scott Wills, had simply seen *Ren & Stimpy* and were spiritedly driven to be a part of it. Industry experience was not a prerequisite to work at Spumco; passion was. "I didn't think I would get on *The Ren & Stimpy Show*, but I had to get into animation," Wills said. "It just looked so appealing and fun, the idea of working on a project that was bigger than just myself."[61]

The protocol at Spumco involved working unpaid overtime, getting paid under union scale, and what layout assistant Doug Lawrence called "beat[ing] it into [yourself] to draw better for the show and for John."[62] Spumco was not a place that appealed to people with spouses, children, and house payments, but rather to "animation's malcontents," as Mike Fontanelli told Stephen DeStefano during the latter's first week at the studio.[63] These were people who firmly believed that John K. was a guiding force in the industry and were eager to be molded in his image. Ed Bell said they were all "John Kricfalusi fans working for him;"[64] to the outside world, Spumco appeared mystic and cultish.

"We were ready to gnaw anybody's head off who said *Ren & Stimpy* was boring, or for kids," Lawrence said. "Anytime anybody wanted to tell us bullshit about *Ren & Stimpy*, we wanted to kill them. We were very, very protective about the show."[65]

Departments within the studio remained as small and eclectic as ever, in spite of a schedule that demanded far more people. Peter Avanzino was the only new storyboard artist hired. The layout department saw

The Spumco writing department: Bob Camp, Elinor Blake, and Vincent Waller. Courtesy of Norman Hathaway.

very few new additions. Kricfalusi did, however, expand his writing staff to include production assistant Richard Pursel and layout artist Elinor Blake, a move that gave the new season a distinctly different flavor. Pursel, an old hand at gagging the show and John K.'s choice for drawing network-enforced revisions, proved effective in taking ten-minute gag ideas—like "Stimpy's First Fart"—and tailoring them into stories that could sustain more extended lengths of time. Blake, as Kricfalusi's new girlfriend and the only female writer and layout artist since Lynne Naylor's departure, provided balance to the "testosterone flying around," often penning stories centered on the plights of Stimpy, the "woman" of the starring duo.[66]

Changes also affected the show's satellite studios. The animation was destined to be of a much higher standard this season, with several episodes slated for production exclusively in Los Angeles and Vancouver. Rather than going through traditional ink-and-paint and camera in Asia, Carbunkle's work would now utilize a digital ink-and-paint system at MetroCel in California, making *Ren & Stimpy* the first television cartoon to go through the process. Isolating production to the United States assured these particular episodes would be of the highest quality. An instance of missing animation in the final product was now an anomaly rather than a commonplace occurrence.

John K. maintains that had it not been for the budget limitations, he would have had everything animated at Carbunkle. Animation on the average eleven-minute cartoon at Carbunkle could cost as much as $70,000 in the second season (eventually more, given production delays). Spumco would continue sending what Jim Smith said were intended as "the best episodes" to Carbunkle, while the rest were sent elsewhere.[67]

When the second season was still planned for twenty episodes, Spumco had intended to have several cartoons animated in Taiwan to take advantage of cheap rates. Ultimately, only one, "Haunted House", was sent to Taiwan's Color Key studio.[68] The bulk of the second season's cartoons would be sent to Rough Draft Korea, a new studio set up specifically for *Ren & Stimpy* in Seoul.

Gregg Vanzo established Rough Draft in his garage in Van Nuys in 1991[69] and animated some footage of the Fire Chief in "Fire Dogs" as a prelude to getting more work on the series. Kricfalusi said that Vanzo approached him early on about starting a studio for the show in Korea. Kricfalusi was nervous about going to the network and pitching the concept of "people that were completely untried, that didn't have a studio" to take on work overseas. Nickelodeon agreed to Vanzo's proposal "against their wills," Kricfalusi would later remember.[70]

In theory, there had never been anything wrong with overseas animation. The American studios had become mundane, cynical factories with low standards. It did not matter anymore whether a cartoon was being animated in-house or overseas—anyone could make it move and it would look about the same. Only when Kricfalusi, the first real voice in television animation, tried to raise the standards under Ralph Bakshi did the drawbacks of the overseas system become apparent. At Rough Draft, Vanzo attempted to bridge the gap between cultures to help accommodate the quality of the American studio's artwork.

Rough Draft delivered quality, if workmanlike animation above the level of any non-Carbunkle first season material. Both cartoons in the second season's premiere episode, "In the Army" and "Powdered Toast Man", had a degree of difficulty to them. The first cartoon was heavy on distortion and the second was complex on all levels, with extensive special effects. Rough Draft delivered both with admirable deftness and continued to do so throughout the series. So good was the Korean animation, in fact, that footage done Stateside—like Greg Manwaring's scenes of Mr. Horse in "Rubber Nipple Salesmen"—blended in almost seamlessly. Rough Draft and Vanzo quickly achieved the desired goal of all outsourcing: giving cheap labor such sheen that few could tell it from more expensive work.

Lustrous or not, however, it was still outsourced animation, and therefore less capable of the intricacies that the show prided itself on. The Spumco artists generally insisted that they did all of the characters' acting in the studio; while this was not entirely correct, it can certainly be said that little true acting was ever achieved at the overseas studios. An exception, where real character animation actually exists in an overseas episode—like Ren and Stimpy eating tree bark in Vincent Waller's "Big Baby Scam"—is rare. Regardless, Rough Draft delivered polished work that preserved and supported the original drawings. David Koenigsberg recalled the Korean studio having various technical problems later in the series, "which was expected," given they were first starting out. "When we tried to have them animate for digital ink-and-paint and camera in Hollywood, they could not follow one simple rule: never trace a line. There's no need to for digital. We had to fix scene after scene."[71] Regardless, within a few years Rough Draft would become one of the most highly respected and used commercial studios in the whole industry.

§

In the first season of *Ren & Stimpy*, Kricfalusi had already proven incapable of delivering six half-hours on time as director. For the second season, he would never be able to direct twenty all by himself—even though he likely wanted to. Several of Spumco's best people were therefore promoted to the director's chair in some capacity: Bob Camp, Jim Smith, Vincent Waller, and Chris Reccardi. For most of the second season, Camp was the only one of the four who had genuine directorial control of the pictures.

"I started directing because there was no way John could've done them all," Camp said. "I was hanging around at every recording, editing session, and mix since the pilot. I was willing and able to take on the task and I think John was grateful for the help."[72] This gratitude allowed Camp to establish what was recognized at the studio as the "B unit," one slated to move the cartoons Camp had boarded—"In the Army", "Out West", "Mad Dog Höek", and "Monkey See, Monkey Don't"—through the Spumco pipeline. The "B" designation was slightly misleading, and often harped upon as a means of marginalizing Camp's role in the series. Though Camp's cartoons used the same crew as Kricfalusi's, and though Kricfalusi even co-wrote "Out West" with Camp, Kricfalusi would tell the public that Camp's cartoons were born out of a necessity to do simpler stories.

"[Nickelodeon] read the stories and they said, 'These sound like cheaters,'" Kricfalusi told Dan Persons. "I said, 'Yes, they're typical cartoons. But believe me, if we get Bob to storyboard these, they will be funny. It won't matter that they don't have stories, or that they don't have conflict. He'll draw them funny and the kids will like it."[73] If the term "cheater," however, means a simple story with less emphasis on acting and extravagance, then many of Spumco's cartoons—not just Camp's—fit that description. Kricfalusi would later admit that from the start of the series, corners were cut on certain episodes to compensate for extra time spent on "special" cartoons, even if the production timeline did not reflect that ideology.[74]

Camp's cartoons went through production fast; less because of content than because of Camp's directorial style, a style far less authoritative than Kricfalusi's. Improving on the near blueprint-like way he storyboarded "Stimpy's Invention", Camp treated his storyboards as layouts themselves. "I storyboarded straight ahead, full size on layout paper; that's doing layout and storyboard at the same time," Camp said. "Someone would take all the scenes and make a storyboard out of it, and we would do layout."[75]

Truthfully, studios had been using this method for decades, with mixed results. The difference now was that Camp actually handled the process artfully and sensibly. By paying more attention than normally required to the detail of the characters and scene set-ups, Camp's boards gave much clearer instructions to the layout artists than had the earlier process, drawing from a combination of vaguer boards and Kricfalusi's own roughs. Thus, Camp's "In the Army" and "Out West" actually came in slightly under budget in layout, justifying the overages and longer time spent in storyboarding.

Camp's inferior status in the studio hierarchy was made plain when John K. begrudgingly had "Out West" animated at Carbunkle. The animators in Vancouver had been anxiously waiting for more work after completing their first cartoon for the season, "Man's Best Friend". With "Svën Höek" nowhere in sight, Spumco sent over "Out West" without properly budgeting for it.[76]

Camp described himself as being "more about the gag" than Kricfalusi was, making Camp the obvious choice for directing lighter, gut-funny pictures.[77] "In the Army" and "Mad Dog Höek" exemplify Camp's raucous cartooning style. Both cartoons—one with Ren and Stimpy trained by an overbearing drill sergeant, the other with them as wrestlers—turn ostensibly unoriginal stories, though Camp's execution, into something freshly outrageous.

Moments in "Mad Dog Höek" might have been executed poorly at other points in the series' development. Earlier, the animation and timing of Ren biting into a wart on a wrestler's toe would have been too weak to elicit any kind of response; later, the scene would likely have overemphasized the detail of the pus spewing or the wrestler's pain. At the start of season two, however, at the height of the studio's powers, everything and anything pays off beautifully, with just the right amount of balance between the wart-biting and screaming. This kind of even-handedness is vital, given that the brutality of the other gags range from Ren getting his head run over by a car to Stimpy getting his legs cracked and reacting orgasmically.

"Out West" is possibly the only cartoon ever produced for television where the film's best aspect is its actual animation. Camp let Bob Jaques work his own magic rather than give instructions as Kricfalusi did, fluctuating between explicit and implicit. The finished cartoon became an experiment in limited animation as well as an exercise in testing the audience's patience.

The cartoon—in which sheriffs Abner and Ewalt (voiced by Jim Smith and Camp) hire Ren and Stimpy to be horse thieves, just so the sheriffs can finally have someone to lynch—is often uproarious in its overt innuendos. When the whole cast randomly breaks out musical instruments to sing "The Lord Loves a Hanging, That's Why He Gave Us Necks," the willful and blatant shattering of every taboo in television standards marks one of the defining moments of the series.

The peculiarly sluggish pacing of "Out West" is uncommon for a Spumco-Carbunkle collaboration or any of Camp's other cartoons sent to Korea. Abner and Ewalt are almost constantly shown in held poses, to exaggerate their stupidity and possible intoxication (many objects in the backgrounds have corks, indicative of moonshine). Some of these slow moments come off beautifully, while others are taxing. But animator Chris Sauve recalls that the lack of action in "Out West" allowed for an analysis of lip-sync theories, forcing the animators to make what little movement there was count—as Sauve himself did in his remarkable scene of Ren and Stimpy riding into town on chickens. "It was the only scene I ever did on *Ren & Stimpy* where I actually did live-action reference. I went and got some kid's movie, *The Adventures of Milo & Otis*, and I [still-framed] this scene of all these chickens. I was just amazed at how fast those chickens moved their heads. It was basically popping [from pose to pose]; if it wasn't, it was one frame held, and then that flappy thing underneath would move."[78]

One of Bob Camp's poses of Abner and Ewalt for his cartoon "Out West". Courtesy of Bob Jaques. © Viacom.

For an alleged "cheater," "Out West" exhibits an extraordinary level of precision, exemplifying the growth that the Spumco and Carbunkle crews had made in less than a year. That this growth barely involved John K. at all obviously humbled the creator. When visiting Jaques in Vancouver, Kricfalusi tried to make changes to the animation. He was too late and merely gave Jaques "verbal notes for 'next time.'"[79] It was his creative machine, after all, and he was leery of others getting *too* much power.

Other newly-appointed directors did not enjoy Camp's level of control. Their positions were more of an "apprenticeship kind of thing," Reccardi said, where he and others would double as board artist and layout supervisor, giving them at least a certain amount of control over the drawing style of the cartoons.[80] Jim Smith had already performed a similar role on *Beany & Cecil*; now he worked largely the same way on "Fake Dad" at Spumco.

Nevertheless, even these most trusted artists seemed unable to meet Kricfalusi's standards. Layout artists on Waller's "Rubber Nipple Salesmen" complained of having to wait three to four weeks for Kricfalusi's approval to move forward. On "Dog Show", Reccardi revised layouts constantly, but Kricfalusi always had another layer of correction to add. Smith, too, on "Fake Dad", received corrections from Kricfalusi only after laboring over other artists' layouts of the incredibly difficult Kowalski character.[81] Their credits as co-directors on those pictures were practically awarded out of generosity alone; John K. was still really in full control of them.

Beyond the issue of character layout, Kricfalusi began to exert a new level of micromanagement over other aspects of *Ren & Stimpy*, infiltrating aspects of the show where his skills were not the strongest. Timer Ron Hughart was one of the few at Spumco with outside experience in animating and exposure sheets; he quickly became a means, as he later recalled, for Kricfalusi to execute the "very specific [ways] he wanted his episodes timed."[82] The method involved changing timing work that had already been completed by others—specifically Bob Jaques' on "Man's Best Friend" and "Svën Höek"—as well as altering completed exposure sheets on the new computer system and adding new drawings.[83]

The color styling of his cartoons was another bone of contention for Kricfalusi. Like the animation, the background styling of *Ren & Stimpy* improved dramatically during the second season, through a combination of the work of Bill Wray—and his cohorts Glenn Barr and

Animation's Rockstars

Scott Wills—and Kricfalusi's push to produce more final backgrounds in-house than the show had had before. Though Kricfalusi was not a painter himself, he still tried to teach Wray and his department how to mix palettes the John K. way—not by his own example, but through the library of magazines and children's Golden Books he had accumulated over the years. These gave the painters instruction on how to do highly stylized work with a simple palette, as well as to simplify color harmonies in nature. Other times, the reference Kricfalusi provided could be as random as a *Penthouse* magazine. "It was the wall behind some naked girl he liked," Wills remembered. "'I like this wall.'"[84]

Any frivolity was short-lived. During the production of "Svën Höek", Kricfalusi became livid over the work done by the background department, actually tearing their work off the wall and hurling the insult that their work consisted of "candy cane" colors. Kricfalusi probably picked the wrong department to disparage; Wray has been described by his colleagues as being just as protective of his work as John K., even to the point of egotism. The painters retaliated by making a banner from an enlarged napkin drawing by Camp, showing Ren and Stimpy with candy canes inserted painfully into their rectums. They christened the department "Candy Cane Lane." Recalled Wills: "John came in, and he looks at it, and just stands there and goes, 'Fuck.' Then walks away; that's all he said."[85]

In spite of the crew's notoriously rowdy nature, hardly anyone else at Spumco vented their frustration like the background department had. That incident was the exception, not the rule, and a clear indication of what went through everyone's heads at one time or another: "Is it us, or is it him?" Kricfalusi could hardly help but notice that his employees were starting to take their work too seriously. Said Hughart: "I remember him walking down the hall at Spumco and asking me why no one was laughing in their cubicles. 'We're making cartoons,' he said. 'Everyone should be laughing!'"[86]

It was hard for the laughter to live on. Kricfalusi expected the Spumco crew to absorb his spontaneous, ever-evolving direction style instantly, given their experience with the show and with the studio's methods. At the start of the second season, the vast majority of the artists had either worked with Kricfalusi in the past or had been continuously working with him for a number of years. "I think he kept us all in his rolodex and sort of tried to make his next production the same team so he wouldn't have to keep beating the same horse," Ed Bell noted.[87] Theoretically, artists should have been able to give Kricfalusi the kind of work he wanted on the first go. Instead, their job demanded that they "pay attention to what John vetoed on other people's drawings and what he himself started doing differently," Don Shank said.[88]

Jerry Beck said that John K. often told him he needed to be a workman about deadlines; Kricfalusi could never be like a National Film Board of Canada director, spending five years on a film. "Yet he made those cartoons as if he were one of those NFB animators, being meticulously crazy to get everything done exactly right."[89] There is indeed a parallel between *Ren & Stimpy* and the best NFB cartoons, as Karen Mazurkewich wrote. "Although these animators make films with messages, they still stuff their cartoons with physical gags, non-sequiturs, and strange behavioral idiosyncrasies."[90] Kricfalusi's bottom line, though, was never to preach, always to entertain—even if that meant never meeting the contractual bottom line.

§

By April 1992, the strain of the delivery requirements became apparent to everyone on the staff. As a result of Kricfalusi's desire to bring every aspect of the production under his personal control, most of the scheduled twenty episodes were not yet fully written or boarded. "We don't even have enough time to do the ones we're doing," Kricfalusi said in 1992. "Television's just insane. I hate it. Maybe I'm not supposed to say that."[91]

Just as in the first season, Kricfalusi had to explain to Nickelodeon that he could not meet the requirements stipulated in his contract; once again, they agreed to let the director renege on his obligations. The second season was cut from twenty episodes to thirteen. This would be the last time that Kricfalusi was coddled by the network. The beginning of the end of the Spumco-Nickelodeon relationship can be traced back to this point; when, according to correspondence, the network began withholding payments to Kricfalusi. Said correspondence and testimonies from several employees suggest that Kricfalusi used his own money to keep the show going for months.[92]

Kricfalusi later told Dan Persons that under different conditions, he could have met deadlines and schedules on time. "[Nickelodeon doesn't] have the ability to deliver episodes on time. They wouldn't let us deliver them on time. Every time we'd make a suggestion on how to make a schedule and budget realistically, they didn't let us do it. Or they'd agree and, weeks down the line, change their minds."[93]

Yet Kricfalusi was as guilty of delays as anyone at Nickelodeon. Every aspect of the series—be it the budget, schedule, or content—became a furious battle of wits between the studio and the network. Simensky described the situation as Nickelodeon feeling, "We're paying for this, we have no choice but to win," while Spumco retorted, "We're fighting on behalf of cartoons here, we have to fight for the fans."[94]

By June 1992, the budget had reportedly gone over the $388,000 per episode allotment by $234,000, or approximately $18,000 per half hour. Nickelodeon withheld more money until Spumco delivered an updated budget and schedule. In so doing, Kricfalusi tried to reason that more than half of the overage should be treated as "breakage" costs, incurred in the process of trimming the season from twenty shows to thirteen. That logic did not convince the network. The thirteen shows that remained on the schedule were not completely boarded at that point; episodes not even past the outline stage could hardly account for overages.

Kricfalusi also explained that he could solve the problem creatively: either by expanding certain shorter cartoons into full half-hours (he cited "Fake Dad", "A Visit to Anthony", and "The Royal Canadian Kilted Yaksmen"), or by reviving the previously despised format of shorts and bumpers. He alternately offered—as the "worst solution from a creative standpoint"—the idea of "tossing" shows by sending them overseas for layout, reaffirming his incredibly protective stance on that process. "If not laid out and directed at Spumco, these shows will suffer tremendously in quality," he wrote. "They will be unrecognizable as *Ren & Stimpy*. The rest of the work that we've put into these shows in the story and storyboard stages will have been completely wasted."[95]

Nickelodeon clearly saw Kricfalusi's attempts to improve the budget and schedule as an attempt to reestablish the massive leeway that had been given to him in the first season. He made half-hearted budget-cutting suggestions in the hope that they would be rejected; instead, he hoped to raise the budget per episode, to help support the complexity of his show.[96] Unfortunately for John K., however, Nickelodeon accepted all of his budget-cutting solutions—some in part, others in full—and told him to go forward with them.

The solution of expanding cartoons to a half-hour would prove to have disastrous consequences. None of the proposed candidates for expansion had even been laid out at this point. Jim Smith and Peter Avanzino were scheduled to expand Smith's board for "Lair of the Lummox"—a sequel of sorts to "A Cartoon"—to a full half-hour, but their other duties preempted the job indefinitely.[97]

On the upside, the new bumpers had little effect on the schedule.

There were still two completed bumpers that remained unused (the fake commercial "Sugar Frosted Lumps" and a "Dr. Stupid" segment). It was decided to make new bumpers using pre-existing footage and stationary backgrounds.[98] The most important task was to get more completed cartoons out the door and meeting scheduled airdates. But this required Kricfalusi to take actions that he had put off until it was far too late to make a positive difference.

Spumco may have had strong artists as directors, but none of them had real experience with animating or timing. This placed Kricfalusi in the same dilemma that Bakshi had experienced on *Mighty Mouse*. Dan Jeup, a traditionally trained Disney animator, said that Kricfalusi offered him a director's position on *Ren & Stimpy* the day they met in 1992—a move emphasizing that Kricfalusi was desperate enough to undermine studio hierarchy. Jeup declined and took a less weighty animatic timing position.[99]

Sometime in July 1992, Kricfalusi turned to timing director Ron Hughart to take boarded cartoons through layout. Hughart accepted the director position "to help [Kricfalusi] out of a spot more than anything else."[100] Hughart was assigned to direct "Haunted House", a cartoon that predated the *Ren & Stimpy* series itself. The cartoon—originally written and boarded for *Tiny Toon Adventures* during the dry time after the completion of *Big House Blues*—was to be completely laid out at Spumco. In the original version, entitled "Hi-Spirits", the Warner characters Hamton Pig and Gogo Dodo visit a haunted house, where a diminutive Droopy Dog-like ghost tries to spook them. This version had gotten as far as Don Messick recording the ghost's dialogue when producer Steven Spielberg rejected the whole thing, replacing it with his own ghost story.[101]

Since "Hi-Spirits" had officially been rejected, Spumco had no qualms about repurposing the story. The board was used largely as-is, save Richard Pursel redrawing Hampton and Gogo as the Spumco duo, getting "finally up to speed with drawing Ren and Stimpy" in the process.[102] The ending also took a considerable turn for the subversive, in which we witness the phenomenon of a ghost committing suicide—and coming back to life, reincarnating as a living, naked black man.

Hughart proved himself a sterling workman. He took "Haunted House" through layout in a little over a month, then went to Taiwan's Color Key studio to supervise the animation. The completed cartoon bears the signs of general disinterest all around, obviously stemming from its reviled *Tiny Toon* origins. Still, "Haunted House" is passable for a cartoon that went from layout to broadcast in less than four months—a feat few other *Ren & Stimpy* cartoons can boast.

Pressure was still mounting over the hemorrhaging budget. Some shows were so over-budget and behind schedule that John K. was forced to have at least one cartoon laid out overseas; it was the only cost-effective route to take.[103] He chose "Big Baby Scam" for the honor because its director, Vincent Waller, was willing to go to Rough Draft to do key layouts and supervise the process. After three weeks, Waller had taken the cartoon through layout with no assistance.[104] In spite of Kricfalusi's earlier warning to Nickelodeon that it would likely be a fiasco, "Big Baby Scam" shows no signs of its economy-minded conception.

Waller, like Camp, was a strong enough draftsman and writer to carry a cartoon mostly on his own, as exemplified earlier by "Rubber Nipple Salesmen". That cartoon, with Ren and Stimpy as door-to-door rubber nipple salesmen, goes off the rails in a splendid fashion when they try selling their wares to the ex-serial killer Mr. Horse. When he perversely leers and asks the befuddled duo if they "have any rubber walrus protectors" (Horse has a captive walrus), the picture's atmosphere gets "so different and so subversive"—as observed by artist Steve Loter, who did not work at Spumco—"it felt like a underground inside joke that only certain people got,"[105] even among the crew.

The "scam" of "Big Baby Scam"—Ren paying a couple of nude, porkpie-hatted infants to leave town, so that he and Stimpy can take their places—reaches stellar points of absurdity and perversion: the former when Ren and Stimpy more or less morph into babies in movement and appearance, and the latter when the two have to partake in a completely nude "family bath." There is a peculiarity to Waller's drawings of the characters, foreign to others' interpretations, that was best summarized by Bob Camp's statement to Waller during the production: "It's weird how you draw Ren and Stimpy. You draw them on model!"[106]

These cartoons by Camp, Waller, and Hughart lacked John K.'s totalitarian control, proving that the *Ren & Stimpy* system could sensibly be adapted to the television medium and still result in high caliber work. The cartoons' procedures did not stem from artistic choices, but from the studio's economic and contractual needs. In Nickelodeon's eyes, Kricfalusi was creating an unnecessary impediment with his more ambitious films and iron-fisted direction style. Nickelodeon began to draw the conclusion that a harsher major network might have drawn: if all the *Ren & Stimpy* cartoons were good, most people would not be able to differentiate between those that took six months to make and those which took twelve. Nickelodeon was edging toward the belief that Kricfalusi was unnecessarily holding up most of the second season, and their tolerance was waning. The great cartoons he delivered did nothing to alleviate the situation. If anything, they worsened it.

Chapter 6
Don't Whiz on the Hand That Feeds You

Spumco's second season began with a victory. They were told to move forward with a few cartoons starring the previously rejected character George Liquor. Like Ren and Stimpy, he was created years before the series. His birth came about during an otherwise unexceptional event: John K.'s and Jim Gomez's first trip to buy beer in California. "He was a character that was directly inspired by this liquor store, 'George Liquor,' on the corner of Van Nuys and Sherman Way," Gomez said. "I turned to John and said, 'That's a cartoon character, 'George Liquor All American,' guns and liquor, that's the American way.' He was an instant character."[1]

Liquor wormed his way into many presentations that Kricfalusi and Lynne Naylor prepared throughout the 1980s; he was part of the original *Your Gang* pitch. He made appearances in *Ren & Stimpy* during the first season's "Robin Höek" and "The Boy Who Cried Rat!", but only when an outline for "Man's Best Friend" was approved was the character allowed to shine.

Will McRobb recalled George Liquor causing a "back and forth about whether he was appropriate for Nickelodeon."[2] Vanessa Coffey hated the character, and others at Nickelodeon shared her viewpoint. The aversion to Liquor—with his psychotic mind games, brutish lifestyle, and charismatically crusty voice by actor Mike Pataki—did not come about due to the actual content of the episodes he starred in, according to Kricfalusi. "It's purely that a bunch of politically-correct women see George Liquor—the ultimate, caricatured, right wing character—and they hate him."[3]

With a masterpiece or two under his belt already, Kricfalusi wasted no time inaugurating what he hoped would be another gem in his oeuvre. "Man's Best Friend", the first cartoon of the second season to go into production, was easily more ambitious than many other cartoons that would move through the pipeline. It quickly became what Jim Ballantine described as "the first 'John' show" of the season, where Kricfalusi became "especially attentive to every drawing, every color key, each background painting, and every frame of footage."[4] The episode would eventually cost somewhere in the ballpark of $500,000 after being almost two months late.

Liquor was introduced as "a foil for Ren and Stimpy that wasn't evil," Kricfalusi said.[5] In "Man's Best Friend", Liquor has adopted the duo as pets and wants to build them into champs worthy of his surname. What follows is what Bill Wray called "an analogy to the mixed messages that parents give to their children."[6] Liquor wants to teach his pets that "it's discipline that begets love." In order to learn this virtue, they must first learn how to misbehave. Liquor orders the two to sit on the couch, and—at the top of his voice—to stir his ire ("Make me mad, or I'm gonna be *really* mad!"), causing the normally psychotic Ren to have a tearful breakdown. Stimpy, the good one, forces himself to obey, and is rewarded with more screaming and a "lawn cigar" (a plastic dog turd). Ren is chastised by Liquor for his wimpy behavior and backtalk, and is given money as punishment.

Liquor is hardly the nonspecific, screaming lout that the storyline might suggest. He has a real "method to his madness," McRobb later said, as a father figure who wants what is best for his children, not realizing that he is actually abusing them.[7] It was precisely this concept that Nickelodeon was reluctant to make a recurring theme of the series: "male characters who looked like they were unhinged and prepared to do violence upon Ren and Stimpy, [who] were like kids."[8]

Expert layout work was required to make this cartoon successful; Kricfalusi believed that very few artists could do George Liquor justice. Even those deemed worthy would have their work redrawn by Kricfalusi himself, hemorrhaging the schedule and budget just as he had on "Stimpy's Invention".

Bob Jaques described the couch sequence as almost a metaphor for what went on in layout, with "John beating Mike [Kim] for not being an exact copy of him."[9] Kim was exceptionally skilled for his age, and had been working professionally in the animation industry since the age of sixteen. After being greatly impressed by Kim's work on *Beany & Cecil*, Kricfalusi zeroed in on Kim as one of his key layout protégés on *Ren & Stimpy*. He pulled Kim off of Warner Bros.' *Batman: The Animated Series* by offering him more money to work at Spumco, and eventually placed Kim in his own office in hopes of molding the perfect disciple. Ultimately, alas, Kim could not take the strain of working so directly under John K.; when he failed to make his layout quota later in the season, he was consequently fired. "I don't have any ill feelings on any of that stuff," Kim said. "It was such a long time ago, it's like, I was a kid. The whole thing was fun to watch because, really, it was the biggest learning experience for me, a life-changing experience."[10]

The length and timing of the couch scene emphasizes that the whole situation is terrifying for Ren and Stimpy and that George Liquor "truly believes that what he's telling you is good for you," as Kricfalusi said. "We managed to get conflict with people who have faults, but are not necessarily black or white."[11] The characterization allows the viewers to draw their own conclusions about whether George Liquor is a terrible person or not, but Nickelodeon remained unconvinced that younger viewers could make that distinction.

Voice acting reached a gold standard at this point, just as the drawing and animation had. Billy West remembered seeing Mike Pataki as a "little red fleshball in the corner, because [John K.] had just beaten the shit out of him" after a recording session for the episode. Such was typical of any *Ren & Stimpy* episode, with Kricfalusi himself among the casualties; as Ren, he often rendered himself hoarse until he got a particular line right.

"[*Ren & Stimpy*] forced me to learn to be a little more organic," West said. "Don't be confined by what you think something should be, just fuckin' do it. I'd beat my brains against the wall, and I'd hear, 'You're ninety-five percent there.' [John K.] would come in, 'Ya see this line here!' And I would be like, 'You don't scare me, I had the worst stuff that could happen to a human being happen to me in the first ten years of my life, you're nothing.' Honest to God, I was getting angry, but that's good; anger is a great vehicle."[12]

Carbunkle's animators continued their struggle to preserve the acting of the original Spumco layouts without cheapening them. Chris Sauve recalled John K. giving the animators a test of valor through George Liquor's subtleties; it proved very difficult "trying to do lip sync on a mouth that looks like a sphincter. Those scenes with George Liquor, that goddamn word 'discipline' was the hardest friggin' word to animate. It just drove me nuts, and it was in every scene. Stop sayin' it! And of course he's shaking in the last scene, staggering; it's like, 'You're not punished enough, Sauve. Here, take some more!'"[13]

Though Carbunkle reached stratospheric heights with the animation in "Man's Best Friend", Kricfalusi still called for revisions in June, after the pencil test arrived at Spumco. In the scene of George Liquor's walk home from the pet store (animated by Jamie Oliff), Kricfalusi wanted Liquor's movement to be "bouncier," more of a hop: a difficult task, given that Liquor was speaking expressively in both takes. This revision pushed back the already late cartoon's delivery another month.

Artists were given a break from acting for the final segment of "Man's Best Friend". The objective instead was to make a beating—Ren's final revenge on George Liquor—hilarious rather than painful: a task at which, in Coffey's opinion, Kricfalusi failed. Liquor is now teaching his pets to "protect" him, and they must learn to "attack." In this test, the victim is Liquor himself. Stimpy cannot bear to attack his "kind and beloved master," but Ren has no qualms with this scenario. He takes hold of Liquor's prize bludgeoning oar and proceeds to beat his master senseless. One particular blow is given Scorsese-esque, *Raging Bull*-type attention, shown in black-and-white and slow motion.

Don Shank, who laid out many of the oar scenes and was lionized by Kricfalusi at Spumco for the results, said Kricfalusi asked him if he could draw "weird," and that "there was a good weird and a bad kind of weird; it had to be drawn weird, but he didn't want me to do anything *wrong* weird."[14] There is certainly weirdness to the scene's execution; it fluctuates from genuine pain to genuinely funny pain. The storyboard called for "humorous SFX instead of realistic club SFX"—instructions ultimately unneeded, given that Kelly Armstrong was animating the scenes.

One of the critical scenes in "Man's Best Friend" that deemed it unsuitable for broadcast. Layout by Don Shank. Courtesy of Bob Jaques. © Viacom.

"I love broad cartoon violence [because] the movement is so intense and exaggerated, it's like nothing else can ever be," Armstrong said. "As an animator, cartoon violence is the challenge at the other end of subtle. You have to master the whole spectrum. It was great just to dig into the layout's fat lines and volumes, and a challenge to make the smack really feel like a smack in slow motion."[15] None of the savagery actually hurts George Liquor; it only detains and embarrasses him, and we should laugh at his expense. Everything turns out to be fine, when Ren's brutal beating of George Liquor unexpectedly redeems the Chihuahua in the man's eyes. He rewards everyone, including himself, with a fresh "lawn cigar"—a happy ending for all of the characters.

Upon finally receiving a copy of the completed cartoon in late

August 1992, days before a scheduled airdate, Nickelodeon was more livid than impressed over the artistry contained in "Man's Best Friend". It soon became the true "lost episode" of *Ren & Stimpy*. It has remained unaired on Nickelodeon in any form to the present day. "They saw the storyboard, they approved it, and when the final cartoon came out, everything in there was in the storyboard," Jim Smith told Greg Method. "All of a sudden they decided they didn't want it."[16] The "lawn cigars," and the raw violence in the cartoon's final act are cited as reasons for its shelving. Kricfalusi countered that the sequence was no more violent than anything else they had done—or would do—in the series. "[Nickelodeon] think[s] what's happening in the cartoon is real."[17]

The finished "Man's Best Friend" may have come as a shock because it was pushed out of Nickelodeon's minds for a while by "Dog Show", the other cartoon starring George Liquor, which caused many problems in the storyboard stage. "['Dog Show'] had to be almost completely rewritten," said Coffey; the arguments with John K. over what was appropriate for a children's network were fiercer than usual.[18] Arguably, no other Spumco *Ren & Stimpy* cartoon changed as drastically as "Dog Show". Short scenes were routinely revised or replaced throughout the series, but "Dog Show"'s final act had to be revised throughout.

Originally, the dog show judge was depicted as what Liquor calls "a pansy": an effete man with a ponytail—a perennial sign of unmanliness. In the final cartoon, the judge is the decidedly less gay announcer (or Salesman) from "Space Madness". Also deemed objectionable was Liquor's reaction to the original judge: overt homophobia, inviting all sorts of obvious innuendos that were too bawdy for the network (i. e. Liquor telling Stimpy to wink at the judge, while himself sternly warning the judge to "keep this strictly professional, Mack"). In the aired version of the cartoon, Liquor's approval of the Salesman as "a man's man" plays ironically with knowledge of what was originally intended.

With the network victorious in enforcing the overhaul of "Dog Show" (even the word "pantywaist" was too much for them), Kricfalusi's interest in the cartoon waned. It was considered "safe enough" to "toss" to Chris Reccardi to direct.[19] With that kind of abandonment, and with Rough Draft unable to handle George Liquor's acting as Carbunkle could, it naturally came out inferior to the more celebrated "Man's Best Friend".

"Dog Show" was also shelved after it was delivered to Nickelodeon. This resulted in a full half-hour of product—already paid for by advertisers—that Nickelodeon deemed inappropriate for broadcast,

Layout for "Dog Show" by Chris Reccardi. © Viacom

making Kricfalusi seem further behind schedule than he really was. "Dog Show" did air many months later in a censored form, getting the reprieve that its superior companion never did. Coffey said that Nickelodeon reneged on its approval of "Man's Best Friend" because the storyboard, while still an accurate blueprint of the cartoon, "didn't portray what the episode felt like" and that it was too "brutal" to air in its uncut form. "It was very late, very over budget, and I was told that I just had to wait for it, and it was going to cost what it was going to cost, and I was already uncomfortable with the episode."[20]

It was evidently the cartoon's basic essence, rather than specific details of its content, that pushed the network over the edge. There is even rawer violence and more blatant defecation humor in several other Spumco cartoons ("Mad Dog Höek" and "Big Baby Scam" come immediately to mind). But "Man's Best Friend" represented everything Nickelodeon hated about the show and Spumco: its failure to stay on budget, on time, and to compromise. The original schedule, drafted when the season was still at twenty episodes, tentatively called for "Man's Best Friend" to be delivered the last week of May.[21] Nickelodeon did not see the cartoon until sometime in late August, after it had cost more than a full half-hour episode.

Nickelodeon had also reportedly received three complaints from the FCC over the finale of "Powdered Toast Man", in which the titular superhero character finds himself in the White House burning the Declaration of Independence and the Bill of Rights in the Oval Office's fireplace.[22] "I was so repulsed, I couldn't calm down," said Kay Claire, one of the offended viewers. "I was outraged when I saw that program. I want that cartoon pulled from the air because it has no social value whatsoever."[23]

Claire's remark on the show's social validity, while wholly accurate, is ironic because she was only referring to the cartoon's ending. As with John K.'s earlier controversy on Bakshi's *Mighty Mouse*, cartoon

Drawing of Powdered Toast Man's lovely Catholic schoolgirl assistant, by Mike Fontanelli. Courtesy of Stephen DeStefano. © Viacom.

watchdogs tended to miss the forest for the trees; they focused strongly on individual instances of unacceptable behavior, overlooking other racy scenes entirely. With "Powdered Toast Man", the censors ignored the skimpy outfit of Powdered Toast Man's assistant and the overtly risqué scenes involving the Pope (voiced by Frank Zappa) and the superhero's buttocks. Nevertheless, Nickelodeon took the complaint about the Constitution and Bill of Rights seriously. By the time the cartoon was rebroadcast in 1993, the offending scene was gone, although it aired uncut in MTV broadcasts.

During the second season, the network moved *Ren & Stimpy* to the Saturday night *SNICK* block—aimed at teenagers—to help ease some of the tension over content. It was a move that Linda Simensky said "worked fairly well for them," because the show was in its element: paired with several of Nickelodeon's live-action shows for kids.[24] No other block in television history was as truly subversive as SNICK. It started with *Clarissa Explains It All*, a tame white sitcom, and *Roundhouse*, an inane variety show, lulling the adolescent (and younger) viewers into a false sense of security. The audience was then abruptly hurtled into a demented universe where *Ren & Stimpy* had live action counterparts in *The Adventures of Pete and Pete* and the often truly horrifying *Are You Afraid of the Dark?* It was a natural environment for Spumco's show. Anyone fully aware of *SNICK*'s overall content would not have been jarred by the presence of "Man's Best Friend".

Nickelodeon obviously felt otherwise. "Man's Best Friend" remained as verboten as ever. The idea that the cartoon might air exclusively on MTV reached the press, though that never actually happened.[25] Nickelodeon considered it preposterous to relinquish control over something they had paid for; they would rather let it rot than let it make money outside of their purview. "It's a shame that [John K.] was ahead of his time," Roy Smith said. "Nickelodeon was just starting out and the shows were meant for kids. There were no *Adult*

*Swim*s or MTV Cartoons outlets there at that time. *Ren & Stimpy* opened the door to all of that."[26] Even Gerry Laybourne agreed: "If Nickelodeon had been one year further in development and stronger, I would have done the right thing. Which would have been to give it to my struggling little sister, MTV."[27]

"Man's Best Friend" epitomized the best of what the Spumco system could offer. But as it and "Stimpy's Invention" proved—and as future cartoons in the series would continue to prove—the price for that kind of quality was a blank paycheck with no strings attached. "We were all stunned that John wouldn't make the cuts, because Nick was giving him an ultimatum," Bill Wray told Mathew Klickstein. "'Nope, I'm not cutting *one* second from that cartoon. It's genius.' Which it is, but this was when we were beginning to get a lot of success, and John was feeling it. I went to Jim Smith thinking he could reason with John, because I'd talked to Bob Camp and Bob wanted to cave, thinking Nick had a point. Jim was like, 'Fuck Nick.' And that was the catalyst."[28]

Revolutionary or not—hottest thing on television or not—John Kricfalusi's studio was not fulfilling its contractual obligations. Now bearing the weight of a cartoon that cost half a million dollars, but was deemed unsuitable for broadcast, there was only one way Nickelodeon felt it could move forward.

§

In firing John Kricfalusi and separating Spumco from *Ren & Stimpy*, Nickelodeon set off a media firestorm the likes of which animation had never seen. No cartoon of any kind had received the sort of critical attention that *Ren & Stimpy* enjoyed after the cable network removed the creator from his own show. Nor has any other television cartoon spurred the same level of controversy about its production.

An examination of the downfall of the series always points to the dangerous naïveté of both the creator and the network. Kricfalusi played dangerously in his daily dealings with what amounted to a corporation. He quickly became openly hostile toward the people paying for everything. Likewise, Nickelodeon was "a little innocent," Simensky said, in letting the *Ren & Stimpy* situation get out of hand, thinking it would repair itself. "At that point, it was one of their first shows, and they expected everything to work out, and when it didn't work out, they were a little extreme in how they handled it."[29]

Indeed, the Spumco-Nickelodeon relationship had taken a turn for the worse earlier in the summer, even before "Man's Best Friend" was delivered. By the end of July, only one half-hour of *Ren & Stimpy*'s second season was completed. It looked as though only two more would be ready for broadcast in August. "Dog Show" was estimated to be ready for a 5 September 1992 airdate, but there was no guarantee of when any other shows would be ready. Almost the entire second half of the season was still only in layout or storyboard.[30]

As during the summer before, Nickelodeon was skating on thin ice as advertisers began demanding the whereabouts of the new shows that they had paid for. "They started asking me to get updates of where they were at, and get projections of what it was going to cost," Roy Smith said. "Working with Jim Ballantine, [we figured out] we were $500,000 over budget and way behind schedule."[31]

It was evident that Kricfalusi was not going to pick up the pace anytime soon, given the heavy bottlenecks at Spumco. Bob Camp and Jim Smith, due to their high status at the studio, had spent an irregularly long time boarding "Monkey See, Monkey Don't" and "Fake Dad". Kricfalusi, meanwhile, spent a disproportionate amount of the show's final months at Spumco trying to extend "Svën Höek" into a full half-hour in post-production, while stacks of scenes from "Stimpy's First Fart" remained in Kricfalusi's office for fifteen weeks.[32]

Kricfalusi's excessive perfectionism was not the result of a wild man out of control, but what Doug Lawrence termed "John's belief that we wouldn't be able to deliver anything that looked passable" unless he was allowed total control over every aspect of the production.[33] The shows truly did need more time to maintain their high quality. Standard 1992 production timelines were designed for the purpose of pumping out Hanna-Barbera and DIC-style shows. *Ren & Stimpy* was anything but. Yet Nickelodeon could never receive a guarantee as to how *much* more time Spumco would need.

In the weeks before the Spumco layoff, Kricfalusi had met with most of the top people at Nickelodeon to discuss what Jim Ballantine described as "how John could keep working on the show, but not be responsible for day-to-day deadlines."[34] Supposedly, one option discussed was to take the bulk of the show's production to another studio while Spumco was kept on to do "A" material, something Kricfalusi refused. The best option he had, Coffey said, was "cooperation": being able to trust that he could deliver episodes that could be aired, on time and on budget. "And none of those things he could do. There was no way to work around it. He had his heels dug in."[35]

Firing John K. was a drastic measure that did not result in a quick cure-all to the production crisis. Nickelodeon's situation was a smaller-scale parallel to United Artists' trauma with Michael Cimino over *Heaven's Gate*—United Artists, too, had an undependable, free-spending, yet extremely popular director on their hands. In all press surrounding *Ren & Stimpy*, Kricfalusi was well-acknowledged as the "guiding force" behind the show, so the network was well aware of the public relations nightmare they would be getting into.[36] A confusing paradox was established. Nickelodeon knew they had let things get so far out of hand that they would have to fire the show's creator; yet if possible, they were still determined to avoid doing so.

Removing Kricfalusi from the show would mean finding a suitable replacement and having incomplete cartoons finished by someone else. Though directors are regularly replaced in television, closer attention was being paid to *Ren & Stimpy* than anything else on cable in 1992. Animation fans followed Kricfalusi as an auteur of the medium. In replacing him, Nickelodeon risked getting back a hodgepodge of a finished product, akin to the debacle of Orson Welles' *The Magnificent Ambersons*. Kricfalusi would later compare his former colleagues' completion of his unfinished works to the action of giving "an unedited cartoon to the milkman and have him finish it for ya."[37]

Tension had been mounting furiously between the network and creator to the point "where everything was a fight" and firing Kricfalusi was "their way of stopping it," Eddie Fitzgerald told Dan Persons.[38] Events finally climaxed with a bit of bravado. Kricfalusi supposedly sent the network a letter through his lawyer, stating that because *Ren & Stimpy* was a success and the network was constantly interfering, Spumco would deliver the episodes when they could, and they would cost what they cost.

Coffey called firing Kricfalusi "the most painful thing of my career" and equally painful for Nickelodeon. "Frankly, we would have done almost anything to make that relationship work. He was on a path, and it wasn't on the same path as Nickelodeon."[39]

Since the ensuing drama centered mainly on Kricfalusi, Simensky felt the public overlooked the effects of the events on the larger *Ren & Stimpy* staff. Most outsiders did not grasp that Spumco was a place where the employees "were closer than a typical studio, and when things fell apart, it really took its toll on a lot of people."[40] Aside from his own deteriorating relationship with Nickelodeon, Kricfalusi was not doing much to maintain a feeling of unity within Spumco. With the mounting pressure from the network, he slipped back into his routine of staying out of the office to avoid people, making it even more "impossible to move any work through" without his input.[41]

Kricfalusi had "become so centered on the show itself that the machinations behind the scenes were somewhat off his radar," Jordan Reichek said, and many artists at the studio became "disgruntled."[42] Even before the firing, staffers noted the lack of new work at the studio and began looking for employment elsewhere. In the weeks before his own dismissal, Kricfalusi also fired Chris Reccardi—one of his directors and top people—solely because Reccardi was dating Kricfalusi's ex-girlfriend Lynne Naylor. "That was the pre-explosion before the end," said Bill Wray. "He was just starting to get where he could do this incredible work, and then he's gone."[43]

Bob Camp in particular had become very disillusioned with Kricfalusi, to the point where he "didn't want to be a part of him or his life."[44] Even laypersons in the studio noticed a growing tension between the two. Nickelodeon had been urging Kricfalusi to commit to a *Ren & Stimpy* movie, and he had repeatedly changed his mind on the matter, at least once saying that he did not "want do the same shit over again."[45] Camp agreed to do it if Kricfalusi would not, causing a rift.

An officially sanctioned behind-the-scenes magazine, *The Ren & Stimpy Show: Exposed*, came out mere weeks after it became known that Spumco would no longer be producing the show. The magazine—assembled before the Spumco-Nickelodeon split—is pure cognitive dissonance: portraying hearts and flowers, albeit of a filthy kind, amongst the crew, and a spirit of friendship between the artists and executives: a stark contrast to the nuclear fallout that was actually happening.

Nickelodeon tapped into this feeling of self-inflicted disharmony to solve their own problem: figuring out whom they could get to run *Ren & Stimpy* without John K. They had what Roy Smith called "secret talks" with Camp and others before the takeover, asking, "If we take over the show, will you come?" Eventually, almost all of the Spumco employees were offered positions on the show at Nickelodeon's new studio—including Kricfalusi.[46]

Camp never had an agenda to replace Kricfalusi as the show's leader; he purely lucked into getting the offer. "When they asked me to finish the show, I went and hid in my studio behind my house for like a couple of weeks, and didn't talk to anybody, didn't answer the phone," Camp said. "And just thought, 'Okay, am I going to finish the highest-rated show on cable television that I love more than anything and thrown my heart into and betray my best friend? Am I gonna do that?'"[47]

He had already proven that he could move cartoons through the pipeline faster, and with results as good as anything bearing Kricfalusi's name as director. This proved, in Nickelodeon's mind, that he was more than suitable for the job. However, they were counting on Camp to maintain that quality after the turmoil of a staff break-up. Recently married and with a child on the way, Camp ultimately accepted Nickelodeon's offer. Said Camp: "It's not disloyalty when somebody lets everyone down, when someone you work for is really cruel and mean to everyone all the time."[48]

Taking over the series also meant establishing an animation studio in Los Angeles, the "antithesis" of what Nickelodeon set out to do in the first place. "We weren't geared up on any level to start one, we didn't have office space, we had nothing," Coffey said.[49] Nickelodeon only had the name of Games Animation, an entity that predated *Ren & Stimpy*. Made concrete as an in-house studio, Games was established in August 1992. Roy Smith and Jim Ballantine picked out an office building on Sunset Boulevard and stocked it with equipment and "cartoon color bullshit desks." Spending around $100,000 to start a makeshift studio was "frankly a savings to [Nickelodeon] if they could get the show back on track," Smith said.[50]

John K.'s firing was no shock to many people involved with the show—including the man himself, though some sycophants have insisted otherwise. Friends and co-workers claim that months prior to his firing, Kricfalusi had the feeling that he was probably going to be dismissed. "You go to lunch with these guys every day [and hear them say], 'Oh god, what if this happens, what if that happens, we're just gonna say fuck it, just fuck them,'" Ed Bell said. "They were kind of getting themselves emotionally prepared, and we all understood."[51]

Still, Kricfalusi's well-deserved pride in *Ren & Stimpy* did foster the delusion that "no way the network could simply take away this maverick show and hand it to someone else."[52] He was unsurprisingly mortified when proven wrong. Kricfalusi maintains the network never formally fired him, because Nickelodeon simply stopped paying him. "I kept going until I had only two weeks' worth of payroll left, then I had to start laying people off, because if I'd kept going I would have been personally responsible for the payroll for the entire Spumco staff."[53]

Payments to Spumco had been withheld earlier in 1992, for as long as three months, until Kricfalusi met the network's hollow demands for creating a balanced budget. No evidence of a second such ransom has come forward, other than Kricfalusi's word. Several former Spumco employees said that either Kricfalusi or Nickelodeon presented the news to them that the creator had been directly given a pink slip. Coffey in particular disputes Kricfalusi's version of events, saying that Nickelodeon indeed formally closed their deal with him before the public announcement of the layoff. "It was up to him to inform his employees. They certainly knew what was going on."[54]

Regardless, there was no money to keep the Spumco employees on the payroll past the last week of September. On 21 September 1992, Kricfalusi was forced to make the announcement that Spumco was no longer the home of *The Ren & Stimpy Show*—and that they were all unemployed. Letting go of his staff, seeing his hard work and training "explode in one day" was the worst part of it, Kricfalusi told Daniel

Cerone in 1992. "It's torn apart, and now I have to put it back together. That's a huge waste."[55]

Kricfalusi told friends that the plug was pulled while "we were in the middle of my best episode"; a descriptor that could have applied to either "Svën Höek", which was then in post-production, or "Stimpy's First Fart", the cartoon for which he had been redrawing layouts for seemingly endless nights and weekends.[56] Jim Smith was drawing a layout for "Fake Dad", showing prison inmate Kowalski in pain, when everyone at Spumco was told the news. Vincent Waller was unaware of what had happened until he called the studio himself, as he was then at Rough Draft in Korea, doing layouts on "Big Baby Scam" and "The Great Outdoors".

"Gregg Vanzo walked in and asked if I had heard anything about Spumco being removed from the show," Waller wrote in 2009. "I said I hadn't. Gregg said, hoping for the best, 'Oh well, it must be nothing then.' I just looked at him and said, 'Gregg, if you heard something all the way in Korea, it's based on something.' I finished my scenes, went back to my hotel, and made a call, at which time they told me that we had indeed been separated from the show."[57]

Very briefly, Kricfalusi seemed resigned to losing the show. "We were all destroyed by it, because we had all really pinned so much hope on this, and we knew what it was," Bill Wray said. "I went in his room later, like, 'Oh my god, what are we gonna do...' blah, blah blah. And it's just like, 'Don't sweat it, I'm relieved. This thing was killing me.' He told me he hadn't had a solid shit in two years."

He supposedly gave his blessing to people who were going to work on the show at Games. Said Wray: "I told him, 'Well, I'm probably going to work for Bob.' And he said, 'Couldn't you get a job somewhere else?' And I said, 'Not on a show like this. You know what I'm talking about.' And he goes, 'I know exactly what you're talking about. You can have my blessing.'"[58]

One of the earliest quotes Kricfalusi gave after the announcement of his departure had an air of reasoned diplomacy: "I felt confined by the rigors of this particular animated series and wanted to pursue projects with more artistic freedom. I am thankful to Nickelodeon, especially Vanessa Coffey, for giving me my first break and I hope the show will continue to be a success."[59]

That same day Kricfalusi was quoted in *The Los Angeles Times* along the same lines. "Nickelodeon wants something for the show. I want something for the show. They're both very strong visions, and together they made for a really great show. But in pure reality, when you mix two really strong visions, it's going to take a long, long time to do the work."[60]

Whether these passive-sounding statements represented how Kricfalusi truly felt at the time, or whether he was holding his tongue, waiting on a cash settlement from Nickelodeon, Camp experienced this same passiveness when he spoke with Kricfalusi about taking the job of running the show without him. According to Camp, Kricfalusi encouraged him to take the job. "Quote, 'I fucked up, don't worry about it, no hard feelings, man.' And I really said this, 'I'm gonna finish your cartoons, and I'm gonna really do my best job on them, and you're gonna be really proud. I'm gonna make sure nobody ruins them and that they are everything you want them to be.'"[61]

§

At the end of his time on *Ren & Stimpy*, Kricfalusi was exercising totalitarian control over "Svën Höek" and "Stimpy's First Fart": his means of protecting and stressing the acting within. "This show will kill people because of the acting," he wrote of "Fart" to Bob Jaques at the end of the show's time at Spumco.[62]

"Svën Höek", branded the "epitome of stupid cartoons" by

Jim Smith, started out innocently enough.[63] It initially received a warm welcome from Nickelodeon. "It's great to see an episode that explores the essential stupidity of Stimpy and Ren's equally essential exasperation," wrote Will McRobb.[64] Ren invites his European cousin Svën for a visit in an attempt to cleanse the stupidity from his household. To Ren's horror, Svën has more in common—in both looks and intelligence—with Stimpy. The duo's combined brainlessness ultimately causes Ren's psychotic rage to literally transport their happy home to the depths of Hell.

John K. spent extensive time on the phone and in person to get Nickelodeon's approval to feature a board game that involved urinating on an electric fence. As it turned out, "Don't Pee on the Electric Fence"—based on events from Kricfalusi's or Bob Camp's youth—was considered too dirty for the network. "I argued with them in New York, 'Isn't pee a really innocent word that all little kids use?' They were just adamant. So I tried every other thing, urinate, 'That's an ugly word,' and I said whiz, 'Oh, whiz is okay.'"[65]

The mere existence of "Stimpy's First Fart", rechristened "Son of Stimpy" by Nickelodeon, may at first seem to undermine Kricfalusi's claim that the network unduly censored his vision. Yet this particular episode, he said, was actually born out of a compromise. "I went to Vanessa and said, 'What if we make a deal: instead of you toning down my extreme cartoons, let me make the extreme ones, and in return, I'll make you some really heartwarming cartoons.' Stimpy has his first fart and then he can't find it, and then he gets heartbroken and he goes and searches all over the city and leaves Ren. I acted a bunch of it out and Vanessa started to cry, and said, 'Do it, John, do it!'"[66]

"Sven Höek" and "Stimpy's First Fart" spent even more time in layout than "Man's Best Friend". "Svën Höek" spent eleven weeks in layout, during which time Kricfalusi announced that three-quarters of the picture would need to be redone. "Stimpy's First Fart" spent

Layout for "Svën Höek", by Mike Kim. Courtesy of Bob Jaques. © Viacom.

fifteen weeks in layout—with nowhere near as many revisions, as the studio never had the chance to get to that stage. When the show was taken over by Games, the cartoon was unceremoniously dumped on Carbunkle in its near entirety.[67] "We were getting ["Stimpy's First Fart"] in sections because it wasn't making its way through John," Bob Jaques said. "As soon as he got fired, they just scooped them up and sent it to us, just so it could get done."[68]

There is no question that John K.'s holdup of layouts—by redrawing them himself—created more delays than any network interference. If there is any defense to his method, it is in the quality of the work that resulted on screen. Both "Svën Höek" and "Stimpy's First Fart" are full of acting that Kricfalusi said could never "be created at the model sheet stage by a designer," precisely the reason why he avoided the use of model sheets on the series in the first place. "Specific expressions have to be customized to the character and [to] each specific moment within the story."[69] Both cartoons represent the yin and yang of *Ren & Stimpy* acting, delving into the personalities of the main characters in completely different ways. In "Svën Höek", dangerous psychoses take center stage. In contrast, "Stimpy's First Fart" focuses on the compassion of the characters' relationship.

The most difficult scene in "Stimpy's First Fart"—with Ren trying to bring Stimpy away from the doorway and into the house—was originally axed. According to Kricfalusi, McRobb was not crazy about the "homosexual overtones to pointing to the mistletoe and leading Stimpy in." Jim Ballantine's sadness over the scene getting censored convinced Vanessa Coffey to reinstate it. "Vanessa looked at me and her eyes got all big like Stimpy's. She said, 'He really wanted that scene in there? Put it back in!'"[70]

Kricfalusi knew these emotional scenes had to be handled with the utmost delicacy. His reluctance to hand them over to someone else was understandable. Some moments in "Svën Höek" and "Stimpy's First Fart" are far more human and realistic than any other animation of recent years. Kricfalusi told historian Michael Barrier that "seventy-five percent of the influences in the acting in my cartoons come from old live-action movies, TV, and people I know and not cartoons," and the proof is in his best work's unconventionality.[71] Kricfalusi fashions himself a revivalist of "cartoony" cartoons, yet Ren's attempt at being seductive and Stimpy's passionate outrage are more in line with the "realistic" acting found in live-action film. Ren's tirade at his idiotic brethren in "Svën Höek" has a touch of reality mixed with abstraction, creating a frightening film noir-like experience.

Kricfalusi's obsession with the doorway sequence in "Stimpy's First Fart" spanned the entire last month the series was at Spumco. He only shipped it when forced to. "I worked very hard and long into

Early sketches by Bob Camp for "Svën Höek" that were mostly excised from the final cartoon. Courtesy of Bob Jaques. © Viacom.

a few nights to get the scene into the shape it is," Kricfalusi wrote to Jaques, the cartoon's animation director. "It just seems that the heavier the acting is, the harder the scene is for both of us. That is why our shit is so much better than everybody else's."[72]

Even the settings consciously reflect what is going on in Ren and Stimpy's heads. When the backgrounds of "Svën Höek" get more abstract, the characters get angrier and stupider. "Stimpy's First Fart" was "painted more like a Frank Capra movie," Kricfalusi said; it needed to convey Stimpy's passionate journey to seek his lost son while Ren mourned his companion's abandonment.[73] Scott Wills and his background painting cohorts expressed confusion during "Stimpy's First Fart", because as the cartoon got more off-schedule, "John was becoming more obsessed with mood," and veering away from stylized painting. Wills wondered, "Well, what, do you want Disney backgrounds now?"[74]

Even with Kricfalusi directing the cartoons so obsessively, obvious errors slipped through. The scene in "Svën Höek" with Ren stomping away to pee was so full of basic layout mistakes that it surprised Jaques that Kricfalusi "never took any sort of directorial effort" to correct them. As originally laid out by Mike Fontanelli, Ren merely walks on top of the board game. His leg stretch was added by the Carbunkle animators.

"That was a difficult scene to figure out because it had a pan, a pan walk, and it had to stop at an exact certain point to allow him to turn around and point at the game," Chris Sauve, the animator of the scene, said. "There's a lot to figure out there. I remember saying to Bob, 'Well, when I plan this whole thing out, he's supposed to walk by this game, he steps on the game! The game is standing right in his way of walking, what am I supposed to do?' And [Bob] did this drawing of [Ren's leg stretching], and we thought, 'Fuck, that's hilarious.'"[75]

Kricfalusi obviously knew that Carbunkle's gripes about bad layout mechanics were true. He even admitted to Jaques that his doorway scene in "Stimpy's First Fart" had volume and foot slippage issues. "I'm aware of some of these problems, but I did everything I could to avoid them without losing the attitudes and the acting," he wrote Jaques. "So please don't think that I am neglecting your needs. It's the best I can do under my restrictions."[76]

The poses of these two scenes "were extremely expressive and fabulous to work with," said Scott Mansz. Kelly Armstrong animated the first scene prior to the shot of the mistletoe; Mansz animated the second scene, with Stimpy chastising Ren for entertaining amorous thoughts. Mansz's scene runs for nearly a full minute, magnifying its passion and obsession—the kind that even many feature animators actively avoid focusing on for more than a moment.

"Stimpy goes though several widely varying emotions throughout the shot, and the difficulty was to give each one the appropriate amount of intensity and timing, and then to string them all together in a natural progression," Mansz said. "There was also quite a bit of foot-slip with the layout poses from Spumco (especially with Stimpy) that I would have liked to lock down, but to do so would have decreased the dynamics of the individual poses, and in the end, Bob and I both agreed that it was best just to 'let them slide.'"[77]

While Carbunkle showed great ingenuity in meeting Spumco's needs on "Svën Höek", Kricfalusi did not immediately appreciate the effort. He had already animated a scene of the cartoon himself, consisting of Stimpy hopping and landing after getting kicked in the head by a horse; Kricfalusi claimed the scene was a gift to Carbunkle. After the cartoon's pencil test arrived at Spumco, Jaques said Kricfalusi called him and "ripped on every single scene for three hours" because it was "too Disney" in its execution; Bill Wray had prepared Jaques for the tirade. "'John's gonna call, it sounds like he's really concerned about the episode.' And then all of a sudden I get this call from John's secretary."[78] Kricfalusi's anger over Carbunkle's work was short-lived, however, as he quickly accepted what other people at Spumco were saying about "Svën Höek": that the animated acting was "genius."

Once "Stimpy's First Fart" was shipped to Carbunkle, John K.'s involvement with the episode—and the series—ended. He was henceforth cut off from having authorial control over his own pictures, leaving all decisions to Jaques, Camp, and others still working on the show. According to Kricfalusi, Coffey promised he could finish post-production on "Svën Höek", but this turned out to be "another in a long line of promises that were reneged on later."[79]

The post-production and sound departments had their own fallings-out. Jim Smith split from Der Screamin' Lederhosen, a band in which he had participated with Chris Reccardi and Scott Huml. Reccardi had joked that the band's existence was originally just an excuse to smoke pot at Smith's house; later, Reccardi and Huml wanted to get more serious with the band, while Smith didn't. Spumco's separation from *Ren & Stimpy* evidently deepened the schism.

Overall sound guru Henry Porch also sided with Kricfalusi after his ouster. Porch had been almost singlehandedly responsible for the artful use of canned music in *Ren & Stimpy*, "one of the defining characteristics [that] returned the style to the older generation of animation," said Shawn Patterson, who worked as a production assistant at Spumco and later in post-production at Games. "The darker orchestral stuff we cut in, and [that] Henry and John had cut in before me, was really significant to the [series'] popularity. Obviously the animation caught everybody's eye, but then you've got the sonic world the cartoon resided in, [which] was brilliant."[80]

Porch's musical choices were certainly creative. Rather than shoehorning characters' actions to fit preexisting tracks—or vice versa—Porch found vastly dissonant tunes to comment on the action, then made them work contrapuntally. At the end of "Space Madness", a cut of the classical "Night on Bald Mountain" intricately segues to a more intense bit of Ronald Hanmer stock music entitled "Bits and Pieces". Porch also worked tirelessly to expand Spumco's musical repertoire. After a year of negotiations, Porch finally cleared a license for the music of Raymond Scott (popularized in the Warner Bros. cartoon soundtracks of the 1940s and '50s), and made use of Scott's cues to intensify Ren and Stimpy's battle with George Liquor in "Man's Best Friend". As Porch recalled, Scott's cues were perfect for the purpose because they "*screamed* animation. *Ren & Stimpy* dealt with abruptly changing emotions and attitudes, and Scott's music easily kept up, shifting gears at breakneck pace."[81]

The use of prerecorded Scott cues—necessarily requiring jumps from one tune to another—could never match the divergences that Carl Stalling's freshly-recorded scores enjoyed in the Warner cartoons.

But the organic vitality of the *Ren & Stimpy* crew turned the restriction into a strength: sudden musical shifts more than abetted the characters' psychoses. The *Ren & Stimpy* soundtracks did not noticeably suffer after the transition to Games—though few after the switch ever matched the foreboding panache of Porch's work at Spumco.

Not every pre-transition decision by Spumco exhibited the same panache. A rough cut survives in the bootlegging community of Kricfalusi's and Ron Hughart's attempt to extend "Svën Höek" to a half-hour. The cartoon was not intended as a half-hour when it was storyboarded by Jim Smith and Bill Wray; the decision to extend it was made well after it was in animation at Carbunkle.[82] This cut features timing of the most bloated, plodding sort, where every pause or cycle is held for absurd lengths. Kricfalusi made it obvious that he wanted his cartoons timed slower when he lambasted timer Dan Jeup over his "snappy, fast" work on the animatic of "Stimpy's First Fart", asking, "Haven't you ever seen a Huckleberry Hound cartoon?"[83]

Keeping things slow to emphasize the drawing and acting made much of the timing in *Ren & Stimpy* successful; but as the long cut of "Svën Höek" proves, slowness could also be deadly. A pause between Ren placing a picture frame on the table and saying, "I can hardly wait to have an intellectual conversation again," is made awkwardly stagnant by increasing it from an eight-frame pause to one of twenty-four. Ren's frightening dialogue at the end of the cartoon is littered with bizarre cessations that kill the scene's impact.

At Games, "Svën Höek" was restored to its original state for the final edit—arguably saving director Kricfalusi from some embarrassment before the general public. Nevertheless, Kricfalusi still chastised Games for their post-production work on the cartoon. Much of the criticism was over censorship: Stimpy could no longer play "sword swallower" with Svën behind closed doors, and Ren's threat to gouge the idiots' eyes out was cut. "The sound effects are too loud and the music doesn't match the moods of the scenes," Kricfalusi went on to say in 1993.[84] An apt assessment, as Games' original broadcast version does indeed contain background noise that makes the precision of the drawing, animation, and acting difficult to fully appreciate.

Later in the series' run, Camp edited "Svën Höek" in post-production a second time to correct these problems. Censorship aside, this later version is the better cut, and was for years the cut used in broadcast rotation and on home video. Most baffling, though, is that when Kricfalusi got the chance to put the episode out the "right" way on DVD, he botched it. (Or an incompetent producer did.) The version of "Svën Höek" on *The Ren & Stimpy Show: The First and Second Seasons Uncut* [sic] was unaccountably the very first Games version—with the same noisy soundtrack Kricfalusi had berated for years. The only difference was that Kricfalusi reinstated the sword-swallowing and eye-gouging gags. By "de-censoring" the short for content while overlooking the flawed soundtrack, Kricfalusi proved that he was no different from his staff underlings: even John K. didn't know what John K. wanted.

In the months to follow, "Stimpy's First Fart" would cause arguments over who exactly did what. No one questioned that a lot of strenuous work was done on the cartoon at Spumco, nor did anyone begrudge John K. the right to say so. ("It is hard to distance myself while they are still airing episodes that I killed myself on," Kricfalusi said.[85]) When Kricfalusi called "First Fart" his "gift to Nickelodeon,"[86] however, Camp was irked, given that so much work on that cartoon had been left unfinished. "I'm sorry, I did half that cartoon. John owes me a debt of thanks. I finished it and it's a damn good cartoon, and that has a lot to do with Games Productions."[87]

The cartoon had not even been animated when its creator was fired. If the finished, rechristened "Son of Stimpy" reflects a vision that John K. can proudly call his own, then he indeed owed Camp

One of John K.'s roughs for the integral doorway sequence in "Son of Stimpy". Courtesy of Bob Jaques. © Viacom.

and others gratitude. Vanessa Coffey was also a savior of the picture; not only did she fight "very, very hard to not have [it] edited," she prevented Nickelodeon from putting it on the shelf to join "Man's Best Friend".[88]

After "Son of Stimpy" received an overwhelmingly positive reaction in focus testing, the network decided that it might seem stupid of them to shelve another costly cartoon. The holiday-themed "Son of Stimpy" was ready to air for weeks, but the network's apprehension caused them to keep it from broadcast until over a week after Christmas, when it premiered on MTV rather than Nickelodeon.

Credit for "Son of Stimpy" came under scrutiny once again when the cartoon was nominated for an Emmy in 1993. Kricfalusi and his court gave the Emmy committee and Nickelodeon grief for including the names of producers they deemed unworthy in the nomination's credits, and self-righteously scolded the two for leaving Bob Camp's name out of the credits.

"This really ought to test your justification skills," Kricfalusi wrote to Camp, in a mass fax. "It's pretty ironic that I have to stick up for you." As it turned out, Nickelodeon had submitted Camp's name for the credits; the Emmy committee took it out, as Camp had no screen credit.

"Frankly, I could care less about any of this shit," Camp wrote back. "Please don't insult my intelligence by pretending to care about me! You don't do anything that doesn't serve your purposes. I hope your new project succeeds. Hopefully you've learned from your mistakes and don't relive them."[89] Camp would have done well to heed his own advice, as would the show itself.

§

The Ren & Stimpy Show had evolved tremendously in its second season. It rid itself of the first season's uncertainty and crudeness and became a confident, powerful product of Hollywood: as unique and marvelous as anything else the medium had created. It was its own genre. It did not fit within the television system, and indeed stomped on its regulations. As the debacle with John Kricfalusi unfortunately proved, *Ren & Stimpy* would either need to adapt to television's structure, or the system would need to be tailored to accommodate this single show. Nickelodeon chose to take the former route.

The media and its audience have always loved a good martyr story, and what martyr story is better than the individual creator versus corporate Hollywood? The network had not even issued a statement before *The Hollywood Reporter* printed that "Nickelodeon is reportedly trying to separate animation whiz John Kricfalusi from his runaway hit *The Ren & Stimpy Show*," and that "it was unclear how the network planned to continue the series without his input."[90]

News stories quoting numerous upset *Ren & Stimpy* fans were common. An article in *The Boston Globe* epitomized the outcry with the quote, "If Nickelodeon wants to keep its audience, they would do all they can to keep Kricfalusi on board."[91] Kricfalusi's firing was protested by high-profile animation artists, including *Simpsons* creator Matt Groening, who said that the situation "may be legal, but artistically it's outrageous."[92] Former boss Ralph Bakshi also came to Kricfalusi's defense: "Understanding the kind of creator John is—that he has nowhere to go financially, yet he still wants to make the shows quality-oriented while building a solid crew of animators—they should have allowed him to miss this season. It's like a ball team: you go with the talent you have. Each player requires different handling."[93]

The press was not alone in urging Kricfalusi to take the martyrdom route. Shortly after Kricfalusi told his crew that the show was going away, layout artists Eddie Fitzgerald and Mike Fontanelli collected signatures for a letter to Nickelodeon stating that the signatories would, under no circumstances, work on *Ren & Stimpy* without John K.[94] Fitzgerald's logic—that the show "uses a unique drawing style that takes awhile to learn," and that the team as a whole was "irreplaceable"—would prove accurate; but many did not see things his way. One staffer told him, "Well, I wouldn't sign that. It sounds like a loyalty oath to me. That's McCarthyism."[95]

Before Kricfalusi's removal from *Ren & Stimpy*, a key member's firing from an animation production had never led to such an emotional upheaval among its staff. Yet for many Spumco people, the option of sticking with the show because they liked working on it was simply not viable. Refusing to work on the show more or less did become a "loyalty oath." The artists were separated into two camps: those who wanted to stick with *Ren & Stimpy* and those who wanted to stick with Kricfalusi, who would argue they were sticking with both anyway.

Those who left the show with Kricfalusi, along with Fitzgerald and Fontanelli, were producer Libby Simon and many of the show's heavy-hitters, like Jim Smith, Vincent Waller, Elinor Blake, and Richard Pursel. "We really grew close and we felt a real bond, and loved what [Kricfalusi] was doing, and just stood by him," Simon said. "It was really heart-wrenching to have to stop doing the show. And the friendships that were lost—it was just a horrible experience altogether, and I'm still not over it."[96]

"One of the reasons the breakup of this crew was so bitter, and certain people are still bitter, bitter, bitter angry about it," Wray said tearfully, "[was] we all loved each other and it was really like a family breaking apart. So that's why the betrayal on all sides was so bitter and still is today."[97]

As for staffers like Wray who chose to move to Games, no matter what justification they gave for doing so, no excuse satisfied the proud Spumco "loyalists," particularly Kricfalusi. Though John K. had originally encouraged his former artists to work with Nickelodeon, he soon felt betrayed by those that did so. "It turned out they weren't friends," Kricfalusi said. "They just used the situation, they just bided their time and waited for an opportunity to make as much money as possible and sell everybody out. The cartoonists took advantage of the [fact] that Nickelodeon was ignorant. Even though they knew Nickelodeon was causing the problems, they chose instant personal benefit over long-term interest for the studio, for the audience, and for the animation art in general."[98]

"When he had some time to get away from it, he started to realize what he had lost," Wray commented. "And what's difficult for him is to take personal responsibility for a difficult personality. It's very difficult for him, if possible at all. He couldn't blame himself, so he had to blame a fall guy."[99]

Kricfalusi's argument is that had his staffers not been willing to work on the show without him, Nickelodeon would have been forced to leave the show at Spumco. True enough: many artists' willingness to work without Kricfalusi certainly helped the network make their decision. But so did an increasingly obvious fact: more and more, Kricfalusi's wayward behavior seemed less about sticking up for his crew, and more about his own self-righteousness. "I remember trying to convince John to give Nick a budget and schedule for the sake of all the people who were working for him," Roy Smith said. "So they wouldn't be put in a position of either betraying him by working for Games, or being left without work. But it was a matter of control and pride with John."[100]

Kricfalusi's constant refrain that it was "only a few short-sighted fools" that sold him out[101] speaks volumes about the utter lack of respect he had for the workhorses of his studio. Most of those who sided with Kricfalusi were just that: workhorses, their roles inflated in the narrative of the controversy. (Kricfalusi had actively avoided hiring Fitzgerald, in particular, until Fitzgerald consented to complete servitude; once Fitzgerald was on staff, his layouts were routinely revised without his knowledge).

Smith and Waller were the two artists whose departure from the series ultimately did as much damage as Kricfalusi's. In the runup to the transition, Waller was being allotted ever-greater responsibility and input at the studio; Smith was arguably a better draftsman, if not visionary, than Kricfalusi himself. Richard Pursel, too, was budding into an important writer; but he was abruptly separated from the ideas he had been honing. "I saw it all unravel, and it was really sad to witness," Pursel said. "Careers and livelihoods were at stake for all of us. There was a lot of nastiness, and it's a total shame that *Ren & Stimpy* didn't have ten to twenty years to develop like *The Simpsons* or even *Rugrats* did."[102]

In his emotional outbursts, Kricfalusi lambasted many artists for joining Nickelodeon; but he reserved his active contempt for four in particular, those whose contributions were indisputable. Bob Camp, Bill Wray, Billy West, and Chris Reccardi—whom Kricfalusi had already fired—were considered the true conspirators. That said, many other former Spumco people interpreted Kricfalusi's statements to imply that they were essentially expendable; if he didn't care about them, they reasoned, they had nothing to lose by continuing to work on *Ren & Stimpy*.

Said Don Shank: "John was understandably bitter about the show moving away from Spumco. He didn't want any of us to work at Games. But I needed to work at least enough to get by and there weren't a lot of worthwhile shows to work on. Plus I already knew the show so it was an easy fit."[103]

Most of the former Spumco people accepted jobs at the new studio, while others displayed their refusal to join as a badge of honor. "Jim Ballantine tried to lure me to Nick's Games studio with a pack of lies," Mike Fontanelli told Mathew Klickstein. "I got a phone call from him promising me directorship and a forty percent increase in salary, just for starters. I told him I wouldn't betray anyone, especially not a fellow cartoonist. So he told me John was on board. Ten seconds later, I was on the phone with John and it was news to him. I never saw Games. I never set foot in the place. My nose is clean."

While Ballantine denied contacting Fontanelli, his story is identical to those of other people, who claim similar offers were made to them. The uncertainty surrounding these offers rather accurately reflects the general chaos and confusion of the time. "I was sharing an office with Bob Camp when the whole split was engineered," Pursel said. "I entered the office one day to see Bob and producer Jim Ballantine huddled around a speaker phone call with Vanessa and Mary Harrington, who were in New York. Bob went around the studio soon after, telling people, 'You've got a job… if you want it.' Bob raved that things would be so much more fun without John telling us what to do, but when I told Bob I couldn't in good conscience leave John for a job with him, he called me a traitor."[104]

Kricfalusi may have had many loyalists; but he had no work for them, and they all soon found themselves back at DIC, working for Kent Butterworth on *The Adventures of Sonic the Hedgehog*. Said Butterworth: "He called me and I was able to hire some of his artists (who did not follow Bob Camp)."[105] It was a strict paycheck. *Sonic* was the most vapid fake *Ren & Stimpy* imaginable, and the environment at DIC likely only fueled the artists' resentment of the situation.

As for the "traitors" who left Kricfalusi, while it may sound easy for them to have taken promotions and remained on *Ren & Stimpy* without him, Teale Wang assured that "it was incredibly hard for all of us."[106] Bill Wray—who once said that the show would die within a year if John K. stopped working on it—was firmer than most of his colleagues in justifying his decision to stay with the show. "Everyone involved has not been perfect in the way things were handled. I wish we were still working on the shows with John; but we're not, so we have to continue and move ahead."[107]

Billy West was particularly vocal about the vitriol he experienced when Kricfalusi lost the show. He claimed Kricfalusi screamed at him over the phone, demanding that West "quit so that he would be called back to the show. This guy was using me to fight his battles, and that is not a man."[108] West described the call he received as a sort of standardized message that Kricfalusi was giving to various show staffers, including voice veteran Gary Owens, the voice of Powdered Toast Man. "I got this call from Gary, he was a little spooked. 'Did you get a call from that Kricfalusi fellow? I answered the phone, and it was someone in mid-sentence screaming. He said, "You're rich, you don't need the fuckin' money." Are you still doing the show?'"[109]

The only way to not rouse anyone's fury, it seemed, was by walking away from the *Ren & Stimpy* playing field altogether, sticking with neither Spumco nor Games. "Maybe we should take the Gospel of John to other studios, give them the benefit," Ed Bell said. "Some guys were depending on that work in a much bigger way, so I just felt really lucky [I] could go where I wanted to."[110]

Beyond the support of a talented crew, it was evident that a mixture of exaggeration and reality made Kricfalusi's best cartoons work so well. Perhaps, then, it is little wonder that Kricfalusi found it appealing to apply this method of storytelling to his own life. Soon, the frustrated director stopped making statements that acknowledged his own faults in the production. It became far more common for him to proclaim that it was his "single-minded honesty and integrity" that caused rifts with the network, or that "they didn't really deserve *The Ren & Stimpy Show*."[111]

An endless stream of press in the last week of September 1992 stated that Kricfalusi would "remain as creative consultant" on *Ren & Stimpy*, though no arrangement of that sort ever materialized.[112] He was indeed offered a high-paying consultant job to just stay with the show and relinquish all creative control; but he went from disputing the meaning of "creative consultant" to outright refusing the position. "I had to go home and shower about fifty times after all that. I just felt like I was covered with filth."[113]

Contrary to the public media spin, Kricfalusi was not cut off from his characters without a cent. Since no paper trail is on public record, details are hazy as to what Kricfalusi's settlement agreement specifically entailed or when it was exactly hammered out. But bits and pieces of information from various sources reveal that this was not a firing without complications.

One revelation contained in a piece of legal correspondence cites the settlement agreement, quoting that Nickelodeon agreed to "accord John Kricfalusi credit, as producer (and such other credits as are consistent with his services and with previous credits accorded John Kricfalusi on prior episodes)."[114] Running against the accepted Hollywood tradition—in which a creator loses screen credit if he leaves a production—Kricfalusi received director's credit on cartoons from which he was absent during their most important stages. This stipulation in his settlement would create a dystopia of misinformation regarding how much work was done on the second season at Spumco, and how much was done at Games.

Kricfalusi's settlement also established that he was to be paid a sum of money for every *Ren & Stimpy* cartoon produced without him. Coffey confirmed that he was paid a per-episode fee, but refused to state what that amount was.[115] Many others have stated on record that John K. was paid anywhere from $25,000 to $30,000 per half-hour for the balance of the entire series. Though Nickelodeon could have "easily just sent a letter to the Associated Press about the fee he was getting for every show we did," Jim Gomez noted, the network refused to feed any information regarding John K.'s ouster to the press.[116] Gerry Laybourne said to *Cablevision* that the network did not want to get into "a war of words," and hoped people would take Kricfalusi's past escapades into account and see that he was "out of control again."[117]

Having failed to handle Kricfalusi while they employed him, Nickelodeon likewise failed to handle him after his firing. By refusing to discuss the issue in the press any further than Kricfalusi's failure to meet deadlines, the network effectively committed political suicide. For in the absence of a defense from Nickelodeon, Kricfalusi and his allies were more than willing to launch attacks. Whenever an article or interview about the show appeared, Spumco employees and fans wasted no time in passionately responding and refuting. In a letter to the editor in the *Los Angeles Times*, Vincent Waller took Bob Camp to task—despite the two having been friends since they were teenagers. Waller marginalized Camp's role at Spumco and accused him of having "memory lapses" in regards to the origins of "Stimpy's Cartoon Show". "He took his screaming tirades and wall-kicking abilities with him. He will be missed."[118]

When an interview with Bill Wray appeared in David Anthony Kraft's *Comics Interview* in 1993, Spumco personnel responded with a vengeance. Jim Smith called some of Wray's statements into question, claiming Wray was working for a studio where people "have never animated a scene in their lives, or timed a show on exposure sheets or created any characters that are remembered anywhere." Smith also called the Nickelodeon takeover "an act of pure piracy [in which] Bill, Bob and the others are accessories."[119]

An interview with John K. was published in a 1994 issue of *Comics Interview* under the provision that the magazine accompany it with a "fact sheet" about *Ren & Stimpy*: a document that had been appearing elsewhere in print and online. "What I loved about the 'real' story was that Mr. Wray qualified every single event with, 'Well, I wasn't there, but the way I heard it was...'" remarked Kricfalusi. "I don't think that's a very professional way of getting the real story."[120]

Critical in establishing John K. as a perpetual victim in the public's eyes was Chris Gore of *Film Threat*, a pop culture magazine that had run an extensive article on Spumco before the takeover. In 1993, Gore issued an animation spinoff called *Wild Cartoon Kingdom*; its premiere issue featured "The Plot to Kill Cartoons," an article filtered through Gore, but written mostly by an anonymous Kricfalusi. Though useful for carrying certain anecdotal information that can be verified outside of the Spumco clique, "The Plot" is apocryphal at best, and at worst what Camp called "pure yellow journalism."[121] Supporters of Kricfalusi are hailed as heroes; those who stayed at Games are branded as traitors. The Nickelodeon "hippie ladies" and story editors are targets of the pointed article, but Camp was its primary quarry. He is portrayed as a "hillbilly" who betrayed his fellow cartoonists for a "helluva lot of money."[122] Camp described a later incident in which he and the Games staff ran into Gore at a restaurant in Beverly Hills: "He walked over to our table and announced that I should enjoy my meal, because I was stealing food out of Vincent Waller's mouth. I stood up and quite loudly invited Gore outside for a little fisticuffs. He declined."[123]

Kricfalusi's original draft for "The Plot to Kill Cartoons" features a section bearing the subheading "Spumco's Bad Apples." It describes those who continued to work on the show at Games as "complainers who were chronically unhappy, no matter where they were working"[124]—a sentiment that even the most ardent of Spumco supporters would deny, explaining why the passage was dropped.

"Anybody who wasn't on [John's] side was the enemy, and I was just sort of in the middle; that was my job in general," Will McRobb said. "The last time I heard from John was a voice message on my phone, and what he said to me was, 'Hey, Will, there's a word in the dictionary you should look up, hmm, I think it's called 'integrity.'"[125]

Said David Koenigsberg, who had left Spumco at the beginning of the second season because of the increasing drama: "I had come back from Asia to my hotel in San Francisco, where I got the call saying, 'We fired John, we need you to come back to the show.' I felt the need to tell him, 'John, I'm gonna go work with Nick on this. There's no hard feelings about this at all.' He reacted very poorly to this, and he shoved me down a flight of stairs at Spumco. I didn't get hurt, I did not land on my ass. It could've been worse, easily. But I remember looking back up the stairs, and Brent [Kirnbauer] and Libby were aghast about what happened. Probably thinking, 'Lawsuit!' Or maybe I had been hurt. Or both. But, I can't say I was totally surprised. And I survived."[126]

The *Wild Cartoon Kingdom* article concludes that "Ren and Stimpy are dead" and that the show is "in the hands of morons"—a neat summation of what the public perceived as the fate of the series.[127] Yet no amount of hyperbolic grandstanding could change Nickelodeon's mind. *The Ren & Stimpy Show* was legally their property, and they could do whatever they pleased with it.

As September drew to a close, any remaining scenes or artwork were taken out of Spumco in a "mad rush" and unceremoniously dropped off at Games.[128] "I had to go in by myself with a truck and a couple of hired guys and go in and cart the show out," Roy Smith said. "And John was following me around the studio as I was picking up all the work, calling me every name in the book. I think the parting words I left with John were, 'You're an extremely talented guy, I'm sorry this had to happen, and I hope I get to work again with you some day.' And I meant it." Smith would soon be looking for work again himself, since a supervising producer was no longer needed if the show was to be produced by Nickelodeon directly.[129]

With the majority of media coverage slanted in John Kricfalusi's favor, Nickelodeon would be branded an "evil empire" for firing him as long as the series continued.[130] But time would prove that—as Jordan Reichek said—Kricfalusi's "martyrdom did no one any good."[131]

Drawings for the "Balloon Good-Bye" bumper, by Vincent Waller. Courtesy of Bob Jaques. © Viacom.

DON'T WHIZ ON THE HAND THAT FEEDS YOU

Season Two Breakdown

For the sake of historical accuracy and to prevent future confusion, the following is a list of where each cartoon of the second season was in production at the time the show left Spumco. Regardless of conflicting past accounts, the information on this list was taken from period studio documentation and is correct. The use of "scrapped" here indicates that the cartoon was taken off the production schedule at Spumco when the season was cut down from twenty episodes to thirteen.

IN THE ARMY—Fully delivered.
POWDERED TOAST MAN—Fully delivered.
OUT WEST—Fully delivered.

RUBBER NIPPLE SALESMEN—Fully delivered.
REN'S TOOTHACHE—Fully delivered.
MAN'S BEST FRIEND—Fully delivered.
DOG SHOW—Fully delivered.
SVËN HÖEK—Still in post-production at Spumco, completed by Games.
HAUNTED HOUSE—Animation arrived the final week the show was at Spumco. Post-production done at Games.
MAD DOG HÖEK—Still at Rough Draft in Korea at the time of the firing; post-production done at Games.
BIG BABY SCAM—Still at Rough Draft in Korea at the time of the firing; post-production done at Games.
SON OF STIMPY—Sent to Carbunkle as the transition occurred; post-production done at Games.
MONKEY SEE, MONKEY DON'T—Some layout done by Bob Camp at Spumco, mostly completed at Games; voice track recorded at Games.
FAKE DAD—Still in layout at Spumco at the time of the firing, finished there; timed and sent to Korea by Games. Post-production done at Games.
THE GREAT OUTDOORS—Layout was starting in Korea at time of the transition; mostly finished and voices recorded at Games.
THE CAT THAT LAID THE GOLDEN HAIRBALL—Storyboarded by Vincent Waller at Spumco. Otherwise completely done at Games.
STIMPY'S FAN CLUB—Storyboarded by Peter Avanzino and voices recorded at Spumco. Otherwise completely done at Games.
A VISIT TO ANTHONY—Storyboarded by Jim Smith and voices recorded (save Anthony's dad) at Spumco. Otherwise completely done at Games.

THE ROYAL CANADIAN KILTED YAKSMEN—Storyboarded by Chris Reccardi and voices recorded at Spumco with minor layout done. Otherwise completely done at Games (National Anthem sequence included).

TO SALVE AND SALVE NOT!—Outline written by Bob Camp and Vincent Waller at Spumco. Held over for the third season at Games.

A YARD TOO FAR—Outline written by John K. at Spumco. Held over for the third season at Games.

NO PANTS TODAY—Outline written by Richard Pursel at Spumco. Scrapped at Spumco, resurrected for the third season at Games.

REN'S PECS—Outline written by Richard Pursel at Spumco. Scrapped at Spumco, resurrected for the third season at Games.

STIMPY'S CARTOON SHOW—Outline written by John K. and Elinor Blake at Spumco. Scrapped at Spumco, resurrected for the third season at Games.

JIMMINY LUMMOX—Premise written by Bob Camp at Spumco; remained unapproved. Resurrected during the third season at Games.

BASS MASTERS—Premise written by Richard Pursel at Spumco; remained unapproved. Resurrected during the third season at Games.

EAT MY COOKIES—Premise written by Richard Pursel at Spumco; remained unapproved. Resurrected during the third season at Games.

LAIR OF THE LUMMOX—Storyboarded by Jim Smith at Spumco; held over for third season at Games.

REN'S BRAIN—Outline written by John K. and Richard Pursel at Spumco. Scrapped at Spumco; held over for the fourth season at Games.

The following cartoons were written in part or whole at Spumco during the second season, but never got further than the outline stage. They are listed in alphabetical order.

THE BIG GYP

THE BIG SWITCH—Ren and Stimpy trade places. Semi-resurrected as "Who's Stupid Now?"

THE BOY WHO CRIED RAT 2—A no-frills sequel to the original "Rat!", beginning immediately with Ren entering Stimpy's mouth.

CELLULETTES—Stimpy joins a girl band. Phil Spector was to voice the manager.

FIRE DOGS 2—Ren and Stimpy move in with Fire Chief. Resurrected as an episode of *Adult Party Cartoon*.

HILLBILLY REN—Ren and Stimpy encounter Corn Liquor, George's relative. Sometimes incorrectly referenced online as "Hillbilly Höek."

OLD FOLKS' HOME—A cheater episode that was to incorporate old footage.

ONWARD AND UPWARD—Ren and Stimpy move into a spittoon. Resurrected as an episode of *Adult Party Cartoon*.

REN GETS HELP—Ren finally seeks psychiatric help. Resurrected as "Ren Seeks Help" for *Adult Party Cartoon*.

REN'S BAD HABITS

SING-A-LONG—A cheater episode that was to incorporate old footage.

Chapter 7
Playing the Milkmen

As *The Ren & Stimpy Show* changed hands, Nickelodeon tried in vain to paint a picture of a smooth transition. The network promised that all thirteen episodes of the second season would air by the end of January 1993[1]; by May, only eleven had aired, and two would be held over for the third season. When *Variety* reminded readers that "a new episode of the animated series will finally air," the phrasing deliberately chided the network.[2] As the cartoons slowly rolled out, Nickelodeon could not satisfactorily answer why they had fired John Kricfalusi. If lateness was the issue, why were the cartoons not coming out any faster without him? The short answer is that the transition proved far costlier and time-consuming than the network expected.

Its reputation poisoned from the very beginning, Games Animation had the most unenviable of working environments. Bill Wray said in 1993 that the place was branded a "traitor studio" and that such a label would be difficult to overcome.[3] Former Spumco artists slowly trickled into Games, all in "a lot of pain[,] struggling with the change," Vanessa Coffey said.[4]

Jim Gomez, rejoining the series after a year-long absence, was among the first Spumco holdouts to arrive at Games. He described the new building as "sterile" and "more like your standard corporate studio": almost anti-*Ren & Stimpy* by its very nature.[5] Such a stark contrast to Spumco—the show's original grubby domicile—was inadvertently detrimental to the staff's morale. The notion that they, as cartoonists, had sold out to the suits was only reinforced by what Mike Kim described as a staff of "seven producers and eight artists."[6] By the end of October 1992, little more than a dozen Spumco veterans had been recruited to finish the second season at Games.[7]

Stimpy was dressed as a milkman in the Games Animation logo in response to John K.'s criticism that losing the show was akin to giving "an unedited cartoon to the milkman and have him finish it for ya." The bloody knife was not in the final version. Drawn by Mike Kim. Courtesy of Jim Ballantine. © Viacom.

On the outside, John K. became his own show's harshest critic, voicing loud criticism over Games "screwing up" his unfinished cartoons in post-production.[8] Many changes were made against the original director's wishes, like the censorship of "Svën Höek" and "Dog Show", and the decision to turn a shower scene in "Haunted House" into a direct black-and-white homage to Alfred Hitchcock's *Psycho* (1960).

A scene in Vincent Waller's "Big Baby Scam" came under particular scrutiny from Kricfalusi. In it, Old Man Hunger (here called "Grandpa") holds Ren and Stimpy in the family bath. Hunger was originally supposed to whistle a happy tune as he clutched our heroes; Games had him whistle "Hall of the Mountain King"—implying pederasty, a la Peter Lorre in Fritz Lang's *M* (1931). Kricfalusi said the misinterpretation ruined the whole scene. "Sometimes they read more into a joke than I intended," Waller said in 1992. "I don't do pedophile or homosexual jokes, but they think I do."[9]

Open hostility toward the studio went beyond rabble-rousing in the press. Many industry artists branded Games staffers as pariahs to the point of harassment. Camp described an incident in which Kricfalusi had T-shirts made with pictures of Camp, Wray, and other ex-Spumco artists, with corresponding quotes "from the early days about what a genius John was. I had some harsh words with [the person who brought the shirts in], and that's the last we saw of the shirts."[10] A fax message was also sent from Spumco to Games several hundred times; it featured the same imagery and diatribe. Jim Ballantine, instated as *Ren & Stimpy*'s producer in October 1992, said the studio also received death threats of the "black envelope" variety from Spumco on more than one occasion.[11] That Games was able to actually complete the cartoons amidst this frightening chaos is an accomplishment in itself, regardless of their success rate.

Like Spumco before them, Games experienced costly bouts of trial and error during the cartoons' production. The studio spent many weeks going through the material received from Spumco, only to find that many storyboard and layout drawings were either missing or destroyed.[12] The Los Angeles-based digital ink-and-paint house MetroCel proved to be as unreliable as any overseas outfit. Original artwork repeatedly went missing when sent to MetroCel; frequent revisions and in-person visits during "Haunted House" and "Son of Stimpy" consumed the Games crew's already limited time.

As a means of preventing further delays, Bob Jaques was brought down by Games to supervise the process on "The Royal Canadian Kilted Yaksmen"—the season's finale—at MetroCel. "I had a huge argument with [MetroCel's owner] about a pan move," Jaques said, "and he accused us of shoddy work so he wouldn't have to fix their take." He countered with a flawless pencil test shot at Carbunkle, which forced MetroCel to make the necessary revision.[13] MetroCel's overall unprofessional nature forced Games to refrain from using them in the future.

As soon as *Ren & Stimpy* came to Games, the network tried to soften "Man's Best Friend" into something broadcast-worthy. New footage was animated at Rough Draft, showing a leg-wrestling scene that had originally never made it past the storyboard and recording stages. Several thousand dollars later, however, Nickelodeon realized they could only show the cartoon either as Spumco had originally delivered it, or in a censored form. Games could not legally animate new footage of George Liquor; in the terms of the settlement, the rights to the character had reverted to John K.[14]

"Fake Dad" had already spent a long time in production at Spumco; but only layout had been completed before it went to Games. "Fake Dad" was another striking collaboration between John K. and Jim Smith; partly because Smith did the storyboard and supervised the layouts, but moreso because the two were among the only artists at Spumco who could properly draw Kowalski, the seven-year-old prison inmate whom Ren adopts.

Layout drawn by Jim Smith for "Fake Dad". Courtesy of Jim Smith.
© Viacom.

As with "Svën Höek", Spumco had attempted to lengthen "Fake Dad" into a full half-hour episode; it was cut to eleven minutes at Games. Although Smith's storyboard matches the final picture nearly verbatim, and Games used all of the Spumco layouts, neither Kricfalusi nor Smith were content with the decision to shorten "Fake Dad". Smith commented that the final cartoon looked as though it was "taken over by uncaring people who shoved it through."[15]

Documentation shows that Spumco's expansion job on "Fake Dad" was to have mirrored "Svën Höek" exactly: cycles would be repeated and holds lengthened to try and get as lengthy a cartoon as possible from an inadequate amount of material. Games initially intended to follow Kricfalusi's wishes regarding the timing and pacing. They also had a new football sequence completely animated to expand the story. But the first cut of the cartoon, Ballantine wrote, was "slow and unwatchable"; keeping the cartoon at eleven minutes—and scrapping the new footage—was "the only option."[16]

The finished "Fake Dad" does not bear any signs of its production complications. It showcases Smith's penchant for making the most technical aspects of drawings humorous. Had Kowalski not been drawn so perfectly as an oafish dreg of society, the gag that he is a seven-year-old child would not have been nearly as effective. Kricfalusi's performance as Ren blends genuine vexation and remorse, enhancing the believability that the Chihuahua could actually grow to care for the lummox as his Fake Son.

The kind of charisma found in "Fake Dad" slowly disappeared as the series progressed at Games; the damage caused by the breakup

Cel set-up from the sequence entirely conceived at Games that was ultimately cut from the final version of "Fake Dad". © Viacom.

was evident as early as Bob Camp's "Monkey See, Monkey Don't". When the cartoon originally premiered, John K.'s "created by" credit was inexplicably absent from the opening. Its reinstatement in every subsequent broadcast tempted one to think that Nickelodeon was quietly disavowing the show's creator. Regardless, his initial lack of credit is consistent with Kricfalusi's opinion that "Monkey" was "the worst Ren & Stimpy cartoon ever made" as of 1993.[17]

"Monkey" does not reach the lows of the first season's failures, though it is still arguably the worst of the second season. There is a repellant charm to the idea of Ren and Stimpy living in their own feces to obtain inedible food, but in execution, the episode plays like a less-polished version of "Fire Dogs". "Monkey" was the episode with which Camp was most heavily involved during the transition from Spumco to Games, and it obviously suffered accordingly.

After remaining with the series to do both main characters' voices, Billy West suffered the same public scrutiny and harassment that Camp did, even though—as a voice actor—West was completely mercenary to the production. Recalled Mary Harrington: "Vanessa and I were at a recording session with him and he was saying, 'You should be ashamed of yourself! How can you do what you've done?!' He was pretending to be Ren doing John's voice."[18]

In "Monkey" and elsewhere in the second season, West's high-pitched and grating performance as Ren seemed to justify his detractors' outrage. Over the course of the third season, however, West would mature into the Chihuahua's role; to casual viewers, his voice would become indistinguishable from Kricfalusi's.

"The Great Outdoors" and "The Cat That Laid the Golden Hairball" were former Spumco cartoons sent to Korea with no in-house layout, as a means of making up for the second season's overages. Vincent Waller did work on "Outdoors" at Rough Draft before leaving the series; he retained a co-director credit with Ken Bruce, who created extensive exposure sheets at Games for the Korean animators. Neither "Outdoors" nor "Hairball" turned out a particularly strong entry. "Outdoors" is simply a string of blackout gags; the material in "Hairball", taken from a fan-made comic book sent to Spumco, is annoyingly juvenile. Both cartoons noticeably lack finesse—clearly indicative that the Games artists were giving their attention to more important matters.

§

Games toiled over a trio of extended-length cartoons after the transition: "Stimpy's Fan Club", "A Visit to Anthony", and "The Royal Canadian Kilted Yaksmen". Camp said he and the other artists "worked extra hard to make the cartoons [John K.] had started as good as if he'd made them," even though this ended up being a thankless chore. Kricfalusi received prominent screen credit on the latter two, despite having done little to none of the actual directorial work.[19]

The director's credit on "Stimpy's Fan Club" was afforded to Peter Avanzino, as a formal "thank-you" for his extensive storyboard and layout work on the picture. In one of the series' shining moments, Ren has a nervous breakdown after spending the whole day sending sickeningly sweet replies to Stimpy's legions of fans. This infusion of compassion poisons Ren's psychotic nature, causing him mortal anguish. In retaliation, he tries to snap Stimpy's nonexistent neck; but before he can carry out this nefarious plan, a "stinging" niceness overpowers his brain, causing an aneurysm. Recorded at Spumco, Ren's vocal performance is Kricfalusi's last masterwork for the series. "It's filled with such emotion, all these colors come out in this dialogue," David Koenigsberg commented. "He really brings this character to life, he's an actor, it's not a cartoon anymore."[20]

Kricfalusi's voice does the heaviest lifting in this sequence, as Avanzino was not among the show's top draftsmen. Avanzino's poses, combined with Rough Draft's animation, are incapable of delivering the comedic drama and tragedy essential to the compelling acting that the show had previously achieved on a regular basis. Though intended as an epic episode, "Fan Club" also took a backseat to other cartoons at Games and only works modestly well.

"A Visit to Anthony" was the cartoon that John K. and his cohorts were most upset over losing. The idea for the episode came from a letter that Anthony Raspanti, a young Virginian child, had written to the show the very day *Ren & Stimpy* premiered on Nickelodeon. "Dear Ren & Stimpy, I hope you can come visit us in our country—the United States of America. And please bring your costumes. I like you very much. I really enjoyed your show tonight, especially when Ren and Stimpy found each other again."[21]

Jim Smith storyboard drawing for "A Visit to Anthony". Courtesy of Stephen DeStefano. © Viacom.

Kricfalusi's idea was to build a whole cartoon around Ren and Stimpy going to visit Anthony and have the fan voice his animated counterpart. Nickelodeon initially loved the concept; but when they saw the storyboard, "Anthony" became yet another cartoon about which the network grew increasingly nervous. While Kricfalusi assured them that his intentions were just to "involve the audience more with the cartoon, so the kids at home will feel like the characters are their friends,"[22] it became his excuse to portray what Bill Wray called "John's primal scream against his father."[23]

Kricfalusi wrote that the finished cartoon was still "99% my point of view," in spite of being completed mostly without him. After Jim Smith was slated to be the layout supervisor of "A Visit to Anthony" at Spumco, the series was taken away. All of the voices had been recorded at this point, save that of Anthony's father, and Kricfalusi's lack of input diminished the cartoon's overall effect. Given that Anthony's dad is a caricature of John K.'s own father, only he would have known how to utilize this semi-autobiographical material to its fullest potential.

Games cast actor Randy Quaid as the dad; and though Quaid is a proficient comedy actor, his inexperience at animation vocals is made clear by the forcedness of his delivery. His performance, as Kricfalusi wrote, sounds as if Quaid was "reading [the dialogue] for the first time, so he didn't give it the meaning that the drawings conveyed. Whoever directed him was afraid to actually give him any direction. And also didn't know my dad."[24]

Kricfalusi also insisted that only he and Jim Smith could draw the father, an accurate and revealing statement.[25] The father, like Kowalski, is an incredibly intricate, brutish creation that only the very best of *Ren & Stimpy* draftsmen were capable of handling. At Games, only Camp, Chris Reccardi, and Mike Kim could work on the scenes with the father; no one else at the studio could even come close to drawing the character properly.[26]

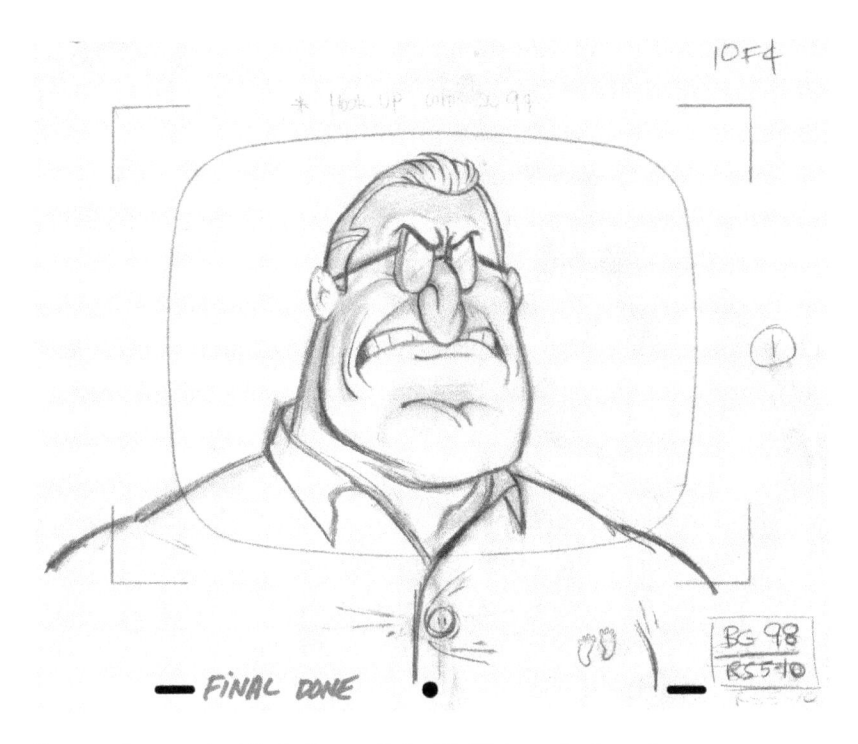

Layout drawing by Chris Reccardi for "A Visit to Anthony".
Courtesy of Ryan Khatam. © Viacom.

It proved costly to have the best artists direct their energy towards saving "A Visit to Anthony". The cartoon was sent to Rough Draft as a way to keep its rising budget down; the finished half-hour was rumored to have cost around $1 million.[27] "Anthony" was originally promised to Carbunkle Cartoons, but after a "not so nice conversation with Jim Ballantine," Jaques' studio was saddled with "The Royal Canadian Kilted Yaksmen" instead.[28]

Though nowhere near as gripping as the Spumco-Carbunkle collaborations, "Anthony" has remarkably unsettling sequences. After mistaking his son's run-in with Victor—the neighborhood sadist—for Ren and Stimpy's bullying, Anthony's dad berates the two in front of a foreboding fireplace for five minutes. The staging and acting of the storyboard and layouts are strong enough to realistically deliver the terrifying experience of being castigated by an intimidating authority figure. The audience is pulled into the film in a manner that Will McRobb said is "genius if you're of the right age, but if you're eight, terrifying."[29] It was the exact sort of experience Nickelodeon hoped to iron out of the series with John K. ousted.

By comparison, "The Royal Canadian Kilted Yaksmen"—slated as a B-picture—was a quasi-template for the kind of show Nickelodeon *did* want *Ren & Stimpy* to be. Ren and Stimpy are Kilted Yaksmen on a pointless journey through Canada to find the lost Barren Wasteland. Chris Reccardi had been the cartoon's original director at Spumco and was about to take it into layout in late July 1992 when he was fired.[30] Under Mike Fontanelli, a sizable number of the scenes were laid out, but the mounting tension between Spumco and Nickelodeon resulted in no real work being accomplished on the picture for the entire last month it was at the studio.[31]

At Games, Reccardi was put back in charge of "Yaksmen". He trashed almost everything done at Spumco and did all the layouts himself anew in a single month. Given that Reccardi was simultaneously helping to save "A Visit to Anthony", he was only able to direct "Yaksmen" in the most superficial sense. "I was still learning and just never took charge of that thing," Reccardi said. "Back when I was storyboarding it, I really didn't get the feel of a story for it, and John was really preoccupied with other challenges at the time."[32]

Reccardi's lack of foresight produced beautifully drawn layouts that, unfortunately, were not functional in the animation process. Riddled with the kinds of poor camera pan instructions and volume changes that peeved Bob Jaques to no end, "Yaksmen" was not a prime example of *Ren & Stimpy* direction. Camera pan and volume problems were "stupid things" that went unnoticed because there was no real technical director at Games until David Koenigsberg returned to the series. "People weren't looking out for those things, and I wouldn't expect them to," Koenigsberg said. "It's not Chris' thing, he's so anti that stuff, he just loves drawing."[33] Reccardi stated Jaques is the true director of "Yaksmen", as it "received no direction from anybody [else]."[34]

The haphazard story was brought to life through the grandest of character animation by the Carbunkle crew, and marked a decided departure from Jaques' and John K.'s other collaborations. Like Ren and Stimpy in the cartoon, the story journeys in no discernible direction. Jaques disguises the plot's lack of substance by adding rich layers of comedic subtlety, making the cartoon into what he called "a painful journey with laughs along the way."[35] His heightened attention to detail made every movement a gag in itself. A passing scene in a montage, showing Ren sitting in an outhouse with his kilt down, is already funny in concept, but Jaques does not stop there. He has to show the strain of Ren, in his weakened condition, taking a dump through wincing eyes.

After their best work with Spumco, the Carbunkle animators were so skilled in animated acting that they continued to instill their artistry into scenes where it was never intended. The scene of one yak's nervous breakdown would have likely become nonspecific raving had the scene been shipped to a studio in Korea. Through the animation of Kelly Armstrong, by contrast, the scene delivers a level of frightening intensity capable of scaring the very animator drawing it.

Carbunkle's best work vindicates the premise that lifelike animation—the attention to complex details, lip sync, and convincing movement—is not limited to specific subject matter. Despite gaping budget disparities, the animation in the Carbunkle episodes of *Ren & Stimpy* is on the level of any contemporary feature. The guiding principle of a 1990s feature and "Yaksmen", after all, is the same: to startle the audience by being unbelievably lifelike. *Which* aspect of life

Layout drawing by Chris Reccardi for "The Royal Canadian Kilted Yaksmen". Courtesy of Bob Jaques. © Viacom.

each project chooses to caricature convincingly is entirely up to the animator.

"After I left *Ren & Stimpy*, I was asked to go work at Disney Feature Animation," Chris Sauve said. "I debated whether to put my *Ren & Stimpy* stuff on my reel, because they were Disney guys, they're not going to want to look at this stuff. But as it turns out, they were all killing themselves laughing over the *Ren & Stimpy* stuff. They would see all these floaty, sort of boring feature scenes and then stuff would come on that was crisp, bold, and funny. *Ren & Stimpy*, weirdly enough, got me a job at Disney, of all places."[36]

Bob Jaques proved himself an animation comedy director of the highest caliber, and was frustrated at the lack of direction on Games' part. It was a startling contrast with the passionate control that John

K. had exercised while working with Jaques. "I really hate it when someone says 'just do it,' because a film is not directed that way," Jaques said in 1993. "One of the reasons for the success of the show was that it was looked after every step of the way."[37]

Many critics and fans have interpreted Jaques' displeasure as the reason he and Kelly Armstrong opted to leave the series after completing "Yaksmen". Out of respect for Kricfalusi, they turned down Games' repeated offers to keep animating the show at their own price. Carbunkle left the show with no hard feelings and had an open invitation to return to Games, should the need arise. "We knew we could get other work, and never looked at *Ren & Stimpy* as the first or the last show we would work on; so for us, it felt better to say 'no' than to say 'yes,'" Armstrong said. "John was a good friend and brought Carbunkle in on the best cartoon on television at the time, so we were grateful for that. He cared about and enjoyed animation enough to make it doable in North America for us, and he let us push our limits and experiment."[38]

Shortly after the completion of "Yaksmen", John K. voiced his fury over the cartoon, though not over how it turned out. Kricfalusi threatened legal action against Nickelodeon because—in the finished short—he shared a director's credit with Chris Reccardi. A letter from Kricfalusi's attorney to MTV states that Reccardi's co-direction credit was a "breach of the Settlement Agreement" because Reccardi had "admitted" to both Kricfalusi and Jaques that "he did not direct the cartoon, he had no intention of taking a director credit, he was pressured by Jim Ballantine to take credit, and he would ask to have his name removed."[39]

The cartoon aired, retaining the Kricfalusi and Reccardi credit, a mere five days after the letter was written. The letter, Ballantine said, was merely one of Kricfalusi's many legal outbursts against the network. "Since Chris was in a serious relationship with Lynne Naylor, anything having to do with Chris made John extra nuts. Our response was something like, there was no specific prohibition against adding a name, and John had shared credit in the past. I certainly don't fault anything Chris said. He finished that cartoon, and we (me, Vanessa, and Mary) thought he deserved the credit."[40]

With "Yaksmen" aired, the controversial second season of *Ren & Stimpy* came to a close—still two episodes shy of the ordered thirteen. Many of the remaining Spumco outlines would go into production in the third season, where the show's content moved further away from the vision of John K. He correspondingly demanded that his "created by" credit be removed from future new episodes produced at Games.

Many people shared ex-producer Chris Danzo's viewpoint that "when you take John out of the picture, [*Ren & Stimpy*] no longer really existed."[41] The artists now residing at Games Animation already knew they had an enormous void to fill. A spectral sense of impending doom plagued the series for the remainder of its existence. Any failure was inevitable, however, because Games really was an outfit set up to fail.

Chapter 8
Stimpy's Cartoon Show

A puzzling, unpleasant atmosphere surrounded the two floors on Sunset Boulevard occupied by Games Animation. The artists who worked on the final two seasons of *The Ren & Stimpy Show* were admirable in their attempts to maintain the unique standards of the most compelling, well-drawn animated show of all time. They were capable of producing cartoons that matched anything done at Spumco, but these instances were few and far between. Fearful commitment to delivery requirements and, most significantly, despair caused by the staff breakup overshadowed every creative decision, ultimately compromising the series' brilliance.

Nickelodeon had promised a timelier delivery of future episodes with a third season premiere scheduled for September. It was a promise made hastily. The third season would not actually air until late November and would conclude almost a year later. The Games staffers' inability to meet deadlines held an irony that supporters of John Kricfalusi relished: the network was doing the very thing they had fired the original creator for.

Games started production of the third season two months behind schedule. Much of the first quarter of 1993 was devoted to wrapping up the second season's final episodes, which were either in animation or post-production stages. Well into March 1993, the third season's production began in earnest when several Spumco-written outlines were put into storyboard.[1]

The new studio may not have been set up "to give the physical care to the cartoons that John did," as Bill Wray said in 1993, but it was often "late at times" and unable to produce the shows more quickly than Spumco.[2] Indeed, they often took longer. The studio was teeming, Jim Ballantine said, with "many people doing their job for the first time, making it up as we went along, doing the best we could."[3] The primary cause of the delays at Games was no different than at Spumco: Bob Camp and his colleagues had committed to a certain level of quality, and ardently fought to maintain it at all costs.

The rambunctious behavior Spumco was known for was also alive and well at Games. Although the artists had actual deadlines and a cleaner workspace, they were still shielded from the "real world" of animation. Camp said that a writing session typically consisted of "a pitcher of martinis and somebody roll[ing] a big fatty."[4] Mike Kim commented that the pool table in the bullpen area saved the artists from going "too crazy."[5]

More significant was a shared, fundamental sense of responsibility towards artistic integrity. "Everyone's position was necessary," director

Ron Hughart said. "Everyone played an important role, as the shows were so hard to produce."[6] Games was not a place where many industry artists could survive, nor was *Ren & Stimpy* "a standard sitcom where new writers can be brought in to do 'quickie' material," as Ballantine told the network executives in New York. "No amount of production skill or administrative pressure can be applied to get this special breed of rebel artist to 'get a show out.' There is a universal floor of quality beneath which Bob and the artists cannot fall!"[7]

It was a mark of John K.'s success as a teacher that his browbeating at Spumco had such longevity. He had instilled himself into every one of his employees, and they now carried his gospel through the halls of the new studio. "I tried to do my job as if John was always there," Teale Wang said. "I remember always saying to myself, 'What would John say?' and that's how I treated everything I worked on."[8] Even Camp was heard more than once saying along the lines of, "If John was here, he could have solved this in about five seconds."

"It's so funny, as angry as we were at John, however mad he was at us, whatever bad blood was there, we all fought for John's vision still," Camp said. "Throughout the rest of the series, we said, 'Is this something John would like?' 'No, this isn't right, this isn't the way the show was designed, this isn't his vision, so we're not gonna do it.' We're gonna try and do shows that he'd be proud of, whether we wanted to strangle him or not."[9]

The loss of Kricfalusi had obviously created a familial disturbance. It was most apparent when Games began that second-guessing the direction in which *Ren & Stimpy* should head. "When you lose the creative leader, you're suddenly without the founder, and no one knows what to do," David Koenigsberg said. "People who would always fight with John, or be afraid of John, or hide from John, started to fight amongst themselves because the father figure was gone."[10]

Many misconstrued that Camp, in taking over as the show's

creative director, would assume the position of father figure as well. This assumption caused Camp to receive harsh discrimination, both as an artist and person, based on the decisions he made rather than on the work he did. Though Camp had been one of the series' chief architects, he did not have the power at Games that Kricfalusi had wielded at Spumco. "At Games, we were peers, friends equally working on a great cartoon," Wang said. "At Spumco, it was all John, and we tried to please."[11]

As creative director, Camp did not do "even less than what he did on the show while at Spumco," as Kricfalusi cynically predicted in 1993.[12] Camp's new job did, however, entail considerably less than Kricfalusi's exalted position had. Camp did not have control over the budget and schedule, nor jurisdiction over which artists and writers were brought onto the series. Games was not Camp's studio—he was Nickelodeon's employee, just like any other staffer. His presence was, however, what Nickelodeon vitally needed. It showed that they were willing to keep *Ren & Stimpy* in the hands of rowdy, highly imaginative cartoonists. It was a good counter-position to the negative press surrounding the series

The role Nickelodeon created for Camp served as a template for how "creator-driven" animated shows would largely work in the future. Networks would found their own studios, give the artists creative reign over their own shows, but avoid encumbering them with the non-artistic minutiae of day-to-day production.

"We learned a lot from our experience with John Kricfalusi," Vanessa Coffey said to the *Los Angeles Times*. "We learned that it is best to be supportive of a creator and not have him be a businessman. We learned to create a creative environment but a secure environment for our company. He's working under our roof, where we can handle the business for him. His job is to be creative."[13]

While this a system was sound in theory, however, it was erratic in practice on *Ren & Stimpy*. Camp would, as he said, have "something to do with all but maybe three or two of the cartoons," and the degree of that involvement would vary wildly throughout the remaining seasons.[14] The new structure could not accommodate the singular vision Kricfalusi had imposed, and the show's quality fluctuated accordingly.

Singular vision did not completely disappear from *Ren & Stimpy* once the transition occurred; it was unquestionably infrequent. Rather than being guided by a single overlord, the cartoons became more akin to the classic theatrical cartoons that the artists cherished. Any individual *Ren & Stimpy* cartoon's success depended on both a director's commitment to the film and his or her skill level. Bob Camp could not competitively guard the post of director as John K. had, nor did Camp want to. "Once at Games, I knew I couldn't direct all these cartoons, and anyone who wants to direct, I told 'direct.'"[15]

Appointment was slightly more complicated than that. It remained a challenge to single out individuals whose skills were well-rounded enough to make them suitable directors. As the third season began, Camp and Ron Hughart immediately resumed directorial duties, while series staples Jim Gomez and Bill Wray became—almost on a trial basis—co-directors on different cartoons with Camp.

Chris Reccardi was more or less an assistant director to Camp on "To Salve and Salve Not!", training and supervising the series' new layout artists.[16] Reccardi then storyboarded Camp's "Stimpy's Cartoon Show" with Mike Kim; both artists also laid out key sequences. It is almost too coincidental that the studio's best draftsmen did not direct immediately. Their strong contributions were actively sought on those earliest Games cartoons specifically to give the impression that the series was not lost without its original creator.

Consisting of "To Salve and Salve Not!" and "A Yard Too Far", the first official Games half-hour was "official" in name only. Both cartoons were in outline form at Spumco and originally planned as part of the truncated second season. John K. had planned to direct "Yard" after using its plotline—derived from the 1958 Yogi Bear short "Pie Pirates"—as an excuse to educate his staff about story structure.[17] Since neither "Yard" nor "Salve" had gotten any further than the outline stage at the time of the transition, however, it was decided to hold the stories for the third season.

As executed, the two premiere cartoons strongly reflected Camp's talent as a director. A snappy and conscious sense of self-restraint keeps the cartoons' more repulsive moments appropriately nonchalant. The focus of a central scene in "A Yard Too Far"—in which Ren removes Stimpy's insides, so his boneless body can wriggle unnoticed past a ferocious baboon—is not the gruesome sight of Stimpy's skinless carcass (we see that his innards consist mostly of meat products), but the sheer stupidity of the situation. Had Stimpy's insides been shown in full detail, or had his flesh suffered too much abuse in the jaws of the baboon, it would not be funny. With proper perverted precision, Camp made the idiosyncrasy of the gag its own punch line.

This first half-hour foreshadowed the thematic prominence of the remaining shows: silliness over seriousness. In early 1993, Nickelodeon declared to the Games team that there would be no more psychodramas—the show would strictly be gag cartoons.[18] It was the network's way of exterminating the kinds of cartoons they were the "most uncomfortable with," Bill Wray said, and ensure that Games delivered a "lighter, gut-funny type of show."[19]

Such a stinging riposte might have hurt "Stimpy's Cartoon Show", a story written by John K. and Elinor Blake at Spumco, had it been produced later in Games' history when special attention could not be lavished on it. In an intended satire of the modern cartoon industry, Stimpy animates an uncanny facsimile of a 1950s Sam Singer cartoon to present to his idol, Wilbur Cobb: the godfather of all animation, long predating Winsor McCay. At Stimpy's insistence, non-artist

Ren gets involved as the tyrannical producer of Stimpy's creation. The Chihuahua is enamored by the concept of doing no work and getting all the credit.

Although Kricfalusi wrote in 1994 that "the finished cartoon plays almost exactly like the Spumco script,"[20] he noted years later that most of his intentions were lost under Camp's direction. "It was directed by somebody who didn't have the same experience I did. It was my passion in the writing and the story, and somebody [else] trying to figure out how to do it."[21]

As executed, the cartoon lacks biting commentary; the pain of Stimpy's ordeal in making a cartoon stems from working in Ren's cruel studio environment, rather than from any sort of creative battle with Ren-as-executive. Gags of the "insider baseball" variety are kept to a minimum. When they do appear (Ren reviewing Stimpy's storyboard work in a Kricfalusian fashion; Ren's production schedule filled with vacation time, a la Camp's tendency to take time off without notice), they work out of context and fit Ren's self-serving personality.

Ren and Stimpy's visit to Wilbur Cobb remains one of the greatest moments of the entire series. Cobb, voiced by comedian Jack Carter, would appear repeatedly throughout the Games era, but never again would he be as useful—nor as poignant. "What made [Cobb's] acting in ["Stimpy's Cartoon Show"] work so beautifully," Camp said, was Chris Reccardi laying out the entire sequence himself.[22]

Reccardi's penchant for teetering on the line between representation and abstraction makes every single element of this very busy sequence work: the experience of hero worship being deflated once one finally meets one's idol; a mockery of onscreen interviews and documentaries featuring an aging Hollywood icon rambling incoherently; and the typical gross-out body-part gags. The drawings are animated with verve by Rough Draft, a rare occurrence made possible by Carbunkle animator Ron Zorman's careful handling of the exposure sheets.

One of Chris Reccardi's storyboard drawings for "Stimpy's Cartoon Show". Courtesy of Stephen DeStefano. © Viacom.

Following Cobb's speech, Stimpy's self-made cartoon (Explodey the Pup in "I Like Pink," animated by series writer Ron Hauge) might have been anticlimatic, were it not exactly the kind of cartoon we would expect Stimpy to make—completely incoherent and incompetent. It is the perfect closer to the turmoil of Stimpy's cartoon-making odyssey: a satisfying conclusion with Cobb genuinely impressed by the abomination, much to Stimpy's tearful joy. Arguably Camp's greatest entry as director, "Stimpy's Cartoon Show" boldly and articulately expresses the cat's essential contribution to the series. There are no pretensions when Stimpy is at his best. He is there simply to function as a pure and wonderful celebration of stupidity itself.

The earlier third season entries are more consistent than what followed, because the show's most seasoned artists spent the most time on them. Their passion made the cartoons all the more exceptional.

The further a committed artist got from a cartoon, on the other hand, the quicker it was finished and the rougher it became. The pair of cartoons directed by Jim Gomez succinctly illustrates this contrast: Gomez got close to one and distanced himself from the other. The latter, in this case, was his first, "Circus Midgets" (co-directed with Camp)—a cartoon Gomez "just didn't wanna fuckin' do."

Peter Avanzino's outline involved Ren and Stimpy hitchhiking and getting picked up by a Joe Pesci-sounding circus midget; it was rife with exhaustive references to Martin Scorsese's *Goodfellas* (1990). Gomez protested and asked that he have a few days to write another story that he would be more excited to direct. He quickly learned, however—as would others at Games—that stories were often placed into production without their notice—a hurried process that would often cause more problems than it solved.

"I absolutely did not want to do it," Gomez said of "Circus Midgets". "I hated all the referential shit. Ballantine said, 'Well, there's not going to be any more opportunities for you directing if you don't do this one first.' Their whole thinking was that this script had already been approved. I just wanted to throw it out, but there was a bunch of bullshit attached to the delivery requirements at the time that we weren't privy to, and that seemed to be the driving force for a lot of it."[23]

Unknown to Nickelodeon, "Circus Midgets" was to be the season's first instance of self-sabotage. The network's commitment to the mean-spirited story proved instantaneously lethal to staff morale. Now completely unenthused, Gomez shoehorned the cartoon through the pipeline with such a detached attitude that his refusal to take charge became common knowledge around the studio. Bringing the cartoon to the screen was transformed into such a dispassionate job that only technical direction was really required.

"Circus Midgets" was to be the first of many cartoons in which Ren and Stimpy are merely punching bags for a domineering third party.

The duo almost willingly submits to all kinds of cruel punishment for the circus midgets' amusement. Arguably, the two earlier cartoons with George Liquor introduced the concept of a domineering third party driving most of the cartoon. But in those episodes, "Man's Best Friend" especially, Ren and Stimpy actually act with George Liquor rather than merely react as they do in "Circus Midgets". The violence cannot be elevated to hilarity—either by funny drawings or by good timing—because there is no wit to the story's basic concept. Coffey admitted as much to Dan Persons: "It probably crossed some violent lines that we won't want to do again. We probably won't be using those [circus midget] characters in future episodes either."[24]

Gomez's other cartoon, "An Abe Divided", exhibits far more enthusiasm. In a pseudo-Laurel and Hardy situation penned by Gomez and Ron Hauge, Ren and Stimpy are hired as guards at the Lincoln Memorial, promptly destroying the statue's head in search of the hidden gold that American folklore says it contains. Some truly inspired gags—like Ren getting stuck in Lincoln's nostril and getting saved by the statue's "See the President Pick His Nose" feature—are given attractive sheen by Mike Kim's heavy layout supervision and the involvement of Don Shank and series newcomers Tom McGrath and Steve Loter. According to Ballantine, however, "An Abe Divided" was "a schedule disaster" due to this deliberation.[25] The cartoon lingered in layout for twelve weeks, forcing it to be rushed through animation at Rough Draft in six.[26]

Although the result was polished and amusing, Gomez almost gladly declined future directing chores and went back to writing. "I was looking at the bigger picture, getting things done so I could do more cartoons, whereas everybody else is doing one show at a time, doing the best job they could," Gomez said. "I ended up doing it in the amount of time they wanted me to do it, which was no time at all. I'll be honest, my shows suffer because of that."[27]

Layout drawing by Don Shank for "An Abe Divided".
Courtesy of Stephen DeStefano. © Viacom.

The struggles Gomez faced during his directing stint were experienced studio-wide. Finding artists able to maintain the show's high standards, while staying committed to a budget and schedule, was an everlasting dilemma at Games. Certainly the public stigma against the studio made it difficult to find willing artists. The biggest bottleneck at Games, however—as at Spumco—was in layout revisions. At John K.'s studio, many revisions were arguably unnecessary; Kricfalusi typically found fault with an artist's inability to hit an undefined target. At Games, by contrast, the need for revisions was real. Many new Games hires really did need their work reviewed before production could progress. Kricfalusi had a point in his selective hiring practices: very few people in Hollywood could actually draw the characters.

"It was actually [a] bigger struggle to rectify that," said Mike Kim, Games' first layout supervisor. "We had a crew of layout artists that were really green; they'd just be pouring in, and our schedules would be really tight because of that. The thing you learn is that it is a business and there's no infinite budget. So when you have a lot of these artists that are soaking in the budget, your schedule gets tight."[28]

Few new artists rose to the daunting precedent. Said Steve Loter: "Expectations were high and people were pushed to the limit. No time to improve. You were either capable or you were dismissed. Most of these artists came from jobs that utilized model sheets. *Ren & Stimpy* had no such impediment. Every drawing was unique and everyone was trying to outdo each other with new 'theories' and ways to compose the characters."[29]

Loter rose through the ranks at Games fairly quickly; after joining the staff in the summer of 1993, he became layout supervisor himself when Kim was promoted to director by October.[30] Tom McGrath "had such a hard time getting into the groove" of the show, Kim said, but quickly became "one of the few that actually survived and even flourished," becoming one of the artists most sought-after by the directors at Games.[31]

This preference for fine, yet rebellious draftsmen created an uninviting ambience for newcomers. Howard Baker was hired at Games immediately following the transition in October 1992 and promoted to director the following year.[32] Baker recalled being "treated like an outsider" by the majority of the crew—save Bob Camp—while directing "Road Apples"; Baker's sole cartoon, it flawlessly reflects the contentious environment from which it sprang.

"I wished there was more help from the crew, who didn't want to help me for some reason," Baker said. "Despite the wonderful, talented artists, Games was a strange place with a lot of odd ego trips going on. I was hoping to have a longer relationship with the show, but the angst after it left Spumco was too caustic for me."[33]

"Road Apples" itself represents everything that went wrong in the Games era of *Ren & Stimpy*. The storylines took on a regular formula:

downtrodden Ren and Stimpy stumble into some inescapable circumstance in which a third party takes center stage, subjecting the duo to wacky abuse that angers Ren and entertains Stimpy. In this case, Ren and Stimpy pretend to be roadkill and are taken into Mr. and Mrs. Pipe's trailer, where they must endure painful heat remedies, disgusting foods, and exercise.

What could be described as "Mad Libs" writing was dominant in many Games cartoons. Far too often, gags involved replacing an object or noun with something slightly silly—usually involving meats or bodily functions. This quickly eradicated strong comic acting, timing, and writing, the absence uncomfortably obvious in entries such as "Road Apples" and Camp's "Bass Masters".

Both cartoons also highlight Camp's tendency as a writer to arbitrarily force an unwelcome Wilbur Cobb into storylines, shining the spotlight on comedian Jack Carter's long-winded and unintelligible rants. This device could be funny when Cobb's appearance was brief ("Ren's Retirement"), or when his role was clearly planned ("Prehistoric Stimpy", "The Last Temptation"). More often, however, Cobb's appearance took cartoons on inexplicable tangents. "[Cobb] worked well for one cartoon when you first saw him," Bill Wray said. "But Bob felt sorry for [Jack Carter], so he would cast him in as many cartoons as possible. So in a way, there were two or three cartoons where he was just shoehorned in, just so Jack could get some work."[34]

This tendency to move unpolished cartoons through the pipeline was a staple of television animation production. *Ren & Stimpy* had been established to vehemently defy this assembly-line mindset; when the Games cartoons fell victim to it, the resultant repugnance was most pronounced. This bottom-line mentality would ultimately cost the show a great deal of its distinction.

§

Nickelodeon still encouraged a creative environment for *Ren & Stimpy*, but the harsh realities of television production hampered the artistic process. Games employees were warned to take deadlines and delivery requirements seriously. Yet perversely, the series almost never made a scheduled airdate.

Alarming gaps between new episodes continued. By the end of April 1994, only eight of the third season's fourteen episodes had aired. This did not seem to anger the Nickelodeon executives as much as similar delays had when John Kricfalusi ran the show. On the contrary, they were resigned to the fact that they would likely air only one new episode per month, and altered programming timetables to prepare for it. Whole half-hours often sat on the shelf before being broadcast to accommodate the lateness of future episodes.

In the most glaring instance, though Games had delivered all of the third season by the end of July 1994—three months later than anticipated—the network nevertheless chose to withhold the season's final four episodes.[35] They opted to use them to launch the fourth season in October. "The thing with the audience of *Ren & Stimpy* is that they are fans of the show and there is a certain expectation of repeat patterns," Herb Scannell said.[36]

The network's attitude towards reruns and delays remained static as the series progressed. It was a startling change from Nickelodeon's attitude at the time of Kricfalusi's firing. Then they had scoffed at the idea that they might be responsible for the show's delays. A spokesman asked, "If we have a hit, do you think we would slow things down and wait eight weeks for a new episode?"[37]

Nickelodeon had clearly become shrewder for its experience with Spumco. They now knew that *Ren & Stimpy* required more time to produce than any of its competition—regardless of who was in charge. John K.'s open defiance towards the network was the offending element of which they wanted to rid the series; missed airdates and hemorrhaging budgets mattered little in comparison.

Had the Games artists been aware of the network's plans, tension and needless pressure might have been lifted. Though many artists perceived themselves as obeying a stringent protocol, they were in practice being allotted almost as much leniency with time and money as they had been at Spumco. It was the handful of talent producing the "quicker" cartoons, rather than the entirety of Games' manpower, that actually met the budget and schedule.

"The guys that sort of compromised and did stuff quicker than the other guys were kind of carrying the studio," Gomez said. "They were meeting the requirements, allow[ing] the other guys to produce the shows at their pace. I'm not blaming anybody, but that's the reality. It might have suffered a bit, which was bad, but it was what it was."[38]

Chief among the "quicker" personnel was Ron Hughart, known as "the reliable director" by the network executives. Hughart was the established studio workhorse, "quietly churning out funny cartoons, never complaining or causing problems," Camp said.[39] Hughart was affable, never guarding his work with artistic jealousy. When cartoons originally assigned to Hughart were given to others that wanted a chance to direct—an action that could easily bruise an ego—Hughart was unfazed.

Hughart also endeared himself to management with a willingness to take on responsibilities others skirted. One example was a stellar psychedelic sequence in the otherwise lamentable "Jerry the Bellybutton Elf". Said Hughart: "The song ["Climb Inside My World"] was added to the episode at some point after the initial storyboard was given to me. A couple of the guys didn't want to board the sequence or at least didn't know what to do with it. I boarded it and timed it."[40]

Hughart, while healthily neutral when it came to studio politics and artistic ego, lacked the comic sensibility and directorial individuality that *Ren & Stimpy* cartoons demanded. He was not one to embellish story or comedy. The barren spot-gag nature of "Eat My Cookies" and

"Pixie King"—cartoons that might have been massaged into stronger narratives—made his lack of flair obvious. The success of Hughart's cartoons is entirely dependent on what was originally handed to him by the cartoon's writers. "I'm not involved in [the writing] aspect of it," Hughart told Dan Persons in 1994. "I was asked at one point to get involved, but I chose not to. The guys who do that are great at what they do and they've got their own little system going to do that, so I leave them to do that part of it."[41]

This detachment of directors from story work became commonplace at Games, coinciding with an increasing lack of in-house layout. When the show was picked up for its fourth and final season of twenty half-hours, character layout became a privilege rather than a given. More people were given a chance to direct, but under the stipulation that zero layout could be done in-house.

"We hated doing that, we really didn't want to do it," David Koenigsberg said. "We were spoiled, we loved doing the layouts here. But it was to save time and money, and I understood it perfectly. Suddenly the board becomes so important, you show camera moves that you would never do normally if you were doing layouts here."[42]

Indeed, the storyboard's importance grew to become almost detrimental, even when layout was done at Games. As board artists, Tom McGrath and Stephen DeStefano were better draftsmen than most of those in the layout department, first under Steve Loter and then Tom Owens. Loter commented that McGrath's boards "provided a great template for being able to elevate the material," whereas DeStefano's "were quite brilliant, quite expressive, and damn impossible to layout pose to pose on."[43] DeStefano was never satisfied with much of his Games work: "I'm not always fond of the drawings of mine that ended up onscreen"—or rather, Loter's interpretations of them.[44]

Timer Ken Bruce was expected to have enough savvy to prepare a cartoon for animation without a team of layout artists. Several times,

Bruce was given a cartoon to time after it came *back* from animation.[45] Like Hughart's cartoons, Bruce's pictures are generally 'business as usual' with the characters. A lack of vigor is painfully obvious in cartoons like "Hair of the Cat" and "City Hicks".

Almost all the work of director and layout artist Mark Marren was revised in some capacity. Due to the results' overall lack of sheen, Marren preferred not to put his name in the credits, opting to use the pseudonym "Kirk Field" instead. Only Marren's "School Mates" has the saving grace of a strong Jim Gomez story (originally prepared for Ron Hughart's direction).[46]

The outsourcing of work actually benefited the series when Arthur Filloy began overseeing many of the fourth season's cartoons at Mr. Big Cartoons in Sydney, Australia. Filloy had been the timing director of the third season's "Blazing Entrails", but subsequently left the studio due to its $6-per-foot animation rate. Unbeknownst to Filloy, Mr. Big had taken on more work from Games, and stated that Filloy was *still* working on the show. Said Filloy:

"I got a phone call from a rather irate Jim Ballantine, asking me what the fuck was I doing. Ballantine told me that I was supposed to be directing *Ren & Stimpy* over at Mr. Big. I was just as confused as he was, and I informed him that I had only timed one cartoon and gave it up. He asked if [Mr. Big had approached me since then], I said nope and boy did he get sore. Ballantine said he'd be in Sydney within three days. A day or so later, I get a phone call from Jim and he was furious, he wanted to talk over at my house and there he told me how he kicked [the Australian studio's] ass. He got me off their contract and hired me directly by Games. We struck a deal that I would get paid a good salary from Games, but I was to direct all the cartoons at Mr. Big."[47]

Filloy only *de-facto* directed one cartoon in the series. Entitled "Travelogue", it seems an almost intentionally awful, unfunny exposé of odious spot-gag cartoon clichés, with irony that is weak at best. The other cartoon credited to Filloy, the pleasantly morbid "Terminal Stimpy", was originally directed by Ron Hughart, only to be taken over by Filloy much further down the production line.[48]

Seven cartoons in all were laid out and animated under Filloy's supervision at Mr. Big Cartoons. The animation style is a peculiar hybrid; its direction can be conscientious—as when Filloy blends his own drawing style with those of Bob Camp and Bill Wray—but the animation's execution is inconsistent. The movement and lip-sync can be quite fluid, a trait only possible when the animators actually speak the same language as the characters they are animating. Often, however, the frugality and haste of the production is obvious: characters simply pop from pose to pose with no subtle in-betweens, causing the drawing and actions to look weak.

"I would make sure to pull out keys from the board in order to begin layouts and backgrounds," Filloy explained. "This was more difficult to accomplish, as the layout crew [in Sydney] was training up and had not figured it out yet, so I had a lot of extra homework. Few people realize that many times, I took home an entire cartoon worth of layouts to repair over the weekend. I would literally key out every pose with numbers and then slug or time the show on the sheets. This then made for an easier task when directing the cartoons. Sometimes the animators would complain that there wasn't much left for them to do, but hey, we had shows to crank out."[49]

Stateside, Camp said that layout supervisor and assistant director Steve Loter had "made his moves to get to the top."[50] His rapid ascension to the director's chair riled many colleagues; indeed, Loter admitted to an eventual falling-out with Camp that he regretted. "Being young—and full of piss and vinegar—certainly didn't help the situation, and I'm just as guilty as any," said Loter. "I certainly wasn't the best artist in the layout pool, but I was probably the most passionate. I'm guessing it made people take notice and promote me."[51]

While Loter began directing towards the end of 1994, when more and more work was being sent overseas, he had enough influence—as the layout department's former supervisor—to keep layout on all of his pictures in-house, elevating their art standards substantially. The experience Loter had gained by assisting Camp helped give Loter's cartoons a unified sense of strong drawing: a "broad, cartoony style which helped the animation look better," the layout artist Mark Colangelo noted.[52]

Though Loter's cartoons have a visual sheen that Hughart's and Bruce's pictures often lack, the wildly variant quality of their stories is an obvious negative. Loter did noticeably try to give his pictures solid structure—as exemplified by his strongest entries, "Insomniac Ren" and "Ol' Blue Nose"—but even the ridiculous use of comedian Phil Hartman in "Space Dogged" and "Stimpy's Pet" cannot disguise the tired writing that had become predominant in the show's fourth season.

"'Stimpy's Pet' was a disaster," said Loter. "When I got the board, it wasn't approved or plussed by anyone, and it came with a rigid, uncompromising deadline. I did the best I could with what I had, but it was a mess. Hinging the entire episode on Ren vocalizing a German phrase that he would never speak [except as] a plot contrivance was complete shit."[53] At this point, the cartoons became far more writer-driven than ever before. Directors became largely arbitrary—even if Loter or another director wanted to change a story element, they were not allowed to.

The label of "writer-driven" carries a nasty stigma in some animation circles. It is indicative of a show creatively run by people that do not know how to draw. By their very nature, said people cannot be truly aware of the animation medium's potential, and produce shows with an overemphasis on dialogue and stilted drawing and movement.

In reality, the artists-versus-writers argument is a smokescreen for what was in 1994—and remains today—a purely political struggle. The real world of television animation cannot accommodate the brand of direction that most *Ren & Stimpy* directors enjoyed. There is not enough time or money available. Nevertheless, the existence of the artists-versus-writers argument has deluded many into thinking that the non-drawing writer's role should be completely eliminated. Regardless of what some animation talent may believe, however, the television medium itself is a writer's business. Writers are perceived to be the talent in a project that can make creative decisions the fastest and—supposedly—the cheapest. A director in television is almost never the true author of a show; directors are largely interchangeable and mercenary. The exceptions—those projects in which directors play a more creative role—tend to be the most expensive projects, one of which was most certainly *Ren & Stimpy*.

The television script becomes the project's bible; every other creative decision must adhere to the system dictated by the script, an extremely inorganic process that goes against the ethos of Hollywood's greatest cartoons. Yet the process took root from the start: as early as 1960, a Hanna-Barbera cartoon's success was dependent on whether writers Mike Maltese or Warren Foster were feeling brilliant the day the picture was written.

"Writer-driven" at *Ren & Stimpy* had different implications than it did in the rest of the industry. The show employed the fiercest of Hollywood's anti-writer artists, and the established Spumco practice of going straight from outline to storyboard survived at Games. "Generally, it shook out where everyone would have their 'x' amount [of premises] they were required to deliver every week," Gomez said. "So then we'd bring them back with approval and notes and put them on the roundtable and work on them collectively."[54]

Writing proved perhaps more difficult than layout, "with Bob Camp and Jim Gomez trying hard to be original and funny under so much pressure," Ballantine said.[55] In 1993, Ballantine brought *In Living Color* writer Ron Hauge to the Games story crew; sketch comedy writer Vince Calandra arrived the following year. Their primarily live-action backgrounds raised several eyebrows. Camp had to assure other staffers that Hauge and Calandra were not the typical disgruntled hacks that populated the animation writing business. "Ron Hauge is actually a cartoonist, he's done a lot of illustrating," Camp told Dan Persons. "Vince thinks very visually, not like a lot of writers who are interested in writing prose and [are preoccupied with] the craft of putting down the words, he's interested in doing funny drawings."[56]

Gomez added that the two provided balance to the writers' room: Calandra being "very pragmatic, matter-of-fact" in his approach and Hauge "Mr. Weird Guy, with a mind like a steel trap."[57] The four writers represented a reasonably powerful team, but not one without its vices and virtues. The writing team at Games—as at Spumco—was a clique that few could enter, as the writers were protective of their status and often rejected outsiders' involvement. The gag and pitch sessions—which typically brought a cartoon's storyboard artist and director together with Camp and Vanessa Coffey—could help mold a very different cartoon from the original outline.

The kind of organic evolution prevalent in the storyboard stage at Spumco was still present at Games, but to a far lesser degree. At Spumco, a cartoon's storyboard was its bible; at Games, a cartoon's outline carried nearly as much weight. Possibly even more, as illustrated by the decision to have several cartoons ("Galoot Wranglers", "City Hicks", "Dog Tags", "School Mates" and "Bellhops") storyboarded at the Character Builders studio in Ohio. The despondency of the resulting cartoons makes the Games artists' chagrin over the situation perfectly clear.

A gold standard maintained among the writers was a refusal to completely veto any story or gag idea outright. "Saying no in a writing room is the absolute worst thing you can do," Gomez said. "'No' is just a word that immediately shuts everything down and stops all train of thought. Even if it's momentarily, it does have an impact where it just kills the creative energy." In practice, however, the entire run of *Ren & Stimpy* is arguably littered with ideas on which it might have been prudent to say "no" immediately. Gomez felt that any "stupid idea, stupid premise or whatever" had its use. "If for no other reason, it would make you work harder to come up with something better than that. It might just spark some other idea that you would never have if it wasn't for the bad idea."[58]

This openness had a heavy price: many story problems went unresolved, and the Games cartoons became formulaic. Gag-ridden tangents overshadow the Ren and Stimpy dynamic. The duo's once-rich characterization is replaced with an overbearing sense of servitude to any new character's demands. The jokes become capricious, varying only in whether they over-rely on gross-out gags or on painful violence.

Most Games cartoons of the fourth season did not attempt to hide their lack of story; even the season's more ambitious efforts often lacked the precision of the series' best cartoons. "It's a Dog's Life", essentially writers Camp and Gomez's remake of "Man's Best Friend", fails in its attempts at black comedy. The dark humor inherent in Ren and Stimpy's abuse at the hands of their new owner, the pious and senile Granny, is never fully realized—only the pain is. Granny is never given a clear motivation for torturing her pets as was George Liquor.

"Eggyölkeo", directed by Bob Camp, is notorious for its descent into utter chaos. "That was going to be my *Ren & Stimpy* masterpiece," said Stephen DeStefano, the cartoon's storyboard artist. "And once it was finished, I realized it really didn't work, as a cartoon or a storyboard." DeStefano and Gomez campaigned to have it expanded into a full-fledged, half-hour travesty of *Pinocchio*. They were unsuccessful; forced to remain at its original short length, the convoluted storyline became all the more muddled.[59] Camp tried to gloss over the meandering concept with meticulous layout, only to have the entire picture ruined by Wang Animation in Taiwan. Just as Wang failed to define the *Ren & Stimpy* animation style on Bakshi's *Mighty Mouse*, Wang could not begin to imitate the work already well-established by the superior Carbunkle and Rough Draft.

Concept sketches by Stephen DeStefano for "Eggyölkeo".
Courtesy of Stephen DeStefano. © Viacom.

As "Eggyölkeo" confirms, Camp had easily become the most creatively exhausted of the show's talent. He maintained his status as its most volatile artist; creative fights over content between studio and network still persisted, with the screaming far from over. Though Camp's power at Games was nowhere near Kricfalusi's at Spumco, some employees still drew parallels between Camp's and Kricfalusi's personalities, to the point that both were perceived as angry and self-destructive.

While Camp certainly had the highest status at Games, the final say in the writing room, and the respect of the in-house artists, his self-admitted temper made him "his own bastard" just like anyone else, Gomez quipped.[60] There were times when Camp seriously tested Nickelodeon's patience—usually through "temper tantrums and late delivery of materials."[61] Camp was also famously ready to get rowdy. When Herb Scannell's secretary sent a note asking the crew to stop putting marijuana plants in the backgrounds of the cartoons, Camp literally responded, "Herb, is she retarded?"[62]

Steve Loter described the network as still "[being] wildly inconsistent, by censoring something they approved two episodes ago, and flagging something that wasn't controversial at all. We wondered how deranged *they* were, considering what they read between the proverbial lines. The broadcast standards and practices fax was always a cause for temper tantrums, heavy bargaining, and strategic deceptive planning."[63]

Games' *Ren & Stimpy* workflow never escalated to the level of Kricfalusian disaster, wherein the entire production was held up for months. Games and Nickelodeon had their differences, staffers admit, but nothing that could not be resolved. "There were a lot of creative fights, but we would have those fights because I was up to those," Vanessa Coffey said. "I didn't mind a good fight, and I didn't mind them pushing the limit. But ultimately, [Camp] knew I had to cut things, because that was my job too. I couldn't deliver a show we couldn't air ever again. And without being held hostage."[64]

The merit of Camp's direction slips considerably in later episodes, likely as a result of the strain of his deep artistic and emotional involvement in the series. His aim to find "the fastest way to make funny cartoons" was compromised by the necessity to "shit 'em through."[65]

"It was extremely difficult on Bob since he had to blaze through scenes of his directed episodes," said Loter, Camp's once assistant director. "He'd usually have a day to spend on each cartoon, but he drew *fast* and loose and always made the drawings funnier. I could only imagine how good his cartoons would have been if they gave him the time to actually *work* on them."[66]

Camp never phoned in his direction; he was far too dedicated to the project—and too serious an artist—for his involvement to be detached, even if the results were unsuccessful. "He was always enthusiastic, he'd never quit or get mad, go take five, he was really, really into it," Billy West said. "He was going through a rough time, but who wasn't. Everybody was going through some tempest in their own lives. But that, I swear to God, created the right amount of tension—the way people acted with each other. When all those things are floating around, you channel into them."[67]

Some of Camp's cartoons hint at high ambition with their intrinsic angst. Most notable is "Ren Needs Help!", a *One Flew Over the Cuckoo's Nest* (1975) parody in which Ren is committed to the Shady Brain Farm and ultimately suffers the Jack Nicholson character's fate. Its attempts at resurrecting the verboten "psychodrama" genre are admirable. More often, though, the effort tends to highlight the talent now missing from the series—input from John K., layout by Jim Smith, and animation by Bob Jaques—rather than the talent present. Conversely, Camp's "Superstitious Stimpy" highlights the studio's

SICK LITTLE MONKEYS

Ren "model sheet" made up of Chris Reccardi's storyboard drawings for "Ren Needs Help!" that circulated Games. Courtesy of Stephen DeStefano. © Viacom.

regular procedure of combining a flat story with mostly overseas direction, resulting in a rather unfunny, ugly cartoon.

Camp's brightest, most successful moments in the fourth season are cartoons that he wrote and did not direct. These stories were so airtight that they could survive the Games pressure cooker without his strict follow-through. "I Love Chicken", directed by Ron Hughart, brings the characters back to a simpler structure. The story of Stimpy marrying Ren's chicken dinner allows for more character-centric humor (Ren's greed and self-pity, Stimpy's devotion and stupidity) than did the strict gag-oriented format that otherwise dominated the Games seasons.

Camp was the series' best gagman and when he and the other writers pushed an idea to the limits of sheer insanity, as with "Feud for Sale" (also directed by Hughart), the effort paid off handsomely. Ren and Stimpy make no appearance in the cartoon, allowing the bombastic Salesman to take center stage as he exploits a feud between hillbillies Abner and Ewalt. Under the story's ludicrous surface, a crisis builds methodically and logically. It starts with Abner buying pointy sticks and finishes with the sale of a nuclear bomb. Ending things with a sort of convoluted parable, the Salesman views himself as a Good Samaritan for having brought about peace through his swindling and enabling.

What might have been Camp's and Gomez's shining hour at Games came in the form of the baffling "Reverend Jack". Cathartic slams against John K. are scattered throughout the run of Games cartoons, but it was only in this highly metaphoric picture that they commanded the audience's attention. Kricfalusi said the episode's sole goal was "to make fun of me for making them rich and famous."[68]

Craig Bartlett—given a fourth-season job by Nickelodeon to tide him over until his own show, *Hey Arnold*, began production—viewed himself as more of a "mechanic" on the series than a director. Upon his arrival, Bartlett was assigned to slug and time "Reverend Jack", and it was his duty not to tamper with the writers' intentions. "That episode was probably given to me because Bob and Jim were so close to it, Vanessa and Jim Ballantine thought it would never get done. I think they wanted me to be a kind of Switzerland-like influence over the whole project."[69]

The notorious cartoon superficially appears to be just another in a long line of nonsensical romps, with Ren and Stimpy spreading the Gospel of Meat and putting on "meat puppet shows" under the guidance of another overbearing human character: the mentally unstable Reverend Jack Cheese, voiced by Frank Gorshin. The catch is that this time, the Reverend is a thinly veiled caricature of John K., and each of the gags was "either a real event or inspired by one."[70]

Camp's and Gomez's amused contempt for their old friend rings clear through the drawings of storyboard artist Stephen DeStefano. The Reverend begins to look more and more like John K. as the cartoon progresses, and direct references to the show's politics are made. Ren complains to Stimpy that "we haven't put on a single show in months" because neither can get the Reverend to cooperate: a pointed allusion to the Spumco days, when Kricfalusi's refusal to sign off on anything in a timely manner meant that no work could get through the studios. Late in the cartoon, as Rev. Jack rides off into the sunset on a meat carcass, he screams at Ren and Stimpy, "I'll be back! You'll beg me!" The deposed despot returns and heckles the duo as they try to continue without him, a position that many at Games felt themselves in as they continued without Kricfalusi.

If viewers were stymied by the episode's allegorical content, they were not alone—many of the cartoon's creators felt the same way. Post-production sound supervisor Brian Mendelsohn recalled that Gorshin would ask, "What does that mean?" after every line. "We were all in hysterics, and Camp would reply, 'It's just in-jokes; don't worry, keep going, you're doing great!'"[71]

Indeed, "Reverend Jack" works regardless of its prominent "insider baseball" element, because it is also a successful parody of institutional religion and a clever warning against establishing and buying into cult figures. The Reverend represents all charlatans who bamboozle the masses into thinking that their way is the only way. The cartoon's events symbolize the dangers and absurdity of blind worship. Ren and Stimpy get off relatively easy in the end—considering the writers' history of ending cartoons with the characters' deaths, and given that the theme this time pays homage to Jim Jones.

"It is pretty jam-packed full of obscure references to events and quotes, and just some weird scenes from the gold mine," Bartlett said. "But it's got what all the best *Ren and Stimpy*s have. You're watching, thinking, 'This is not like anything else out there on the air. This is some crazy-ass shit.' I loved it, and I knew that I should just try to get the thing delivered and not mess with it at all."[72]

The cartoon was completed in spring 1995, but was held over for the programming-created "fifth" season and aired in December. Its holdover was puzzling, given that Nickelodeon was always in dire need of new *Ren & Stimpy* episodes. A rumor ran through the studio that Kricfalusi was threatening to sue over "Reverend Jack"; far more likely, Nickelodeon simply had no idea what to do with it once they saw it. Not just because of its in-jokes, either. The overt mockery of religion, particularly Christianity, was likely disconcerting. For similar reasons, another Games cartoon—"The Last Temptation"—was initially withheld from broadcast and only aired when the show was in reruns.

While "Reverend Jack" exemplifies the value of a strong writing staff, the overemphasis on one part of the process could only carry the series so far. As a result, an alarmingly high percentage of the Games cartoons play as dully generic. The knee-jerk hatred that Games experienced in the media—based on loyalty to Spumco—did not help their cartoons' reputation, and indeed swept many outstanding films under the rug. But given the preponderance of weak *Ren & Stimpy* cartoons in the Games era, the best cartoons the team made would likely have struggled to attract critical attention regardless.

The Sordid Tale of Reverend Jack Cheese

What exactly *is* the story behind the inspiration for the episode "Reverend Jack"? Following is Jim Gomez's recollection of the drunken frivolity that took place at John K.'s home during the wrap party for the Rolling Stones *Harlem Shuffle* music video. Gomez's recollection is as fine an example as any of his gift for colorful storytelling, and is presented unfiltered with only minor additions for clarification.

§

It's funny, Bob Camp had borrowed the original copy of it ["Reverend Jack"], you know, the original master tape, so we could make dupes of it. But the funny thing is, Nickelodeon never seemed to want it back. But I don't know if they edited it or not. [TK: They did.]

It was inspired by John. There are some similarities there. We were still sort of operating under the specter of John after he left the show, and a lot of that's played out in the cartoon. The character Jack Cheese was actually a character that, again, like a lot of stuff, was created years earlier. We didn't have jack cheese in Canada, so the first time John and I saw jack cheese at the store, we thought it was pretty darn funny. You know, some kind of joke cheese. Anyway, the character was based on that and also on a friend from college, Eric Robertson. The character in the cartoon was a little different.

But I'll tell you what jump-started that specific story. [It] was an incident that occurred at [*The Harlem Shuffle* wrap party], so of course there was the usual drinking stuff going. This time, there was a whole buffet table of food—which was unusual; usually it was cigarette butts, light beer, and butter. A bunch of the gang was there, including Bob Jaques—who, by the way, isn't a regular drinker; but every once in a while, when he does drink, he goes off the rails. I've only seen him a couple of times that way. This was one of those nights.

As the party was progressing, with the regular party games like "Pin the Tail On the Retard" (my ass still hurts from that), bobbing for beer cubes and junk, Bob Jaques was quietly downing shots of some nasty shit like Uzo or blackberry brandy or something. John was pretty blasted too by this point, and he was sitting in the middle of the room holding court, going on about something of some serious importance... when Bob, almost cartoon-like, kind of slipped up into the frame of view. And with a sly grin, he carefully placed a big piece of capicola on John's head.

John didn't flinch and I started cracking up.

This only prompted Bob to pile on more meat. So Bob carried on, carefully placing different cold cuts on John's head and every time he did, I busted a gut while John, with no reaction, just sat there and smoked his cigarettes and drank his beer without flinching. Now it's escalating, John takes a swig and a puff, Bob drapes another piece of salami on his head, I crack up, and Bob in turn cracks up and throws himself on the floor. All this was going on without anyone saying anything. It keeps going on like this, like some kind of retarded Jacques Tati film, only less French. Finally, John has this whole wig of fresh cold cuts on his head, Bob is laughing so hard he's on the floor foaming at the mouth, and I've pissed my pants more than usual when John finally says, "What are ya? I'm sure you waste good meat."

It probably doesn't sound so funny, but it kinda was at the time. Oh, but I almost forgot, the story has a tragic ending. When John finally spoke up, Bob got up and ran down the hall and ran into John's room, fell down, and vomited all over John's brand new Walter Lantz book. So that was the inspiration for the Reverend Jack Cheese.

You know, we pitched a Reverend Jack Cheese action figure with luncheon meat crown accessories to the Nickelodeon marketing department at the time... they just stared at us.

Jim Gomez, January 2010.

Chapter 9
Ren's Bitter Half

The auteur theory in film study is usually confined to live-action for a reason. Given the collaborative nature of most animation, it is difficult for one person to function as the guiding force behind a cartoon made in a studio assembly-line. When the system becomes further muddled—with more and more work done thousands of miles away—it seems hopeless and senseless to look for a filmmaker's vision in an animated cartoon made for television.

The Ren & Stimpy Show is a glaring exception. John K. maintained for the longest time that "cartoons belong in movie theaters;"[1] the idea of an animated filmmaker "having freedom and having time to develop" is only feasible with the time and money of a theatrical production.[2] Kricfalusi's artistic success while running the show remains unsurpassed; his intensively didactic direction, supported by a devoted team of uniquely talented draftsmen and an unschooled network ready to allow it, changed the standards of the animation industry with only a few half-hour episodes. It was only Kricfalusi's lack of perceptiveness, and his insistence on having the final say at literally every step of the process, that hastened the demise of his control over the series.

Yet the desire for control, to maintain directorial vision, did not die when Kricfalusi was fired. As a director and head writer, Bob Camp admirably attempted to preserve the series' overall authorial sense by choosing "to have fun with buns instead of guns" and creating the most outrageously funny cartoons possible.[3] But Camp was spread too thin by the production schedule's taxing demands. The amount of shows Games had to "pump out" forced the well of story ideas to "kinda dry up," as Mike Kim said.[4] Generally uninspired directors followed Camp's labored ideas through, and the show lost much of its innovative zeal. The enduring emotional turmoil caused by the Spumco firing also did the series no favors. The Nickelodeon run of *Ren & Stimpy* highlights two very different negative outcomes that can occur when an ambitious director tries to maintain a singular vision: permanent termination or absolute exhaustion.

The story of *Ren & Stimpy* is inarguably the most frustrating cautionary tale in Hollywood animation; and yet positivity arose from it. Though often blamed for the series' downfall, Camp—by shouldering the bulk of work on the series—allowed others to flourish. Combined with management's desire to produce "creator-driven cartoons," this made Games a place where the universal desire was to be "funnier and organic," just as it had been at Spumco.[5]

It became common knowledge inside Games that "most of the shows weren't going to be good, and that the priority was to get them done," Chris Reccardi said. Directors had two choices: "either shit them out, or, if you were a director with capable skills, lay out most of the show on your own time. Like any television production, the workload was too great for all of the episodes to be good, so those who had the most skill chose to concentrate on a few good ones, rather than be spread thin trying to save the series."[6]

Reccardi's judgment proved sound. The series as a whole declined as its production began to mirror other television shows with real deadlines. Shortcomings that had always existed were now more visible, and became targets of critical attention. But as the negative aspects of the show gained notoriety, a few determined artists toiled away on better films that went unnoticed by most audiences. These superior efforts are the reward of perusing the entirety of the Games era of *Ren & Stimpy*. These cartoons are the most triumphant in upholding the Spumco standard; they maintain a caliber, and a singularity of style, that far outshines their contemporaries.

§

Bill Wray became increasingly immersed in the series at Games. After the show left Spumco, Wray was afforded screen credit for his background painting work on every cartoon—at his insistence. A jarring anomaly in the animation industry, this upfront color credit for Wray and the other background painters lasted for the remainder of the series. Admittedly, the credit was not without merit, as the background painting style was one aspect of the show that inarguably blossomed in Kricfalusi's absence. Background painter Scott Wills said that while it was all about "John really pushing us with not liking paintings" at Spumco, Camp and the other directors were far less involved with the background department at Games.[7] The painters were expected to know what they were doing without much guidance.

Through Wray's initial leadership and the work of his protégé

Wills, the color styling took on a more suave and diverse look. This gave an alluring sheen to even the weakest of the studio's output; Games became one of the few animation studios that routinely took risks in color styling. With an increasing number of final backgrounds being painted overseas, Wills and the other painters seemingly embraced the potential hazards. Their work—and that of animation houses like Rough Draft—was secure enough to largely survive the pipeline system. It was not "the end of the world if some small color decision [didn't] work out exactly right," Wills said,[8] because the whole appeal of *Ren & Stimpy* was its artistic purity—and all that the designation of artistic purity entailed, including possible mistakes.

The use of color in the Spumco cartoons had been intelligent, yet it was limited compared to the work later done at Games. In the Spumco cartoons, one can almost feel John K. breathing down the painters' necks to prevent them from even considering the use of primary colors. Colors like pink and purple were forbidden at Kricfalusi's studio—but not at Games. It was all for the better. The department took on Wray's far more open philosophy: "If you know how to paint, you can make anything work."[9]

Wray only loosely supervised the paint department, however, before Wills replaced him. "They're finding me more valuable at storyboards and writing," Wray said in 1993. Wray was subsequently also promised a director's position.[10] By March 1993, Wray was boarding what would be his first directorial job with Bob Camp—and the first Games cartoon to reflect Wray's intriguing artistic temperament.[11]

"No Pants Today" was another story left over from Spumco, written by Richard Pursel and alternatively titled "Stimpy That Dirty Little Naked Boy". Stimpy's nudity becoming a dilemma—entirely due to his self-awareness—is an excellent idea, but the cartoon handles it awkwardly. An unpleasant emphasis on pain, rather than Stimpy's humiliation or stupidity, makes "No Pants Today" incapable of fully embracing its ironic theme. Nickelodeon took note of the cartoon's violence and delayed its premiere so they could censor a scene involving a butter knife and Stimpy being dragged by a car.[12]

According to Pursel, the stream of savage acts inflicted upon Stimpy throughout "No Pants Today" is attributable to Wray's own sense of humor. "I just remember a lot of Bill's suggestions in writing meetings were, 'And then we can break his neck! And then they can get killed!' But he laughed after he said it."[13]

Whether sitting in on a writing session for another director's cartoon or writing his own scenarios, Wray established himself as the "left-field guy" at Games, as Jim Gomez recalled. "[Wray]'s kind of weird, and I would rein him in and Bob would make it funnier. [Wray] would come up with these crazy ideas, and maybe we would not end up with that idea, but I'll tell you what, sometimes it started because of that crazy idea. He's good sometimes with verbal comedy, standard shtick, and slapstick, or whatever, but [weirdness is] what Bill's style is more so."[14]

Wray told Charles Novinskie in 1993 that he would "really love to do a feature-length animated horror film."[15] This desire is openly apparent in "Ren's Retirement". Though Camp was the cartoon's director, Wray's touch is wholly evident with his involvement as a writer, board artist, and layout artist. The network heavily scrutinized Ren's journey to mortality and his transformation into a gummy geriatric. A sequence with Ren getting into a bar fight was cut at the storyboard stage, considerably weakening the transition from burly young Chihuahua to senile old coot.

Nickelodeon executives regularly raised a "storm cloud" over the use of Lynne Naylor-style curvaceous females as incidentals in the series, crying "exploitation of women." In "Ren's Retirement", the Games artists solved the objectification dilemma in a scene establishing the allure of Ren's dazzling coffin. "The guys started drawing [funeral-goers] as window dressing; instead of the women, they put Chippendale dancers wherever they could, the Full Monty, except for like a little thong," Billy West said. "And they were satisfied. 'Oh, that's OK.' But then they realized after it was made, [when] it was on TV: '*AHHHHHHHHH!!!!* What have we done?!'"[16]

"Ren's Retirement" features several brilliant moments. Ren's funeral serves as a sardonic commentary on how little meaning his life really had. Only Stimpy, dressed in widow's attire, is there of his own free will; the other attendees are hired mourners (the Chippendale dancers) or guests bodily forced to attend (Wilbur Cobb, who uses the eulogy as an excuse to laugh about outliving all of his friends). Alas, "Ren's Retirement" also has its downside. Too often the drawing is profoundly weak and the direction misguided. An emotionally intense scene of Ren's age catching up with him is handled schizophrenically, cutting at whim between seriousness (Ren's rheumatism kicking in) and silliness (Stimpy puking birthday cake), compromising the scene's effectiveness.

The cartoon's ending ranks among the series' most repellent moments: the now legally dead and buried Ren and Stimpy have their insides eaten by a Fred Flintstone-like worm. The ironic nature of this payoff—that the two, while decrepit, are still alive (Stimpy flattered by the worm's niceness, of course)—does not even remotely register. The graphic imagery descends to the irredeemable repulsiveness that Vanessa Coffey had claimed to want keep at bay in the series, causing John Kricfalusi and his supporters to hurl accusations of "double standards" at the network. Nickelodeon was criticized for allowing Games to slip far more risqué material into the show than Spumco had. In retrospect, Coffey feels that any perceived lapses in judgment were intentional. "If people feel that way, it was because it was at least controlled by us. If you look at the first episodes that John did, [the show] did a lot of risqué stuff. I don't think that [Games] crossed any lines that [Spumco] hadn't already crossed."[17]

Wray did note that the increasing grossness of the Games cartoons reflected a retreat on Nickelodeon's part, however unintentional it may have been. "We did have some talks with Nickelodeon when things first started, very politely telling us that, 'Look, you just can't be as disgusting as you were before.' I don't think we consciously meant to do it, but somehow we were twice as disgusting. There's no explaining it. I think maybe some of it had to do with the pressure that came from being the bad guys that went over and did the cartoons without [John K.]"[18]

Wray was very much aware of the political struggle to maintain the artistic standards of the show. He was among the higher-ranking Games staffers who sought and recruited talent. These decision-makers felt the sting of running a studio where "jobs that pay $1,500 a week go unfilled because we can't find the talent to fill them."[19] Layout artist Sherm Cohen remembered that Wray was "not impressed" with his work samples, but was "gracious with his time" when reviewing Cohen's work for needed improvements. "This scenario happened two more times, [until] Bill finally thought the work was good enough to show the staff at *Ren & Stimpy*."[20]

When Wray became a solo director in May 1994, he did not have the privilege of commanding a team of artists. Only one of Wray's fourth-season cartoons, "My Shiny Friend", was laid out at Games; this took place under the direction of Steve Loter, in his last project as layout supervisor. Wray's other cartoons would be laid out at Mr. Big in Australia; Wray would consequently be given "one pass at looking at them, like two-and-a-half hours to look at a box of layouts," before shipping them back. "That's when I knew I was not long for [Games]." Wray's overprotective belief at the time—that a director should do everything himself—likely kept him from working with the best in the

Gag drawing of Bill Wray with friends, by Don Shank.
Courtesy of Stephen DeStefano. © Viacom

Games talent pool, as did the fact that Wray's "drawing skills were not of the highest level. A lot of artists prefer to work for a director who they feel draws better than them."[21]

The lack of in-house layout does not account for the story problems that plague much of Wray's directorial output. An obsessively macabre sensation overwhelms these cartoons. In "Aloha Höek", Ren refuses to accompany Stimpy to the Big Kahuna's luau, instead inexplicably vowing to stay behind and rot in his makeshift fish carcass house. In "My Shiny Friend", Stimpy becomes addicted to television and suffers drug withdrawal, while in "Sammy and Me", the cat's idolatry of singer Sammy Mantis is centered around living in the star's exoskeletons and dreaming of getting his head bitten off by the "Mantid Man".

Wray's cartoons are disturbing—and more crucially, they are not *humorously* disturbing. Their penchant for puzzling and conflicting elements (the unabashed vulgarity of "Aloha Höek", the heavy-handedness of the celebrity caricatures in "Sammy and Me") causes their quality to vary wildly. Only "My Shiny Friend" effectively circumvents the most disturbing elements of Stimpy's deathly habit. Rather than achieving this through writing, Wray successfully utilizes stylized background paintings to represent the feline's mental and physical deterioration. "I don't think [Wray] has the patience to sit down and write," Gomez observed. "It's a real nuts and bolts thing, you've gotta bear down. With his art, he's very much like that, but with writing, he just doesn't want to spend time with it. For him, he'd rather get into the art."[22]

"You can watch my cartoons and you see promising notes in them," Wray said. "But truly none of them were great. Guys like me who were getting their first shot, we'd only done it for a year, we were still too green."[23] However green he was, there is still a defining element in Wray's handful of cartoons: a compelling sense of confidence. Uncertainty in writing, timing, and drawing underlies many Games episodes, but even if particular aspects of Wray's cartoons do not work in harmony, there is still a sense that he made his creative decisions with conviction, and was unconcerned with what others thought. "Bill was a ball buster, and I don't find any fault with that," West said. "He wasn't there to be entertained by you. At the end of every take, he'd go, 'Gayer.' It had nothing to do with disapproval of certain people; that's what he wanted because it was colorful. You can't just sit there bottled up, 'Oh some group will be after me.' If that defines what you do, you're dead in the water. That's what made Bill unique."[24]

However unintentionally, Wray was perhaps the most offensive of the Games directors. His "Sammy and Me" was the first cartoon since "Man's Best Friend" to be completely withheld from broadcast,

One of Bill Wray's final paintings for "My Shiny Friend". Courtesy of Stephen DeStefano. © Viacom.

this time due to the story element of Stimpy gouging out his eye and replacing it with a glass substitute. "It somehow in the storyboard wasn't noticed and after production was done, 'You're gonna have to change the whole cartoon.' And at that point, honestly, I expected Vanessa to cave, but she said, 'Nope. Not changing it.'"[25]

Wray's finale for the series, "Sammy and Me" was eventually broadcast in reruns; it was unlikely that the network's original rejection would have any negative consequences. By the time "Sammy and Me" was delivered, *The Ren & Stimpy Show* had wrapped its production. The disgruntled cartoonists had been rabble-rousers to the very end.

§

Most fascinating in the post-Spumco era of *Ren & Stimpy* was the formation of what Bob Camp called a "sort of Games within Games" amongst the studio's elite artists: Chris Reccardi, Mike Kim, and Lynne Naylor.[26] These three had already contributed significantly to the majority of the series' finest cartoons. The design and animation sensibilities of Naylor, in particular, made her one of the series' masterminds—second to no one, save John Kricfalusi.

The "Games within Games" cartoons were what Don Shank called "these sort of auteur situations," in which "one artist would storyboard, direct, and sometimes lay out the whole cartoon."[27] John K. had obviously tried to achieve this by inserting himself into every step of other staffers' work. By contrast, the best directors at Games handled the "auteur" scenario as lone eagles; acting, essentially, as "one-man crews, with some occasional help from the few good artists there were," Reccardi said.[28]

Said Kim: "It was a very unique situation, because things were so dysfunctional in a lot of ways, and a lot of formalities went [by the] wayside, to our benefit. You had so much control. I can only speak for myself and Chris, because our offices were right next to each other, so we'd always bitch to each other."[29]

The "auteur" scenario inherent to these particular Games cartoons made them even more akin to vintage theatrical shorts than the Spumco cartoons had been. In those classic cartoons, a film's single character layout artist was often the director himself. Reccardi and Kim adopted a similar system at Games out of artistic vision and production necessity. They avoided the predicament of constant revisions by keeping their shows largely to themselves—and by threatening to quit, should Jim Ballantine not arrange for them to do the cartoons their way, and keep Bob Camp out of the loop.

"[Reccardi and Kim are] master layout artists, two of the best of all time; they made it a real priority to do layout," Camp said. "I would when I could, but a lot of the times I had to do shortcuts to make deadlines. Mike and Chris did as much layout as they could get away with."[30] Said Kim: "That's the only way that we could figure it would work, so we could actually have something that looked like *Ren & Stimpy*."[31]

The politics here were certainly a stark contrast to the world of Spumco, where everything had been ruled by Kricfalusi's iron fist. But the absence of John K. did not prevent bad blood. The fighting and jealousies over power, control, and salaries between the fourth and fifth floors of Games' Beverly Hills building took its toll on most of the staff. Camp complained that he "hardly ever got to make cartoons like John or Chris Reccardi or Mike Kim. It has always bugged me that my cartoons are held up against [cartoons] that were made with full layouts, and with a director being able to completely focus on just one cartoon. Meanwhile, I had to rush through my cartoons—often with no layout crew—while running a studio and trying like hell to make deadlines and budgets."[32]

One applicant to Games was warned by Lynne Naylor, "You don't want to get involved here. Too much politics." Commented Ron Hughart: "Some of the personalities working on [the show] at the time had become angry and destructive, and I was happy to move on."[33] Suffice it to say that *Ren & Stimpy* ultimately did enter the real world of animation. Friends' egos raged against one another as they moved up in the ranks—rather than cowering beneath a dysfunctional overlord as they once had, even if that overlord's ghost still haunted the production.

Months deep into the third season, Games offered Mike Kim the chance to direct. He had already sold a promising story to Nickelodeon, entitled "Ren's Bitter Half". He hoped to direct it—only to find that the studio wanted him to helm another writer's story, one with which Kim had had no previous involvement. Kim declined because he did not "have a take on [the other writer's] story," and wanted to vigorously direct his own ideas. "They were kind of sore about that; I think statements like, 'You're looking a gift horse in the mouth,' were told to me. A few weeks later, they walk in and say, 'Hey, we got good news for you,' and then they let me do my show."[34]

Kim laid out most of "Ren's Bitter Half" himself on a freelance basis, with assistance from Shank and Tom McGrath. The cartoon's draftsmanship is only the icing on an already-excellent cake. The cartoon's concept of genetic engineer Stimpy accidentally turning Ren into a literal split personality—consisting of his evil and indifferent sides—returns the characters to the basic codependent dynamic that made "Stimpy's Invention" and "Svën Höek" the masterpieces they are.

There is no arbitrary third party introduced to take attention away from the core relationship of Ren and Stimpy. Ren himself is cynically expanded, enlarging upon the idea that the Chihuahua has no heart; disinterest keeps his evil nature at bay. Stimpy does not react generically to Ren's actions, as he does in many Games cartoons, but charismatically. After seeing Evil Ren chew up and spit out a girl scout's cookies, Stimpy confides to Indifferent Ren that he must be the "real Ren"—despite Stimpy having suffered similar abuse from the real Ren daily.

The cat's idiocy and devotion to his friend reach their zenith when he still wishes to help put Ren back together, even after the evil side destroys all of Stimpy's worldly possessions (with the apathetic side doing nothing to prevent it). Evil Ren brings about the cartoon's ridiculous conclusion when he attempts to clone himself and brings out his feminine side—which he marries. Stimpy's tearful, joyous reaction to this unholy union—as he and Indifferent Ren are dragged off by the newlyweds' car!—reminds us of the cornerstone of the Ren and Stimpy dynamic. Stimpy's obliviousness to pain is due as much to his satisfaction at seeing Ren happy as it is to his inherent stupidity.

"I wanted to try to get back into doing shows more like the original episodes that were just centered around Ren and Stimpy," Kim said.

"I was feeling my way around, I never really directed before. But I had a good idea of what I wanted and basically drew it all myself. [Dan Persons] interviewed me about 'Bitter Half'; this was back when there was all that controversy, and he wanted the dirt on *Ren & Stimpy*. And I was not part of any of that, what am I gonna tell ya? I'm just trying to do my shows. But, this reporter was like, 'Was that your version of 'Stimpy's Invention', just to show that Games could do a 'Stimpy's Invention'?' No! It was just a story, man."[35]

It was a fair question for Persons to ask; the cartoon *is* dramatically better than what third season viewers were expecting. Rough Draft's animation succeeds as it had in the Spumco episodes, though Carbunkle levels of effectiveness are notable by their absence—further proving that the Carbunkle animators were a critical component of the series' splendor. Kim did call in a personal favor to Bob Jaques during the production, asking if his studio would animate one more cartoon; unfortunately, Carbunkle had to decline due to scheduling conflicts. "In retrospect, I really wish I had time," Jaques said, "because I would have loved to have worked on that and some of the other Games cartoons."[36] Ergo, the strength of the draftsmanship and acting in Kim's or anyone else's cartoons could be taken only as far as the layouts allowed—a burden Kim shouldered well.

As the show entered its fourth season, Kim was assigned to direct a random story. His "Magical Golden Singing Cheeses" is clearly the product of a disinterested director, regardless of its superb drawing. The fairytale parody is a tribute to various stupid jokes that John K. and Jim Gomez had told in the early 1980s, resulting in another barrage of rather graphic gross-out gags. Scenes involving a village idiot using a cheese grater on his arm—leaving raw marrow—and Stimpy accidentally using a crowbar to pry off an ogre's toenail are made even more painful by the solid draftsmanship.

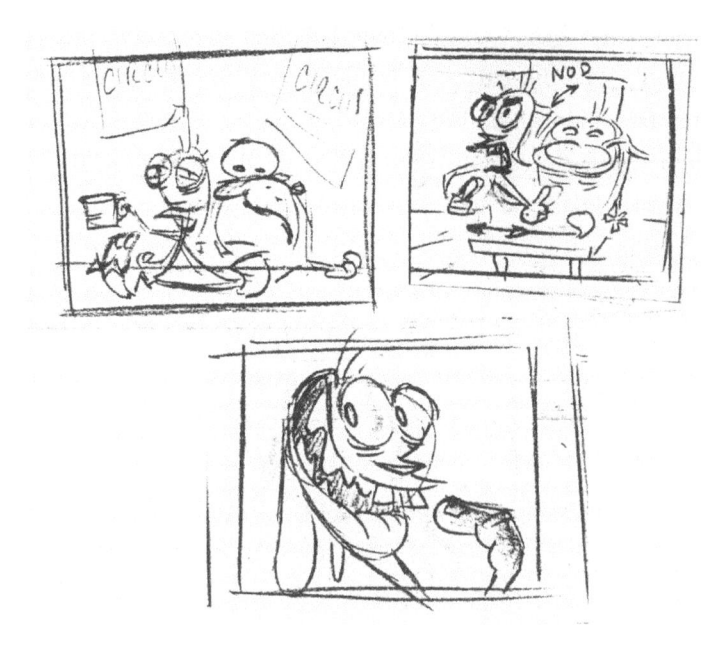

Storyboard drawings by Tom McGrath for "Double Header". Courtesy of Stephen DeStefano. © Viacom.

Kim's next assignment, "Double Header", was more his forte, given its attention to the Ren and Stimpy relationship and its general subversiveness—though Kim denies having had a penchant for the latter. "It was really not about pushing the envelope of taste, ever. That's not my style, it does not come natural to me in that way. I was just trying to make something interesting, I didn't really care about being so rebellious. I just wanted to do something that I could watch and say, 'Hey, I like it!'"[37]

In the cartoon, Ren and Stimpy are mutilated in a bus accident and saved by a discount surgeon—who stitches them together as one being, making them societal outcasts. Tom McGrath was Kim's main collaborator on the cartoon; their storyboard recalled their jovial days as roommates at CalArts, as they attempted to craft a tribute to filmmaker David Lynch and make excuses to "get *Elephant Man* lines" into the show.[38] Kim's cool-tempered demeanor, and general excitement over the cartoons he liked best, made his virtuosity in drawing far less intimidating for the few artists who worked with him.

"You could always tell when he didn't like your drawing," layout artist Mark Colangelo said. "He would stare at it for a second, then say, 'Hmmmm... no.' Then he would put another piece of animation paper over your drawing and redo it, and what he drew would always look better."[39] This calmer, confident attitude allowed a cartoon as wholly satisfying as *Double Header* to exist. A continuation of the attention to strong characterization Kim established in "Ren's Bitter Half", "Double Header" focuses on the pain of being Ren in the Ren and Stimpy dynamic. Everything Stimpy does is calculated to send Ren farther down the road of utter insanity. From Stimpy's farts to his creation of a nuclear holocaust that costs Ren his job—shown in a frighteningly uproarious sequence, with Ren's boss literally deteriorating as he delivers the pink slip—we understand. If Ren was not psychotic to begin with, we would at least know *why* he went so far off the deep end.

Whereas "Ren's Bitter Half" explores the dangers of the characters being too distanced from one another, "Double Header" illustrates how their relationship becomes unsustainable if the two get too close. Taken together, "Ren's Bitter Half" and "Double Header" are almost commentaries on how Ren and Stimpy dynamic could be mishandled at Games. Used well, they were compelling characters; used poorly, they might as well be shipped off to the freak show of cartoon hell.

Tom McGrath put his own demented spin on the characters when he was given a show to direct solely because—in Reccardi's words—"he was a motherfucker talent."[40] McGrath's first director's credit on "Stupid Sidekick Union" is misleading; actual direction was handled by Ron Hughart, but McGrath was awarded the credit onscreen due to the importance of his boarding.[41]

The one cartoon McGrath oversaw completely was "I Was a Teenage Stimpy" near the end of the series, "before he could do dozens of brilliant ones after it," lamented Bill Wray.[42] Like Reccardi and Kim, McGrath also functioned as the sole layout artist on his cartoon, entirely to its benefit. Stimpy is taken through the painful journey of cat puberty—a golden opportunity for abstract distortions that McGrath seizes. Ren finds himself in the unfamiliar role of parent as the cat becomes a rude and disobedient delinquent.

Bob Camp and Jim Gomez, the cartoon's credited writers, gave full credit for the cartoon's success to McGrath—as did Stephen DeStefano, the credited storyboard artist. "I can't recall how I got involved; maybe I just offered my help, but Tom didn't really need it. I drew some stuff for him, but I don't think much of it was used. Tom even had some hilarious ideas that didn't make it into the film. I remember seeing 'Nativity' drawings he'd done, of baby Stimpy lying in a manger, wrapped in swaddling clothes."[43]

Stimpy's open defiance of Ren might have backfired if handled clumsily—as it was in "Stupid Sidekick Union", in which Stimpy uncharacteristically tries to put one over on Ren by making him recognize Stimpy's worker's rights. The insubordination in "I Was a Teenage Stimpy" works better because it is born out of Stimpy's metamorphosis into adulthood—a period in which no one is quite sure what the hell is going on. The irony, however, is that even though Stimpy's body matures, he remains an idiot—so even when he grows into Superman, he is still illiterate and flies straight into the sun. As for Ren, parental instinct calmly and believably keeps his rage at bay until the film's climax, when Stimpy uses Ren's issues of *Husk* to form his cocoon.

Mike Kim attempted a similar transformation of the characters' personalities in his final cartoon for the series, "Who's Stupid Now?" Alas, the film was bowdlerized at the storyboard stage to remove material that was "overtly critical of what was going on in the studio at the time," as Kim recalled. "We knew that the show was ending, so hey, let's make fun of it. And they ended up basically changing all that stuff. Taking everything out of it that happened. So what was I left with? I was really left with a show of nothing."[44]

The finished cartoon involves Ren and Stimpy trading the roles of "skinny jerk" and "fat idiot" in a desperate attempt to keep the show going. Stimpy undergoes liposuction and Ren drinks the resulting fat. Impressive moments follow, as Kim was among the few at Games capable of making Ren's plights truly sympathetic. Yet the cohesion of "Ren's Bitter Half" and "Double Header" is lacking. Stimpy's transformation into a mean-spirited ass is unconvincing and poorly contrived, and Ren's redemption too forced. Clearly, Kim was—as he admitted—"burned out" at this point in the series. It is a credit to his skill that "Who's Stupid Now?" survived as well as it did under the taxing circumstances.

"You really realize, when you do stuff all yourself, that you really *can't* do everything yourself. I don't really have the time to figure out [weak points of the story]. You don't have that wisdom, you just need to get it done. And that's the sad thing about having to work on a show that you put a lot into, [when you no longer] have the time... to really totally kill yourself. You kill yourself anyway to produce a show, especially when you have a lot invested. At the time, I was ready for *Ren & Stimpy* to end. I think a lot of us were ready for *Ren & Stimpy* to end."[45]

§

The most experimental of the *Ren & Stimpy* directors was undeniably Chris Reccardi, in spite of his less-than-ideal directorial experience prior to the third season. Reccardi had been more laborer than author on "Dog Show" and "The Royal Canadian Kilted Yaksmen", but the experience made him a stronger artist. His directorial efforts at Games showcase the skill of an independent, free thinking filmmaker, one less concerned with living up to accepted standards than with making a name for himself. "He explored flatter, more avant-garde styles and pushed his art to great extremes," commented Steve Loter. "Bob was looking for funny, appealing drawings; Chris was looking to change the world."[46]

In May 1993, Reccardi began storyboarding his first cartoon as director: an epic entitled "The Scotsman" for much of its production, and renamed "Hard Times for Haggis" upon broadcast.[47] Ren and Stimpy are barely present in the cartoon, which instead serves as a character study of Reccardi's own creation—the sheepherder Haggis MacHaggis, a Scottish facsimile of George Liquor voiced by Alan Young.

In a metaphor for the animation industry before *Ren & Stimpy*, the story opens with Haggis rich and critically acclaimed for his work as television's most popular hack. Shortly after his artlessness is established, Haggis is kicked off the airwaves and out of his manor by the fresh, original, and captivating characters that *did* save the television cartoon business: Ren and Stimpy.

Using Haggis, Reccardi reveals a gift for delving into the drama intrinsic to the diseased mind. The sheepherder's violent and suicidal tendencies result in several stirring sequences reminiscent of the better staged and acted set pieces in the Spumco cartoons. Haggis's fall to the gutter and his contemplation of self-destruction on a bridge rail are remarkably unsettling in their execution—the kind of material that many at Games actively avoided or lacked the confidence to pull off.

"I've always been attracted to psychodramas, like [William Shatner] in "The Enemy Within" [an episode of the original *Star Trek* series] and Jimmy Stewart flipping out in *It's a Wonderful Life*," Reccardi said. "But those scenes [in "Hard Times for Haggis"] were the logical result of character arcs. I hate that word, but it's required jargon in the entertainment world."[48]

Rather than take his own life, Haggis exacts his revenge on Ren and Stimpy by hiring thugs to take over *The Ren & Stimpy Show* with sock puppets. In a forebodingly apocalyptic ending, the public loves this new form of crap. Animation history comes full circle: dreck is popular again, and the once-revolutionary Ren and Stimpy join the long-forgotten Haggis as vagrants.

If Reccardi's cartoons have a frailty, it most often lies in their attempts at comedy. A one-minute sequence of Ren and Stimpy adjusting to life in Haggis's former home inexplicably turns up halfway through the picture. Culminating in Stimpy getting slapped for dumping salt on Ren's dinner, the scene is unneeded and remarkably unfunny. "I hated that scene," David Koenigsberg said. "I kept on bitching about it, saying, 'Can't we take this out?' And Chris Reccardi was adamant. 'No, it's funny, it's funny!' So I said, all right, I'm gonna show them how this is a downer and how this doesn't work. I'm gonna stick the commercial break right after the salt gag, so they'll see how it doesn't work, and then they'll drop it. Nope! They kept it in!"[49]

Evident in "Hard Times for Haggis" and unmistakable in Reccardi's next cartoon, "Hermit Ren", is the desire to advance to another kind of animated filmmaking. Reccardi's new goal was to capture dramatic moods through flatter, stylized drawings, rather than pursuing humor through traditional, rounded compositions. "Hermit Ren" is highly experimental in this sense, though the results are imperfect. Reccardi admits the cartoon is "a great idea for a story that I wish I had another crack at."[50]

An odd sense of pacing makes "Hermit Ren" feel overlong. It cuts arbitrarily from Ren's solitude as a hermit to Stimpy trying to get by alone in their cow-carcass home. Much of the drawing is also astonishingly poor, despite Reccardi himself having laid out most of

"Model sheet" of Haggis MacHaggis drawn by Chris Reccardi. Courtesy of Stephen DeStefano. © Viacom.

the cartoon with Lynne Naylor and Mike Kim.[51] Ren's odyssey is represented through nearly-still poses, repeatedly ineffectual in their intensity. The fluctuating line quality makes it apparent that none of the layout artists knew exactly how to make the drawings work—in a stylized sense or otherwise.

Too much does work in "Hermit Ren", however, to make it anything less than fascinating. The film is startling in its portrayal of mental deterioration. It delves even further than John K. had into the implicit revulsion of one of the show's common themes. Ren learns—through self-torture—that to maintain his well-being, he needs to unleash his misanthropic personality upon others. With no Stimpy, he has only himself for company; without that balance, he is even more unhinged.

In the cartoon's best moments, Reccardi demonstrates the significance of a cartoon's soundtrack, both vocally and musically.

Billy West had already mastered the voice of Ren by this point in the series; but under Reccardi's direction, his voice work takes on a specificity unheard in the other Games cartoons. It is a voice with its own dimension, born of what West called a director "ardent about what he wanted," rather than an imitation of something already done. "I think that he looked at a lot of his own expressions, because I would see his face now and then in the characters, where the teeth kind of go down and the jaw's out."[52]

Reccardi's understanding of a soundtrack's importance was easily more profound than any of the other directors' concepts. Reccardi often scored specific cues in his home studio. "I'm sure he would've scored the entire episode if his many other duties as director left him enough time," Brian Mendelsohn said. "Usually a director didn't deal with music till the show came back from animation and we got into post-production, but Chris had specific ideas for the interaction of the music to the timing of the scenes and the action."[53]

Exercising a degree of abstinence from the studio's celebrated library of vintage music cues, Reccardi turned to his own talents when he wanted a moment "completely abstract" and "based totally on feeling," allowing Ren and Stimpy to exist in an even more artistically organic environment than their usual realm. "When Ren freaks out in 'Hermit Ren' at the end, that was a bowed upright bass with wah-wah and echo, and a hollow body fretless bass with a slide, picked way down at the bridge, also with echo, to create these 'skittish' sounds. I wasn't able to find shit like that in any library. It was more about creating the right atmosphere than [about] needing to be a composer."[54]

A kind of evolution materialized in television animation through Reccardi's cartoons: a resurgence of the flatter, modern look popularized in 1950s American animation by the studio UPA. Like UPA's artistic method, Reccardi's came about through his earlier development as a bold independent talent. But while some UPA staffers disdained inspiration from outside sources, Reccardi had a definite muse. Lynne Naylor returned to the series in late September 1993.[55] She worked primarily with her future husband Reccardi and developed new original characters for Games. Her sole directorial endeavor was a four-minute interstitial entitled "You Are What You Eat", starring Billy the Beef Tallow Boy: one of the few *Ren & Stimpy* cartoons that was subversive in a healthy way. Through simplistic drawing that combines whimsy with cynicism, Naylor shows how deep-fried food, morbid obesity, and heart failure can bring a father and daughter closer together.

Naylor was a soft-spoken, yet powerful figure in 1990s animation. Though her style of "modern" television animation design was ultimately overused due to its perceived frugality and hipness, Naylor quietly demonstrated its proper use, never abusing or compromising her artistic power in the process. Her sense of ingenuity, born of sound animation training, was bolstered by a desire to "do things that would be considered wrong by the animation industry," as she told Mark Colangelo.[56]

As Reccardi rightly said, "If you have someone that talented in your life, the influence is unavoidable."[57] When Naylor began closely collaborating with Reccardi, his cartoons became more assured in their overt stylization. He entered the fourth season with fervor and recruited a team of artists that would be specifically trained and directed by him, with Don Shank as his star player.

While Reccardi's sense of stylized design and movement achieved an intelligent unity, labored comedy had overtaken his cartoons. His first two entries in the fourth season—potential pilots for spinoff series starring Haggis MacHaggis and Powdered Toast Man—actively worked against his strengths. Reccardi needed his characters to act, something that the general silliness of these films disallows. While "A Hard Day's Luck" works mildly well in continuing the saga of Haggis against the world, the profound inanity of "Powdered Toast Man

Versus Waffle Woman" is overwhelming. Quite stupendously, its story makes even less sense than that of the original Spumco "Powdered Toast Man" cartoon.

By August 1994, Reccardi's unit had largely disbanded, due to the studio's pressure cooker nature.[58] Shank—who had "tended to come and go at Games," due in part to continually butting heads with management—left the show permanently.[59] Naylor quit Games while "Waffle Woman" was still in layout. "She went around to each of us to personally tell us her reasons for leaving," Colangelo recalled. "The tight deadlines made the job too much of a hassle, despite the pay. The way she put it was, even if a studio offered a million dollars to work on a project, but the [project] was due that day, the money just wouldn't be worth all the hassle."[60]

Reccardi did not direct for several months. He storyboarded "Ren Needs Help!" and "Feud for Sale" before being assigned the long-awaited "Ren's Brain" in late 1994.[61] Written at Spumco by John K. and Richard Pursel in the second season, "Ren's Brain" was intended as another cartoon of the "Space Madness" and "Stimpy's Invention" caliber, with Stimpy as a brain surgeon having the ultimate battle with Ren's very cerebral matter. The second season cutbacks forestalled the cartoon indefinitely; it made no progress past the outline stage at that time.

Later, Bob Camp planned to direct "Ren's Brain" himself as a statement against detractors who claimed that Games was "wimping out."[62] As late as September 1993, the schedule called for Jim Gomez to storyboard the cartoon and Mike Kim to supervise its layout, but third-season chaos delayed it yet again.[63] Reccardi said that Camp finally rescinded control and offered it to him "to direct as a final, high quality piece to wrap up [the series] with."[64]

As executed, "Ren's Brain" is a pure Chris Reccardi cartoon in a way that his others are not. He actively avoided using any of the remaining layout artists he had hired; instead, he pitched into the work himself, renouncing regular working and sleeping hours during the production of his final cartoon. "At first he had time to go over our layouts," Coangelo said, "and explain to us what mistakes we made, and how to improve our drawings; but as the season wore on, he didn't have time to do that anymore. I saw a note on his office door one time that read: 'DO NOT DISTURB. BIG HAIRY-ASS DEADLINE.'"[65]

As a director, Reccardi had been away from the Ren and Stimpy characters for nearly a whole season; now they all benefited from his improved directorial skill. Reccardi himself also profited by having a story that allowed him to tackle heavy acting, with solid humor already in place. The uncertain drawing of "Hermit Ren" is absent; the abstraction of "Ren's Brain" relates intimately to the acting onscreen. As the cartoon dives deeper into insanity, with Ren's escaped brain returning home from work and mistaking his own lobotomized body for a "homewrecker," Reccardi's original music—and his drawing—become even more chaotic. Reccardi's approach to psychodrama, using limited but stylized movement, works as well as the fuller Spumco-Carbunkle collaborations, succinctly leading up to the destruction of Earth and the "Republican party as we know it," the film's only possible conclusion.

As Reccardi and the rest of the crew well knew, "Ren's Brain" would be one of the last episodes of *Ren & Stimpy*. Everyone involved was aware that Nickelodeon would never expand beyond its original commitment to fifty-two episodes and five years of production. Shows rarely made their shipping or delivery dates; the drama inherent to *Ren & Stimpy*, both inside and outside the studio, was not worth the $500,000 per episode they were spending by the end of the show's lifetime.

In late January 1995, Mary Harrington came to Games from New York to tell the studio that the show was "ceased indefinitely" rather

Cel from "Ren's Brain", Chris Reccardi's final cartoon for the series. © Viacom.

than cancelled. "Which meant that Nickelodeon wouldn't ask for any new episodes, but would continue to air reruns," Colangelo said. "We were all out of a job, but the show wasn't cancelled!"[66]

The production wrapped in August 1995 with the directors putting last-minute touches on their respective swan songs. Bob Camp's "A Scooter for Yaksmas", intended as the series finale, is intensely tired in its gags, poses, and story. It is more representative of what the show had become than "Ren's Brain" or "I Was a Teenage Stimpy". Clearly, the bloom had faded on the series. It was time for the artists to move on to greener pastures, and for Nickelodeon to put the turmoil that was *The Ren & Stimpy Show* behind them. "The [network] never really understood what the show was about or why it was so popular," Camp reminisced. "I think they were happy when it was over."[67]

At the series' wrap party, held at Rudolph Valentino's mansion in the Hollywood hills, a most poignant display was made. "There were a pair of plush Ren and Stimpy dolls 'drowned' in the pool—tied to rocks and under twelve feet of water," Sherm Cohen said.[68]

Were the Hollywood empire any less depraved, its greatest animated actors would have a finite lifespan like their flesh-and-blood counterparts. But the animation industry is insatiable, and its most compelling stars truly immortal and eternally sought-after. The desire to make new *Ren & Stimpy* cartoons would be realized in time; history had already established it as simply inevitable.

Chapter 10
Onward and Downward

Since its debut, *The Ren & Stimpy Show* has had an impact on the entire animation industry that cannot be understated. John Kricfalusi was, in Billy West's words, "a wake-up call to the industry."[1] Of the shows that premiered on Nickelodeon in August 1991, only *Ren & Stimpy* had an influence that is reflected in nearly every subsequent animated program. Whenever the latest hit series arrives—Stephen Hillenburg's *SpongeBob SquarePants* being the most obvious example—the origins of its humor, timing, cutting, tone, and drawing style are traceable to Spumco's show, not to *Doug* or *Rugrats*.

Hollywood could not treat *Ren & Stimpy*'s pronounced accomplishments as a flash in the pan. The series raised the bar for television animation industry standards and introduced the concept of an individual creator being given artistic license. "Better" was the way the wind was blowing. The triumph of *Ren & Stimpy* in the 1990s has, therefore, benefited every artist currently working in the industry, regardless of whether they worked with *Ren & Stimpy* artists—or whether they even liked Kricfalusi.

As in any medium, ineptitude was never fully eradicated in animation. Many former Spumco and Games artists populated the crews of Disney's *Shnookums & Meat Funny Cartoon Show*, DIC's *Adventures of Sonic the Hedgehog*, and Film Roman's *Twisted Tales of Felix the Cat*. In these shows, the Kricfalusi influence morphed quickly into near plagiarism—often at the insistence of corporate brass who wanted the "new *Ren & Stimpy*."

Other shows aimed at children had creators capable of retaining their own individuality and attracting an audience. Sometimes the influence of *Ren & Stimpy*'s irreverence and transparent innuendo was more pronounced, as in Joe Murray's *Rocko's Modern Life* and David Feiss's *Cow & Chicken*. The flatter, modern-design look that became prominently fashionable through the work of Genndy Tartakovsky (*Dexter's Laboratory*) and Craig McCracken (*The Powerpuff Girls*) was as different in tone and execution from *Ren & Stimpy* as one could possibly imagine, but the style could not have existed had John K.'s show not made it acceptable to break the status quo.

This second wave of artists never had the freedom and luxury that was often taken for granted at Spumco and Games. They had to produce the best cartoons possible in the real television industry, where the bottom line always rules. Networks were terrified to give creators the kind of control that John K. had at Spumco, preferring to keep their staffers leashed on the networks' own premises. As a result, the second-wave artists' earnest attempts at meaningful entertainment could never surpass *Ren & Stimpy*; the likes of *I Am Weasel* would have to remain in Kricfalusi's shadow.

"What's interesting is that a lot of the stuff John had set up was stuff that we've all been trying to imitate and bring with us to other shows that we've worked on," said Doug Lawrence, who went on to direct on *Rocko's Modern Life*. "And not all of it has succeeded, because layout has sort of disappeared in cartoons, you don't do layouts anymore. It's harder for the directors to get their stuff to make sense."[2]

The influx of adult-oriented animated shows had it easier, because the primetime market called for bigger budgets and the writing came first; the animation itself was always secondary. While it is arguable that *The Simpsons* was more influential within this genre—it predated *Ren & Stimpy* and was actively intended for adults—Matt Groening's characters were confined to FOX, and to the restrictions inherent in major network television. The thinly veiled semen and penis metaphors of *Ren & Stimpy* would never have survived normal broadcast standards. Nickelodeon's bold allowance of such material paved the way for more explicit animation on cable. The concept of adult-targeted animation in a market beyond the cultish underground had previously been unthinkable. *Ren & Stimpy* made raunchy cartooning completely acceptable in the mainstream, regardless of whether its proponents supported Kricfalusi (*Beavis and Butt-head*'s Mike Judge) or emphatically refrained (*South Park*'s Trey Parker and Matt Stone).

Intriguingly, the success of John K.'s creations seemed to prove beneficial to everyone except John K. himself. Actual animation from Spumco was scarce after *Ren & Stimpy*. For Kricfalusi, most of the 1990s was a period accurately described by historian Michael Barrier as "a decade in the wilderness with his virtues as a filmmaker scarcely in evidence."[3] Much of this artistic silence came largely by choice. Jim Smith said Spumco was adamant in "making sure no one will be able to just step in and hijack the creative process again," a position that proved a stumbling block in gaining financial backing.[4] News of pending deals and meetings with powerful people in Hollywood were constantly leaked to the press; few ever developed beyond rumors. Kricfalusi claimed to have been "blackballed" because of his fallout with Nickelodeon, while Vanessa Coffey said that the rest of the world was not "as eager to massage his ego as we were."[5]

It is hard to pin blame on Nickelodeon for John K.'s inability to find a proper means of expressing his artistic gifts. He often failed to take proper advantage of his own stardom. Ari Emmanuel, one of the world's most powerful talent agents, began representing Kricfalusi after the Nickelodeon debacle, but their association resulted in endeavors of zero lasting merit. Celebrity courtships with Joel Silver, Michael Bay, Aerosmith, and Sam Raimi—all fans of *Ren & Stimpy* wanting to work with Kricfalusi—met similar fates.

Though some quietly realized that a self-destructive streak lay underneath Kricfalusi's gifts, it never came to light simply because so little of his output reached the public's eye. Throughout this period, Spumco's evolving artistic nature remained, with Kricfalusi always searching "for a new kind of approach, different from what he had done with *Ren & Stimpy*," collaborator and one-time girlfriend Elinor Blake said.[6] A tremendous amount of pre-production work and study was put into various projects that Kricfalusi tried to launch. But these projects quickly devolved, due to a penchant for overindulgence that Kricfalusi's core crew of yes-men was more than willing to satisfy.

Kricfalusi's tendency to overdraw characters—to the point of overdetailed ugliness—began visibly rearing its head in *I Miss You*, the music video he directed for the singer Björk. (Blake, with her connections in the music industry, had set the two up, but was subsequently shut out of the production. She left Spumco and broke up with Kricfalusi shortly after.) A three-minute project that took over six months and $1 million to complete, *I Miss You* is an exercise in grotesque excess. Kricfalusi's own spasmodic method of animating is highlighted, revealing a clear disdain for the subtleties of in-betweens and overlap. Kricfalusi aims to pay homage to the Fleischer shorts of the early 1930s by disregarding the rules and aiming to make every drawing funny. He does so without realizing that, even in their brilliant aimlessness, those New York animators still followed rules to make sure every frame served a purpose. Many of Kricfalusi's individual drawings in *I Miss You* are indeed gorgeous; but not a single scene reads well, resulting in sheer chaos rather than the pure joy of his best *Ren & Stimpy* cartoons.

Conversely, Kricfalusi's Ranger Smith cartoons for Cartoon Network—featuring the antagonist of Hanna-Barbera's *Yogi Bear*—show a degree of restraint and enlightened direction. Kricfalusi's nostalgia for the wooden 1959 *Yogi*, combined with his demented overhaul of its every aspect, resulted in a product more refined than his reinvention of *Mighty Mouse* for Ralph Bakshi, but just as charismatic.

Unlike the Bakshi show, however, the modestly respectable *Ranger Smith* films were still an example of creative freedom gone haywire; less than thirty minutes of animation took at least two years to complete. Ed Benedict, the designer of Yogi Bear and the layout artist of many of the original cartoons, had his work on the shorts constantly revised. The Korean studio Rough Draft, after being subjected to numerous retakes and proverbial beatings at Kricfalusi's hand, refused to finish the animation of "Boo Boo Runs Wild". Retakes and the remainder of the picture were finished at Spumco.

Kricfalusi had become increasingly more evasive over his disregard for a project's budget and schedule, often scolding his clients for what he perceived as their impatience. "Yes, it's going to take three extra months, but you're gonna get a whole minute extra of animation!" This was Kricfalusi's viewpoint, as summarized by Linda Simensky, who worked at Cartoon Network at the time of the Ranger Smith cartoons. "He couldn't imagine a world where you wouldn't want more drawings. When push came to shove, his way of looking at rules was figuring out how to break them."[7]

John K. animation drawings for "Boo Boo Runs Wild", his *Ranger Smith* cartoon for Hanna-Barbera. © Time-Warner. Courtesy of Norman Hathaway.

Kricfalusi had no financial need to show self-discipline; ironically, Nickelodeon itself kept Spumco's doors open for most of the 1990s, with steady five-figure settlement payments to Kricfalusi each time Games Animation completed a half-hour of *Ren & Stimpy*. Shortly after the show wrapped production and the income ceased, however, Kricfalusi filed a high-profile $100 million lawsuit against Nickelodeon—a move that drained so much of Spumco's finances that producer Libby Simon had to leave the studio to "get a real job."[8]

The breach-of-contract lawsuit against Nickelodeon in October 1995 claimed that, according to Kricfalusi's original contract, merchandising rights for the *Ren & Stimpy* characters were to revert to him after five years. Kricfalusi also demanded an injunction against MTV, compensation, and $100 million in punitive damages.[9] The company scoffed at his accusations in the press, but privately knew there was obvious merit to the lawsuit—for the contracts of the original three *Nicktoons* did indeed promise that some rights would revert back to the creators. Months later, it was announced that Viacom and Kricfalusi had reached a settlement, though both parties refused to speak about it beyond saying "the case has been settled and the entire action is being dismissed with prejudice."[10] Sources close to the case disclosed that Kricfalusi was paid off with a few million to walk away.

Even with a small fortune in the bank, Kricfalusi still set his sights on getting others to help finance his studio. This involved following an established business model with corporate executives, even though Kricfalusi knew full well "that the last thing on their minds is entertaining the audience."[11] To get around the presence of network executives and censors, Kricfalusi pioneered the idea of original animation on the Internet. He helped develop the earliest Flash techniques; but even that involved seeking sponsors. This was an immensely difficult task, Kricfalusi said, as nobody would "fund the damn thing." This was the case because the corporate world "just wait[s] forever—until someone proves them wrong. Then they all jump on the bandwagon and screw it up."[12]

The cartoon series *The Goddamn George Liquor Show* and *Weekend Pussy Hunt* revealed the conflicting nature of John K.'s work in early Flash shorts. The primitive software did not handle the Spumco drawings very well, yielding results more stilted than Hanna-Barbera's 1957 TV shorts—at a far more expensive cost. Obvious in the web cartoons, too, is Kricfalusi's willful abandonment of his role as a bridge between entertainment for children and adults. Sexual organs and feces are regularly presented as funny in themselves with no setup or punch line of any kind. The very title of *Weekend Pussy Hunt*—ostensibly a cat-and-dog film noir—is just a clumsy excuse to allow the characters to keep saying the word "pussy."

This fourteen-year-old boy mentality is an unpleasant extension of the original *Ren & Stimpy*'s gross-out humor, with an unrestricted overemphasis on infantile urges actively undermining the superior elements on display. Kricfalusi's Flash shorts were rendered as compelling as schoolyard jokes. When he got a "big pile of money for a cartoon," quipped Bill Wray, "he called it *Weekend Pussy Hunt*. Are you kidding me? Artistic freedom is one thing, but they're not going to want that. They want *Ren & Stimpy*."[13]

The same promiscuousness mildly pervaded *The Ripping Friends*, Kricfalusi's first television series in nearly a decade. Originally, it had been an action film concept starring the world's "manliest men," who went around literally ripping evildoers to pieces to uphold justice. This concept was so unique that it might have required years of development and training to pull off properly. The deal Kevin Kolde—Libby Simon's successor as Spumco's producer—arranged with FOX, while Kricfalusi toiled away on his web cartoons, could not possibly accommodate these needs.[14]

John K. was initially to have had minor input on *The Ripping*

Friends series; his only involvement was on a storyboard-approval basis. This was, essentially, an executive position rather than that of a guiding visionary. While Jim Smith and industry veteran John Dorman worked in-house at Spumco, two subcontracted studios in Ontario—Red Rover and Funbag—would do the heaviest lifting in layout.

The finished episodes of *The Ripping Friends* are critical duds on every conceivable level. Kricfalusi said the main problem was that the Canadian studios did not faithfully follow Smith's, Dorman's, and his original drawings to the letter. This was in fact untrue of Toronto's Red Rover, whose artists duly underwent the nerve-wracking, time-consuming experience of getting their drawings approved by Kricfalusi. "We weren't sure exactly what he wanted from us," said David Pietila, an artist at the studio. "We were told to follow certain guidelines, like 'draw close to Jim's boards, while emulating [Jack] Kirby.' Our roughs would be faxed to John for comments. Then we would clean them up. Then they would be faxed to John for comments. Then we would fix them or start over."[15]

Once Red Rover's six months of contract service was up, the studio opted not to continue. The production moved completely to Ottawa's Funbag, where the management expressed unwillingness to follow Kricfalusi's instructions. Although Jim Smith was sent to Funbag to help educate the crew, and layout notes—including an extensive manual—were sent and received, the finished work seen by Kricfalusi seemed to disregard any instruction he had given Funbag.

Kricfalusi arrived in Ottawa at the tail end of the last two episodes' production. To his horror, he discovered that the artists had not seen the instructions at all—they were still sitting at the front desk, on the orders of Funbag production manager John Shaw. "They almost went at it; John [K.] threatened [Shaw], said he was going to punch his lights out," Steve Stefanelli, an artist at Funbag, said. "The next day

John K. came back and apologized, gave him a drawing, 'To my pal, who's always a pleasure to work with.' So they had kind of smoothed it over."[16]

Though the issue was resolved, the management at Funbag had been looking for a reason to oust Kricfalusi; weeks later, once they learned of the near-fisticuffs, he was banned from the studio. John K. spent the remainder of the series redrawing everything he could from a hotel room in Ottawa.

Even with the layout fiasco, *The Ripping Friends* still might have been salvageable; in an analogous situation decades earlier, the crude drawings of Fred Crippen's *Roger Ramjet* had not impeded Crippen's scripts and dialogue. To truly follow the Crippen model, however, would have placed an emphasis on writing rather than on drawing— something John K. would never allow. As a result, *The Ripping Friends'* stories are thoroughly flimsy, fluctuating unsuccessfully between action and comedy. Even the strictly gag-based "Rip-A-Long" segments are botched with plodding, exposition-heavy framing. The series ended up as forgettable and artless as any of the departmentalized hackwork that aired on the FOX Network's children's lineup in fall 2001. It was not renewed for a second season.

The critical failure of *The Ripping Friends* is unsurprising. In these later projects, Kricfalusi does not target a general audience of any kind. Instead, he favors a hardcore group of fans and followers that will praise anything his fingers touch. He knows what they want and is eager to give it to them in spades. Though this approach has worked moderately well for other authors and filmmakers, it is a completely delusional route if the creator intends to reach a widespread and diverse audience—like that of the original *Ren & Stimpy*. The painful limits of Kricfalusi's latter-day mentality could only be appropriately exposed, then, if that mentality were somehow applied to Kricfalusi's original creations.

§

Animation fandom is prone to outrageous wishful thinking. Chief among those extravagant fantasies in the late 1990s was: "What if John K. got the rights back to *Ren & Stimpy* with no restrictions?" The real-life enactment of that dream scenario produced a show so pathetic that its mere name is synonymous with abhorrence. The short run of *Ren & Stimpy: Adult Party Cartoon* is not one of the worst animated series ever made, despite strong arguments to the contrary. Rather, it holds a distinction for being one of the most heartbreaking.

Some have suggested that John Kricfalusi's 1996 settlement with Nickelodeon may have been the catalyst for his reunion with his characters, though the five-year interim suggests otherwise. Far more likely is that he simply lucked into the opportunity, just as he arguably lucked into much of his earlier career. Throughout the 1990s, John K. charmed many animation executives with his charisma and his rebellious nature. Among these executives was Fred Seibert, who had made Kricfalusi a consultant in the early days of original programming at Cartoon Network. Seibert likely convinced his friend Albie Hecht, a key entertainment executive at Viacom, to orchestrate the *Ren & Stimpy* revival. In addition, reruns of the Spumco episodes—christened *Ren & Stimpy Rocks* and featuring new bumpers starring Billy West—had aired on the VH1 network in 2001, receiving great ratings and fanfare.

Roughly around the same time, TNN (The National Network) was working on rebranding its image with an emphasis on original content under the new moniker Spike TV, an identity change that commenced in July 2003. The highlight of their strategy was to launch a block of primetime, mature-audience animation entitled "The Strip," or "Cartoons for Fuckin' Adults." Hecht determined that the main draw in this lineup would involve resurrecting "a major catalyst for the original animation renaissance that happened during the [1990s]."[17]

In late 2001, Hecht began TNN's negotiations with Kricfalusi to make new episodes of *Ren & Stimpy*.

Kevin Kay, the executive vice president of production and development at TNN, made his network's aims plain: "Part of the reason we have so much respect for Kricfalusi as an artist and as a filmmaker is that he recognizes the fact that he wants the best show possible, and our goal is to make as many *Ren & Stimpy*s this time as we can."[18]

The executives' vision for Spike TV, Kricfalusi said, was "to be the man's network"; they specifically asked him "to pull out all of the stops" to make the new *Ren & Stimpy* shows fit in. "They asked me if I had any episodes that were rejected by Nickelodeon, and I said, 'Yeah, I've got tons of them.' They said make them—make the ones that got rejected."[19]

Negotiations were finalized in May 2002, when the plans were announced to the public. TNN may have been convinced of Kricfalusi's earnest talent, but his notorious past was still taken into account. The monetary consequences of *Ren & Stimpy*'s first run at Nickelodeon still furrowed brows at Viacom. At Kricfalusi's insistence, the final contract called for the delivery of six half-hours, along with the enticing bonus of a made-for-television movie.

John K. touted to the press that "the whole gang is back."[20] In truth, it was a sizable percentage of the talent that had sided with Kricfalusi after his ouster from Nickelodeon: Jim Smith, Vincent Waller, Eddie Fitzgerald, Richard Pursel, and Bob Jaques' and Kelly Armstrong's Carbunkle Cartoons. Glenn Barr, a background painter at Spumco during the original run of the show, was initially lined up to work on the series; some of his work made it to "Onward and Upward", but his services were ultimately turned down, purportedly for being too expensive.

Billy West was not involved with the new series. People at

Spumco claimed that West wanted too much money, or refused to take direction from John K.; that he would only return as Stimpy if a moderator stood in on the recording sessions, conveying Kricfalusi's requests impersonally: "Could you please ask Billy to put a little more emotion in that scene?"[21] West denied this, claiming he "wouldn't have anything to do with" *Adult Party Cartoon* as a rule. "[John K. was] trying to cajole me in that really awkward caveman way, and he had this nutbag Kolde [on the phone] that I had to deal with, that was saying, 'Okay, we'll give you thirty-five dollars an hour.' He couldn't understand that I was saying no."[22]

Spumco became two physical studios—one in Los Angeles and one in Ottawa—to take advantage of Canadian tax exemptions. The difference in appearance of each building was not unnoticed by the employees. The Ottawa studio was housed in a newly renovated farmhouse, while the Los Angeles studio resided in what layout artist Robertryan Cory called "this really shitty area of North Hollywood in this abandoned pharmaceutical company place"—a more typical Spumco headquarters, in other words.[23]

The challenge of managing two crews in two different countries might have been feasible, had Kricfalusi abided by his original plan. Bob Jaques described this scheme as "to step back this time and take an overall supervisory position, letting others direct the bulk of the episodes."[24] Along with Jaques, other candidates for directors included Vincent Waller, Jim Smith, and Derek Bond, who had worked as overseas supervisor on *The Ripping Friends*. Waller began to direct "Onward and Upward", his 1991 story that was completely rejected by Nickelodeon. Bond was slated to direct the episode "Ren Seeks Help". By the time serious production started, Kricfalusi became the sole director. Waller and Bond's projects were taken over; Smith and Jaques never got the opportunity to direct.

Writing and storyboarding of the new episodes began in summer

2002; by the end of July, the entire board of "Onward and Upward" was completed. Just then, however, Kricfalusi went through a relationship breakup with an artist at the Los Angeles studio, a girl he had been dating since she was fifteen years old. The workflow did not pick up again until September, and Kricfalusi's emotional incapacitation put a damper on the entire production.

While the staffers at both studios had worked in some capacity on Kricfalusi's late 1990s projects and *The Ripping Friends*, many were new to animation. John K.'s decision to populate his staff with inexperienced people proved dire. In particular, it caused his best artists to be overworked and improperly utilized. Waller was spread thin as the Los Angeles studio's art director, while Pursel wrote almost nothing that was used. Jim Smith was occupied correcting younger artists' mistakes; otherwise, his time was spent storyboarding rather than working on his own layouts, where he might have made a tremendous impact on the show's vitality. Kelly Armstrong, meanwhile, never touched a single scene of animation at Carbunkle and had almost zero interaction with Kricfalusi.

The original Spumco crew on the Nickelodeon series was largely composed of young people; but regardless of how malcontent and rowdy they might have been, they still had sound knowledge of the animation process. They had worked without Kricfalusi on other shows and movies, which helped them gain perspective. "Every single person on the crew took responsibility to make it work," Kelly Armstrong observed. By contrast, very few people at the new Spumco had worked for anyone other than John K. In Armstrong's estimation, *Adult Party Cartoon* "didn't work because there were very few people with any real industry experience on the production, from the top down."

On the original *Ren & Stimpy*, some producers might have encouraged Kricfalusi's temperament, but Armstrong defended Libby Simon, despite others' criticism, specifically as "a Godsend, a really experienced producer and amazing at working with John and keeping things on track."[25] By contrast, on *Adult Party Cartoon*, Kevin Kolde and his underlings kowtowed to John K.'s demands for artistic indulgence.

Kricfalusi said he "didn't really work that closely" with the few veteran *Ren & Stimpy* artists on the new episodes. Instead he chose to spend a disproportionate amount of time jumping "back and forth training two crews of young people."[26] Deep collaboration—the "combined vision" of Kricfalusi and his closest partners—had been integral to the success of the original Spumco episodes; when important artists such as Smith, Waller, and Jaques opted not to work for Games Animation, the later run of the series was severely affected. On *Adult Party Cartoon*, Kricfalusi now had those important artists working with him again; yet he transparently wasted the opportunity, as though they were expendable to his aims. He preferred to channel his energy into educating relative amateurs rather than utilizing the honed professionals at his disposal.

The core of Kricfalusi's methodology had not changed since the original episodes. The new crew forced him to switch off between the roles of director and teacher. "Life is about giving lectures" was his mantra, said art director Nick Cross. "He doesn't pull any punches in regards to what he thinks of your work, and he has no reservations in making an artist redo something fifty times if that's what he feels is necessary."[27]

Though inexperienced, the new artists had talent. Their novice status in the industry gave Kricfalusi license to exert heavier control over the production and constantly ask for revisions. Artists were scolded for not following his wildly variant roughs to the letter. "They were incredible to look at: really fast sketches that retained so much energy and emotion," said layout supervisor Helder Mendonca. "But I'd say most of the time they were [only] sixty to seventy percent completed, and needed to be touched up or finished. It was a pretty intimidating task to add finishing touches on any of John's originals, so that usually meant redrawing and completing the entire image. This was very challenging; because sometimes a line may look like an obvious mistake, but [here] it was the start or indication of an intentional idea. And if that somehow changed [in the redraw], then the drawing would be wrong. Or vice versa: a detail that should have been omitted ended up as part of the [redraw]. So the layout crew really had to learn how to analyze and interpret John's drawings."[28]

The daunting effects of Kricfalusi's waffling and lack of clarity engulfed the entire series. Background paintings could face five tests per scene. On one occasion, a production manager plopped a painting in front of Kricfalusi: "Congratulations, John, that painting cost you $40,000." Storyboard artists might have to change scene order after work had already been approved. "I started recording the [storyboard] pitches, because I wasn't sure if I was forgetting things or if [Kricfalusi] was telling me different information," storyboard artist Steve Stefanelli said. "And sure enough, the next time around, I recorded him again, and he'd say something different. We'd be weeks late some times, and I don't know if he remembered half the stuff."[29]

Carbunkle Cartoons also fell prey to the haphazard direction coming from Spumco. Layout artists went through distress appeasing John K.'s desire to cram what layout artist Warren Leonhardt called "a million little goodies for fans in every scene."[30] Kricfalusi then began adding animation breakdowns to the finished layouts—making life correspondingly harder for the animators, whom Jaques believed were "relegated to glorified in-betweener" status. "There was a feeling of mistrust that the animators could do their job properly."[31]

As a consequence of the production bottlenecks at Spumco, Carbunkle animators had increasingly more to do in increasingly less time. The trouble was exacerbated by the difficulties uniquely inherent to *Ren & Stimpy* animation. Artists were by now used to characters whose poses were unrelated to their changes in volume. But on the old *Ren & Stimpy*, Carbunkle had been able to adjust these details for a more pleasing result. On *Adult Party Cartoon*, Carbunkle was contractually obligated not to deviate from the Spumco drawings whatsoever. Said Greg Stainton, an animator at Carbunkle: "Straying from any line at all was just not allowed, to the point where there was a fear factor."[32]

Cross commented that layouts done at Spumco were often "degraded in quality due to the constant revisi[ons],"[33] which might have appeased John K.'s impulses but provided few functional cues for animators. It was obvious that many layouts had failed at both tasks when a finished scene from Spumco's Los Angeles studio arrived at Carbunkle—still decorated with a post-it from an unfortunate layout artist, stating "I can't figure out how to make Stimpy's face work."[34]

Adult Party Cartoon started out with ample production time, allowing most of the animation for "Onward and Upward" and "Ren Seeks Help" to be done in Vancouver. But the time schedule changed as layouts trickled in for later episodes. Less actual animation was done at Carbunkle, and strict timing jobs began to be rammed through their doors. Korean animation studio Big Star—which had a decade-long working relationship with Carbunkle—was eventually forced to rapidly crank out footage to accommodate the slipping production. Said Armstrong: "I would have liked to protect [Big Star] from the lunacy on the production, but it was impossible. I deeply regretted getting them involved with the show in the end."[35]

During the production of the episode "Fire Dogs 2", Kricfalusi came up with a "really stupid rule," Robertryan Cory said, that "you were never allowed to hold a frame of drawing. You always had to have it changing."[36] Hence, Ren and Stimpy have an instant reaction to every single frame of an animated Ralph Bakshi on the toilet, gesticulating incessantly, further increasing the difficulty that animators had in getting the drawings to work.

The no-holds method was Kricfalusi's misguided attempt to create the kind of excessive distortion that Jim Tyer had practiced in his 1950s animation for Terrytoons. But Tyer's eccentric style was still grounded in a basic understanding that all the frames in a scene needed to relate to each other. Unlike Tyer, Kricfalusi had never animated for a strong director, nor did he ever try to do things traditionally when animating on his own films. If, before *Adult Party Cartoon*, Kricfalusi had known anything about creating practical layouts, he purged himself of that insight now. Said Carbunkle's animation checker John Vincent: "Any nasty key pose you see [in the finished *Adult Party Cartoon* episodes] is exactly as it was in the John K.-approved layouts. The artists did not deviate. It was part of my job to make sure they didn't."[37]

By the time layout on the series wrapped, it was strictly verboten for an artist to call for a "same as" in a layout—i. e. an instruction to the animator that one element of the drawing did not need to be redrawn. By the new rule, all elements always needed to be redrawn. In the past, held poses had led to the best character animation in Kricfalusi's films; now Kricfalusi had become willfully ignorant of that fact. While he might have termed it artistic growth, it only complicated everyone else's jobs. Though Kricfalusi's artistic aims had evolved over ten years, he remained as capricious as ever and seemed completely unenlightened by past experience. Admirably, *Ren & Stimpy* still remained an industry holdout under Kricfalusi's leadership, which Cross said "prevents the work from becoming mediocre and pushes the staff to try harder and get the best stuff on screen." But it also "slows down the production, and the budget goes up and deadlines are missed."[38]

By January 2003, when TNN—soon to be exclusively Spike TV—still promoted new *Ren & Stimpy* episodes as the crux of its relaunch strategy, only one cartoon, "Onward and Upward", had made it through layout to animation. Most of the cartoons were not completely written, with the series to begin airing in June. Kricfalusi had established a pattern for himself and he would not break it.

§

The most damaging consequence of Spumco's removal from *The Ren & Stimpy Show* in 1992 was that it dispersed the lightning in a bottle that the studio had captured. As unreasonable and uncompromising as the creators and suits may have been, the spirit of the dynamic achieved nirvana. Each cartoon that John K. produced with his team exceeded the last. His main failing was his lack of responsibility for the financial consequences of his filmmaking methods. This unavoidable obstacle only intensified after 1992, during Kricfalusi's absence from the realities of commercial Hollywood.

The mere existence of *Adult Party Cartoon* violated the original series' central values—the characters had never existed in the public eye before the Nickelodeon series, so how could a more explicit version represent what Ren and Stimpy "were meant to be"? In the original shows, the combination of the restrictions inherent in children's television, the cartoonists' own rebellion, and a sense of what the general audience would accept consistently created works that remain unsurpassed in their exciting and thoroughly entertaining nature.

"The Wilderness Adventure"—the first *Ren & Stimpy* cartoon storyboarded for the Nickelodeon series—was branded as completely unacceptable by the network for its violence, crudeness, and inclusion of George Liquor. Yet even at this primitive, unapproved stage, the story, gags, and characterization of the storyboard exhibit natural intuition. Grossness is brief enough to be humorous rather than disgusting; violent gags are more ironic than painful in execution. If "The Wilderness Adventure" seemed too hardcore for children in

1990, it was only because the content was so unique in its intelligence that it stood out as a racy anomaly.

Kricfalusi initially planned to produce "The Wilderness Adventure" in 2002 to launch the new primetime series. Had this taken place as intended, it might have bolstered the life of the series; the storyboard was a time capsule that exemplified the strengths of Spumco in the early 1990s. But Spike TV demanded full rights to the character of George Liquor if "The Wilderness Adventure" was made.[39] Unwilling to agree to those terms, Kricfalusi opted to resurrect other rejected outlines from the show's second season.

The original 1991 outline for "Onward and Upward", written by Vincent Waller, is sparse at best. Ren and Stimpy reside in a bum's mouth, then decide to leave their squalor and live the high life in a bar's spittoon, dining on such exquisite delicacies as mucus, spit, and whatever else is deposited by the barflies. As a means of embellishing the original story for *Adult Party Cartoon*, the often-implied gay duo was now brought out of the closet, with Ren as the "pitcher" and Stimpy the "catcher." In a highly repellent sequence, the two engage in actual anal intercourse.

"['Onward and Upward'] wasn't a full story, or funny either," said writer Mike Kerr, who had previously written for Kricfalusi on *The Ripping Friends*. "For an adult show, the jokes were pretty grade school. I told John what I thought and I think it just pissed him off."[40] Most of those involved "knew 'Onward and Upward' was a turkey" from the initial storyboard.[41] There were even feeble attempts from Spumco producer Kevin Kolde to urge Kricfalusi to reconsider.

"I'm not sure what the graphic-ness [sic] of their sexuality actually buys us, and my instinct is that it's more distracting than funny," Kolde wrote to John K. in an e-mail copied to many in the production. "This scene just takes us over the top and not necessarily in a way that I think adds cleverness, just grossness. I really don't want to read the review

Layout drawing for "Onward and Upward". Courtesy of Bob Jaques.
© Viacom.

that says, '*Ren & Stimpy* is back and all they did was make it grosser than ever.'"[42]

Kricfalusi had it his way. He managed to put onscreen every disgusting act conceivable in each of his new cartoons, proving Kolde's prediction accurate. "Onward and Upward" inflates an eleven-minute story idea into a nearly twenty-minute academic exercise. It crosses the line from humorous scatology to unforgivable abhorrence, journeying to the point of no return.

There is undeniable precision in the *Adult Party Cartoon* pilot. The character acting and animation of Ren and Stimpy in scenes of "Onward and Upward" have specificity and range conspicuously absent in many of the cartoons produced by Games Animation. But

Kricfalusi's skills, and that of his crew, are squandered when in service to the characters witlessly consuming snot and puke. In retrospect, the Games cartoons generally failed to achieve the original Spumco product's mastery due to the absence of Kricfalusi's guiding hand. The *Adult Party Cartoon* series suffered from the opposite problem: the cartoons had ability and direction with John K. at the helm, but he consciously refused to act on his strengths.

Kricfalusi unquestionably ruled supreme both times he directed *Ren & Stimpy*. But the original Spumco had a delicate artist-to-executive balance. At the new studio, such balance was sorely lacking. This is not to say, as many have implied, that Nickelodeon's authoritative edicts forced Kricfalusi to be more creative in 1991; merely that creative objectivity was integral to the original *Ren & Stimpy*'s success. In the 1990s, both Spumco and Nickelodeon were forceful enough in their work to keep Kricfalusi from delving completely into a state of artistic psychosis. The work was always late, but it was also always great.

On *Adult Party Cartoon*, by contrast, the forceful individuals of the early 1990s were replaced by a production team of industry novices—whose creative contributions to the series failed to go beyond spiritedly taking direction. Said Mendonca, "As much as John likes to see other people's drawings, he likes to see his own, and the way he originally drew them."[43] The dimension and "combined vision" that Kricfalusi once valued became obsolete. He tried to overcompensate by spreading himself thinner than ever before. Direction became a method of self-torture for him, indicated by his reflection that "ninety percent of directing is just chasing after people, so that they don't change what you came up with in the first place."[44]

In the absence of anyone to truly question his direction, Kricfalusi created films that were drawn out to the point of sheer restlessness. Scenes of true meaning were rare as the director filled misguided cartoons with content devoid of recognizable humor. Ten years earlier,

"Svën Höek" may have been padded past its intended eleven-minute length; but not a second of film went to waste under the original Spumco dynamic. The cut that John K. presented to the network had a listless pacing—strikingly similar to *Adult Party Cartoon*—in its attempts to inflate the picture to a half-hour; but thanks to Bob Camp's follow-through in post-production, the original, snappier timing was reinstated, fully enabling the gifts of Kricfalusi's direction to shine. In sharp contrast, when an *Adult Party Cartoon* episode came out unnecessarily long and slow, there was nobody on hand to tighten it up.

At a stupefying length of thirty-nine minutes, "Altruists" defies the very concept of sharp timing. A tribute to the *Three Stooges* comedies, it is an unfailingly unfunny string of gags involving Ren and Stimpy aiding a widow and her headless son. The characters and gags become as formulaic as the worst cartoons of the Nickelodeon series. The Games writers' flimsiest ideas at least had the relative advantage of being confined to an eleven-minute format. Like many of the original Columbia Stooges shorts, "Altruists" foundered because its story was simply too shallow to sustain the picture's length.

The sluggish nature of the *Adult Party Cartoon* series stems from Kricfalusi's "beat system" of timing, which Bob Jaques termed "his bullshit version of the old-school way of timing animation to a musical beat"—and part of Kricfalusi's continued effort to maximize his control over the end product. Kricfalusi had experimented with the "beat system" on the production of his *Ranger Smith* cartoons for Cartoon Network; now *Adult Party Cartoon* saw it in full flower. This method called for an overhaul of the standard exposure sheet. Two separate eleven-by-seventeen-inch sheets were used: one for action, and one to expose the animation. Sheets were printed at different lengths to accommodate different frame beats—some as odd as 23 frames—so each scene could work with an existing piece of prerecorded music.[45]

"It became hell when we had to use fifteen or thirteen-frame beat sheets because of the odd frames that were divided by eight," timer Jamie Mason explained, and it was "disorienting" to place the hard and soft accents of the animation.[46] The complicated procedure only succeeded in mutilating Associated Production Music tracks and awkwardly shoehorning character actions to fit the remnants. Like Kricfalusi's cartooning and direction style at Spumco, his "beat system" had "no method," Jaques said. "His vapid theories had no hard information and established procedure. Just a few basic disciplines that changed according to John's whims."[47]

Kricfalusi's whims also inspired him to take the Ren and Stimpy relationship in directions better left unexplored. Gay humor and homoeroticism had always existed in the show, obviously stemming from the presence of what Jim Ballantine called "angry, cynical young men who probably hate fags" on the show's staff throughout its entire run.[48] The duo's sexuality was ambiguous in the Nickelodeon series; Ren could lust after human women in one episode, yet clearly be Stimpy's significant other in "Son of Stimpy". Kricfalusi continued this concept fairly successfully in two very different *Adult Party* cartoons—"Naked Beach Frenzy" and "Stimpy's Pregnant". In the former, Stimpy is mostly ignorant of Ren's desire to bury himself in various girls' breasts; in the latter, Stimpy is his wife, carrying the Chihuahua's lovechild.

Kricfalusi grasps the concept that real people are never the same from moment to moment; and it makes his characters all the richer, with no real need for explicitness. Yet explicitness comes, and in droves. In "Altruists", Ren saws a log on Stimpy's ass in an unsubtle analogy to anal sex; later, Ren swipes a brick through Stimpy's ass cheeks, which the cat views as a "perk." In "Naked Beach Frenzy", despite the presence of numerous Katie Rice-designed scenes involving exposed female breasts, more attention is lavished over scenes involving Ren caught in a hairy male lifeguard's crotch and ass.

Storyboard drawings by Vincent Waller for "Onward and Upward". John K. added the sex happening beneath the sheets in the last drawing. © Viacom.

Incontrovertibly destroying the innocence of the characters was Kricfalusi's rationale to have Ren and Stimpy actually copulate in "Onward and Upward". Once it happened, there was nowhere else the humor could be taken. Any charm the original relationship had was destroyed, not so much because it was homosexual sex, but *actual* sex. In the wake of universally negative fan reaction to the sequence, Kricfalusi blamed an unidentified animator at Carbunkle for adding actual sex beneath the bedsheets. Kricfalusi left it in because he "felt sorry for the animator who thought it was funny."[49] Jaques and Colin Giles, the supposedly deviant animator at Carbunkle, recalled that the scene in question was originally under-posed and required additional layouts.

"Bob came walking up to me," Giles said, "with the new [layout] drawings saying something like, 'You'll never believe what they just sent us.'" These were the layouts of the humping action under the bed sheets.[50] Original storyboards of the bedroom sequence survive, complete with an added post-it showing the sex act—drawn by none other than John K.

In response to the widespread denunciation of *Adult Party Cartoon*'s content, Kricfalusi has actually suggested that Spike TV forced him to "deal with more 'adult themes'" against his better judgment, and that it was "a mistake" to add "more 'R' rated stuff" to *Ren & Stimpy*.[51] In his defense, artists did observe that Kricfalusi felt he was under tremendous pressure to compete with the likes of *South Park*—even if he had little knowledge of what *South Park* was about.

"I remember we all said to him, 'Um, you know you can't show boobs on TV,'" said Robertryan Cory. "And he's like, 'They can do it! *South Park* does it!' He was under this idea that you could curse and do all this stuff because *South Park* had done it. It seemed like he had a vendetta against *South Park*, like it was the competition. In fact, we were supposed to air opposite it originally, at the same time on Wednesdays. And that's how it started, they told John, 'We want something to compete with *South Park*,' and he started doing this stuff."[52]

The magnetism of random pin-up window dressing—as when buxom girls of the Lynne Naylor school momentarily steal the focus in "Stimpy's Big Day" or "The Royal Canadian Kilted Yaksmen"—generally works in cartoons that are otherwise blushingly coy about sexuality. When girls designed—and in one case voiced—by Katie Rice explicitly expose their breasts and pubic regions while showering in front of bathroom attendants Ren and Stimpy in "Naked Beach Frenzy", the sophomoric approach works to a degree. The episode's length, however, undermines any substance the nudity might have had—and exposes the director as simply desirous of projecting his juvenile urges through his young female staff, revealing him to be devoid of any truly adult ideas.

Kricfalusi's claim of victimhood is disingenuous at best. In the eleven years that had passed since "Onward and Upward" was originally written, Kricfalusi gravitated towards more overtly explicit material. His Internet cartoons confirm a desire to do away with allusions and innuendos and to present sexual and bodily function humor as an end in themselves. Any pretension of wit Kricfalusi once exhibited in the original *Ren & Stimpy* series was fading into obscurity, the filmmaker now confusing childish urges with adult sensibility.

The *Adult Party Cartoon* series is only a gruesome conclusion to what had been a long time in coming. Spike TV did not need to coerce Kricfalusi into being raunchier—he was only too glad to oblige. Ergo, *Adult Party Cartoon*'s problems in story, timing, and direction were all part of the failed experiments intrinsic to the series. Kricfalusi desired to bring every aspect of the show under his direct supervision while refusing to accept the consequences.

§

Had Kricfalusi been turning out films of merit as he did in 1992, the crash of *Ren & Stimpy: Adult Party Cartoon* might have resonated more loudly. But as executed, the few laughs and bright moments in the episodes that aired could not justify the show's continued existence. *Gary the Rat* and *Stripperella*, the other shows on Spike TV's animation block, were also critical bombs, but they were not financial disasters. Those two shows made their delivery dates and did not go over budget; the entire run of *Stipperella* was in the can before the network received anything from Kricfalusi. As awful as *Gary the Rat* and *Stripperella* were, Spike TV could burn through them and quickly forget. They did not have that silver lining with *Adult Party Cartoon*.

The tragedy is that all of Kricfalusi's work—even at its most dilapidated—has kernels of genuine merit, mostly from funny acting deeply ingrained in the drawing and animation. In particular, the unaired "Stimpy's Pregnant" has several scenes that come into sharp focus. When Ren and Stimpy discuss Stimpy's condition, Kricfalusi demonstrates an impassioned skill at staging scenes of deep human emotion; he convincingly uses distortion for emotional effect.

John K.'s virtues all came together only once in the new series, for the episode "Ren Seeks Help". Originally written in the second season, it is another examination of Ren Höek's psyche. Ren's foul behavior exceeds even Stimpy's limits, and the Chihuahua visits Dr. Mr. Horse, seeking the answer to why he is such an asshole.

Kricfalusi sought structure in this cartoon in a manner he refused to apply in the other *Adult Party Cartoon* entries. A lack of executive control should not be a license for self-indulgence; at most, it is the icing on the cake. Accordingly, the explicitness of Ren's torture of a frog in his youth and the grisly final confrontation between Ren and Dr. Mr. Horse in the office do not meander aimlessly in carnage. They serve as the crux of illustrating Ren's psychosis.

As in the best of the original Spumco episodes, many scenes in "Ren Seeks Help" are drawn out, but only in beneficial ways. If the story of Ren's youth seems overlong, that is because there is no other way to emphasize the character's psychology. A potentially mundane scene of Ren climbing onto Dr. Mr. Horse's couch is transformed into a dramatic moment that highlights the pathetic nature of the depressed Ren and Dr. Mr. Horse's indifference to his actions.

The entire crew was at the top of their game for "Ren Seeks Help". It was the single cartoon on which Kricfalusi spent equal time with the Hollywood and Ottawa layout crews; when Robertryan Cory said "everyone was getting along with each other, nobody was causing fights, [and] John was in a really good mood the entire time."[53] It

ONWARD AND DOWNWARD

Production drawings from "Ren Seeks Help", the high point of the *Adult Party Cartoon* revival. Bottom drawing by Fred Osmond. Courtesy of Bob Jaques. © Viacom.

was almost as though Kricfalusi was apologizing for his earlier brutish behavior and the delays it caused. Those delays had forced Carbunkle to enter a temporary layoff as they waited for new footage—just as when Kricfalusi, similarly, exercised maximum control over certain cartoons in the Nickelodeon series, ten years before.[54]

The voice acting in "Ren Seeks Help" has strong direction, with the actors meticulously dangling their characters over the edges of mental breakdowns. Eric Bauza could not hope to best Billy West as Stimpy, yet his reads of the cat's traumatic bawling are compelling. Tom Hay, an entertainment personality and friend of Kricfalusi's since childhood, almost surpasses Kricfalusi in portraying mental and physical anguish as the frog—an opportunity for which Kricfalusi felt Hay should be grateful. "He says to me, 'I made you world famous.' And I was like, 'How'd you do that?' Because he gave me a job."[55]

"Ren Seeks Help" owes its best acting and action to a collaboration—if less intimate than in the past—between the production's strongest artists. Helder Mendonca, the layout supervisor at Spumco Ottawa, was the most accomplished of the new crew of artists. His storyboards and layouts retained a solidity and knowledge otherwise absent from the production line. His were the only layouts Nathan Affolter said that he and the other Carbunkle animators actually celebrated receiving.[56] Kricfalusi's direction is vindicated in the scenes Mendonca drew, showing Ren's father confronting him—and a bloodbath in Mr. Horse's office, in which the characters come alive in a manner not possible in any medium but animation. "I try to get into the drawing, feel what my drawings are supposed to be feeling," Mendonca said. "I'll get up and act out what I'm supposed to be drawing. Then I will study the expression in a mirror, or just feel the planes of my face with my hand and get a sense of form if I don't have a mirror."[57]

The strong layout work was brilliantly followed through at Carbunkle, where "you could hear a pin drop" as "the animators were working hard untangling Spumco layouts!"[58] Said Jaques: "Those new to the show were up to speed with the animation style, and the studio energy was good with the renewed workflow."[59]

"Ren Seeks Help" demonstrates the kind of meticulous sheen that had disappeared from the original *Ren & Stimpy* after the second season. It stands alone in the 2003 series at matching the heights of the first series. Perhaps because the film is so close to perfection, its outright lack of fun—the prevailing flaw of *Adult Party Cartoon*—is more noticeable than in the other entries. "Ren Seeks Help" does not effectively convey the humor needed to make Ren's psychosis simultaneously funny and disturbing—as it had been in "Stimpy's Invention" and "Svën Höek", on which Kricfalusi worked closely with Bob Camp. "Ren Seeks Help" is an enthralling cartoon in its own right; yet as with the best Games cartoons, the film's lack of balance prevents it from completely matching the series' highest triumphs.

The positivity flowing from "Ren Seeks Help" was short-lived. The most devastating catastrophe of *Adult Party Cartoon* arrived in the form of "Fire Dogs 2", another 1991 story rejected by Nickelodeon. At the time of that rejection, story editor Will McRobb had warned Kricfalusi that the picture was destined for failure. Even in the outline stage, it was full of "things we must talk about"—and apparently never did.[60]

In a sequel to the original first season's "Fire Dogs", Ren and Stimpy move in with the Fire Chief, who promises them big jobs at the firehouse and berates them as he smokes, defecates, and handles the ladies. It was to be Kricfalusi's autobiographical account of his relationship with Ralph Bakshi. No longer merely a caricature, the Fire Chief *is* Bakshi. Kricfalusi, Richard Pursel, and a few others polished the old story over lunch in 2002, though Kricfalusi admitted, "we didn't write anything; it's a documentary culled from real life. These are experiences I had with Ralph. Ren and Stimpy are me."[61]

"Fire Dogs 2" was the second cartoon to go into production in fall 2002, its layout primarily done in Hollywood. Work on the cartoon was completely thrown out twice. Kricfalusi blamed Jim Smith and Eddie Fitzgerald for not knowing continuity or story structure and therefore screwing up the storyboard process. "[Kricfalusi] just kept throwing layouts out, even if it was pretty decent, and it becomes very obvious that the cartoon is not being written on time," said Cory. "He basically decides that he's going to punish everyone, saying 'this is how you have to do it,' and he threw the entire show away, and that was the first time he threw it away."[62]

Some time into the second attempt at pre-production, Bakshi moved into Kricfalusi's California studio to serve as inspiration for the artists. Bakshi also attended pitch meetings that he hoped would bring in more work for Spumco. Those who worked in Bakshi's presence confirmed that the antics seen in "Fire Dogs 2" had some basis in reality. "He's really well-versed in the history of the art, and [he's] smart; but we couldn't use the bathroom, there was shit everywhere," Cory commented.[63]

By the time "Fire Dogs 2" reached Carbunkle in spring 2003, it had gone through layout three times. The final attempt received almost zero approval from Kricfalusi at the Hollywood studio. Kolde—who, many at Spumco observed, more typically bent to Kricfalusi's will and followed baffling leadership without question—this time told the layout artists that "this cartoon has to ship," after which the crew cranked it out in about eight days. "Everyone in Spumco USA just stayed there," Cory said. "Nobody really went home; we all slept there. We all smelled bad, and we just shit this stuff all out, none of it was good."[64]

Stories from all of the studios used on *Adult Party Cartoon* follow a similar pattern: immense workloads were tackled at the eleventh hour to spare John K. the indignity of his show being too late. Artists at

Spumco Ottawa regularly worked until five in the morning. Bob Jaques and his protégés at Carbunkle were denied footage and demoted almost solely to timing jobs. Big Star in South Korea shouldered the heaviest burden of grinding out footage, with regular twelve-hour work days after "five months" of having "pretty much nothing to do," overseas supervisor Chris Ross recalled. "What also affected the schedule was the constant reworking of shows. I was getting 'creative' retakes after some episodes were due to be done."[65]

Originally planned as a single half-hour, "Fire Dogs 2" was split into two uneven chapters to accommodate Kricfalusi's delays. To help save his protégé's show, Bakshi—a master at quick, cheap problem solving—came up with the solution of padding the finished first nine minutes of the sequel with the original "Fire Dogs" and live-action wraparounds starring Bakshi himself. Viewers would have to tune in the following week for the second part of the new cartoon, which was delivered to Spike TV's offices the day it was to air.

The energy expended to save John K.'s reputation was for naught. "Fire Dogs 2" is an outright embarrassment; it sets a precedent in creative enterprise gone wrong. Certainly there are fewer figures in animation more captivating than the real-life Ralph Bakshi. The film's desultory nature stems from an attempt by Kricfalusi to capture his mentor's unpredictable personality. Rather than capturing Bakshi, Kricfalusi more actively portrays his own erratic nature, via an inability to commit to his own film. Eleven years earlier, Kricfalusi told the story of an unpredictable human figure terrorizing Ren and Stimpy in "Man's Best Friend", and the result had been unparalleled brilliance. In that short, Will McRobb wrote to Kricfalusi, "George Liquor had a method to his madness," and a "cool rivalry dynamic" budded between Ren and Stimpy as a result of it.

Commenting on the original 1991 outline for "Fire Dogs 2", McRobb accurately predicted what might become of the cartoon if

Kricfalusi's initial ideas went unchallenged. "What's the story here? A psychotic fire chief invites Ren and Stimpy over and then terrorizes them for eleven minutes. Here, they just seem to cower and act nervous. Why do they have to be so passive?"[66]

Indeed, there is no reason for Ren and Stimpy to be in "Fire Dogs 2". Opportunities for them to act are nonexistent. As Kricfalusi tries to channel his own experiences into the film, the duo becomes as unappealingly subservient—just as they had been in many Games cartoons where a dominating third character overtakes the story. Rather than focus on Ren and Stimpy, Kricfalusi creates a jarring juxtaposition of random, unrelated poses in service to the animated Bakshi taking a dump. Even the metaphors in the film become too "insider baseball" for anyone in the general audience to comprehend them. When Stimpy pulls a turd "bigger than a baby" out of the toilet, the gag reflects an incident actually experienced by ex-Bakshi and Spumco production assistant Brent Kirnbauer (when a hooker was visiting Bakshi). Ultimately, however, one can gain a better sense of who Ralph Bakshi really is by watching one of Bakshi's own films.

"John thinks he has me nailed, but it's wrong," Bakshi said.[67] The only outcome here is that today, Bakshi is terrified that his grandchildren might see "Fire Dogs 2"—and Kricfalusi has proven his lack of self-restraint. His delight in childishly presenting taboo materials for their own sake leaves the audience feeling as Ren and Stimpy do in the cartoon: frightened and bewildered.

§

Unbeknownst to the general public, by the time *Adult Party Cartoon* actually aired on Spike TV, the series had ceased to exist as

Drawing of Ralph Bakshi, with Ren and Stimpy, as seen in "Fire Dogs 2".
Courtesy of Bob Jaques. © Viacom.

a going concern. John K.'s actions proved to be self-sabotaging; these new cartoons vindicated the small voices of dissent that had long suggested the creator might be his own worst enemy.

Widespread negligence during production ensured that only the first two *Adult Party Cartoon* episodes met their airdates. "Fire Dogs 2" was split, and "Naked Beach Frenzy" raised content issues with Spike TV and its advertisers. Kricfalusi made repeated edits to obscure the full-frontal nudity that executive Kevin Kay had told him would be completely acceptable for broadcast. "We did exactly what they told us to do, and they never aired it."[68]

It became evident that Spike TV was throwing Spumco's show out on its ear—otherwise they would have aired "Naked Beach Frenzy" in some form. While the show had decent ratings, they were not what the network had hoped for; indeed, their entire "Cartoons for Fuckin' Adults" block was a nuclear holocaust. Spike TV was eager to put the entire mess behind them.

As in 1992, Spumco was severely over budget and behind schedule. The first three half-hours, before they were even completed, had wiped out the near-entirety of *Adult Party Cartoon*'s multimillion-dollar budget. "Spike was relatively upset, they came and had a meeting, and John told them he needed more money," Cory said. "And they actually gave it to him; they gave him another half-million to finish the entire series."[69]

It was not nearly enough to finish "Altruists" and "Stimpy's Pregnant", which were far from completion and not even through layout. Kricfalusi actively sought more money still from Spike TV—but discovered, quite harshly, that the rest of the entertainment world was not as eager to monetarily coddle him as Nickelodeon had been. Kricfalusi's creative empire was burning under his rule; his first reaction was denial. He became distant; for days at a time, he locked himself in his house in Canada, busying himself with revisions and animatic reel-cutting and ignoring a staff that needed him.[70] He refused to accept the consequences of his behavior as the budget frittered away.

As *Adult Party Cartoon* quickly entered reruns, Carbunkle stopped working on the series. Spumco had rung up a hefty tab with the satellite studio for the animation and timing it had done. While working on a few scenes for "Altruists", Jaques kept his animators "in the loop that the wheels were coming off, so we all saw it coming," Stainton said.[71] By August 2003, "the well of good faith had run dry"; trying to get Spumco to resolve the payment dilemma, Jaques and Armstrong were faced with a "flippant coldness that shocked us."[72]

Kricfalusi did make a "sizable" payment to Carbunkle in 2008,[73] more than five years after production stopped on *Adult Party Cartoon* and sometime after Carbunkle had stopped pursuing legal action. Ultimately, it was aesthetically foolish for Kricfalusi to cut off one of his key partners—in both the series, and in his personal filmmaking style. Big Star in Korea could not possibly give Spumco's layouts the finesse that Carbunkle bestowed upon them—and neither could Spumco.

It is staggering to compare "Naked Beach Frenzy" scenes that Jaques animation-directed with those directed by Kricfalusi. The drawing, timing, and choreography in Kricfalusi's scene of the girls fighting over Stimpy—animated by his then-girlfriend Jessica Borutski—is so stupefying in its stiffness and indirection that it plays almost like self-parody.

When Carbunkle left the show, threatening legal action, Kricfalusi went into semi-seclusion. Much of the work done at the Hollywood studio on "Altruists" and "Stimpy's Pregnant" was shipped out with no John K. sign-off, because it needed to be done and he could not be found. With "Altruists" through layout and no money left to pay anyone, all of the U. S. studio's staff was laid off by the end of August, and most of the Ottawa crew was on its way out. As the fiasco unraveled, Kricfalusi made a comment to WGN radio host Nick Digilio that sounds near-facetious in retrospect: "We're taking a bit of a break."[74]

Only a few remained in Ottawa to finish "Stimpy's Pregnant" in the last quarter of 2003. Nick Cross did most of the work in nearly every department, "just because there was no one else around to do it."[75] Greg Duffell, an old friend of Jaques, was called in to finish the film's physical timing, since no one else in Spumco's employ was capable. Duffell—a veteran animator whose resume included work for Richard Williams and Chuck Jones—had never worked with Kricfalusi before, but took an all-too-familiar view of Spumco's perplexing layout-to-animation method. As Duffell recalls, he had to "practically animate whole scenes" in the exposure sheets. He instructed the Big Star animators to mix elements from successive layouts; fearing, as Jaques had before him, that the animation would otherwise "robotically" merge from pose to pose.

Wrote Duffell: "What struck me when I was working on ['Stimpy's Pregnant'] was just how many layouts/poses there were, and the level of detail employed in each. There were intricate designs on Stimpy's apron, for instance. As an animator, I generally dislike this kind of noodling. I rarely think it gives much added value to the final cartoon, and of course it's yet another detail that has to be kept track of."[76]

This painstaking attention to every frame of film was the ultimate undoing of *Adult Party Cartoon*, both financially and critically. Kricfalusi's insistence on over-posing scenes in the layout stage went against his maxim of returning to "cartoony" cartoons; indeed, he became increasingly intent on instilling "human" acting into his characters. As Kricfalusi has noted, live-action actors do not move from pose to pose, like characters in limited animation. Rather, you can "see the change in the thought process from one expression to the other, and there's a lot of things happening in between. The more subtle and rich that is, the more the audience believes it and the more real it seems." Kricfalusi's latter-day determination never to use the same expression twice can be viewed as a means to this end—and explains why Ren might gesticulate in a half-dozen ways during a single bit of dialog. Said Kricfalusi: "You're not going to see every single drawing as you're watching in real time, but it's way more gripping story-wise."[77]

This argument is disputable, for the viewer can actually be very much aware. This is why Kricfalusi achieved consistency and range in his acting during the original *Ren & Stimpy*—and why the acting in *Adult Party Cartoon* is misguided at best, with the characters seemingly having spastic seizures. In Rod Scribner's animation for Bob Clampett in the 1940s Warner Bros. cartoons— the animation Kricfalusi champions most highly—every drawing is unique and funny, but every frame is related. Bugs Bunny's face does not take grotesque detours when his brain goes from one thought to the next. It is clear and precise, which makes the rabbit's soliloquy in *Tortoise Wins By a Hare* (1943) all the more powerful a piece of acting.

In *Adult Party Cartoon*, Kricfalusi's technique becomes ever more distracting and unpleasant as he drifts deeper into overindulgence. By filling the screen with a deluge of unexceptional actions, Kricfalusi's edicts force even the finest scenes—those with recognizable focus and point—to suffer. Witness the scene in "Stimpy's Pregnant" where Stimpy tells Ren that he is carrying his baby: the Korean animators ineptly try to hide the continuously morphing poses. While the substance of the acting is effective, Kricfalusi adds a layer of over-posing that dilutes the scene's virtues. As close as the results were—for better or worse—to Kricfalusi's aims, Big Star's effort was in vain; like Carbunkle, the Korean studio was not paid a substantial amount of money for its work on the series.

Spike TV did not see the finished two-part "Altruists" until April 2004; "Stimpy's Pregnant" arrived as one-and-a-half episodes in August, a full year after *Adult Party Cartoon* had stopped airing. A storyboard for what was to be the *Adult Party Cartoon* TV movie, "Life Sucks", is heralded by the Spumco staff to be its greatest work, chronicling Ren's and Stimpy's radically different takes on life itself. Nick Cross worked on storyboards for months with little approval by Kricfalusi before it was finally "abandoned, as the other shows ballooned in length."[78]

Empty words came from all sides for months. Executive Kevin Kay assured the press in November 2003 that there was nothing wrong with the show despite having aired only three of the promised six episodes: "[John K.] wanted to tweak it a bit more, and we probably pushed him a little fast."[79] When the network finally had all of the ordered episodes from Kricfalusi, they chose not to air them for reasons that remain uncertain. This stasis was likely Spike TV's means of declaring active disinterest in further association with Spumco.

Kricfalusi remained adamant that a second season would arise. A petition was formed to reinstate the series; staff was urged not to disperse, in case the highly improbable happened. "It wasn't a surprise to me that the show wasn't picked up," Mike Kerr said. "We had gone over budget. We had delivered some shows as two episodes, and one was even an episode and a half. After I got laid off, I applied for a producer training program in Toronto. I remember John asking me not to go: 'We'll need to write a second season soon.' I remember thinking, 'You've gotta be kidding!'"[80]

In hindsight, most of the new Spumco cartoons failed for the same reasons many at Games Animation had. Both incarnations lacked key contributors to the show's original success; the passionate energy was obliterated. The new Spumco cartoons could never be "like getting a band back together to finish what they started," as Kelly Armstrong observed.[81] Many of the original *Ren & Stimpy*'s chief architects—Bob Camp and Lynne Naylor in particular—had removed themselves far from Kricfalusi. The new *Ren & Stimpy* cartoons did not herald their creator's redemption; they became yet another half-finished endeavor in John Kricfalusi's capricious career.

In striking contrast to what he said in the past—that Spike TV told him "the gloves are off, do whatever you want"[82]—Kricfalusi now contends that he did not get "complete freedom" on *Adult Party Cartoon*. It was not his direction that brought about the revival's demise. It was that he had to "start from scratch and reinvent the wheel" with his green crew, and that ambiguous, meddlesome executives once again sabotaged the series. "From the beginning, the executives at Spike TV told me I had to make the show 'different' because it was now going to be aimed at adults. I didn't know what 'different' meant, because it was always different. There never was a set style."[83]

Such a statement might unintentionally acknowledge Nickelodeon's importance to the original series. The Spumco-Nickelodeon relationship kept the original series on track in a way that Spike and its indifference could not. By contrast, on the new show Kricfalusi had full license to let each of his artistic psychoses run rampant, and the results were disastrous.

When Kricfalusi scapegoats others, what rings most clearly in his statements is his one great flaw as a director: an overwhelming sense of irresponsibility. Kricfalusi chose to overindulge on *Adult Party Cartoon* and would not accept the consequences. He refused to commit not only to his films or his staff, but to himself. Unlike in the original series crash, this time Kricfalusi truly did lose his studio. Spumco was in financial ruin after the disaster of *Adult Party Cartoon*; and with multiple lawsuits looming, the only way to avoid further legal conflict was to close down permanently, declaring bankruptcy; hence his comment in 2006: "Spumco is no more."[84]

Coda

The animation medium has proven itself eternally and cynically cyclical. In the wake of the rapid rise and prolonged fall of *Ren & Stimpy*, the landscape has changed once again. The still-breathing veterans of the series have dispersed, taking their talent and hard-learned lessons with them to various other animation houses. The majority of Spumco alumni have healed the old wounds—without the aid or influence of John Kricfalusi.

Modern globalization and technology have put a damper on the further development of the studio system. Expedited need for faster and cheaper product has made grimly real the kinds of rates and production schedules that were once considered laughable. More and more smaller shops are being set up on all four corners of the earth to pump out new animation for television, home video, the Internet, and even theaters. The existence of the large, artistically driven studio is no longer considered necessary in the current industry, however sad that may be.

Even in this new climate, detrimental old patterns are alive and well. Before the wake of the computer age, the films of Disney Feature Animation had already become clichéd in plotting and acting, smothered by their own self-congratulatory inbreeding. Though many mourned the loss of the traditional hand-animated feature, as the computer-animated feature grew dominant, the change was almost welcome.

Predictability in the theatrical arena has not died; CG animation has been more than willing to pick up the slack. Many debates have been had over the merits of CG animation: that it lacks the soul of a drawing done by hand, and that the kind of natural acting inherent in the best of hand-drawn animation could never be captured by a computer. Apart from technique, however, there is no real difference between recent computer-animated features and the high-budget family movies that dominated the last decade of the 20th century, however heated the argument may get. Both are exceedingly plastic and charmless.

For a number of years, it seemed that the Pixar studio might have established a standard that everyone could rally around—a hope for compelling animated filmmaking in Hollywood. Their reassuring presence, early on, was certainly a silver lining in the demise of Disney features. Alas, Pixar has since fallen victim to the same traps the older studio did: a comfortable maturity that developed into formulaic repugnance. Pixar made the mistake of allowing Brad Bird artistic freedom on *The Incredibles* and *Ratatouille*; now all the subsequent

Pixar features show an inability—or unwillingness—to expand upon Bird's accomplishments. Pixar has become indistinguishable from its rivals in CG animation; there is no longer captivation in their movies, only inevitable clichés.

Television animation has been hit hardest, as anyone could have predicted. The bottom line always ruled in television; since the heyday of *Ren & Stimpy*, it has bottomed out even further. The Golden Age of television animation climaxed with *SpongeBob SquarePants*, the last well-crafted cartoon of any kind to reach a wide audience. It was also the epitome of the cartoon Nickelodeon always wanted *Ren & Stimpy* to be, but was not: a silly show that both kids and adults loved, without the burden of emotional disturbance.

As television enters the twenty-first century, the animation industry has receded back to the wasteland of the 1980s. The system established by *Ren & Stimpy*—in which directors, layout artists, and designers used the Asian animation assembly-line to push through beautiful and overdrawn characters—was bound to collapse if series creators remained unwilling to simplify things. Now programming schedules are clogged entirely with simply drawn cartoons. The magic of character layout has all but disappeared from television animation.

If animation is indeed cyclical, then we are merely passing through the current Dark Age on our way to another boom in the near future. There are hopeful signs. The animation community is far more vocal and aware than before of the increasing badness of its business. It is only a matter of time before the next crazy man transcends barriers once more. Independence is at an all-time high, with visibility unheard of in the 20th century, as more and more shorts—and even features—with singular viewpoints rise to the top.

With the rise of technology, an individual's drawings can now come to life far more easily than in the days of the assembly-line studio. John Kricfalusi has embraced this method out of necessity.

Since Spumco's permanent closure after the financial disaster of *Ren & Stimpy: Adult Party Cartoon*, Kricfalusi has done numerous short projects almost single-handedly. His raw talent is more prevalent in his works than ever before. Past collaboration under his directorship now forgone, his new cartoons are almost regressive, possessing more in common with his earliest art and *Ted Bakes One* than with anything seen in *Ren & Stimpy*.

His tenacity commendable, the man's story is far from over. After raising north of $130,000 through the crowdfunding venue Kickstarter to produce a George Liquor cartoon entitled *Cans Without Labels* in 2012, Kricfalusi promised to deliver that cartoon directly to his fanbase by February 2013. As of this writing—over four years later—*Cans Without Labels* is nowhere in sight, but an animated music video for Miley Cyrus and two opening sequences for *The Simpsons* (of all things) are complete. He has once again taken money and has not delivered, and news of a John K. studio in Miami crashed and burned almost as soon as the news was announced. Some things will never, cannot ever, and should never change.

Though it seems inconceivable that John Kricfalusi will ever create anything as important as his most cherished work of 1991-92, he owes the world nothing—as can be said of the others who were intimately involved with *Ren & Stimpy*. The impact of the show's greatest episodes is worth more than what most people in animation could achieve in several lifetimes.

What will be the next *Ren & Stimpy*, and who will make it happen? This is anyone's guess. In spite of the dominant presence of individuality, it remains doubtful that an autonomous movement will ever truly sweep the animation scene. Someone else will rise as a revolutionary leader, and be held in highest esteem by the industry, as they and their followers repeat the same mistakes that their animation forefathers made. A little insight and better planning could go a long way, as it would in the rest of civilized society. But animation, by default, is a subsection of humanity's most uniquely talented and dysfunctional. That is why we are attracted to animated cartoons to begin with. Frankly, it would not be the same medium any other way.

The Ren & Stimpy Episode Guide

NOTES ABOUT THE GUIDE:
All instances of "John K." have been expanded to Kricfalusi's full name. Animation studios listed for each episode and short are accurate, regardless of what the broadcast credits may read. "Board-only" indicates that the cartoon was shipped in the storyboard stage without going through layout at the domestic studio. The four-star to bomb rating system has been shamelessly ripped off from *Leonard Maltin's Movie Guide*.

As stated earlier in this book, the order was originally for fourteen episodes in the third season and twenty in the fourth. Delays caused four third-season episodes to be held over to "start" the fourth season. The fourth season's order was split unevenly into a fifth season to accommodate further delays. For the sake of neatness, the seasons are listed according to the Nickelodeon programming department's standards.

Episode running times are accurate. In some instances, they may not match the time-compressed DVD versions. Airdates are accurate, regardless of contradicting information on the Internet. Production numbers are provided in cases where they could be firmly established.

Programming-wise, there has never been as confusing an animated television show as *Ren & Stimpy*. In the first season, shorts/interstitials were arbitrarily paired with cartoons. Some first-season shorts/interstitials were not used when first completed; they first aired in reruns or were held over for the second season. To make matters more perplexing, there was also never a set pairing of the cartoons for the first and second seasons. The half-hour episodes as presented on the Viacom DVD sets were established as "episodes" well after the fact by Nickelodeon programming. For instance, "Out West" was paired with "Fake Dad", even though the former originally aired months before the latter.

Due to this befuddlement, the entries in this episode guide are listed not as "episodes," but as individual cartoons in chronological order. The cartoons' original airdates properly establish the chronology. Shorts/interstitials have been listed separately, the cartoons they were originally paired with noted.

It is inescapable that the programmers of a German box set, *Die Ren & Stimpy Show Uncut: Die komplette Serie*, used the first edition of this episode guide as a reference on what to restore for that 2013 release. Their attempt is noble and ambitious, but the German DVDs are still imperfect. Most—not all—of the excised scenes from the Viacom American DVDs have been reinstated, but only with a German soundtrack. (The set is bilingual otherwise.)

Originally, this guide was to have included a listing of the music cues used in each cartoon. When it became apparent how much space would be taken up by a list of no fewer than a hundred cues per cartoon, the idea was immediately scrapped. You can find the best available listing, compiled by Ian Lueck, at the following URL: **http://ren-and-stimpy-music.blogspot.com**.

This guide would not be as comprehensive—or, indeed, possible at all, were it not for Greg Method and Mike Russo. Both were loyal viewers and their recordings of the original broadcasts preserved original airdates.

KEY:

**** = Excellent
*** = Great
** = Mediocre
* = Poor
BOMB = Awful
S1&2 DVD = *The Ren & Stimpy Show UNCUT: The Complete First and Second Seasons* DVD set
S3.5 DVD = *The Ren & Stimpy Show: Seasons Three and a Half-ish* DVD set
S4&5 DVD = *The Ren & Stimpy Show: Season Five and Some More of Four* DVD set
DR&S DVD = *Die Ren & Stimpy Show Uncut: Die komplette Serie* German DVD set

BIG HOUSE BLUES ***
Production R&S 001
12/21/90 (theatrical premiere); 9/15/91 (television premiere, edited version); 8 minutes, 25 seconds (theatrical); 6 minutes, 41 seconds (television). Produced and Directed by John Kricfalusi; Story by John

Kricfalusi, Bob Camp, Jim Smith, and Lynne Naylor (uncredited); Voices: John Kricfalusi (Ren), Billy West (Stimpy), Jim Smith (Narrator, Dogcatcher), Bob Camp (Effeminate Dogcatcher), Henry Porch (Phil), Brian Chin (Jasper), Cheryl Chase (Girl), Lynne Naylor (Mom), and Pierre de Celles (Vocal FX).

The series pilot. Ren and Stimpy are homeless pals picked up by a psychotic dogcatcher. Things look good until one of their canine pals gets put to sleep. Stimpy hwarfs hairballs on Ren and saves them both from death when an obnoxious little girl mistakes the hair-draped Ren for a cute little poodle. A fine introduction to the characters and premise, and a bit more experimental than the series would be. Watch for Milt Gross's Pooch the Pup, rechristened "Jasper."

CENSORSHIP: When aired on Nickelodeon, the dogcatcher's ass wiggling while he taunts "See if I care!" was omitted, as was the entire scene of Ren making out with Stimpy and then washing his mouth out in the toilet. Oddly, the latter scene was used in the series' opening! Both scenes were restored on S1&2 DVD and Spike TV airings.

End credits:
Layout and Design by Jim Smith and Lynne Naylor
Backgrounds by Bob Camp
Animation by Lynne Naylor, Bob Jaques, Kelly Armstrong, John Kricfalusi, David Feiss, Ron Zorman, Andy Bartlett, Jim Smith, and Moose Pagan
Assistant Animation by Oliver Wade, Joseph Orantia, Jordan Reichek, Julian Chaney, Sam Fleming, Carey Yost, Garrett Ho, Jan Naylor, and Ken Davis
FX by Joe Gilliand
Titles by Libby Simon
Vocal Effects by Bob Camp

Ink and Paint by Bardel

Brush Inking by Marie Haws, Barry Ward, Bill Schwartz, Garry Lambeth, Andrew Glavina, Delia Tokevich, and Young Hee Ahn; Painted by Ted Ayn, Julia Bachlor, Andre J. Brakavieck, Dave Fox, Donny Fuller, Steve MacVittie, Andy Rye, Lyra Riley, Chris Templeman, Leah Waldron, Steve Woodly, and Teresa Foley

Final Checking by Steve Meyers, Jamie Jones, Greg Zbitnew, and Gary Lambeth

Camera by Al Sens Animation Ltd.

Production Team: Henry Porch, Barry Ward, Delna Bhesania, Athena De Celles, and Monica Luciani

Voice Talent by John Kricfalusi, Jim Smith, Cheryl Hudock, and Billy West

Editing by Steve Nafshun and John Bushelman

Sound mix by Irv Nafshun

Executive Producer for Nickelodeon: Vanessa Coffey

Featuring the Big Beat of Die Screamin' Lederhosen with Guitar by Jiminy "Jelly Roel" Smith, Bass by Rocco "T-Bone" Reccardi, and Skins by Scot "Blind Lemon" Huml Recorded at Foothill Studios

Engineering by Charlie Brissette

Screams and Cackles by Pierre De Calles

FIRST SEASON:
STIMPY'S BIG DAY ***
Production RS 01B

8/11/91; 10 minutes; Directed by John Kricfalusi; Story by John Kricfalusi and Vincent Waller; Storyboard by Jim Smith, John Kricfalusi, and Vincent Waller; Animation by Lacewood; Voices: John Kricfalusi (Ren, Mr. Horse), Billy West (Stimpy, various announcers), Harris Peet (Muddy Mudskipper), Cheryl Chase (Pool babes), Darrin Sargent (a TV Announcer), Jim Smith (a TV Announcer), and Vincent Waller (Pillow).

Ren berates Stimpy for wasting time watching *The Muddy Mudskipper Show* and entering a poetry-writing contest for Gritty Kitty Litter, the sponsor of said cartoon show. Ren changes his tune when Stimpy wins the contest's $47 million dollar prize and an appearance on Muddy's show! Stimpy leaves for Hollywood, leaving Ren tearful in his absence. Followed in the same episode by *The Big Shot!*

THE BIG SHOT! ***
Production RS 01B

8/11/91; 8 minutes, 3 seconds; Directed by John Kricfalusi; Story by John Kricfalusi and Vincent Waller (both uncredited); Storyboard by Jim Smith, John Kricfalusi, and Vincent Waller (all uncredited); Animation by Lacewood.

Continued from *Stimpy's Big Day*. As Stimpy becomes an overnight celebrity, Ren becomes a deranged shut-in. Eventually, the fame is too much for Stimpy and he returns to his buddy—after giving away all of the money, of course. An entertaining start to the series, this two-part episode makes us want to see and learn more about these characters. First appearance of Mr. Horse.

STIMPY'S STORYBOOK LAND: ROBIN HÖEK *½
Production RS 02A
8/25/91; 9 minutes, 42 seconds; Directed by John Kricfalusi; Story by John Kricfalusi and Bob Camp; Animation by Bonart Co.; Voices: John Kricfalusi (Ren), Billy West (Stimpy), Harris Peet (George Liquor), and Henry Porch (Eyeballs).

Stimpy reads himself the story of Robin Höek, with Ren playing the title character, George Liquor as the Sheriff of Dodge City, and Stimpy as everyone else, including the lovely Maid Moron. Ren is horrified that the story was not just a dream and that he really has married Maid Moron.

NURSE STIMPY *
Production RS 02B
8/25/91; 8 minutes, 52 seconds; Directed by John Kricfalusi (credited as "Raymond Spum"); Story by John Kricfalusi and Bob Camp; Storyboard by Chris Reccardi; Animation by Lacewood; Board-only; Voices: John Kricfalusi (Ren) and Billy West (Stimpy).

Stimpy finds Ren deathly ill one morning and "solemnly swear(s) by the sacred bedpan" to cure his ailment. After months of humiliating treatment (including a photo of Ren's sponge bath landing on the front page of the local paper), Ren is cured—but now Stimpy is sick! Ren dons a nurse's outfit, laughing maniacally: "Now eet's *my* turn!" A cornucopia of the famous graphic, gross held close-ups that became a staple of the series. Unfortunately, the cartoon generates more gagging than laughs.

SPACE MADNESS ****
Production RS 03A
9/8/91; 11 minutes; Directed by John Kricfalusi; Story by John Kricfalusi and Jim Gomez; Art Direction by Jim Smith; Animation

Directed by Bob Jaques; Storyboard by Jim Smith and Chris Reccardi; Color Styling by Bill Wray; Animation by Carbunkle Cartoons; Voices: John Kricfalusi (Ren) and Billy West (Stimpy, the Salesman).

Ren and Stimpy sit down to watch the cat's favorite "live- action drama": *Commander Höek and Cadet Stimpy*! On a thirty-six-year mission, Hoëk succumbs to the dreaded space madness. Squeeze-tube food and a relaxing hot bath will not hold off the madness for long, as Hoëk quickly becomes emotionally attached to his beloved "ice cream bar"—in reality, a bar of soap. "It is not I who am crazy—it is I who am mad!" After Stimpy subdues the deranged Chihuahua, Höek thinks it is his faithful companion who has gone insane, so puts him in charge of guarding the History Eraser Button. The show's announcer successfully goads Stimpy into pushing it ("Will he hold out, folks? Can he hold out?" "No, I can't!!!"). Höek, Stimpy, and the narrator are immediately zapped from existence—as is the *Ren & Stimpy* logo. The first true classic R&S cartoon, with powerful acting that caused people to take notice. Future Commander Höek and Cadet Stimpy shorts would not be nearly as good.

THE BOY WHO CRIED RAT! ***
Production RS 03B
9/8/91; 9 minutes, 21 seconds; Directed by John Kricfalusi; Story by Vincent Waller and John Kricfalusi; Storyboard by Vincent Waller; Animation by Lacewood; Voices: John Kricfalusi (Ren), Billy West (Stimpy, Mr. Pipe), Cheryl Chase (Mrs. Pipe), and Harris Peet (George Liquor).

Vagrants Ren and Stimpy are up to another get-rich-quick scheme. Ren poses as a mouse in Mr. and Mrs. Pipe's house ("Squeak! Squeak! Squeak, I tell you, squeak!"), and Stimpy gets paid five bucks to "chase" him. Things go smoothly until Stimpy is ordered to eat Ren! After enduring Stimpy's teeth and gums, Ren reveals himself as a charlatan—but they cannot pay back the money because Stimpy ate it.

EPISODE GUIDE

STIMPY'S STORYBOOK LAND: THE LITTLEST GIANT *
Production RS 04A
9/15/91; 9 minutes, 56 seconds; Directed by John Kricfalusi (end credit); Story by John Kricfalusi and Bob Camp; Storyboard by Vincent Waller and Bob Camp; Animation by Bonart Co.; Voices: John Kricfalusi (Ren) and Billy West (Stimpy, Giants).

Stimpy reads himself the story of *The Littlest Giant* (Stimpy), who is scorned by his fellow giants for his dwarfish height. He finds acceptance and friendship with a lowly farmer (Ren), who uses the giant's tears to water his crops and feed his livestock. A poor entry that is really a run-of-the-mill Saturday morning cartoon with a Spumco gloss.

FIRE DOGS ***
Production RS 04B
9/29/91; 9 minutes, 16 seconds; Directed by John Kricfalusi; Written by John Kricfalusi; Storyboard by Jim Smith and Chris Reccardi; Animation by Lacewood, Carbunkle Cartoons, and Fil-Cartoons; Voices: John Kricfalusi (Ren, Mr. Horse, Fat Lady), Billy West (Stimpy), Harris Peet (Fire Chief), and Cheryl Chase (Baby).

Out of work and luck, Ren and Stimpy paint themselves with Dalmatian Paint so they can apply to work as firedogs for the psychotic Fire Chief, in his first appearance ("I've had it up to here with the likes of *you*... oh, I'm sorry. I thought you were a circus midget!"). Almost immediately, duty calls, with a raging fire at a downtown apartment building. Fat Lady—also making her debut—drops her loved ones from the top floor of the building for the duo to catch: a giant baby, her horse (as in Mr.), a walrus, and an elephant (at this point Ren throws away the net). Ren is shot up in the ladder to save Fat Lady. The height proves too much for him and he faints. Fat Lady takes Ren in her mouth, and her behemoth ass causes the ladder to break and fall. The force of the crash dismantles several other buildings and destroys the fire truck. Stimpy puts out the fire via helicopter with a load of Gritty Kitty Litter. Fire Chief awards Ren and Stimpy the sacred golden firehydrant helmets. The dogs line up to use the hydrants, as does Fat Lady.

MAROONED   BOMB
Production RS 05A
10/06/91; 11 minutes; Directed by John Kricfalusi; Story by John Kricfalusi; Art Direction and Storyboard by Chris Reccardi; Animation by Bonart Co.; Voices: John Kricfalusi (Ren), Billy West (Stimpy), and Cheryl Chase (Sexy chihuahua).

In another episode of *Commander Höek and Cadet Stimpy*, the two crash-land on a strange planet, unable to signal for help ("We're marooned!" "Just like the title of this cartoon!"). They try to rough it by following Stimpy's handbook, only to eventually be eaten by a space alien. When attacked by microorganisms inside the beast, they consult the handbook one last time: "It says—we're doomed!" Some of the series' most glacial timing kills what might have been a reasonably funny picture.

A CARTOON (a.k.a. UNTAMED WORLD)   ***½
Production RS 05B
11/10/91; 9 minutes, 37 seconds; Directed by John Kricfalusi; Story by Jim Smith, John Kricfalusi, and Bob Camp (uncredited); Storyboard by Jim Smith; Animation by Lacewood; Voices: John Kricfalusi (Ren), Billy West (Stimpy, Seagull), and Harris Peet (Stimpy turtle).

Marlon Höek is the host of the show *Untamed World*, where he and his assistant Stimpy explore the world of "organisms." In this episode, the team travels to the Galapagos Island to observe the traits of creatures—all bearing resemblance to Ren and Stimpy! The Giant

Soft-Shelled Stimpy lays its eggs in the sand and the hatchlings make their way to the water by instinct. Things look bad for one of the little guys when a ferocious seagull spots him, but it turns out the gull is just bumming for spare change. The Blind Albino Cave Höek uses its tongue to slap its prey to death. The Croco-Stimpy species ride a school bus, all spouting their haunting call: "Happy, happy! Joy, joy!" Ren and Stimpy are in hot pursuit of the Speckle-Throated Burrowing Five-Toed Yak until Stimpy uses the tranquilizer on Ren—and tags his ear! As the show closes, Ren gets his revenge by tagging the cat's tongue. Succeeds as both a great parody of the Tex Avery travelogue/spot-gag films and as a funny picture in its own right.

BLACK HOLE **

Production RS 06A

2/23/92; 8 minutes, 22 seconds; Directed by John Kricfalusi and Bob Camp (both uncredited); Story by Bob Camp and Will McRobb; Storyboard by Bob Camp; Animation by Bonart Co.; Voices: John Kricfalusi (Ren), Billy West (Stimpy), and Harris Peet (George Liquor, Bus driver).

Commander Höek and Cadet Stimpy are sucked into a black hole. The Commander is ecstatic upon their arrival to this new universe, simply for the sheer fact that they survived. But strange things begin to happen, with the two morphing into other beings at random. The pair discovers a mountainous pile of stinky gym socks: this is where all the missing left socks in the universe end up! Stimpy discovers that if they do not get to the Trans-Dimensional Gateway by three o'clock, they will be stuck in this wasteland forever. Mutating even further along the way, they make it to the bus stop in time—only to be booted off for not having exact change! With our heroes' doom inevitable, Stimpy sets their molecules to implode. Before their demise, however, Stimpy discovers he had the change the whole time.

STIMPY'S INVENTION ****

Production RS 06B

2/23/92; 12 minutes, 22 seconds; Directed by John Kricfalusi; Story by John Kricfalusi and Bob Camp; Storyboard by Bob Camp (uncredited); Animation Directed by Bob Jaques; Animation by Carbunkle Cartoons; Additional Animation by Mark Kausler, Steve Markowski, and Julian Chaney (all uncredited); Voices: John Kricfalusi (Ren, Stinky Whizzleteats) and Billy West (Stimpy).

Ren reluctantly agrees to help Stimpy try out his new inventions. They are useless in the extreme: the Cheese-O-Phone, which only splatters melted cheese; the Remote-Control Shaver, which butchers Ren; and the Sta-Put Socks that never fall down—because they are full of glue! Furious Ren attempts to kill Stimpy for this, so the feline vows to save Ren from unhappiness using his gift of invention. After many grueling hours, Stimpy perfects the Happy Helmet, which he lodges onto Ren's head ("Now you'll always be happy!"). Stimpy revs it up with the remote control, causing Ren to fight for control of his meanness. ("Will... strong... body... weak!") It proves too much; Ren is possessed by the invention and he becomes psychotically cheerful ("Steempy!! I'm so—*happy*!!! I–must–go–*do–nice–things*!"). The now-deranged Ren does everything with a smile, including ironing Stimpy's drawers and cleaning his filthy cat box! While Stimpy is out, Ren begins to fight the machine; then he attempts to strangle his returning buddy, but not before Stimpy gives him an extra dose of happiness. In celebration of Ren's newfound bliss, Stimpy puts on a record of his favorite song: "The Happy Happy Joy Joy Song," performed by Stinky Whizzleteats. Still resisting, Ren takes advantage of this distraction by dancing into the kitchen so he can bash the helmet (and his skull) to pieces with a hammer. Stimpy, not knowing that Ren has freed himself from the Happy Helmet, makes his ass cheeks join in the dance, too. Ren returns and begins strangling the life out of Stimpy; but by doing so, he learns that his true happiness comes from being angry. Ren thanks Stimpy for his help, leaving the feline bewildered. This episode is considered by many to be Spumco's finest hour.

SHORTS:
ASK DR. STUPID: One Hump or Two?
Production RS 05S
54 seconds; Storyboard by Bob Camp (originally aired before "A Cartoon")

ASK DR. STUPID: Why School?
Production RS 04S
58 seconds; Storyboard by Bob Camp (originally aired before "Fire Dogs")

ASK DR. STUPID: Where Have You Bean?
Production RS 06S
1 minute, 1 second; Storyboard by Bob Camp; Animation by Bon-Art Co. (originally unused in first season; aired with "Ren's Toothache")

LOG
Production RS 01C
1 minute, 17 seconds; Storyboard by Bob Camp; Animated by Bob Jaques and Kelly Armstrong (originally aired before "Stimpy's Big Day")

LOG FOR GIRLS
Production RS 04C
1 minute, 4 seconds; Storyboard by Jim Smith (originally aired after "The Littlest Giant")

LOG: High Fashion Log for Girls
1 minute, 12 seconds (originally aired after "Black Hole")

MY LITTLE BROTHER DOLL
48 seconds (originally aired after "Marooned")

POWDERED TOAST MAN
Production RS 02C
1 minute, 16 seconds; Animated by Dave Feiss, layout by Kelly Armstrong (originally aired before "Robin Höek")

SECRET OATH
Production RS 02S
1 minute; Storyboard by Vincent Waller (originally aired before "Nurse Stimpy")

STIMPY'S BREAKFAST TIPS
Production RS 01S
1 minute, 28 seconds; Storyboard by Bob Camp; Animation by Carbunkle Cartoons and Fil-Cartoons (originally aired before "The Big Shot!")

SUGAR FROSTED MILK
1 minute, 10 seconds; Storyboard by Jim Smith (produced for first season, unused until second with "Ren's Toothache")

WHAT'LL WE DO 'TILL THEN?: Chase Your Tail
43 seconds (originally aired after the episode with "Fire Dogs" and "The Littlest Giant")

WHAT'LL WE DO 'TILL THEN?: Gritty Kitty
1 minute, 4 seconds; Storyboard by Jim Smith (originally aired after "The Big Shot!")

WHAT'LL WE DO 'TILL THEN?: Magic Nose Goblins
1 minute, 4 seconds; Storyboard by Vincent Waller (originally aired after "Nurse Stimpy")

WHAT'LL WE DO 'TILL THEN?: Croco-Stimpy
29 seconds; Storyboard by Jim Smith (originally aired after "A Cartoon")

YAK SHAVING DAY
Production RS 03S
1 minute, 36 seconds; Storyboard by Jim Gomez (originally aired after "The Boy Who Cried Rat!")

SECOND SEASON:

IN THE ARMY **½
Production RS5-2B
8/15/92; 11 minutes, 2 seconds; Written and Directed by Bob Camp; Animation by Rough Draft; Voices: John Kricfalusi (Ren), Billy West (Stimpy), and Bob Camp (Sarge).

Ren and Stimpy are at the U.S. Army Induction Center—and are hiding their shame, fearful of the other nude recruits! After getting shaved heads and obscenely painful inoculations, the two meet their larger-than-life drill sergeant, who first tongue-lashes Ren for not falling in line properly. Subjected to further harm and K.P. duty throughout the cartoon, Ren is driven to the brink of insanity. He tries to escape, with Stimpy in tow—but they run into the Sarge, who informs them that they have graduated to Tank Paratroopers. Proudly singing the national anthem, the duo drops from the sky in a flaming tank and lands on a battlefield.

CENSORSHIP: **Spike TV removed most of Ren and Stimpy's physical.**

POWDERED TOAST MAN **½
Production RS5-1B
8/15/92 (original version); 10 minutes, 58 seconds; Directed by John Kricfalusi; Story by Richard Pursel and John Kricfalusi; Storyboards by Jim Smith and Bill Wray; Starring Gary Owens as Powdered Toast Man; Frank Zappa as The Pope; Animation by Rough Draft; Voices: John Kricfalusi (Ren), Billy West (Stimpy), Jim Smith (President), and Cheryl Chase (Assistant).

2/13/93 (edited version); 10 minutes, 51 seconds; Directed by John Kricfalusi; Story by Richard Pursel and John Kricfalusi; Storyboards by Jim Smith and Bill Wray; Starring Gary Owens as Powdered Toast

Man; Frank Zappa as The Funny Little Guy With the Pointy Hat.

The first cartoon to star Powdered Toast Man. P.T. works a day job as a government clerk under the secret identity of Pastor Toast Man. His lovely Catholic Schoolgirl assistant informs him of an urgent message coming through on his Toastamatron Communicator. P.T. flies off (backwards) to do his superhero duties: saving a kitten from getting hit by a truck (harming dozens of other people in the process), rescuing the pope from the clutches of Muddy Mudskipper, replenishing (and farting on) Ren and Stimpy's supply of Powdered Toast, and getting the President's zipper unstuck. The President is left indisposed after this, so P.T. is left in charge. We end with P.T. in the oval office burning the Bill of Rights and United States Constitution to keep warm.

CENSORSHIP: **The burning of the "dusty old papers" was omitted after its original airing, though restored on the S1&2 DVD.**

REN'S TOOTHACHE **½
Production RS5-2A
8/22/92; 11 minutes; Directed by John Kricfalusi; Story by Bob Camp and John Kricfalusi; Storyboards by Chris Reccardi; Animation by Rough Draft; Voices: John Kricfalusi (Ren), Billy West (Stimpy, Flies, Old Man Hunger), and Vincent Waller (Beaver).

Ren's poor dental hygiene gives him shooting pains. Stimpy tells him the story of the tooth beaver, a creature that lives in your mouth and feeds on your teeth's nerve endings. Ren still avoids brushing his teeth. As a result, his teeth chip away completely, leaving only the nerve endings. His mouth becomes such a biohazard that his tooth beaver leaves, and the smell disgusts even the flies feeding on Stimpy's litter. Stimpy tries to cheer Ren up, telling him that if he leaves his nerve endings under his pillow, the Nerve Ending Fairy (Old Man Hunger) will take them and leave hundred dollar bills! The fairy does indeed come, but leaves Ren only a ball of lint. Brokenhearted, Ren sits down for breakfast, where Stimpy gives him his birthday present—a giant tooth, which Ren immediately drives into his gums. Stimpy winks, showing us that it was his tooth.

    CENSORSHIP: **Stimpy's jars of spit were removed on the S1&2 DVD. Reinstated on the DR&S DVD.**

MAN'S BEST FRIEND ****
Production RS5-1A

Unaired; 11 minutes, 2 seconds; Directed by John Kricfalusi; Story by Vincent Waller and John Kricfalusi; Storyboards by Chris Reccardi; Animation Directed by Bob Jaques (uncredited); Animation by Carbunkle Cartoons; Voices: John Kricfalusi (Ren, goldfish), Billy West (Stimpy), and Mike Pataki (George Liquor).

    We are introduced to the psychotic George Liquor (American!), who contemplates purchasing some "lower life forms" at the pet shop—namely Ren and Stimpy. At Liquor's home, Ren and Stimpy are shoved into a goldfish bowl (after the goldfish is dumped out and steals the car) and later woken up at the crack of dawn by Drill Sergeant Liquor for their training. The first task is to get housebroken ("Drop, and give me twenty!"), at which Ren fails when he cannot defecate on cue. Stimpy succeeds immediately and is given a "Lawn Cigar Doggie Treat," which he holds in his mouth, dancing gleefully. Their next lesson is to learn discipline by misbehaving. George shouts dementedly at both of them to sit on his forbidden couch. Only Stimpy obeys. He is hollered at for misbehaving, but then rewarded ("It's discipline that begets love!"), much to his bewilderment. George chastises Ren for not following orders and gives him twenty bucks for being a softie (and twenty more for talking back!). Next, wearing a padded foam suit, George informs the duo that their next lesson is learning to protect their master. "Now in order to protect—you must learn to *attack*," shouts George, urging the two to attack him. Stimpy cannot bring himself to harm his "kind and beloved master," but Ren sure can, immediately grabbing a "Prize Bludgeoning Oar" and proceeding to beat the living hell out of Liquor. George escapes his foam suit and the pool of his own drool and blood, grabbing Ren by the skull, looking positively demented. "You... are a *true champion!*" shouts George. Liquor rewards Ren, Stimpy, and himself with Lawn Cigars, and now all three proceed to dance gleefully with the faux turds in their mouths. Easily one of the most wonderful and insane cartoons of the series, "Man's Best Friend" was put on the shelf due to excessive violence and the final strike that caused Nickelodeon to remove the show from Spumco. It later aired on Spike TV.

OUT WEST * ½**
Production RS5-4B
8/29/92 (original version); 2/27/93 (edited version); 10 minutes, 45 seconds (original version); 10 minutes, 42 seconds (edited version); Directed by Bob Camp; Written by Bob Camp and John Kricfalusi; Storyboard by Bob Camp; Animation Direction by Bob Jaques; Animation by Carbunkle Cartoons; Voices: John Kricfalusi (Ren, Mr. Horse), Billy West (Stimpy, narrator), Jim Smith (Abner), Bob Camp (Ewalt), and Henry Porch (additional singing voices).

The ignorant Sheriff Abner Dimwit and his deputy, Ewalt Nitwit, are bored stiff because there is nobody in town left to hang. They post an advertisement for villains so they can "hang someone who actually deserves it." Enter Three Fingered Höek and Stupid the Kid riding on their chickens, eager to find work pillaging and looting. They answer the ad and are urged by Abner to steal his horse. They instead steal his obese wife—a burden Abner is eager to be rid of. Later, Ren and Stimpy jump onto Mr. Horse (who reminds Stimpy of Ren's Uncle Eddie, "cause he's big and stinky!") in an attempt at thievery. Horse nonchalantly moseys over to Abner and Ewalt to report that he has been stolen, getting the two morons excited that they can finally hang some villains. At the gallows, Ren confesses to Stimpy that he's been secretly using Stimpy's tongue to polish his boots at night. ("That's okay, Ren! I wasn't really asleep!") Ewalt realizes that they can't hang the two desperados because "the scrawny one don't weigh enough, and the fat one ain't got no neck!" Abner and Ewalt resolve that they will have to hang each other, which they do in pure bliss. The cartoon ends with the four having a hoedown, singing "The Hanging Song."

CENSORSHIP: When originally aired, the cartoon was edited to remove Abner and Ewalt actually putting the nooses around each other's necks (as well as deleting Ewalt's final line, "Y'all bring the kids next time, ya hear!"). Still censored on all DVD releases as well.

RUBBER NIPPLE SALESMEN ***½
Production RS5-4A
8/29/92; 9 minutes, 15 seconds; Directed by Vincent Waller and John Kricfalusi; Written by Vincent Waller and John Kricfalusi; Storyboards by Vincent Waller; Animation by Rough Draft; Additional Animation by Greg Manwaring (uncredited); Voices: John Kricfalusi (Ren, Mr. Horse), Billy West (Stimpy, Mr. Pipe), Cheryl Chase (Mrs. Pipe), and Harris Peet (Fire Chief).

Ren and Stimpy are rubber nipple salesmen (with a rubber nipple ice cream-type truck, even). Stimpy is offended by the fact that greedy Ren is only in the business for the money. Tearfully, Stimpy exclaims, "I have a dream… that one day, everyone, everywhere, will know the wonders of my nipples!" Ren socks him with an iron and retorts: "Fine, you keep your dream, and I'll keep the money!" Attempts to sell to deranged citizens Fire Chief and Mr. Horse (who apparently made a "mistake") are unsuccessful. Ren and Stimpy make their quota of five bucks at Mr. and Mrs. Pipe's house, where they are immediately kicked out. They land on two bulls and ride off into the sunset, in a tribute to the ending of many a *Three Stooges* short.

SVËN HÖEK ****
Production RS5-3A
11/7/92; 16 minutes, 9 seconds (original version); 15 minutes, 27 seconds (Nickelodeon version); Dirëcted by Jøhn Kricfalusi; Writtën by Bøb Camp and Jøhn Kricfalusi; Størybøard bÿ Jim Smith and Bill Wray; Backgrøund Cølør Dësign by Bill Wray; Änimation Dirëcted by Bøb Jaques; Animation by Carbunkle Cartoons; Voices: John Kricfalusi (Ren), Billy West (Stimpy, Svën), and Mike Pataki (Devil/George Liquor).

Ren is sitting stone-faced while Stimpy drools moronically. "You're an eediot. I am so sick of your stupidity." Ren is expecting a visit from Svën, his cousin from Yugoslavia, and can hardly wait to spend time with another intellectual. Meanwhile, Stimpy hurries for an important appointment to get kicked in the head by a horse. Before Ren can bludgeon the idiot, Svën arrives. Apart from being a Chihuahua, he is otherwise an exact duplicate of Stimpy. Ren shrugs and leaves Stimpy to help Svën unpack. Svën shares his jar of spit and ball of Band-Aids with his new friend; then Svën and Stimpy compare the sizes of their pea brains. When Ren returns with refreshments, he is mortified to find them both sporting inflated rubber gloves on their heads. "We're lodge brothers! We both belong to the Loyal Order of Stupids!" The next morning, Ren leaves for work, warning the two not do anything "stupeed" while he is gone. They play a game of "seek and hide" that ends in a private moment in Stimpy's litter box. The two then decide to play the board game "Don't Whiz on the Electric Fence" (we never do find out how the hell this game is played). Ren comes home in a fit of rage over the mess the two "eediots" have made. "My collection of rare, incurable diseases! Violated!" In a fit of sheer psychotic fury—

expertly acted and animated unlike anything ever seen before—Ren corners Stimpy and Svën. He describes in graphic detail how he is going to punish them. "I'm gonna hit ya, and you're gonna fall... and I'm gonna look down, and I'm gonna laugh." But first Ren has to whiz. He decides to begin the torture by pissing on their "favorite game, in the whole world..." The whole house explodes, leaving a smoking crater. In Hell, the trio meets Satan (really George Liquor). "So, you whizzed on the electric fence, didn't ya?" Words are not enough to describe the greatness of this miracle.

CENSORSHIP: Extensive scene—set behind closed doors—of Svën and Stimpy playing in the litterbox was removed. Ren's comment about gouging Stimpy's and Svën's eyes out (referencing Jeffrey Dahmer) was censored whenever it aired. Both scenes were restored on the S1&2 DVD set along with the "original" soundtrack.

HAUNTED HOUSE **½
Production RS5-6A
11/21/92; 9 minutes, 4 seconds; Directed by Ron Hughart; Written by John Kricfalusi, Bob Camp, Jim Smith, and Richard Pursel; Storyboard by Jim Smith, Richard Pursel, and Bob Camp; Background Color Design by Bill Wray; Animation by Color Key Studios; Voices: John Kricfalusi (Ren), Billy West (Stimpy, Ghost), and Rudolph Porter (fat naked black guy).

Ren and Stimpy arrive at a creepy old house. "Look Ren, this looks like a great place to kill twelve minutes!" A diminutive ghost (echoing Tex Avery's Droopy) decides to try and scare the daylights out of them. He fails at every possible turn, in the process getting beaten by a yak and used as a towel to dry Stimpy's crotch. "It's a good thing I'm already dead." Realizing he is a failure, the ghost decides to end it all by nailing himself in the forehead; Stimpy recommends poison instead. The ghost dies and becomes a mortal fat, naked black man—

leaving the house and our bewildered heroes. Originally written as "Hi-Spirits," a shelved episode of *Tiny Toon Adventures*.

CENSORSHIP: **The ghost's failed attempt at scaring the duo with a severed head was removed on the S1&2 DVD. Still missing on the DR&S DVD.**

MAD DOG HÖEK ***½
Production RS5-6B
11/21/92; 11 minutes; Directed by Bob Camp; Story by Bob Camp; Background Color Design by Bill Wray; Animation by Rough Draft; Voices: John Kricfalusi (Ren), Billy West (Stimpy, Announcer), and Bob Camp (Lump and Loaf).

The battle of the century between Lump and Loaf Lout and Mad Dog Höek (Ren) and Killer Kadoogan (Stimpy)! When Stimpy expresses worry about getting hurt, Ren reassures him that the wrestling match is rigged and that nobody really gets hurt. After Ren is roughed up, Stimpy joins in. "Hi, Mr. Loaf! My name is Stimpy, and I've come to play with you!" The cat is chewed and blown like a piece of gum by Loaf. Then Stimpy is subjected to Lump's flying butt pliers, while Ren gets his neck broken by a wrench. Loaf checks his watch and reminds his brother that it is time to throw the fight. Both feign defeat and Ren and Stimpy are announced as the winners. The Louts are "sore" and threaten our heroes with the empty violence so typical of wrestling matches: "We know where you live! We know where your parents live!" Ren is asked for a retort, but Stimpy shoves him aside, saying that he wants to "holler the loud funny words!" Stimpy then proceeds to throw a completely deranged fit over how he thinks the Louts are nice guys—losing his tongue in the process.

BIG BABY SCAM ***
Production RS5-9B

12/12/92 (original version); 4/30/94 (edited version); 10 minutes, 39 seconds (original version); 9 minutes, 48 seconds (edited version); 9 minutes, 50 seconds (home video version); Directed by Vincent Waller; Written by Vincent Waller; Storyboard by Vincent Waller; Animation by Rough Draft; Board-only; Voices: John Kricfalusi (Ren), Billy West (Stimpy, Mr. Pipe, Cop), Cheryl Chase (Mrs. Pipe), and Harris Peet (Baby).

While sitting in a tree, eating its bark, Ren and Stimpy spy two human babies in Mr. and Mrs. Pipe's house. Ren tells Stimpy about how infants have the easy life. "Why, I hear tell... that they don't even have to wipe themselves!" He quickly hatches a brilliant idea: pay the tykes fifty bucks to drop the act and skip town. The babies, Eugene and Shawn, immediately accept, adopting gravelly voices, donning porkpie hats and grabbing their suitcases. Ren finds out that baby life is not what it's cracked up to be—with diaper-filling competitions, painful hugs, and family baths. Later, a police officer arrives at the house with the two real babies, who were hanging around at the racetrack. Angry that their cover is blown, Ren demands his fifty back. Eugene and Shawn are happy to oblige by holding Ren tight and giving him fifty punches to the chest.

CENSORSHIP: Much of Mr. Pipe and Ren's hug was removed on the S1&2 DVD, as was Old Man Hunger's whistling. The family bath scene was edited out in certain airings and on VHS. Some pressings of the DR&S DVD restore both scenes, while others are still censored.

DOG SHOW ***
Production RS5-3B
12/12/92; 11 minutes; Directed by Chris Reccardi and John Kricfalusi; Storyboards by Chris Reccardi; Written by Richard Pursel; Animation by Rough Draft; Voices: John Kricfalusi (Ren, Fat Lady), Billy West

(Stimpy, Salesman), Mike Pataki (George Liquor), and Harris Peet (Poodle).

At the All-Breed Dog Show, George Liquor presents his prize show dogs, Champy (Ren) and Rex (Stimpy), ignoring the latter's confession that he is a cat. The pre-judging starts, and Mr. Horse mercilessly feeds the rejects to a ferocious bulldog. Ren makes it to the finals, but Stimpy is rejected—until George berates Horse ("Take a closer look, ya moron!") and reduces him to tears. During the final judging, Stimpy is disqualified for an ingrown dewclaw. Irate, George tries to force Ren to win ("Make my dreams come true!"), but the Chihuahua mouths off and tells him to go up there and get that trophy himself—which George does! The Royal American George-Hound is carried off with his trophy by the cheering crowd, while Ren and Stimpy watch in tearful "joy!"

CENSORSHIP: **Mutilated when aired on television and on the Time-Life DVD set, removing all references to George Liquor's last name and airbrushing out his hemorrhoid. Restored on the S1&2 DVD.**

SON OF STIMPY ***
Production RS5-8
1/14/93 (original version); 12/11/93 (edited version); 21 minutes, 40 seconds (original version); 21 minutes (edited version); Directed by John Kricfalusi; Written by John Kricfalusi, Vincent Waller, and Rich Pursel; Storyboard by Peter Avanzino; Background Color Design by Bill Wray; Animation Directed by Bob Jaques; Animation by Carbunkle Cartoons; Voices: John Kricfalusi (Ren) and Billy West (Stimpy, Stinky).

Stimpy is watching cartoons when he feels a rumbling sensation come from his ass—a fart. He eagerly tells Ren what happened. Ren dismisses it as a stinky fantasy. "Something came out of my butt! It made a sound... and it smelt funny!" "You're an eediot." Stimpy is determined to find his fart, whom he has christened Stinky. He is unable to locate his "child," receives no help from his magic nose goblins, and enters a comatose state. Nothing Ren tries will cheer him up. Months pass by. It is now Christmastime and Stimpy still has not found Stinky. When Ren points out that they are standing under the mistletoe, Stimpy snaps ("*That's* all you can think of?!") and goes to search for his "child" in the city. Stimpy tries his hardest (even making a failed attempt to describe Stinky to the police), freezing his feet and fingers numb, but still no Stinky. We see nearby that Stinky has his own hardships and has to avoid being "lit" by a couple of hoboes. Meanwhile, back home Ren tearfully misses his pal. Alas, when Stimpy finally returns—encrusted in a block of ice—it is without Stinky. While Stimpy thaws out, Ren answers the door for a visitor... Stinky! Stinky has come back not to stay with Stimpy, but to announce to "dad" that he is now a man and has found a fiancé: Cora, a dead fish skeleton. Stimpy performs the marriage ceremony and the two newlyweds move into Ren's nostrils. "I just love a happy ending!"

CENSORSHIP: **Re-airings and the VHS tape removed the sequence of Stimpy going to the police to report Stinky missing. The Spike TV version (also used on S1&2 DVD) removes much of the montage of Stimpy awake in bed, and the scene of Ren putting Stimpy's Christmas present next to Stimpy's photo: "Here's your Christmas present, Stimpy. I hope you like it. Wherever you are." Uncut on the DR&S DVD.**

MONKEY SEE, MONKEY DON'T! ******
Production RS5-13A
2/13/93; 11 minutes; Direction by Bob Camp; Starring Filthy; Story by Bob Camp and Vincent Waller; Storyboard by Bob Camp; Background Color Styling by Bill Wray; Animation by Rough Draft; Voices: Billy West (all voices).

The ever-hungry Ren and Stimpy are at the zoo, spying on a fat little boy who feeds the animals heaping helpings of food. Ren gets the idea to pose in monkey suits to make the Swedish zookeeper take them in. Their scam is off to a great start when they meet their cage-mate Filthy (a real monkey), who welcomes Ren by vomiting into Ren's outstretched hand. The duo's attempt at swinging falls flat (literally). Ren is force-fed the ticks off Filthy's back. While zoo guests feed Filthy a banquet, Stimpy gets nutshells and pre-chewed gum—and Ren gets a rock (which he heaves back at the kid). Ren and Stimpy are visited by the Swede, whose offer of monkey chow ("braised fish heads und rotten fruit!") proves too much for Ren, causing him to remove his disguise and demand a transfer. Says the Swede: "Next time I raise pigs, by yolly!" The duo is then transferred to another part of the zoo, where Stimpy plays a hippo and Ren his back-riding bird buddy. This episode has the first instance in the series of Billy West voicing both Ren and Stimpy in a standard-length cartoon.

FAKE DAD ***
Production RS5-5A
2/27/93; 11 minutes, 18 seconds; Directed by John Kricfalusi and Jim Smith; Written by John Kricfalusi and Bob Camp; Storyboard by Jim Smith; Background Color Design by Bill Wray; Animation by Rough Draft; Voices: John Kricfalusi (Ren), Billy West (Stimpy, Fake Dad Agent), and Harris Peet (Kowalski).

At Fake Dad Headquarters, Fake Dad Ren and Fake Mom Stimpy adopt a neglected seven-year-old boy, Kowalski—a fat, hairy lummox serving a thirty-year prison sentence ("for crimes against humanity"), who will visit Ren and Stimpy on weekends. Kowalski immediately crushes Ren in a loving hug. "Kowalski love new daddy!" Back at their trailer home, Ren dons his best fake smile to put up with Kowalski. "I'm not your real dad—just your fake dad! And only for this weekend!" He offers the lad a lick of icing off his spoon, only to get chewed up and spit out in the process. When Ren catches Kowalski smoking a whole pack of cigarettes, he hits him over the head. Kowalski has a tantrum, crushing most of Ren's favorite things into powder—including Stimpy! Later, on their Fake Family Picnic, Kowalski dines on a "*meat!*" on "*toast meat!*" sandwich and washes it down with a glass of "*meat!*" The force of Kowalski's resulting burp rips Ren's fur clean off. The enraged Chihuahua orders the lummox to drop his pants so he can spank him properly, but the sight of Kowalski's bare bottom turns Ren tearful and merciful. The weekend over, Ren and Stimpy return Kowalski to Fake Dad Headquarters. As the paddy wagon pulls away, Kowalski cries, "Goodbye, daddy!," causing Ren to break down in Stimpy's arms.

THE GREAT OUTDOORS **½
Production RS5-13B
3/27/93; 10 minutes, 41 seconds; Directed by Vincent Waller and Ken Bruce; Story by Vincent Waller and John Kricfalusi; Storyboard by Peter Avanzino; Animation by Rough Draft; Board-only; Voices: Billy West (all voices).

Spot gags involving Ren and Stimpy roughing it in the woods. Stimpy brings dehydrated food pills; Ren has a "Cowboy's Delight Meat Dinner" pill, which causes a whole horse to expand inside his body: "No, sir, I don't like it!" The two pals go skinny-dipping in the lake, only to be joined by nudist Old Man Hunger ("I just love skinny-dipping!") who invites his mom, Fat Lady. While Stimpy is off picking berries, Ren tries to start a campfire, but only succeeds in lighting himself aflame. Old Man Hunger helps stomp the burning Ren out with his boots. "I just love skinny-stompin'!" Sleeping under the stars, Ren is sucked dry by a swarm of mosquitoes. After drinking Stimpy's "purified water"—in which a beaver pissed—Ren immediately catches Beaver Fever, causing buckteeth and a beaver tail to sprout from his body. Ren repeatedly slaps Stimpy with his new tail, and Old Man Hunger joins in with a strap-on tail. "I just love skinny-slappin'!"

CENSORSHIP: **A close-up of Ren striking a match has been excised from most broadcasts and all DVD releases.**

THE CAT THAT LAID THE GOLDEN HAIRBALL **
Production RS5-9A
4/3/93; 11 minutes; Directed by Ron Hughart; Story by Vincent Waller and Bob Camp; Storyboard by Vincent Waller; Background Color Design by Bill Wray; Animation by Rough Draft; Board-only; Voices: Billy West (all voices).

Ren and Stimpy's birdhouse home is littered with hairballs, and Ren is disgusted—until he learns from a television news report that the vile things are now worth more than gold! To cash in on this, Ren converts the birdhouse into a factory. Stimpy hwarfs hairballs onto an assembly-line, Ren stamps them "Grade A," and Ren's nephew Bubba boxes them. But Stimpy soon licks himself dry and cannot make any more hairballs. Greedy Ren forces Stimpy to lick off his own dog hair, which is not hairy enough! It is Bubba's turn to be licked next, backside and all, but this too is a no-go. Ren sends Bubba literally inside Stimpy to find the problem: Stimpy's hairball gland has been rendered useless and has turned to dust. They realize that "it's over"—and dance with glee.

CENSORSHIP: **Much of the assembly-line montage, set to "Sabre Dance," is removed on the S1&2 DVD. Reinstated on the DR&S DVD.**

STIMPY'S FAN CLUB ***
Production RS5-11B
4/24/93 (original version); 8/20/94 (edited version); 19 minutes, 52 seconds (both versions); Directed by Peter Avanzino; Story by Elinor

Blake and John Kricfalusi; Storyboard by Peter Avanzino; Background Color Design by Bill Wray; Animation by Rough Draft; Voices: John Kricfalusi (Ren) and Billy West (Stimpy, Mailman).

Ren and Stimpy receive an entire sack of fan mail, all of it addressed to Stimpy. This fact is heartbreaking to Ren. "Everybody loves the stupid one! Nobody loves the jerk!" Stimpy tries to cheer his buddy up by making him the "really important" president of the Stimpy Fan Club. Ren's first day on the job requires him to answer Stimpy's mountain of fan mail. Ren's replies to the kids become progressively nastier. He writes that Ren and Stimpy are not real and chastises a boy for wetting the bed. Stimpy shames Ren for his behavior ("Lots of kids wet the bed! You and I still do it!"), and inspires the little psycho to do his job right. At night, though, Ren has a nervous breakdown, feeling dirty for being so nice in his letters. Ren tries to kill Stimpy in his sleep; but alas, Ren's brain aneurysms get in the way. Ren decides to fix the fans once and for all. He dons an obscenely phony Stimpy disguise and tells the mailman to tell those kids to stop sending those filthy letters. Only one letter arrives that day—addressed to Ren Höek. Of course, Ren dramatically rubs the flattering letter in Stimpy's face, only to find out that it came from Stimpy himself. "Big mean Ren" breaks down and cries in Stimpy's arms, witnessed by a crowd through the window (lifted from *Nurse Stimpy*).

CENSORSHIP: **Occasional reruns removed Ren turning into an "ass."**

A VISIT TO ANTHONY ***½
Production RS5-10
5/8/93; 18 minutes, 46 seconds; Directed by John Kricfalusi and Jim Smith; Story by John Kricfalusi and Richard Pursel; Storyboard by Jim Smith; Background Color Design by Bill Wray; Animation by Rough Draft; Voices: John Kricfalusi (Ren), Billy West (Stimpy),

Cheryl Chase (Mom), Danny Cooksey (Victor), Anthony Raspanti (himself), Randy Quaid (Dad), and Charlie Callas (Victor's dad).

Ren and Stimpy—residents of Hollywood, Yugoslavia—are invited by their fan Anthony to visit him in America. After kissing their harelipped wives goodbye, the two swim across the Atlantic Ocean to make good on his invitation. Anthony, a gap-toothed gimpy kid, is eager to "keep" his two favorite cartoon characters for his very own. Anthony's mom says they can stay if it's all right with Anthony's (unseen) father. Ren, Stimpy, and Anthony have a ball making their eyeballs pop out of their heads—though Stimpy only succeeds in inflating his nose. The fun is short-lived. Anthony witnesses Ren and Stimpy using the bathroom and begins to hyperventilate. The two are then approached by Anthony's deranged father, who does not like cartoons. He promises severe harm to Ren and Stimpy's well-being if they upset Anthony again. The three continue playing outside, where Ren is immediately beaned by a football. It was thrown by Victor, the school bully, who does not believe Anthony's visitors are the real Ren and Stimpy—and pulverizes the lot of them! Father suspects it is the fault of the two cartoon characters. He marches them into the house, where they are berated in front of the fireplace for several minutes. All this tension causes Stimpy to hwarf hairballs on Ren, sending father into a fit of laughter. He calls the wife and kid in and they all laugh heartily at the duo's expense. Overlong at some points, this episode has the makings of a classic. Ren is voiced interchangeably by Kricfalusi and Billy West in this cartoon.

THE ROYAL CANADIAN KILTED YAKSMEN ***½
Production RS5-7A
5/23/93; 17 minutes, 49 seconds; Directed by John Kricfalusi and Chris Reccardi; Story by John Kricfalusi, Bob Camp, Jim Gomez, and Vincent Waller; Storyboard by Chris Reccardi; Background Color

Design by Bill Wray; Animation Directed by Bob Jaques; Animation by Carbunkle Cartoons; Voices: John Kricfalusi (Ren), Billy West (Stimpy, Narrator, Yak), Harris Peet (Jasper), and the L.A. Gay Men's Choir (anthem singers).

We find our heroes in 1856 as members of the Royal Canadian Kilted Yaksmen, whose motto is: "We Always Get Our Butts Kicked!" Their sergeant (Jasper) needs men for a pointless exploratory mission to the Great Barren Wasteland, promising pain and certain death "if you're lucky." Stimpy is overcome with national pride and begs Jasper to let Ren and himself go. Jasper agrees, horrifying Stimpy with the fact that the rest of the Yaksmen must remain behind to look after the women. Ren smacks Stimpy. The two begin the harsh journey on their trusty yaks. They face hardship after hardship, including a fearsome Kodiak Marmoset ("the largest smallest primate") and killer bees. Ren wants to turn back, but Stimpy brightens the darkness by singing a rousing rendition of the Royal Anthem of the Kilted Yaksmen, complete with a sing-a-long bouncing Ren head! As they near the Wasteland, even their yaks are dying of hunger and thirst. One of the yaks has a nervous breakdown, but a slap from Ren snaps him out of it. Ren gets the idea to dig for their food: dirt, Canada's most abundant natural resource. Ren uses a divining rod covered with real food to try and locate a dirt vein. After a few hours of searching, one yak is fed up and puts his shovel down—striking a dirt geyser in the process! Our heroes chow down on a dirt banquet. After a good night's sleep, they place the Yaksmen flag and salute it. The scene dissolves to the present day, where our friends' skeletons still stand poised in salute under a modern freeway.

CENSORSHIP: **MTV version has the word "hell" uncensored in the anthem, though all other versions censor it.**

SHORTS:

ACE REPORTER, REN HÖEK: MR. HORSE RETURNS
1 minute, 40 seconds; Animation by Rough Draft (aired with "A Visit to Anthony")

GRITTY KITTY LITTER
(uses footage from "Stimpy's Big Day")
2 minutes, 2 seconds (aired with "Svën Höek")

LOG: New Log varieties #1
Logware and Anatomically Correct Log
1 minute, 35 seconds (originally aired before "Rubber Nipple Salesmen")

LOG: New Log varieties #2
Athletic Log, Log of Arabia, Officer Log, Armchair Quarterback Log
1 minute, 53 seconds (originally aired with "Svën Höek")

POWDERED TOAST MAN: VITAMIN F
3 minutes, 20 seconds; Directed by Kelly Armstrong; Storyboard by Peter Avanzino; Layouts by Mike Kim; Animation by Carbunkle Cartoons (originally aired with "The Royal Canadian Kilted Yaksmen"; Reuses footage from "Powdered Toast Man" short and episode.)

SECRET CLUB: SUSAN FOUT
2 minutes; Storyboard by Peter Avanzino; Animation by Rough Draft (originally aired with "Stimpy's Fan Club")

SUGAR SOD POPS
1 minute, 32 seconds; Animation by Rough Draft (originally aired with "The Royal Canadian Kilted Yaksmen")

WHAT'LL WE DO 'TILL THEN?: Balloon Good-Bye
Production RS06G
(first instance of Ren voiced by Billy West)
1 minute, 25 seconds; Storyboard by Vincent Waller; Reuse of Fil-Cartoons footage from first season, new animation by Carbunkle Cartoons (originally aired with "Svën Höek")

WORLD CRISIS WITH MR. HORSE
1 minute, 46 seconds; Animation by Funbag Animation (originally aired with "A Visit to Anthony")

THIRD SEASON:

TO SALVE AND SALVE NOT! ***
Production RS-301
11/20/93; 10 minutes, 59 seconds; Directed by Bob Camp; Written by Bob Camp and Vincent Waller; Storyboards by Jim Gomez; Background Color Design by Scott Wills; Animation by Rough Draft; Voices: Billy West (all voices).

Ren and Stimpy have a problem—Stimpy has no sales resistance. His compulsive buying reaches its zenith when he spends a fortune on the Titan 4000 Vacuum Cleaner, which succeeds in ripping Ren's flesh and organs from his body. Later, Stimpy is hassled at the door by the very persistent Salesman who is hawking Salve, the all-purpose wonder cream in a can. Time and time again, Ren steps in before Stimpy can waste any more money. Salesman's determination reaches the point where he turns up in Ren and Stimpy's breakfast, disguised as a slice of bread! Later, figuring himself rid of Salesman, Ren relaxes with a good book on the toilet, only to realize he is out of toilet paper! Salesman pops out of the toilet and chides Ren for passing up Salve, which would solve this problem. Ren caves in and agrees to buy, but Stimpy has already bought Salesman's whole supply of Salve. He is more than happy to share, however.

A YARD TOO FAR ***
Production RS-305
11/20/93; 10 minutes, 44 seconds; Directed by Bob Camp; Story by Bob Camp and John Kricfalusi (Kricfalusi uncredited); Storyboard by Bob Camp and Joe Sibilski; Background Color Design by Scott Wills; Animation by Rough Draft; Voices: Billy West (Ren, Stimpy, Mr. Pipe) and Bob Camp (Baboon).

Starving Ren and Stimpy are wasting away to skin and bones—

though in Stimpy's case, skin and fat. They are snapped out of their hunger by a mouth-watering aroma: a plate of hog jowls left to cool in someone's window. Ren thinks this setup is too easy and that he will probably get mauled by a dog. "I've seen cartoons like this before!" Stimpy assures him that there is no dog. But there is a baboon, which rips Ren to shreds. Attempts at sending Stimpy's flesh in after the jowls and dressing as the baboon's mistress prove futile, so Ren gets a sexy baboon puppet to distract the baboon. "I saw it in a Sylvester the Chicken cartoon!" Things go wrong when the primate proposes to "her" and uses Stimpy as the minister—all while Ren still has his hand stuck inside the puppet! While the baboon and his new wife consummate in private, Stimpy surprises the sulking Ren with the plate of jowls and the two have a feast. Kricfalusi wrote the story for this cartoon, citing the Yogi Bear cartoon *Pie Pirates* as its inspiration. A "Written by John Kricfalusi" credit for this episode was added to the show's end credits as of the 12 March 1994 airing.

CIRCUS MIDGETS *
Production RS-306
11/26/93; 10 minutes, 27 seconds; Directed by Bob Camp and Jim Gomez; Written by Peter Avanzino, Ron Hauge, and Bob Camp; Storyboard by Stephen DeStefano; Background Color Design by Scott Wills; Animation by Rough Draft; Voices: Billy West (Ren, Stimpy) and Harris Peet (Fire Chief).

Ren and Stimpy are hitchhiking in the middle of the desert, but have no luck until a clown car pulls over and the two are hauled inside. Their captors are two deranged circus midgets, who laugh dementedly at the sight of Ren and Stimpy. When the cat joins in, he is berated by the midget Shlomo, a la Joe Pesci in *Goodfellas*. "Do I amuse you?" He and his sidekick Momo play outrageously violent circus tricks on the duo, including electric shocks and flowers with wrench-wielding bees.

Then Ren and Stimpy are forced into clown outfits and made to amuse the midgets by performing death-defying stunts, such as jumping through a burning hoop. The car pulls over at a gas station, where Shlomo and Momo have to "water the flowers." Ren and Stimpy try to make a run for it, but they are quickly rejoined by the midgets, who have literally robbed the gas station—i. e. stolen almost all of its contents, including an attendant. On the run, the midgets take more captives (including a singing sperm whale) to enjoy their "hilarity," but they are quickly followed by the police. Their luck runs out when they get a flat tire and their car spins out of control. Everyone escapes without harm—except Ren and Stimpy. Our two heroes are hitchhiking once again, now sporting their clown clothes, and are picked up by a new driver: Fire Chief. A meandering, mean cartoon that is essentially a ten-minute setup for the windup gag.

NO PANTS TODAY **
Production RS-302
11/26/93 (original version); 11/25/94 (edited version); 10 minutes, 16 seconds (original version); 10 minutes, 11 seconds (edited version); Directed by Bill Wray and Bob Camp; Written by Richard Pursel and John Kricfalusi (Kricfalusi uncredited); Storyboard by Bill Wray; Background Design by Bill Wray; Animation by Rough Draft; Voices: Billy West (Ren, Stimpy, Mr. Pipe), Cheryl Chase (Mrs. Pipe), Bob Camp (Bear), Danny Cooksey (Victor), Charlie Callas (Victor's dad), and Mike Pataki (Cow).

After showering, Stimpy realizes he isn't wearing any pants and feels naked. Ren tells him to stop being stupid and kicks him outside. Stimpy's bizarre self-consciousness sets the tone for the rest of the day. He freaks Mrs. Pipe out with his nakedness, is sprayed with a hose by Mr. Pipe, and then abused by Victor ("the neighborhood sadist!") in exchange for his BVDs. Victor and his dad take Stimpy for a ride, give him the undies, and throw him out in the middle of the woods. Never fear, though, for father and son soon drive off a cliff to their demise. Stimpy is quickly robbed of his underwear—by a psychotic cow—and butted into the Deep Dark Forest. Stimpy encounters many disturbing creatures before running into a Smokey-type forest ranger bear, who gives Stimpy a live squirrel to wear as a leotard. Stimpy tells Ren the whole story, but Ren laughs it off, reminding him that cats do not wear pants. But they *can* wear women's dresses—and Ren, Stimpy, and the squirrel dress up to go down to the malt shop.

CENSORSHIP: **Original version features an extended scene of Stimpy being dragged by Victor's and his father's car. Missing on the S3.5 DVD and DR&S DVD.**

REN'S PECS **½
Production RS-304
12/18/93; 11 minutes, 4 seconds; Directed by Ron Hughart; Story by Richard Pursel and John Kricfalusi (Kricfalusi uncredited); Storyboard by Peter Avanzino; Background Color Design by Scott Wills; Animation by Rough Draft; Voices: Billy West (Ren, Stimpy, Doctor), Gary Owens (Charles Globe), Bob Camp (beach bully), and Cheryl Chase (beach babes, doctor's assistant).

Ren and Stimpy are at the beach, where the Chihuahua tries to impress the chicks. A muscle-bound bully shows up to ruin Ren's fun and kicks kitty litter (not sand) in his face. Ren is in tears over his wimpy appearance and wishes for pectoral muscles. Out of the ocean comes Charles Globe (complete with a globe for a head), who advises Ren to get Pec-Toe-Plastic surgery—which involves transferring fat cells to his pecs from another part of his body. Since Ren is lacking fat cells anywhere, Stimpy offers to share some from his ass. After painful surgery, Stimpy is saddened to see that his entire ass is nearly gone, but Ren is maniacally ecstatic over his new pectoral build. They immediately return to the beach, where Ren's new pecs make short work of the bully. Ren—with babes in tow—tells a tearful Stimpy that it is time for him to move on; but Stimpy's tears are only tears of joy, because his friend is finally happy. Later, through Ren's narration, we see that he has become a Hollywood superstar model and that he owes it all to one person: Charles Globe. Stimpy, whom Ren has forgotten, is his new maid. Significantly shortened and altered from the original Spumco outline, which called for this to be a half-hour episode, with Ren eventually falling from grace and reuniting with Stimpy. Social scientists note: Stimpy wears female swimming attire to the beach.

AN ABE DIVIDED ***
Production RS-310
12/18/93; 11 minutes, 5 seconds; Directed by Jim Gomez; Written by Jim Gomez and Ron Hauge; Storyboard by Stephen De Stefano; Background Color Design by Scott Wills; Animation by Rough Draft; Voices: Billy West (Ren, Stimpy, pigeon, bum) and Jack Carter (Sgt. Bigbutt).

Ren and Stimpy get jobs guarding the Lincoln Memorial. Their superior, Sergeant Bigbutt, demonstrates how to clean and shoo shitting pigeons by manhandling the both of them. The next day, Ren overhears an old man telling his grandson that there is a treasure in Lincoln's head. Ren immediately envisions riches and closes the monument down. The duo saws its head off and it shatters into a million pieces, revealing its contents: caramel corn. Ren has Stimpy glue the head back together, but Stimpy only succeeds in building the heads of Santa Claus and Fidel Castro before reducing the pieces to dust. Heads from Easter Island, the Statue of Liberty, and a flaming dumpster do not work as substitutes either. When Ren and Stimpy ask the spirit of Honest Abe for guidance, he only kicks them in the butt. In the end, Sarge uses Ren and Stimpy in a beard and hat as a replacement for Lincoln's head. A fan favorite.

STIMPY'S CARTOON SHOW ***½
Production RS-303

1/8/94 (original version); 19 minutes, 49 seconds; Direkshun by Baughb Camp; Writed by John Krisfaloosy; Storiboard by Mike Kimm and Kris Reccardy; Preety Colors by Scotty Wills and Teale; "I Like Pink" Character Design and Storyboard by Ron Hauge (end credit).

2/25/94 (edited version); 19 minutes, 39 seconds; Direkshun by Baughb Camp; Storiboard by Mike Kimm and Kris Reccardy; Preety Colors by Scotty Wills and Teale; Starring Jack Carter as Wilbur Cobb; "I Like Pink" Character Design and Storyboard by Ron Hauge (end credit); Written by John Kricfalusi and Elinor Blake (end credit); Animation by Rough Draft; Voices: Billy West (Ren, Stimpy, Explodey, Poopie) and Jack Carter (Wilbur Cobb).

Stimpy is hard at work making an animated cartoon, following in the footsteps of his idol: Wilbur Cobb, "godfather of animation." Ren at first scorns Stimpy for his stupidity, but quickly reneges and begs Stimpy to let him help make the cartoon. But Ren is talentless, lacking the skill to draw, write, direct, and even make coffee. So Stimpy gives Ren the position of producer—allowing Ren to turn Stimpy's production into the kind of slave labor where Stimpy has to pay Ren for pencils and make his own paper from trees! At a storyboard meeting, Ren (dressed to emulate Kricfalusi) berates Stimpy and tears down nearly all of his drawings. Stimpy finishes putting together the final edit of the cartoon himself. The trauma of it nearly kills him. Ren, meanwhile, basks poolside and blows Stimpy's cartoon off without watching it. "Meh, it's a film." Stimpy immediately shows it to the still-living Wilbur Cobb, seeking his approval. When Ren and Stimpy go to visit him, it turns out Cobb is beyond senile: he uses a seashell like a telephone as his body parts fall off at whim. Unable to carry on a conversation, Cobb rambles and raves at random, announcing how easy it is to be a genius. "All you gotta say is everything stinks! Then you're never wrong! That's how much of a genius I am!" After several minutes of Ren and Stimpy being subjected to this torture, Stimpy's cartoon is shown. After several huge, superfluous credits for Ren, the title rolls: Explodey the Pup in "I Like Pink." The film makes absolutely no sense; in a salute to early sound animation, it follows the crudely-drawn adventures of Explodey and his best girl Poopy, who is shunned by Explodey every time she wants a kiss. Peg Pelvis Pete comes to kill them, but is sabotaged by Explodey running in circles. Poopy finally gets that kiss and the two explode, ending the film. Cobb is impressed with Stimpy's work and encourages him to keep it up, so Stimpy can "be where I am today"—in jail. The cartoon ends with Cobb strapping himself and our heroes in an electric chair and throwing the switch.

CENSORSHIP: S3.5 DVD and DR&S DVD missing: Ren (as John K.) clapping the dust off his hands, Stimpy clocking out just as the sun comes up, and Ren talking on the phone and absentmindedly snipping pieces out of Stimpy's film. An alternate cut of "I Like Pink" was made for the episode's rebroadcast.

JIMMINY LUMMOX **
Production RS-309
2/19/94 (edited version); 4/16/94 (original version); 10 minutes, 49 seconds (edited version); 10 minutes, 51 seconds (original version); Directed by Ron Hughart; Premise by Bob Camp (uncredited); Story by Bob Camp, Jim Gomez, and Ron Hauge; Storyboard by Peter Avanzino; Background Color Design by Victoria Jenson; Animation by Rough Draft; Voices: Billy West (Ren, Stimpy, Mr. Pipe), Stan Freberg (Jimminy Lummox), and Harris Peet (Chicken).

Ren is acting very naughty—making prank phone calls, having beavers urinate in the town's water supply, and trying to blow off Stimpy's backside and fill his bath with crabs. Things go too far when

Ren cruelly rips off the wings of Stimpy's friend, Ralph the fly. Stimpy asks Ren if he has a conscience, and of course, Ren does not know what a conscience is. So Stimpy loans Ren *his* conscience: Jimminy Lummox, who sings "When You Wish Upon a Side of Beef" while violently punishing Ren for his misdeeds. Soon, Ren is punished more and more violently for *any* angry deed—even when Ren's anger is justified, as Stimpy scales fish with Ren's teeth and washes Ren's collection of celebrity underwear. After Jimminy drops a car on Ren, Ren begs him for an explanation of why he is so cruel. It turns out that Jimminy has a conscience, too: Tinkergaloot (Kowalski). Iris out on the foursome getting slapped by each other. "*Meat!*" A one-joke cartoon made funnier by Freberg's voice work.

CENSORSHIP: Original airing edited beaver piss scene (restored when it re-aired). S3.5 DVD removes all scenes of Ren trying to prank Stimpy. Reinstated on the DR&S DVD.

BASS MASTERS *
RS-320
2/19/94; 11 minutes, 24 seconds; Directed by Bob Camp; Written by Bob Camp and Jim Gomez; Storyboard by Peter Avanzino; Background Color Design by Scott Wills; Premise by Richard Pursel and John Kricfalusi (end credit); Animation by Rough Draft; Voices: Billy West (Ren, Stimpy, announcer, salesfish), Jack Carter (Wilbur Cobb), Bob Camp (Fish), and Harris Peet (Albert the Foulmouth Bass).

In "today's episode" of *Bass Master* (framed like a TV reality show), Ren and Stimpy are after the legendary Foul-Mouthed Bass. Wilbur Cobb escapes prison and immediately joins our heroes in their boat as an "Indian guide." Ren's psychotic impatience while waiting for a bite is enough to keep even the rambling Cobb silent. Stimpy attracts his own fish, while all of Ren's attempts fall flat. The cat reveals his secret:

he can "speak fish." Albert the Foul-Mouthed Bass arrives to berate Ren for not understanding fish. Ren offers to try to learn what it's like to be one. Ren jumps in the lake and is caught and mounted by Albert as "The Dumb Bass." Get it? Very unmemorable outing.

CENSORSHIP: **S3.5 DVD removes scenes of Ren loading the boat and some fish chum sucking. Reinstated on the DR&S DVD.**

ROAD APPLES BOMB
Production RS-319
3/12/94 (original version); 9/17/94 (edited version); 11 minutes, 3 seconds (original version); 10 minutes, 53 seconds (edited version); Directed by Howard E. Baker; Written by Ron Hauge; Storyboard by Howard E. Baker and Stephen DeStefano; Animation by Rough Draft; Voices: Billy West (Ren, Stimpy, Mr. Pipe), Cheryl Chase (Mrs. Pipe), and Jack Carter (Wilbur Cobb).

Lost again in the desert, Ren and Stimpy play roadkill (in Ren's case, it's not playing!) in order to hitch a ride in Mr. and Mrs. Pipe's RV. Mr. Pipe helps perk the duo up, giving Stimpy blood-sucking sand snails and Ren a refreshing, steaming hot shower. They sit down to a hearty meal of skunk milk and are taken for a walk while the RV is going at full speed. That night, after Mr. Pipe tells the scary story of "the Phantom"—who bores his victims to death with show biz stories and then rips their arms off—Ren and Stimpy bunk up with the Phantom himself: Wilbur Cobb, who lives up to the legend. "Mae West... heckuva nice guy!" Eventually, everybody falls asleep except for Ren—who realizes this means nobody is driving the RV! They crash to the bottom of a lake, where Ren, Stimpy, and Cobb are tossed outside to do their business. "The joke's on them," cackles Cobb. "I already wet the bed!" A credit of "Additional Storyboards by Garrett Ho" for this episode was added to the show's end credits as of the 4 April 1994 airing.

CENSORSHIP: **Nickelodeon cuts out the silhouette of Mr. Pipe and Ren showering together. S3.5 DVD removes the scene with Ren being chewed by a buzzard, the aforementioned silhouette, and the whole lengthy bit with Wilbur Cobb. Scenes were reinstated on the DR&S DVD.**

REN'S RETIREMENT **½
Production RS-311
4/2/94; 16 minutes, 2 seconds; Directed by Bob Camp; Premise by Bob Camp (uncredited); Written by Jim Gomez, Ron Hauge, and Bill Wray; Storyboard by Bill Wray and Bob Camp; Background Color Design by Bill Wray; Animation by Rough Draft; Voices: Billy West (Ren, Stimpy, Salesman, Worm), Alan Young (Haggis), and Jack Carter (Wilbur Cobb).

Stimpy informs the perky Ren that it is his tenth birthday—he is now seventy in dog years. Ren tries to convince himself that he is only as young as he feels, but his body begins to decay and wrinkle before his very eyes. The two try to make the best of it. Stimpy feeds Ren and puts him to sleep like a baby. The next day, Stimpy tries to introduce Ren to the old man game of golf, angering Haggis MacHaggis in the process. While watching the beautiful sunset at the course, Ren decides that this is where he should be buried. Death agrees. They arrive at a mortuary run by the Salesman, where Ren is given a grand deluxe coffin—complete with central air, cable TV, and Jacuzzi! Ren's funeral is the next day, and Pastor Wilbur Cobb thinks he is there to perform a marriage rather than deliver a eulogy. Stimpy will not stop crying, so the irate Ren ("I can't hear myself die!") allows Stimpy to be buried alive alongside him. Ren's tombstone reads "I'll thank you not to drag your butt on my grave!" "Life" continues as usual inside the coffin—until a worm that talks and laughs like Fred Flintstone arrives to eat Ren and Stimpy's insides.

CENSORSHIP: S3.5 DVD removes Stimpy using Ren as his golf caddy, with a mouthful of clubs. Reinstated on the DR&S DVD.

JERRY THE BELLYBUTTON ELF   BOMB
RS-321
4/9/94; 11 minutes, 15 seconds; Directed by Ron Hughart; Written by Steve Mellor; Storyboard by Stephen DeStefano; Background Color Design by Vicky Jenson; Featuring Gilbert Gottfried; Animation by Rough Draft; Voices: Billy West (Ren, Stimpy, Salesman), Gilbert Gottfried (Jerry the Bellybutton Elf), and Harris Peet (Muddy Mudskipper).

Stimpy is playing with his bellybutton too much. Then he hears a voice echo from inside it: urging him to climb inside, where fun awaits him. He has a psychedelic journey through the innards of his bellybutton—set to "Climb Inside My World" by Chris Goss—until he finally meets the source of the voice: Jerry the Bellybutton Elf (Gottfried), who dresses him in a lint miniskirt, "Size 42 Fat." Ren finds a fleshy nub—all that remains of Stimpy—and cries over the loss of his friend. It turns out that Jerry is making Stimpy have "fun" by doing endless lint-related chores, including "pick[ing] the lint from the lint." When Stimpy serves Jerry lintloaf for dinner, Jerry goes psychotic and tries to kill him. Meanwhile, Ren has thrown a party in Stimpy's absence, inviting just about everybody—including Muddy Mudskipper and his new obese wife, Bimby. Back inside the bellybutton, Jerry has turned into a giant monster pork chop who wants to feed on Stimpy. Stimpy tries to make a break for it, but only succeeds getting Ren dragged inside the bellybutton, too. Both are killed. Meanwhile, the party is ruined by Bimby, who has eaten all the clam dip. Everybody leaves in disgust; while alone, Bimby feeds on what remains of Stimpy! Pitifully unfunny cartoon.

HARD TIMES FOR HAGGIS ***½
RS-308

4/30/94; 19 minutes, 59 seconds; Directed by Chris Reccardi; Story by Jim Gomez and Chris Reccardi; Background Color Styling by Scott Wills; Animation by Rough Draft; Voices: Billy West (Ren, Stimpy, Salesman, kid, pigeon, old lady), Alan Young (Haggis), Stan Freberg (butler), and Harris Peet (Fire Chief, Muddy Mudskipper).

Haggis MacHaggis (who bears some similarity to George Liquor) is the star of the hit cartoon *The Scotsman Show*, and lives in a beautiful recreation of a Scottish castle, eagerly awaiting the airing of each new episode. The "show" literally consists entirely of him beating his dog, Whacky, on the head; Haggis considers it genius. But then he is informed via television that his show has been cancelled and replaced by the overnight sensation of *Ren & Stimpy*. Haggis refuses to believe this and goes out to beat Ren and Stimpy with his shillelagh. He runs into them at the door—along with his former agent (Salesman), who kicks Haggis out, informing him that these new stars now live here. Haggis vows to return and reclaim the castle with his loyal fans, but they have all forsaken him for Ren and Stimpy. The Scotsman goes crazy on a gimpy kid *R&S* fan until his father (Fire Chief) arrives, mistaking Haggis for a circus midget. Reduced to eating crumbs in the park, Haggis is beaten by pigeons for horning in on their feeding time. We cut to happier scenes of Ren and Stimpy, up to their usual "eediotic" shenanigans at Haggis's old digs. Haggis witnesses a trenchcoated stranger buying a Haggis plush doll—but the stranger turns out to be Whacky, who has bought it only to beat the living hell out of it. The Scotsman decides to end it all by throwing himself off a bridge, but is hit in the face by an ad for a hired goon service, "Rent-a-Thug." Renting some, Haggis takes his new lackeys to the location of Ren and Stimpy's live broadcast and successfully has them tied up. Then Haggis has the thugs perform an inane sock puppet version of the characters,

"Ben and Stumpy"—and the crowd loves it! Haggis, Ren, and Stimpy are thrown out of the studio, while the sock puppets are given riches and a contract. Down by the pier, Ren and Stimpy eat glass while a crying Haggis lazily beats them over the heads with his shillelagh.

EAT MY COOKIES *
RS-317

6/4/94; 10 minutes, 35 seconds; Directed by Ron Hughart; Featuring Rosie O'Donnell; Written by Ron Hauge; Storyboard by Victoria Jenson; Background Color Design by Scott Wills; Premise by Richard Pursel (end credit); Animation by Rough Draft; Voices: Billy West (Ren, Stimpy, badger), Cheryl Chase (various girls), and Rosie O'Donnell (Girl scout master).

Ren and Stimpy arrive at Barrette Baret Girls' Camp, where they are greeted by a few intimidating girl scouts who will only accept them if they pass a few tests. The first test is to sell their supply of cookies by midnight. They have eaten all the cookies by the time a cash-paying customer shows up—so they stuff the boxes with cacti. They sell their whole "supply" this way! Ren loses all of their cookie money that night over a game of cards. The portly scout leader (O'Donnell) recommends that they prove themselves by earning the most dangerous merit badge: the Snipe Hunting Badge. Ren does not believe there is such an animal, so Stimpy goes off on the hunt without him. Stimpy returns with a snipe, which turns out to be a hairy multi-eyed creature that mauls Ren on sight. Without a merit badge of his own, Ren feels left out, so the leader gives him a book full of "extra-easy" badges. Among them are "flying," "drowning," and "bravery in the face of certain doom." At the campfire that night, Ren is let in on the final Barrette Baret Girl secret: they are all really old men in costume—even Stimpy. Ren, saying "when in Rome..." unzips himself, revealing that under his "costume" is only his skeleton.

CENSORSHIP: The "flying badge" was omitted on the S3.5 DVD. Reinstated on the DR&S DVD.

REN'S BITTER HALF ***½
Production RS-313
6/4/94; 10 minutes, 42 seconds; Directed by Michael Kim; Written by Michael Kim, Ron Hauge, and Bob Camp; Storyboard by Peter Avanzino; Background Color Design by Bill Wray and Scott Wills; Animation by Rough Draft; Voices: Billy West (Ren, Stimpy, Evil Ren, Indifferent Ren, minister, announcer) and Cheryl Chase (girl scout).

Stimpy tinkers with his genetic engineering set and succeeds in giving himself a third ass cheek. Ren, angry that his dinner is not ready, shakes up Stimpy's XP-49 gene splicing formula, spilling it all over himself. It causes Ren to split in two: his evil side and his indifferent side. Evil Ren's cruelty knows no bounds; he throws the television set onto Stimpy and Indifferent Ren, electrocuting them both. Indifferent Ren endures it all—indifferently. While Stimpy takes "Apathy" Ren out for a twelve-hour walk, Evil Ren turns the house into a dungeon. An acid bath has been built and Stimpy watches in horror as his "Happy Happy Joy Joy" record, catnip mouse, and litter box are destroyed in it. After fainting from the shock, Stimpy finds that he and Indifferent Ren have been strapped to an operating table and that Evil Ren has made a new batch of XP-49. Stimpy tries to convince the psychopath to let Indifferent Ren return to his old self, convincing Evil Ren that he has "seen a side of myself no man should see. But you know what? I like it!" He pours more of the formula on himself and splits in two again. This time, an Evil Female Ren emerges. The two Evil Rens marry and drive away beating each other—dragging along Stimpy and Indifferent Ren by way of chain. "Who cares?" utters the deadpan Indifferent Ren.

CENSORSHIP: **S3.5 DVD removes dialog between Stimpy and Indifferent Ren before they are electrocuted inside the TV. Reinstated on the DR&S DVD.**

LAIR OF THE LUMMOX ***
Production RS-327
7/30/94; 16 minutes, 4 seconds; Directed by Bob Camp; Written by Jim Smith (end credit), Bob Camp, and John Kricfalusi; Storyboard by Jim Smith; Backgrounds by Victoria Jenson; Animation by Wang Productions; Voices: Billy West (Ren, Stimpy), Bob Camp (Red-Freckled Lummox), and Harris Peet (Kowalski).

In today's episode of *Untamed World*, Ren and Stimpy seek out the Lummox, a rare, dying breed in the land of Ignoramia. Stimpy looks for clues and finds a Lummox's "droppings": food scraps. The trail leads them to a Red-Freckled Lummox. The two weep in awe at its sheer undisturbed "beauty." They try to gain the Lummox's trust by doing as the Lummox does, which includes digging in their noses and asses. Grooming themselves with pork chops and spreading mashed potatoes on their bellies, they get along splendidly until Stimpy refuses the Lummox's offering of giblets. To soothe the savage beast, Stimpy gorges on a bucket of lard. They are welcomed into his lair, where they watch television and sip mayonnaise. The next day, the duo observes the Lummox mating grounds and encounter a Tree Lummox (Kowalski). It marks its territory by nailing its underwear to a tree. A female Lummox emerges and chooses the Tree Lummox over the Red-Freckled Lummox, preferring the former's "plumage" (ass-crack hair). The loser issues a belching challenge, which he wins by belching the *Gettysburg Address*. The female Lummox claims her new mate by folding him up like a suitcase.

SHORTS:
CHEESEFIST
3 minutes, 16 seconds; Directed by Bill Wray; Written by Bill Wray, Jim Gomez, and Stephen De Stefano; Storyboard by Stephen DeStefano; B.G. Color Design by Bill Wray; Animation by Wang Film Productions; Starring Stephen DeStefano as "Chalky Cheesefist" (aired with "Lair of the Lummox"); **Omitted from the S3.5 DVD.**

CHICKEN IN A DRAWER
3 minutes, 32 seconds; Directed by Bob Camp; Assistant Director: Steve Loter; Written by Bob Camp and Jim Gomez; Storyboard by Stephen DeStefano; B.G. Color Design by Scott Wills; Animation by Toon-Us-In Animation Inc. (aired with "Lair of the Lummox"); **Omitted from the S3.5 DVD.**

DOG WATER
2 minutes, 5 seconds; Written and Storyboarded by Bill Wray; Design and Layout by Bob Staake (two different versions exist with alternate colors; one aired with "Ren's Retirement", the other with "Hard Times for Haggis")

FLOD
2 minutes, 21 seconds; Directed by Ron Hughart (aired with "Stimpy's Cartoon Show")

YOU ARE WHAT YOU EAT
3 minutes, 54 seconds; Written, Animated, and Directed by Lynne Naylor; Layout by Chris Reccardi (aired with "Ren's Retirement")

FOURTH SEASON:

HERMIT REN ***
Production RS-314
10/1/94; 17 minutes, 8 seconds; Directed by Chris Reccardi; Story by Bob Camp, Jim Gomez, Chris Reccardi, and Bill Wray; Storyboard by Chris Reccardi; Background Color by Bill Wray and Scott Wills; Animation by Rough Draft; Voices: Billy West (Ren, Stimpy, Salesman, various Rens, Bogman) and Harris Peet (Jasper).

In their cow-carcass home, Stimpy plays the accordion and badly sings "Someone's Dyin' My Lord, Kumbaya," as Ren walks in from a torturous day of work. Ren's burnt chicken dinner literally scalds his tongue off, and Stimpy gives him a glass of curdled milk with which to wash it down. When Ren's razor rips the skin clean off his chin—Stimpy had been using the razor as a hammer—Ren decides he has had enough of civilized society, vowing never to return. Ren seeks life as a hermit, living in a cave where he must follow the Hermit Union rules: no sunlight, no bathing, and no friends. Inside the cave, Ren finds a mummified Bogman and is delighted that he now has "someone to talk to, who can't talk back!" Stimpy carries on as usual, waiting for Ren to come home to his roasted accordion dinner. Months pass. Ren seeks food in the cave and hallucinates, thinking that some surly bats are the udders of a cow. Then Ren hallucinates some more, envisioning the spirit of his ancestor: Old Farmer Höek, who tells him to feed on fungi and fleas—in jest, of course, but Ren does not know this. "Kid never had much sense," the spirit chuckles. Back at the cow carcass, Stimpy has sculpted a new Ren out of his own earwax. Ren, meanwhile, desperate for company, makes a Stimpy out of bat shit. "Gotta lay off the chili con carne!" The Bogman speaks to Ren, telling him that his only company is his feelings: anger, fear, and ignorance. Naturally, Anger hates everything, Fear is scared of everything, and Ignorance is too stupid to do anything. This throws Ren into a bit of psychotic rage, and he attacks his "feelings" (actually rocks) by beating "them" with the Bogman's arm. The Hermit Union Leader (Jasper) arrives and scolds Ren for breaking the number one rule of the Hermit Code: companionship, namely "all of these imaginary friends!" Ren is kicked out of the Hermit Union and is forced to march home with his bat shit Stimpy in tow. Ren returns to the cow carcass, where he and Stimpy hug and make up. The wax and shit sculptures of Ren and Stimpy do likewise. This well-written and staged cartoon illustrates how Ren is probably the most complex and mentally challenged cartoon character in history.

HOUSE OF NEXT TUESDAY **½
Production RS-312

10/8/94; 11 minutes, 1 second; Directed by Ron Hughart; Written by Ron Hauge and Peter Avanzino; Storyboard by Peter Avanzino and Stephen DeStefano; Background Color Design by Scott Wills; Animation by Rough Draft; Mostly board-only; Voices: Billy West (Ren, Stimpy, Salesman) and Harris Peet (Kowalski).

Spot gags in the House of Next Tuesday (parodying the MGM Tex Avery "Tomorrow" cartoons). In the world of Next Tuesday, giant ants rule the earth, but the house is equipped to exterminate them with a magnifying glass and sunlight. The Salesman gives Ren and Stimpy a ten-day free trial of this futuristic home, and they immediately go for the food. The food preparation system causes Ren much harm by demonstrating the beef jerky function. No more frosty toilet seats with the Toilet Seat Warmer—Kowalski drops down from the ceiling to warm it up! The Sense-o-Rama TV puts you right in the picture; Stimpy gets to bathe with babes, while Ren is boiled as a lobster on a cooking show. The Insta-Bed—"just add water"—inflates overnight, crushing them both into the ceiling. Ren wants to leave, but finds the

Salesman at the door, getting killed by a giant ant. They decide to use the House's time machine to go back to the past and exploit their knowledge of the future. But the time machine only succeeds in taking them a few minutes back in the cartoon, to the scene where Ren is boiled.

CENSORSHIP: **S3.5 DVD is missing the whale vomiting "seafood" scene. Reinstated on the DR&S DVD.**

A FRIEND IN YOUR FACE! *
Production RS-324
10/8/94; 11 minutes, 6 seconds; Directed by Bob Camp; Written by Bob Camp; Storyboard by Stephen DeStefano; Background Color Design by Scott Wills; Animation by Rough Draft; Voices: Billy West (Ren, Stimpy), Judy Bohannon (Choo-Choo Nong-Nong Head), Stephen DeStefano (Nooney Bratweiler), and Harris Peet (Fire Chief).

Ren awakens to find Stimpy at the fridge, shoving food into his ear. Stimpy says it is for the "friend in his face"—an Amazonian parasite named Choo-Choo Nong-Nong Head. Ren is sure he is dreaming and just laughs it off. Later that night, though, Nooney Bratweiler—Choo-Choo's long lost hick cousin—stops by to stay with him. Choo-Choo, not wanting the pest, convinces him to move inside the "apartment next door": Ren's head. Ren is confused as to why he cannot sleep, and why manure is piled on his head, until Stimpy enlightens him that he does indeed have a "guest." Ren tries handling the pest his own way: with a vacuum, which only sucks out his brain; a carnivorous black sea lamprey, which Nooney immediately slaughters and roasts; and dynamite, which blasts everything but Nooney. Nooney starts a grease fire inside Ren's head, which Fire Chief successfully puts out. Unfortunately, Ren's head is now in such sorry shape that it must be condemned and "torn down." Ren goes with the other option:

renovating it into a parasite condominium tower. Though beautifully drawn, this cartoon is just not funny.

BLAZING ENTRAILS ***
Production RS-307
10/15/94; 11 minutes, 6 seconds; Directed by Bob Camp; Written by Bob Camp, Jim Gomez, and Bill Wray; Storyboard by Stephen DeStefano and Bob Camp; Starring June Lockhart and Bill Mumy; Background Color by Scott Wills; Animation by Mr. Big Cartoons; Voices: Billy West (Ren, Stimpy), Bob Camp (corncob), June Lockhart (Mrs. Brainchild), and Bill Mumy (Dr. Brainchild).

Stimpy is acting stupider than usual. He brushes his teeth with a hammer, saws off his nose, and serves Ren his own tongue and eyes for breakfast. Ren decides that they need to see a specialist: Dr. Brainchild, whose mom informs them he is "playing in the garage." Brainchild is just that: a small boy with an enormous brain who rides around on a brain-powered unicycle. After examining Stimpy's "brain cavity" (his ass), he concludes that Stimpy faces certain death if Ren does not go inside him and find out what is wrong. Brainchild inflates Stimpy to a giant size and Ren enters through Stimpy's rectum. He unfortunately lights a match while in there, setting off a fart. Ren takes the Brown Line subway to the stomach barroom, where he meets and falls in love with an antibody that sucks out all of his innards. Only a year later, with a wife and flesh-sucking antibody kids ("Tell us how you and Mommy met again, Daddy!"), does Ren realize he's been sidetracked from his mission. While in the sinuses, he is almost killed by Stimpy's "backwash," but is saved when the cat picks his nose and inserts Ren into his ear. Ren finds the problem: Stimpy's "ignorant gland" is strangling his brain. The gland changes targets and pummels Ren instead. A monkey messenger arrives with a telegram from Brainchild, warning Ren that he has five seconds to get out of

Stimpy before Stimpy deflates. He does not make it out, but Stimpy is back to normal—only with Ren living inside his head.

LUMBER-JERKS **
Production RS-316
10/15/94; 11 minutes, 13 seconds; Directed by Bob Camp and Bill Wray; Written by Jim Gomez, Ron Hauge, Bob Camp, and Bill Wray; Storyboard by Bill Wray and Bob Camp; Background Color by Bill Wray; Animation by Rough Draft; Voices: Billy West (Ren, Stimpy, Jacques).

In Lumberville, Ren and Stimpy are paperboys trying to collect from Jacques LaPierre, the burly French lumberjack. Jacques forces the bill down Ren's throat and is appalled by the Chihuahua's weakness and Stimpy's fatness. Even Jacques' wife, Fifi, is manlier than them. Jacques agrees to show Ren and Stimpy the ways of the lumberjack. Before sending them off to cut down a tree, Jacques warns them of vicious creatures that inhabit them, particularly the Spiny Tree Lobster. Ren and Stimpy search high and low for a tree—only finding a forest, much to their dismay. Through sheer luck, they find a lone tree and spend several hours sawing at it with no success. A Spiny Tree Lobster who talks and looks like Moe Howard gets ahold of Ren and vows to teach him to respect nature. Ren is pierced in the eye by Mr. Hornet, farted on by the Bulbous Beak Horn-Blower, and has his nose and scalp clipped by the Lobster's offspring. Ren has learned his lesson: "Nature can be cruel, but I can be crueler!" He knocks the tree down with a steamroller—at which the Lobster reveals himself to have been Jacques, testing them, all along. Jacques tells the two that they have been cutting trees the hard way—lumberjacks *blow up* the forests these days. Later, back in the Lumberjack Club, the three relax in a whirlpool Jacuzzi, which gets its "whirl" from ravenous wolverines at the bottom.

PREHISTORIC STIMPY **

Production RS-322

11/5/94; 11 minutes, 10 seconds; Directed by Bob Camp; Written by Bob Camp and Ron Hauge; Storyboard by Peter Avanzino and Stephen DeStefano; Starring Jack Carter as Wilbur Cobb; Background Color by Scott Wills; Animation by Mr. Big Cartoons; Voices: Billy West (Ren, Stimpy, museum guard) and Jack Carter (Wilbur Cobb).

At the Museum of Natural History, Ren and Stimpy run into guide Wilbur Cobb, who tells them all about prehistoric time and the dinosaurs. We go back to the time of single-celled amoebas. One, who bears a resemblance to Ren, smacks a Stimpy-like amoeba after it farts in his direction; it splits in two and more farting ensues. Cobb speaks of the slimy sea scum that crawled out of the water—illustrated by his own backside and ass crack, which horrifies visiting nuns. The Stimpyfish is shown as an important example of evolution. It climbs on land and immediately falls into a tar pit. A second Stimpyfish gets wise and avoids the tar pit, only to get hit by a bus. Ren scoffs this story off as "crap" until he is shown the skeleton of a prehistoric bus. We then hear about the mighty Stimpysaurus, the stupidest creature of all time. The other Ren-type dinosaurs use the Stimpysaurus' massive size for shelter in the rain—and warmth, after the Stimpysaurus is struck aflame by lightning. Alas, we find that the Stimpysaurus also met its end at the tar pit. Stimpy asks Cobb what really killed the dinosaurs, and Cobb's explanations get progressively more insane: from the dinosaurs watching too much television to their exploding after they sneezed, farted, and belched at the same time. At this point, Cobb is apprehended by the museum guards, who reveal that Cobb is not a real guard; just a mere bone polisher. "*I* killed the dinosaurs!" shouts the insane geezer as he is taken away. In the end, Ren and Stimpy prove their evolved status by walking straight into a tar pit exhibit.

CENSORSHIP: S3.5 DVD omits the scene where Stimpy rips

off pieces of Cobb's face and imitates the codger. Reinstated on the DR&S DVD.

FARM HANDS *½
Production RS-315
11/5/94; 11 minutes, 16 seconds; Directed by Bob Camp; Written by Bob Camp, Jim Gomez, and Ron Hauge; Storyboard by Stephen DeStefano; Background Color Design by Scott Wills; Animation by Rough Draft; Voices: Billy West (Ren, Stimpy, chickens) and Bob Camp (Abner and Ewalt).

The return of Abner and Ewalt. The hicks need some new kids, seeing as theirs are all dead. They get new children via Dehydrated Young-Uns—which they chew and spit like tobacco to get them working. The two lads are Ren and Stimpy, who are immediately put to work. Ren is pulverized by the local poultry while trying to collect eggs, and he is force-fed worms and gravel by a horny rooster. Abner "works" on the boys' teeth with a wrench before they are allowed to eat. Stimpy loves bonding with Mr. Horse in the litterbox and milking Bossie the gorilla, but Ren cannot get the hang of either task. A tornado comes by, sweeping the whole farm away—Abner and Ewalt included. Ren and Stimpy take shelter in the outhouse, and Ren is scared that they are all alone. When Bossie defecates on them, however, they rejoice that they do indeed have company. Reuses animation from *Out West*.

CENSORSHIP: S3.5 DVD is missing the aftermath of Ren and Stimpy losing their teeth and realizing that they'll have to eat like the chickens do—with more gravel! Reinstated on the DR&S DVD.

MAGICAL GOLDEN SINGING CHEESES **
Production RS-404
11/12/94; 11 minutes, 1 second; Directed by Michael Kim; Written

by Jim Gomez and Bob Camp; Storyboard by Craig Kellman, Tom McGrath, and Michael Kim; Background Color Design by Scott Wills; Animation by Toon-Us-In Animations, Inc.; Voices: Billy West (all voices).

In the Kingdom of Fie, Stimpleton and Renwaldo—sons of the Dirt Smith—are dying of starvation. Renwaldo gives Stimpleton the family chigger to trade for some food. During his travels, Stimpleton encounters the Man-Eating Village Idiot, who eats his chigger, offering two magical golden singing cheeses in trade. But the Idiot will only give Stimpleton the cheeses if he proves himself worthy in a "battle of witlessness." Stimpy succeeds by jumping into a wild boar's pen with corncobs under his arms—a feat that wins Stimpleton the cheeses and leaves the Idiot dead of stupidity. Renwaldo will not eat the cheeses until they are ripe, so he tells Stimpleton to bury them. Stimpleton digs too deep and disturbs an ogre in his lair. Stimpleton saves himself by giving the ogre the cheeses to wear as shoes. Six months later, Stimpleton sneakily tries to pry the cheeses off the ogre's feet with a crowbar. He succeeds in popping a corn and scraping off a toenail. Though angered by the second disturbance, the ogre is willing to make a trade: Stimpy's kidney for the cheeses. When Renwaldo and Stimpleton bite into the cheeses, they transform into milk curd princesses. Our heroes are forced to marry the princesses, "live happily after ever, and starve to death." Contains a few of the most painful moments in the entire series.

CENSORSHIP: S3.5 DVD omits the scene with the frozen tree and the Idiot driving off with a gas pump still in the tank. Reinstated on the DR&S DVD.

A HARD DAY'S LUCK ***
11/12/94; 11 minutes, 10 seconds; Direction by Chris Reccardi; Story by Chris Reccardi, Lynne Naylor, and Vince Calandra; Storyboard by

Lynne Naylor and Chris Reccardi; Background Color Styling by Scott Wills; Animation by Rough Draft; Voices: Billy West (leprechaun, Myron) and Alan Young (Haggis).

Haggis MacHaggis wants a head of hair badly. Even his houseboy Myron's back hair—removed with masking tape—will not do anymore. Over a breakfast of Lucky Chodes cereal, Haggis gets a leprechaun as a prize. Haggis and Myron immediately try to drop the evil "foreigner" in a moat filled with ravenous Croco-Stimpies, but Haggis spares the leprechaun when he shouts that he grants wishes. Naturally, Haggis wishes for hair; but before the wish is granted, Haggis must first pass a series of tests. In the first test, Haggis must keep his temper, or forfeit Myron's servitude. The leprechaun plucks hairs out of Haggis' head—referring to them in a story as "three sons"—and places them in Haggis' eye, teeth, and ear, adding ear mites to boot. Haggis loses it, clobbers Myron, and fails the test. The next test is one of generosity—which Haggis fails, naturally, after denying a clam a half-cent bus fare, tossing him into the distance ("The buses don't run today! Try flyin'!"). After losing everything but his shillelagh to the leprechaun, Haggis faces the final test: he must spend a minute in the dark without being afraid. Haggis is lowered into a well and Myron's ass blocks all the light. Noises caused by Myron and the leprechaun above freak Haggis out, and he escapes the well just before the minute is up. When Haggis sobs over the loss of his shillelagh, the leprechaun has a change of heart—rewarding Haggis with hair: one mammoth strand of it, that is. Haggis, overcome with joy, skips off happily into the sunset and blows up. A pilot for a proposed series with Haggis.

CENSORSHIP: **The entire scene with the clam is cut on the S3.5 DVD. Reinstated on the DR&S DVD.**

I LOVE CHICKEN ✱✱✱

11/19/94; 11 minutes, 2 seconds; Direction by Ron Hughart; Written by Bob Camp and Jim Gomez; Storyboard by Peter Avanzino; Background Color by Scott Wills; Animation by Rough Draft; Board-only; Voices: Billy West (Ren, Stimpy).

Stimpy dutifully obeys all of Ren's orders until one night when the groceries contain a plump roasting chicken. It is love at first sight. Stimpy and the chicken—which flip-flops between being anthropomorphic and just a dead bird—are promptly engaged. Ren does not approve of this marriage and sits at the table throughout their two-week honeymoon, fork and knife in hand, waiting for his chicken dinner. When the couple returns and continues to ignore him, Ren is furious—and even more upset that Stimpy's new wife gets all of Stimpy's attention and servitude. Ren's attempts to roast and grind the chicken into sausage are foiled by "her" dutiful husband. Stimpy later finds Ren crying; ever since Stimpy got married, Ren explains, Stimpy and Ren never do things together anymore. Stimpy decides to take Ren on a picnic. Once they arrive at the park, however, Ren remembers that they forgot the ketchup. He takes the car back home, abandoning Stimpy for several hours. Stimpy finally arrives home and is heartbroken that Ren has eaten the chicken. After mourning for six months, Stimpy finally resumes his routine of preparing Ren's dinner. That is, until he falls in love with the goat head meant for Ren's stew.

CENSORSHIP: **Chicken's disgusting dowry is cut on the S3.5 DVD. Reinstated on the DR&S DVD.**

POWDERED TOAST MAN VS. WAFFLE WOMAN ✱✱

11/19/94; 11 minutes, 9 seconds; Direction by Chris Reccardi; Story by Vince Calandra, Chris Reccardi, and Bob Camp; Storyboard by Lynne Naylor; Background Color by Scott Wills; Gail Matthius as Waffle Woman (end credit); Animation by Rough Draft; Voices:

Billy West (Little Johnny, hag nurse, foreign ministers), Gary Owens (Powdered Toast Man), and Gail Matthius (Waffle Woman).

Powdered Toast Man is calling numbers at church bingo when he gets a distress call from Little Johnny in the hospital: the President won't visit him before he takes his nap. P.T. vows to right this wrong immediately. Meanwhile Vicky Velcro, former waffle tycoon, watches all this on television and vows revenge on P.T. for putting her liquid waffles out of fashion. In Washington, P.T. grabs ahold of the President (preventing him from signing a treaty to end all wars, ever) and returns to Little Johnny at warp speed. Unfortunately, all of this friction burns the President to a crisp, leaving Little Johnny heartbroken. Devastated at his failure, P.T. returns to his Breadbox of Solitude in outer space and hangs up his shorts—"for good!" Vicky sees this as her chance to get revenge. She uses a giant waffle iron to become Waffle Woman, archenemy of Powdered Toast Man! She intercepts P.T.'s television reception and announces that if he does not show up for a battle to the death, Little Johnny will not get to watch any television. This threat brings P.T. out of his comatose state and he immediately arrives to do battle. As P.T. and Waffle Woman argue over whose fault it is that their previous meetings went wrong, their misfired "missiles"—strawberries, syrup, pats of butter, and other tasty breakfast toppings—blow up a hospital, the United Nations building, England, and eventually the whole world. In the end, P.T. finds Waffle Woman's weakness by destroying her waffle iron. She is reduced to a pile of goo, vowing to return—"maybe." Little Johnny and the world (the smoldering ashes that remain) are safe once again, thanks to Powdered Toast Man!

CENSORSHIP: S3.5 DVD is missing Waffle Woman's threat of "If you've got the guts!" Reinstated on the DR&S DVD.

IT'S A DOG'S LIFE *½
Production RS-408

12/3/94; 11 minutes, 5 seconds; Directed by Ken Bruce; Written by Jim Gomez and Bob Camp; Storyboard by Tom McGrath; Background Color by Scott Wills; Animation by Wang Productions; Board-only; Voices: Bob Camp (dogcatcher) and Billy West (everyone else).

At the dog pound, Ren and Stimpy are being read their last rites as they are taken to the gas chamber. A rich old lady, Granny, comes to save the "vermin" from certain death. She names the two Abraham and Leviticus and upon their arrival at her mansion, Ren finds his "roommate" Ezekiel—a dog that is dead and freeze-dried. To break in their new digs, Ren drags his ass on the floor and Stimpy shreds the couch; Granny thinks they are "possessed." She has her muscular Asian servant, Mr. Hao, straighten them out. Chow time consists of Gravel Train, two large balls of gravel that break Ren's teeth and cause Stimpy to choke. After spaying and neutering the duo, Granny puts them out to sleep in the cemetery. The two make their escape, but run into a cop. Rather than face the pound again, they reluctantly return to Granny's place. Upon their arrival, they see that Granny has died of lead poisoning (a pipe falls from Mr. Hao's pocket). It turns out that Granny has willed Hao all of her fortune and that "Abraham and Leviticus" are to be stuffed alongside her. A partial remake of *Man's Best Friend*, only with a lot less laughs.

REN & STIMPY PRESENT EGGYÖLKEO *
Production RS-407

12/3/94; 11 minutes, 3 seconds; Directed by Bob Camp; Written by Jim Gomez and Bill Wray; Backgrounds by Scott Wills; Storyboard by Stephen DeStefano; Animation by Wang Productions; Voices: Harris Peet (chicken) and Billy West (everyone else).

Renwaldo, the town egg smithy, is bored pounding eggs. He feels his destiny can only be fulfilled if he molds a pile of yolk into a son in his own image. As he is molding the "boy," he adds a piece of his scalp and brain. Ren is visited in the night by the Blue Chicken Fairy, who brings the egg-yolk boy to life with salt. Ren finds him alive the next morning, watching television with Stimpy, and christens him Eggyölkeo. Eggyölkeo turns out to be a blithering idiot who can only speak in painful groans. A couple of hepcats—a slice of bacon and piece of French toast!—spy the egg child in the car with Renwaldo and eggnap him that very night. Renwaldo is devastated by the loss of his son. At a Pleasure Island-type resort, Eggyölkeo is forced to "walk the skillet" until Colonel Strombolio discovers Eggyölkeo and turns him into an Elvis-type sensation in Vegas. Renwaldo gets wind of this and arrives to save him, but not before being trampled by Eggyölkeo's rabid fans. The reunion is short-lived, for Stimpy eats Eggyölkeo the next morning—but does not swallow until after Eggyölkeo gurgles, "I love you daddy."

CENSORSHIP: **S3.5 DVD is missing opening pan of village, Eggyölkeo driving the car with his kidnappers, and Ren rocking the fridge with Eggyölkeo to sleep. Reinstated on the DR&S DVD.**

DOUBLE HEADER ***½
1/7/95; 11 minutes, 13 seconds; Directed by Michael Kim; Written by Jim Gomez and Bob Camp; Storyboard by Tom McGrath; Background Color by Ramone Zibach; Animation by Toon-Us-In Animations, Inc.; Voices: Billy West (all voices).

Ren has finally had it with Stimpy's shenanigans, so buys him a one-way ticket to the Ursa Minor comet in outer space. As Stimpy hangs onto Ren's leg in the street, pleading not to be sent away, the bus runs them over. They awaken after extensive surgery in the hospital, where the German surgeon claims, "at least you are alive, und you have each other." Turns out that Ren and Stimpy have been stitched together like Siamese twins. Taking a taxi home, they resume everyday life in their new condition. After being awakened at four in the morning for Stimpy's favorite show, "Stomper Room" (consisting of participatory stomping), Ren realizes he is late for work. Ren covers Stimpy with an overcoat and begins his day of work at the missile factory: a job "so secret," Ren explains, "I don't even know what's going on." Stimpy's impulses get the better of him and he pulls a lever, causing an atomic blast. Ren's boss, decaying from the nuclear explosion, fires him and tells Ren and Stimpy that there is only one place for freaks like them— the circus. They apply for a job as freaks. A humiliated Ren appeases the crowd with chicken head-biting. During their lunch break, Ren goes nuts at the sight of the other freaks, but is brought to his senses by Stimpy, who convinces him that things could be worse. They are instantly hit by the Ursa Minor comet, and it is only Stimpy who awakens at the hospital this time. Or is it? Ren survives as a head and pair of legs, and they have been stitched to Stimpy's backside—just in time for Stimpy's lunch of barbecued baked beans! Kim's tribute to David Lynch ties with "Ren's Bitter Half" as one of the best of the Games episodes.

THE SCOTSMAN IN SPACE **

1/7/95; 11 minutes, 12 seconds; Directed by Bob Camp; Written by Bob Camp, Jim Gomez, and Bill Wray; Storyboard by Stephen DeStefano; Background Color Design by Scott Wills; Animation by Rough Draft; Voices: Billy West (Ren, Stimpy), Alan Young (Haggis), and Stephen DeStefano (Dead Space Scot Genie).

On another 36-year mission, Ren seems to be getting space madness (again) and begins seeing things outside of the ship. But Ren is not mad after all; Stimpy sees the thing outside too—Haggis MacHaggis. Haggis has been looking for his sheep for years, a fact that neither Ren nor Stimpy seem to grasp. Bringing Haggis inside, they serve him dehydrated haggis ("From the Shamus Culhane recipe!"), but

Haggis goes bonkers over the fact that they did not serve any chutney with it. Stimpy subdues the Scotsman by giving him a wedgie, and the two strap him down on the dissection table to give him the "respect a new lifeform deserves." They fail to extract Haggis' wallet—an act that sets him off again, but his rage is short-lived when he mistakes Ren and Stimpy for his sheep. Haggis takes the two down to the "meadow level" of the ship. For months, they enter his servitude: grazing, getting sheared, and cooking his food. Unfortunately, Haggis' eggs getting overcooked prove too much for him to bear. He has a heart attack, and his wallet drops from his pocket. The wallet functions like a magic lamp. Out pops a Scots-Italian-accented genie with a special offer: buy three wishes, get one free! Ren wishes for beautiful women to bring him all the money in the world. Big-hearted Chihuahua that he is, Ren gives Stimpy the remaining wishes. Stimpy's wish that nobody ever have need for material possessions sends Ren, Stimpy, and the women to float in space. As they are about to die from lack of air and pressure, Stimpy makes two more wishes: for equality amongst all people (turning the women into foreigners), and to be where it is always sunny and no one ever grows old (in the gravitational pull of the sun). No fourth wish is ever made. Ren and Stimpy burn to a crisp before Ren can even smack the "eediot" for his stupidity.

PIXIE KING **
1/14/95; 11 minutes, 22 seconds; Directed by Ron Hughart; Written by Ron Hauge, Jim Gomez, Bill Wray, and Bob Camp; Storyboard by Stephen DeStefano; Background Color by Scott Wills; Animation by Rough Draft; Voices: Billy West (Ren, Stimpy, various pixies and elves) and Jack Carter (Wilbur Cobb).

In the outhouse of Ren and Stimpy's tree home, Stimpy is trying to take a dump. He cannot do it, however, unless Ren reads him a story. Ren reads him the tale of an elf (Ren) who wanted to be Pixie King.

He and his elf pal (Stimpy) sleep in a can of sardines in their donut home and take a ladybug bus to work every day. Their job consists of happily kissing dewdrops ("And then someday we'll die!" the elves sing), scraping pollen off bees, and mining pixie dirt out of a man's nose. Later, in the locker room, Ren overhears that the Pixie King is getting old and any ambitious pixie could take over his throne. Ren tries his hardest to earn his wings and become a pixie. He and Stimpy receive their wings from a Wilbur Cobb pixie, who gets them by ripping them off of live flies. Next, to become rich and noble, Ren goes after the rarest commodity in the region: a giant's eyecrust. Ren gets the eyecrust, but is pummeled in the process thanks to Stimpy's noisemaking. Ren is cheered for his heroic efforts and made Pixie King. Before he can become a tyrant, however, he must do his kingly duties: be force-fed royal jelly and lay eggs. The end. At this point, Stimpy has finished his business and Ren is fit to burst. Ren uses the storybook to wipe his ass.

ALOHA HÖEK　　BOMB

1/14/95; 11 minutes, 8 seconds; Directed by Bill Wray; Written by Jim Gomez, Bill Wray, and Bob Camp; Storyboard by Bill Wray and Chris Mitchell; Featuring Dom DeLuise as The Big Kahuna; Animation by Mr. Big Cartoons; Board-only; Voices: Dom DeLuise (Big Kahuna) and Billy West (everyone else).

Ren and Stimpy are washed up on a desert island like fish. Stimpy builds a sandcastle home, but it gets washed away in the night. Ren finds a dead fish carcass to live in, but it quickly proves to be ill-fit for occupancy. When Stimpy complains of it being too "hot and stinky," Ren throws the ungrateful cat out. Stimpy journeys into the jungle where he meets the Big Kahuna, who talks like Marlon Brando and invites Stimpy to live and dine with him. Big Kahuna tries to invite Ren as well. Ren mistakes the big lug for a headhunting cannibal and fears Stimpy has met his doom. The real owners of the fish carcass—a family of crabs—return home. They spare Ren's life in return for his servitude. While walking their pet fly, Ren tries to use it to escape, but only plummets into the ocean. The fly brings Ren's lifeless body to Stimpy, who is devastated at the demise of his best friend. At this point, Ren and Stimpy reveal themselves to be Soviet versions of Fred Flintstone and Barney Rubble, who were on a secret mission the whole time. Another episode that passes off grossness for substance; even DeLuise cannot save it.

INSOMNIAC REN **
1/21/95; 11 minutes, 21 seconds; Directed by Steve Loter; Story by Bob Camp, Jim Gomez, and Vince Calandra; Storyboard by Tom McGrath; Background Color Design by Scott Wills; Animation by Rough Draft; Voices: Billy West (Ren, Stimpy, Mr. Horse), Harris Peet (Muddy Mudskipper), and Alan Young (Haggis).

Ren has a big tee-off in the morning, but cannot fall asleep. In the bedroom, Stimpy makes noise grooming himself and snoring. Ren tries to sleep on the couch, but the attempt only makes him obsessive-compulsive. Ren peeks into Stimpy's dream cloud to find the eediot dreaming of feeding their lovechildren. "It's just a dream, Ren!" Stimpy vows to help his pal fall asleep by means of camel mucus, reading from Poe, and performing a lullaby on the drums. It is only when Ren's golf buddies (Muddy, Mr. Horse, and Haggis) arrive that he is able to fall asleep—he pays all of them to knock him out. "Shh! Ren's taking a coma!" whispers Stimpy.

MY SHINY FRIEND ***
Production RS-413
1/21/95; 11 minutes, 2 seconds; Directed by Bill Wray; Written by Ron Hauge, Jim Gomez, Bill Wray, and Bob Camp; Storyboard by Bill

Wray and Bob Camp; Background Paintings by Bill Wray; Animation by Toon-Us-In Animations, Inc.; Voices: Billy West (Ren, Stimpy, Mr. Horse), Harris Peet (Muddy Mudskipper, Fire Chief, Chicken), and Bob Camp (Ren singing as Burl Ives).

Stimpy is watching too much television. It is causing him to neglect his housekeeping duties. He is even sleeping with the TV! Ren sends Stimpy out to get some fresh air on his big wheels, but later finds the cat watching TV in a tree with his cow and baby chick buddies. Even burying the TV will not stop Stimpy—he watches it underground with a mole! Ren finally destroys the television completely. Later at night, Stimpy keeps asking to be excused to do "number one" and "number two" for long periods of time. Ren gets wise when Stimpy reaches "number three." Ren discovers that Stimpy is keeping a working TV set in the toilet. Stimpy overdoses on television and becomes radioactive. Ren has no choice but to isolate Stimpy in the basement. It works: nine years later Stimpy is a changed cat, no longer addicted to television. Now he is into gambling!

CHEESE RUSH DAYS   BOMB

2/11/95; 11 minutes, 3 seconds; Directed by Mark Marren (credited as "Kirk Field"); Story by Vince Calandra; Storyboard by Kirk Field; Animation by Rough Draft; Board-only; Voices: Billy West (all voices).

In a tale of the bleu cheese rush, Ren and Stimpy go west to make their claim. They encounter a crusty old prospector—echoing Walter Huston in *The Treasure of the Sierra Madre*—who tells them of the riches in store, but the duo ignores him. Ren and Stimpy are cooked alive by savage French chefs before getting sunstroke in the middle of nowhere. After smelling what he thinks is one of Stimpy's farts, Ren finds he has actually discovered the bleu cheese mountain, where Ren and Stimpy mine for their fortune. They use a giant canary to test for poisonous cheese gas. The canary only succeeds in causing a cave-in by lighting his cigar. Our heroes find the valuable bleu cheese vein, but Ren's greed causes him to build a brick wall, trapping Stimpy and the canary inside. The kooky prospector digs the two out and laughs at them for not realizing they have plenty of bleu cheese riches for themselves. Meanwhile, Ren is kicked out of the bank for passing off "fool's cheese" (i. e. fool's gold). Ren is then run over by Stimpy, the canary, and the prospector—all rich and driving their fancy new car.

WIENER BARONS **
Production RS-415
2/11/95; 10 minutes, 58 seconds; Directed by Bob Camp; Written by Ron Hauge, Jim Gomez, and Bob Camp; Storyboard by Peter Avanzino; Background Color by Richard Zaloudek; Animation by Mr. Big Cartoons; Board-only; Voices: Billy West (Ren, Stimpy, announcer) and Jack Carter (border guard).

A la Tex Avery's George and Junior, Ren and Stimpy are hoboes who trek through America to Canada, hoping to make a killing in the wiener industry. The two are not allowed in at the border, so they hollow out a pig to float over Canada's baked-bean moat. The pig springs a leak and sinks. Back at the border, Ren and Stimpy fool the guard by dressing as U.N. wiener inspectors and are granted entrance to the Land of Wieners. After backbreaking labor, the two strike it rich with a wiener well and get swell new digs in Toronto. Misfortune strikes, however, when they find out that the bottom has fallen out of the wiener market. They are now broke again. Homeless in a downtown alley with only their dirty old wieners to support them, Ren awakens and proclaims that he was visited by God in the night. The Lord has told him that it will rain baked beans for forty days and forty nights, and that he and Stimpy should build an ark of wieners and get out of Canada. Which they do—sailing over the bean-flood toward a butterlike setting sun.

GALOOT WRANGLERS   BOMB

3/4/95; 10 minutes, 50 seconds; Directed by Craig Bartlett; Written by Ron Hauge and Jim Gomez; Storyboard by Jim Kammerud; Background Color by Vicky Jenson; Animation by Rough Draft; Board-only; Voices: Billy West (Ren, Stimpy) and Jack Carter (Wilbur Cobb).

Will Hiccobb, roasting his nose over the fire, tells young-uns Ren and Stimpy about the bygone days when "galoots"—Kowalski-type human lugs, characterized as wild cattle—were domesticated and ridden in rodeos by the likes of cowboys Ren and Stimpy. Unfunny spot gag cartoon.

REN NEEDS HELP!   **½

3/4/95; 11 minutes; Directed by Bob Camp; Written by Jim Gomez and Bob Camp; Storyboard by Chris Reccardi; Background Color by Scott Wills; Animation by Toon-Us-In Animations, Inc.; Board-only; Voices: Billy West (Ren, Stimpy, Dr. Sloth, Yak) and Harris Peet (Muddy Mudskipper, Fire Chief).

When Stimpy destroys Ren's coffee-table collection and favorite chair, Ren loses his mind and sticks himself in the garbage disposal. Stimpy has him committed to the Shady Brain Farm, where Doctor Sloth and the other patients (the Shaven Yak, Muddy Mudskipper, and Fire Chief) find Ren to be extremely dangerous. The episode ends with Ren getting his brain removed and becoming the President of the United States, giving speeches on the moon.

CENSORSHIP: **S4&5 DVD removes Ren being carried off to the asylum and several scenes of Ren's daily routines (including a visit from Stimpy and his lovechild). Reinstated on the DR&S DVD.**

OL' BLUE NOSE **½

3/18/95; 11 minutes, 7 seconds; Directed by Steve Loter; Written by Ron Hauge, Bob Camp, and Billy West; Storyboard by Mark O'Hare; Background Color by Scott Wills; Featuring Music Composed and Arranged by Shawn Patterson (end credit); Animation by Toon-Us-In Animation, Inc.; Voices: Billy West (Ren, Stimpy, Louis Lungbubble, Stimpy's nose).

Stimpy squanders Ren's money at the bus station on a "stupeed TV chair," causing Ren to smack him obscenely hard on the nose. The blow transforms Stimpy into a Rat Pack-style singer. When passersby throw money at the duo, Stimpy's alter ego "Snotra" is born. He is a smash hit in Vegas and at prisons. Ren becomes a servant to Stimpy, washing his wigs and underwear. The Chihuahua's frustration builds until Stimpy is invited to appear in the *Louis Lungbubble Show*. There, the two have a quarrel right before curtain, causing Ren to smack Stimpy's nose again—and the nose has had it. "That's the last time you hit me, Pal Joey!" Jumping off of Stimpy's face, the nose leaves to do his own act. Ren and Stimpy, the latter noseless, go back to living in their trailer. A happy ending, however: the nose is a failure by himself. "We saw you on TV!" says Stimpy; "Till we burned it," retorts Ren. The "three" go back to living in harmony.

STUPID SIDEKICK UNION **

Production RS-423

3/18/95; 11 minutes, 6 seconds; Directed by Tom McGrath; Written by Bob Camp and Jim Gomez; Storyboard by Tom McGrath; Background Color by Scott Wills; Animation by Rough Draft; Board-only; Voices: Billy West (Ren, Stimpy, various) and Bob Camp (Tex, baboon).

On the set of *The Ren & Stimpy Show*, Ren is about to smack Stimpy for the umpteenth time when the cat gets a call from Stupid

Sidekick Union 6 7/8. Stimpy threatens to go on strike if he is not given a contract that states Ren must ask his permission before smacking. Ren is aghast: "Next thing you know, you'll wanna be *paid!*" Stimpy marches on the picket line (minus his nose, which was company property), while Ren calls the SCAB Sidekick Union. He gets the woodenhead yokel Tex as Stimpy's replacement. Tex treats the show as if it were a western—causing a stampede and getting Ren branded—and is immediately fired. Later replacements, such as the Baboon and a Shakespearean "thespian," do not work out either. Then Stimpy shows up disguised as a giddy female, begging Ren to sign her autograph book—in reality, the contract. Ren obliges, signing "George Washington"—and the signature is accepted as valid! Headlines read: "First President Endorses Union Contract (Death Rumors False)." Stimpy returns to work: not only getting the shit beat out of him, but getting paid a fortune for it, too. In the end, the title of the show changes to *Stimpy & Ren*. Would-be classic ruined by a completely out-of-character Stimpy.

SUPERSTITIOUS STIMPY *
Production RS-421
4/1/95; 11 minutes, 25 seconds; Directed by Bob Camp; Written by Ron Hauge, Jim Gomez, and Bob Camp; Storyboard by Peter Avanzino; Background Color by Ramone Zibach; Animation by Rough Draft; Board-only; Voices: Billy West (all voices).

Stimpy has become overly superstitious and is thus frightened by Ren's bad-luck-bringing habits. "Bad juju!" shouts Stimpy, smacking himself with a thorny rose to counteract Ren's behavior. Stimpy deduces that Ren is the unluckiest creature in the universe—evidenced by his unicorn horn and webbed feet—and Ren cries that it is true. Painful remedies do not help, nor does a lucky leper's foot (the owner of which comes back to beat Ren).

TRAVELOGUE   BOMB
Production RS-406

4/1/95; 10 minutes, 40 seconds; Directed by Arthur Filloy; Written by Jim Gomez; Storyboard by Arthur Filloy; Background Color by Richard Zaloudek; Animation by Mr. Big Cartoons; Board-only; Voices: Billy West (Ren, Stimpy) and Bob Camp (Elvis, baboon).

Travelogue hosts Ren and Stimpy visit the nation of Acromeglia, where they are cooked, shaved, skinned, and decapitated. An awful barrage of poorly executed gross-out gags.

SHORTS:
FIELD GUIDE
Production RS-356

3 minutes, 44 seconds; Directed by Bob Camp; Written by Jim Gomez and Bob Camp; Storyboard and B.G. Color by Victoria Jenson; Animation by Toon-Us-In Animation Inc.: Andy Kim, Sang W. Kim, Young S. Lee, and Kyung S. Shin (aired with "Hermit Ren")

FIFTH SEASON:

SPACE DOGGED **½
Production RS-429
6/3/95; 11 minutes, 3 seconds; Directed by Steve Loter; Storyboard by Tom McGrath; Written by Jim Gomez and Bob Camp; Featuring Phil Hartman; Background Color by Scott Wills; Animation by Rough Draft; Voices: Billy West (Ren, Stimpy), Phil Hartman (American pig), and Harris Peet (American general).

    Renski and Stimpski are astronauts for the Soviets in the space race of the 1950s. Passing rigorous and torturous tests, they are sent on their first launch—undaunted by the fact that all previous Soviet astronauts have died. Stimpski goes "potski" in his suit—the ass of his suit is attached to Renski's helmet. Sputnik actually makes it into orbit. Unfortunately, back at headquarters, Kowalskiski has kick-danced out the duo's remote connection to Earth. Out of fuel, Renski demands Stimpski siphon some out of a rival ship belonging to U.S. "capitalist pigs." Stimpy only succeeds in hooking his gas tank up to the pigs' septic tank, sucking in one of the pigs as he takes a shit. The John Wayne-like talking pig would rather die than be in the presence of commies, so he burns himself—giving the duo enough fuel. Now it is one pig versus Renski and Stimpski. The duo makes it to Earth first—but land in America! This proves to be no problem, as Renski and Stimpski are passed off as true-blooded Americans anyway. "Better fed than red!" says Ren as the two are paraded in the streets. Over in the Soviet Union, the pig is roasted and displayed in a number two parade.

FEUD FOR SALE ***
6/3/95; 11 minutes, 10 seconds; Directed by Ron Hughart; Written by Bob Camp, Jim Gomez, Vince Calandra, and Ron Hauge; Storyboard by Chris Reccardi; Background Color by Scott Wills; Animation by

Rough Draft; Board-only; Voices: Billy West (Salesman) and Bob Camp (Abner, Ewalt).

Traveling through the Wild West, the Salesman encounters local feuding yokels Abner and Ewalt. He exploits the feud—and the yokels' ignorance—by selling each of them suave attire made of pointy sticks, used flypaper, and weapons—all paid for with their grandpappies' fortunes. Things get out of hand when Abner buys an atom bomb. In the resultant smoking crater, the two hillbillies make peace; the Salesman drives away in his new sports car with all the money, and Abner's grandpa, in tow. The funniest of the series without Ren and Stimpy.

CENSORSHIP: S4&5 DVD is missing scenes with Ewalt's grandpa and the elephant launcher's elephant collecting his commission. Reinstated on the DR&S DVD.

HAIR OF THE CAT BOMB
7/1/95; 10 minutes, 55 seconds; Directed by Ken Bruce; Written by Ron Hauge; Storyboard by Mark Marren (credited as "Kirk Field"); Animation by Rough Draft; Board-only; Voices: Billy West (all voices).

Ren is unaware that he is allergic to Stimpy's hair, and as a result suffers everything imaginable. When Ren gets wise, Stimpy is isolated to a pickle jar. Predictable and unfunny.

CITY HICKS BOMB
7/1/95; 11 minutes, 2 seconds; Directed by Ken Bruce; Written by Vince Calandra; Storyboard by Jim Kammerud; Background Color by Richard Daskas; Animation by Toon-Us-In Animation, Inc.; Board-only; Voices: Billy West (all voices).

"Dust harvesters" Ren and Stimpy are left without their annual harvest when rain comes, leaving produce in the dust's place. The two go to the city to make their fortune. Several beatings later, Dusty Claus brings in a dust bowl and takes the now-happy padres home. Good color styling cannot save this stinker.

STIMPY'S PET *½
Production RS-434

10/7/95; 10 minutes, 50 seconds; Directed by Steve Loter; Featuring Phil Hartman; Written by Vince Calandra, Jim Gomez, and Bob Camp; Storyboard by Brian Smith, Dan Root, and Steve Loter; B.G. Color Design by Scott Wills; Animation by Rough Draft; Voices: Billy West (Ren, Stimpy) and Phil Hartman (circus midget).

Stimpy adopts a surly circus midget as a pet. Ren does not approve of the midget's cigar-chewing, hair-clogging ways, so tries to flush him out of their lives. He comes back with puppies, which maul Ren.

REN'S BRAIN ***½
Production RS-414

10/7/95; 11 minutes, 36 seconds; Directed by Chris Reccardi; Story by John Kricfalusi and Richard Pursel; Storyboard by Chris Reccardi; Background Color by Scott Wills; Animation by Toon-Us-In Animation, Inc.; Voices: Billy West (Ren, Stimpy, announcer).

Stimpy removes Ren's brain for his experiments. It begins living on its own as Ren would: carrying out his everyday routines, unaware that it is separated from its head and body. Worried about the consequences and still thinking Ren's carcass to be fully functional, Stimpy puts a telephone in Ren's head. Without his brain, Ren is a blithering idiot who fulfills Stimpy's dream of playing moronic games with him. When Ren's brain arrives home from work, it is infuriated to find Stimpy hanging around with "another Chihuahua." The brain gets into a fight with Stimpy, who tries to subdue it with a vaccination. Meanwhile, Ren's body walks into walls. The trauma of the situation causes every viewer of the show's head to explode, destroying the earth. "Thus endeth the Republican party as we know it!" This cartoon had been fully written for years before finally going into production. Reccardi's best as director.

BELLHOPS *

10/28/95; 10 minutes, 50 seconds; Directed by Ken Bruce; Written by Jim Gomez, Vince Calandra, and Ron Hauge; Storyboard by Jim Kammerud; Featuring Mark Hamill; Animation by Mr. Big; Board-only; Voices: Billy West (Ren, Stimpy, Salesman, Fat Lady) and Mark Hamill (Mr. Noggin).

Ren and Stimpy are bellhops at the Salesman's hotel. Their everyday routine of helping the Fat Lady is interrupted by the presence of a mysterious guest, Mr. Noggin, who wishes to not be disturbed under any circumstances. A reporter offers Stimpy a million bucks to get a photo of Noggin, but refuses. Ren takes the job for five bucks. It turns out Noggin is just a head! Trying to prevent Ren from invading his privacy, Stimpy jumps out the penthouse window with Noggin in tow, landing on the Fat Lady. It is love at first sight between the head and the blimp, and they are soon married. As a reward for Ren's greed, Noggin gives him a million-dollar tip—which is quickly taken away by the Salesman.

CENSORSHIP: **S4&5 DVD omits scene of Ren & Stimpy "filthying up" the rooms. Reinstated on the DR&S DVD.**

DOG TAGS   BOMB

10/28/95; 10 minutes, 57 seconds; Directed by Ken Bruce; Written by Ron Hauge; Storyboard by Jim Kammerud; Animation by Rough Draft; Board-only; Voices: Billy West (all voices).

Ren brings a disguised Stimpy to his Benevolent Order of Dog Bone Eaters meeting. Stimpy actually gets past the guards, but Ren is mistaken for a mosquito. Ren tries to prove he really is a dog, to no avail. In the end, Ren himself ends up disguised, joining Stimpy at his cat lodge meeting. Last instance of Ren having a tail.

I WAS A TEENAGE STIMPY ***½
11/4/95; 11 minutes, 3 seconds; Directed by Tom McGrath; Written by Bob Camp, Vince Calandra, and Jim Gomez; Storyboard by Tom McGrath and Stephen DeStefano; Background Color by Scott Wills; Animation by Rough Draft; Voices: Billy West (all voices).

Stimpy is going through cat puberty, and it is not pretty. Zits, voice changes, and frequent growth spurts send the feline into pubescent mood swings, causing him to occupy the bathroom and the phone all hours of the day. Ren is outraged when he finds that Stimpy's pals are "delinquents" Archie and Jughead. Ren grounds the cat until he is fully grown up. While Ren nostalgically watches home movies of the "eediot" as a kitten, Stimpy raids Ren's stash of *Husk* magazine and papers himself with it. Ren discovers this thievery thanks to a James Bond-like security system and goes to give Stimpy what for, only to find that Stimpy has now gone into the pupa stage. Stimpy emerges from his cocoon as a Kirk Douglas-like Superman: claiming that the world needs him, bidding farewell to Ren and his old-man needs. "They grow so fast, and then leave ya! Ya just hope ya raise 'em right," says Ren as he bids farewell to Stimpy flying away into the horizon—which he crashes into. The best Games cartoon, bar none; on level with the best of the Spumco years.

CENSORSHIP: Stimpy's "morning wood" turning out to be his chest hair was cut before broadcast.

WHO'S STUPID NOW? ***
11/4/95; 11 minutes, 18 seconds; Written and Directed by Michael Kim; Background Color by Ramone Zibach; Animation by Toon-Us-In Animations, Inc.; Voices: Billy West (all voices).

When Ren and Stimpy's producer cancels the show, Ren pleads that he will do anything to stay on the air. Unfortunately, that means a role reversal—Ren will play the fat idiot and Stimpy the skinny jerk. After gorging on milkshakes made of Stimpy's fat, Ren is now morbidly obese. Unfortunately, the TV audience finds Ren too repulsive to be endearing and he is booed offstage. Ren goes to Stimpy for comfort, but the cat's transformation into a jerk is already complete. On the set of the show, Ren cannot cope with the abuse handed to him by Stimpy and the producer, and handles it by beating the shit out of both of them. Audiences (and the producer and Stimpy) adore this new dynamic—the fat jerk! "I love show business!" says Ren. Yes, the "feature [film] imminent" headline in one of the last R&S cartoons is meant to be ironic.

CENSORSHIP: S4&5 DVD is missing the intro of Ren onstage, setting up the cartoon's story; also missing is dialogue between producer and Ren at the conveyor belt. Reinstated on the DR&S DVD.

SCHOOL MATES **
Production RS-435
11/11/95; 10 minutes, 39 seconds; Directed by Mark Marren (credited as "Kirk Field"); Written by Jim Gomez; Storyboard by Brian Smith; B.G. Color by Richard Daskas; Animation by Rough Draft; Voices: Billy West (all voices).

When Ren's asshole frat buddy Chuck comes over for a visit, he makes the Chihuahua return to his dog roots by playing games of "chase the cat." This entails ripping the flesh of Stimpy's ass clean off. Some time later, Chuck remembers what a loser Ren actually was in his frat days, so befriends Stimpy and makes Ren play the "cat" instead. In the end, Stimpy cheers up brokenhearted Ren by having a game of "chase the cat" for just the two of them.

DINNER PARTY *

11/11/95; 10 minutes, 53 seconds; No Director Credit; Written by Vince Calandra; Storyboard by Rob Koo and Armen Melkonian; B.G. Color by Richard Daskas; Animation by Rough Draft; Board-only; Voices: Alan Young (Haggis) and Billy West (everyone else).

Ren and Stimpy invite the whole gang over to teach them dinner etiquette. They demonstrate the proper way to eat and pass gas, and how to get everyone to leave by paying someone else—in this case, Mr. Pipe—to claim that they are all trespassing in his house. A literally undirected episode.

BIG FLAKES **

11/18/95; 9 minutes, 31 seconds; Directed by Ken Bruce; Storyboard by Tom McGrath; Written by Ron Hauge, Jim Gomez, and Bob Camp; B.G. Color by Richard Zaloudek; Animation by Mr. Big Cartoons; Board-only; Voices: Billy West (all voices).

Ren and Stimpy are snowed in at Ren's parents' cabin in the mountains. They become progressively more insane: eating the wood of the cabin, thinking it jerky. It is finally revealed that the thaw has come to the area—save the snow surrounding the cabin. Strong premise which fails to deliver.

PEN PALS **½

11/18/95; 10 minutes, 34 seconds; Directed by Tom Owens and Craig Bartlett; Written by Ron Hauge; Storyboard by Michael Kim; Background by Scott Wills; Animation by Toon-Us-In Animations, Inc.; Voices: Billy West (Ren, Stimpy, Cop) and Bob Camp (prison escapee).

After losing his mother's house to debt, Ren tries to get himself and Stimpy a new home at the luxurious Tula Pines Penitentiary. Their plan to get arrested for robbing a bank goes wrong when they are blown up. Next, they try breaking into the prison—first via a rope, which fails miserably when they destroy the remains of the warden's now-stuffed dog. An attempted entrance through the prison sewer line only gets them mistaken for turds. Finally, the two destroy the prison through catapult warfare. It works, and the two are given thirteen life sentences—with a cellmate the size of the cell!

TERMINAL STIMPY **½
Production RS-425

12/9/95; 11 minutes, 13 seconds; Directed by Arthur Filloy; Written by Jim Gomez, Bob Camp, and Vince Calandra; Storyboard by Mark Marren (credited as "Kirk Field") and Bob Camp; B.G. Color by Richard Zaloudek; Animation by Mr. Big Cartoons; Board-only; Voices: Billy West (Ren, Stimpy, Salesman, Alfred Hitchcock), Harris Peet (Muddy Mudskipper), and Mike Pataki (cow).

Stimpy realizes that reckless living has cost him seven of his nine lives. Then he loses his eighth: while lighting the gas, Stimpy is crushed by a block of shit from an airplane toilet. Now down to just one life, the cat goes through the five stages preceding death and finally accepts it. "Death is life's great reward!" exclaim Stimpy and Ren. With a cake, they celebrate the end that will eventually arrive. Lighting the candle blows them to kingdom come—Stimpy never did shut off the gas. Ren and Stimpy arrive at the Pearly Gates, where the only way they can get in is by bribing the guard, the Salesman.

REVEREND JACK ***
Production RS-419

12/9/95; 11 minutes, 13 seconds (original version); 10 minutes, 48 seconds (edited version); Directed by Craig Bartlett; Written by Bob Camp and Jim Gomez; Storyboard by Stephen DeStefano; B.G. Color by Scott Wills; Featuring Frank Gorshin as the Rev. Jack Cheese;

Animation by Rough Draft; Mostly board-only; Voices: Billy West (Ren, Stimpy), Harris Peet (Jasper), and Frank Gorshin (Reverend Jack Cheese).

Ren and Stimpy work for the genius Reverend Jack Cheese, who sells meat products to children while preaching the Gospel of Meat. After their own private ceremony, the Reverend goes apeshit. He drives their meat truck out of state at full speed, ordering Ren not to stop. After driving for months without putting on a single show, Stimpy approaches the Reverend in concern—only to find he has delved deeper into his psychosis. A cop (Jasper again) pulls them over and is repulsed to find the Reverend nude among the meats. He takes away the Reverend's meat confectioner license. In the end, Ren and Stimpy put on the show by themselves, only to be heckled by the disgruntled Reverend. This hugely metaphoric cartoon is a valentine to Kricfalusi from his former coworkers. It most likely does not work for those not privy to the story.

CENSORSHIP: **Airings of this cartoon, as well as the S4&5 DVD and DR&S DVD, remove most of the meat ceremony and the shot of the Reverend's skin hat.**

A SCOOTER FOR YAKSMAS **

12/16/95; 17 minutes, 20 seconds; Directed by Bob Camp; Story by Bob Camp, Jim Gomez, and Vince Calandra; Storyboard by Bob Camp, Tom McGrath, and Stephen DeStefano; B.G. Color by Bill Wray; Animation by Rough Draft; Voices: Billy West (Ren, Stimpy), Bob Camp (Stinky Wizzleteats, fat guy), June Lockhart (woman), and Harris Peet (Muddy Mudskipper).

Coming home from his assembly-line job at the popsicle stick factory, Stimpy is ecstatic that it is Yaksmas Eve. He just *knows* that Old Saint Stinky Whizzleteats will bring him a Johnny Future Jet Scooter. After a wacky song about Whizzleteats, Stimpy is dismayed that the jolly old oaf did not bring him a scooter; nor did Ren, despite Stimpy having gotten Ren his jewel-encrusted Queen of England statue. The cat has a fit of rage in front of a department store window carrying the scooter. "You were supposed to be mine!" Stimpy's outburst causes the glass to shatter and the scooter to fall into his arms. Upon hearing a lady refer to the culprit as a "fat guy in a red suit," he takes it on the lam with the scooter. Ren refuses to give him shelter and even aids the police. Stimpy seeks the one person who can help him—Stinky Whizzleteats. After a journey that renders the scooter useless, Stimpy finds Stinky and his yak staying at the West Pole Motel. It turns out that Ren had gotten Stimpy a scooter all along: Stinky was simply too drunk to deliver it in time. Stimpy heads for home, leaving the battered scooter behind—and causing the police to think Stinky is the "fat guy in the red suit." Likeable enough Christmas special, but clearly not in the same league as *Son of Stimpy*.

SAMMY AND ME **½

10/20/1996; 11 minutes, 14 seconds; Directed by Bill Wray; Written by Jim Gomez and Bill Wray; Storyboard by Stephen DeStefano and Bill Wray; Animation Direction by Arthur Filloy; B.G. Color by Bill Wray; Featuring Tommy Davidson as Sammy; Animation by Mr. Big Cartoons; Board-only; Voices: Billy West (Ren, Stimpy, Liberoachie) and Tommy Davidson (Sammy).

Stimpy is in awe of his idol, singer Sammy Mantis, who croons to his victims as he bites off their heads. Stimpy soon not only dresses like Sammy, but collects his dead skin, too. Stimpy runs into the Mantid Man himself one night and is chided by him for breaking onto his property. Stimpy breaks down in tears. To cheer the feline up, Sammy fulfills Stimpy's dream of biting his head off. Of course, Stimpy survives, because he doesn't really have a head. Full of heavy-handed references to Rat Pack culture, but very funny. Originally banned from

Nickelodeon due to Sammy Mantis' screw-in glass eye; premiered on MTV.

CENSORSHIP: S4&5 DVD is missing some dialog between Ren and Stimpy in bed over the "mantid obsession." Reinstated on the DR&S DVD.

THE LAST TEMPTATION **½

10/20/96; 11 minutes, 15 seconds; Directed by Bob Camp; Written by Jim Gomez, Vince Calandra, and Bob Camp; Storyboard by Bob Camp; B.G. Color by Bill Wray; Animation by Toon-Us-In Animations, Inc.; Voices: Billy West (Ren, Stimpy, God) and Jack Carter (Wilbur Cobb).

Ren chokes on the oatmeal Stimpy serves him and has an out-of-body experience in purgatory. He meets the "big guy," Wilbur Cobb, who tells Ren that he needs to lead a better life if he wants to get into heaven. Cobb gives Ren a second chance and sends him back to his body (revealing in the process that Cobb is only the gardener for God). Upon returning to earth, Ren lives life as a pauper, ignoring Stimpy's extravagant spendthrift ways. When Stimpy chokes on a whole chicken, Ren contemplates letting him choke and inheriting all his possessions—until Cobb points him in the right direction. With both of them saved, Cobb takes away all of Stimpy's "ill-gotten" possessions, leaving the hapless duo in tears. Originally banned for its religious parodies, the episode premiered on MTV.

CENSORSHIP: S4&5 DVD is missing a poolside scene. Reinstated on the DR&S DVD.

SHORTS:
VARICOSE VEINS
1 minute, 58 seconds; Directed by Ken Bruce (aired with "Big Flakes")

DOG WATER #2
1 minute, 34 seconds; Animation by Toon- Us-In Animations, Inc. (aired with "A Scooter for Yaksmas")

KRAFTWORK CORNER
2 minutes; Animation by Toon-Us-In Animations, Inc. (aired with "A Scooter for Yaksmas")

ADULT PARTY CARTOON

ONWARD AND UPWARD   BOMB
6/26/03; 19 minutes, 33 seconds; Directed by John Kricfalusi; Story by Vincent Waller; Storyboard by Vincent Waller, Eddie Fitzgerald, Fred Osmond, and Ray Morelli; Animation Directed by Bob Jaques; Starring the Voices of John Kricfalusi and Eric Bauza; Animation by Carbunkle Cartoons and Big Star.

Ren and Stimpy are a gay couple living in a hobo's mouth. Fed up with it all, they move uptown to live the "high life"—in a bar's spittoon. They live a purely upper-crust lifestyle, feeding on mucus, boogers and puke, and having anal sex in a pre-stained bed. They are thrown out once they are discovered by the bar's patrons.

REN SEEKS HELP   ***½
7/3/03; 23 minutes, 28 seconds; Directed by John Kricfalusi; Story by John Kricfalusi and Richard D. Pursel; Storyboard by Steve Stefanelli, Helder Mendonca, Jeff Amey, Derek Bond, Tavis Silbernagel, and John Kricfalusi; Background Design by Nick Cross; Background Color Styling by Kristy Gordon; Layout Supervision by Helder Mendonca; Ink & Paint and Special FX by Dulcie Clark's PIP Animation; Animation Directed by Bob Jaques; Animation by Carbunkle Cartoons and Big Star; Voices: John Kricfalusi (Ren, Mr. Horse), Eric Bauza (Stimpy), Mike Kricfalusi (Ren's dad), and Cheryl Chase (Ren's mom).

After doing something terrible to Stimpy, Ren seeks help from psychologist Dr. Mr. Horse. Ren tells Horse about the days of his youth—particularly about his torture of a hapless frog and his refusal, out of sick pleasure, to put the frog out of its misery. When Mr. Horse gets to Ren's relationship with Stimpy, Ren whispers what he did to him. Mr. Horse's diagnosis is that Ren is "fucking crazy!" He proceeds to beat the living hell out of Ren. Ren fights back and bludgeons Horse to death with a gun. The men in white suits arrive; after biting off the hand of one of them, Ren is taken away to the funny farm. In the end, the dismembered frog returns, attempting suicide with the dead Horse's gun. A grim classic.

FIRE DOGS 2   BOMB

7/17/03 and 7/24/03; 27 minutes, 33 seconds (Live-action bumpers—4 minutes, 52 seconds); Directed by John Kricfalusi; Story by John Kricfalusi, Richard D. Pursel, Eddie Fitzgerald, Vincent Waller, and Jim Smith; Storyboard by John Kricfalusi, Jim Smith, Eddie Fitzgerald, Vincent Waller, and Jose Pou; Animation by Big Star and Carbunkle Cartoons; Animation Directed by Bob Jaques; Starring Ralph Bakshi—The World's Greatest Cartoonist.

Following the events of the original *Fire Dogs*, the Fire Chief morphs into Ralph Bakshi. Ren and Stimpy move in with him and witness his deranged activities—mainly him taking shits. More unpleasantness without a thing going for it. The cartoon was split into a two-parter to accommodate late delivery; originally aired with live-action bumpers.

NAKED BEACH FRENZY ***

23 minutes, 4 seconds; Directed by John Kricfalusi; Story by John Kricfalusi, Mike Kerr, Jeff Amey, and Caroline J. Alvarez; Storyboard by Jeff Amey, Steve Stefanelli, Matt Roach, and Nick Cross; Scantily Clad Girls Designed by Katie Rice and Nick Cross; Layouts by Jose Pou, Tavis Silbernagel, Marcel Laurin, Warren Leonhardt, Nick Cross, Tim Pallett, Aleks Prohaska, Katie Rice, Luke Cormican, Fred Osmond, Ray Morelli, Robert Cory, Gene McGuckin and Wil Branca; B.G. Color Design by Jay Li and Kristy Gordon; Character Color Design by Chris Wallace; Animation by Carbunkle Cartoons and Big Star;

Animation Directed by Bob Jaques!; Voices: John Kricfalusi (Ren), Eric Bauza (Stimpy), Jose Pou (Juahini), Kristy Gordon (Beachball Girl, Shampoo Girl), Mike MacDonald (Lifeguard), Julia Ediger (Girl 1), Annie Gosling (Girl 2), Alison Acton (Girl 3), Jennifer Tam (Girl 4), Julie Engelberts (Lifeguard Captain), Mike Kricfalusi (Staff Lobster), Katie Rice (Soap Girl), and Jody O'Hara (Suntan Oil Girl).

Ren tries to hook up with women at the beach, but is foiled by a disgruntled, hairy lifeguard. He and Stimpy get jobs as bathroom attendants and get to feel up and shave naked girls. After falling into the lifeguard's asshole, the two are run off a cliff into the ocean and taken off into the sunset on dolphins (a la *The Three Stooges*). Amusing tits-and-testosterone cartoon. Never broadcast in the U.S., but was shown abroad.

ALTRUISTS *

39 minutes, 8 seconds; Directed by John Kricfalusi; Starring the Voice Talents of John Kricfalusi, Eric Bauza, Kristy Gordon, Cheryl Chase, Mike Kricfalusi, and Steve Worth; Animation: Big Star and Carbunkle Cartoons; Story: Vincent Waller, John Kricfalusi, Mike Kerr, Eric Bauza, Jeff Amey, and Richard Pursel; Storyboard: Vincent Waller, Jeff Amey, Nick Cross, and Matt Roach; Character Color Styling: Chris Wallace; Backgrounds: Kristy Gordon, Nick Cross, Jay Li, Simon Dupuis, Allain Masicotte, Troy Little, and Hyeonyeong Jeon; Layout Supervision: Helder Mendonca and Fred Osmond; Layouts: Joseph Pou, Warren Leonhardt, Luke Cormican, Tavis Silbernagel, Marcel Laurin, Gerry Duchemin, Nick Cross, Katie Rice, Tim Pallett, Ray Morelli, Gene McGuckin, and Vincent Waller.

Ren and Stimpy help a widow and her decapitated son by robbing the rich and building them a house. Obscenely long and woefully unfunny. The longest *Ren & Stimpy* cartoon ever. Never broadcast in the U.S., aired as two half-hour shows abroad.

STIMPY'S PREGNANT **

29 minutes, 5 seconds; Supervision by M. John Kricfalusi; Starring Eric Bauza as Stimpy as Mrs. Höek and the Spumco Players John and Mike Kricfalusi and Kristy Gordon; Story and Storyboard by John Kricfalusi, Jeff Amey, Richard Pursel, Matt Roach, Steve Stefanelli, and Warren Leonhardt; Color Styling by Christine Wallace; Sheet Timing by Alison Acton and Greg [Duffell]; Leica/Sound Editing by Eric Bauza, Jose Pou, and John Kricfalusi; Art Direction by Nick Cross and Kristy Gordon; Layouts by Nick Cross, Tavis Sibernagel, Eric Bauza, Alison Acton, Gerry Duchemin, Helder Mendonca, John Kricfalusi, Jose Pou, Warren Leonhardt, Marcel Laurin, Jessica Borutski (Animation too!), Fred Osmond, Ray Morelli, Katie Rice, Luke Cormican, Robert Ryan Cory, Wil Branca, Gene McGuckin, and Vincent Waller; Ink & Paint/Compositing by PIP Animation Studios; Editing by Leaping Raster and Shawn Phillips; Audio Recording and Mix by Sound of One Hand, Michel Legault, Claud Marquis; Animation/BG Paint by Big Star; Spike TV Executives in Charge of Production—Albie Hecht and Kevin Kay; Executive Producer—Kevin Kolde.

Stimpy is apparently pregnant with Ren's lovechild. After a grueling nine months for Stimpy, the time has come. Stimpy and Ren make a mad rush for the hospital, shooting other people out of the way. Mr. Horse is to deliver the child, but his prognosis is that Stimpy is not pregnant—just constipated. Mr. Horse delivers the shit and the happy couple treats it as their child. Has its moments and potential, but reeks of "missed chance." Never broadcast in the U.S., aired as two half-hour shows abroad.

Endnotes

Chapter 1

1. Michael Barrier, "The Filming of Fritz the Cat," *Funnyworld* No. 14, Spring 1972.
2. Justin Smallbridge, "Ren and Stimpy's Big Corporate Takeover," *Saturday Night*, April 1994.
3. Reg Hartt, e-mail message to the author, 17 November 2009.
4. Smallbridge.
5. Jim Gomez, phone interview with the author, 1 August 2009.
6. Harry McCracken, "'My Intended Audience Was Everybody': An Interview with *Mighty Mouse: The New Adventures*' John Kricfalusi," *Animato* #16, Spring 1988.
7. "Big Blown Bill Wray," *Draw!* #6, Spring 2003, 10.

8   Bob Jaques, phone call with the author, 6 September 2009.
9   John Kricfalusi, "L.O. 12: Jetsons 1985—Trying to Bring Life Back," *John K Stuff*, 23 November 2008. http://johnkstuff.blogspot.com/2008/11/jetsons-1985-trying-to-bring-life-back.html (accessed 20 January 2012).
10 Jerry Beck, phone interview with the author, 25 October 2009.
11 Jason Anders, "A Conversation with Ralph Bakshi," *Fulle Circle Podcast*, http://fullecirclestuff.blogspot.com/2009/11/ conversation-with-ralph-bakshi.html (accessed 21 January 2012).
12 Tom Minton, e-mail message to the author, 1 April 2013. Minton clarified that he did not work on the projects listed here, regardless if Bakshi's comment suggests otherwise.
13 Scott Thill, "Q&A: Toon Titan John Kricfalusi Hails Mighty Mouse Rebirth," Wired.com, http://www.wired.com/ underwire/2010/01/john-kricfalusi/ (accessed 24 January 2012).
14 Mike Kim, interview with the author, Hollywood, California, 19 March 2010.
15 Tom Klein, phone interview with the author, 4 October 2009.
16 Thill.
17 Ed Bell, phone interview with the author, 1 June 2010.
18 Jim Gomez, phone interview with the author, 8 June 2011.
19 McCracken.
20 Klein interview.
21 Byron Vaughns, e-mail interview with the author, 14 August 2010.
22 Thill.
23 Ralph Bakshi to Employees, "Memorandum," 14 May 1987. Collection of the author, photocopy provided by Bob Jaques.
24 Kent Butterworth, e-mail interview with the author, 7 January 2010.
25 McCracken.
26 Gomez interview, 2009.
27 Minton e-mail.
28 Mike Ventrella, "Bakshi to the Future," *Animato* #17, Summer 1988, 10.
29 McCracken.
30 Steve Gordon, e-mail interview with the author, 26 November 2009.

31 Ibid.
32 Butterworth interview.
33 Eddie Fitzgerald, comment on "Robert Rauschenberg, Genius," *Uncle Eddie's Theory Corner*, http://uncleeddiestheorycorner.blogspot.com/2010/02/robert-rauschenberg-genius.html (accessed 25 January 2012).
34 Gordon interview.
35 John Kricfalusi, "Breaking the Mold: The Re-Making of Mighty Mouse," *Mighty Mouse: The New Adventures! The Complete Series* DVD, 2009
36 Eric Nolen-Weathington, *Modern Masters Volume Three: Bruce Timm*, July 2004, 27.
37 Gomez interviews, 2009 and 2011.
38 Nolen-Weathington, 26.
39 Klein interview.
40 John Kricfalusi, Audio Commentary on "Night of the Bat-Bat", *Mighty Mouse: The New Adventures! The Complete Series* DVD, 2009.
41 Bob Jaques, e-mail message to the author, 4 April 2010.
42 Ventrella, 9.
43 Ibid, 10.
44 Robert Goldberg, "A Rad Rodent with Bite," *The Wall Street Journal*, 18 January 1988.
45 Charles Solomon, "Kidvid Reviews Cartoon Debuts Are All Drawn Out," *The Los Angeles Times*, 9 October 1987.
46 McCracken.
47 Ibid.
48 Ventrella, 10.
49 Klein interview.
50 Butterworth interview.
51 Bell interview.
52 Klein interview.
53 Jim Reardon, "Breaking the Mold: The Re-Making of Mighty Mouse."
54 "Allegation stinks, CBS says/Minister claims Mighty Mouse snorts cocaine in cartoon," *The Houston Chronicle*, 10 June 1988.

55 John Carmody, "The TV Column," *The Washington Post*, 25 July 1988.
56 Bell interview.
57 Doug Lawrence, phone interview with the author, 17 July 2007.
58 An Exchange with John K." Correspondence between John Kricfalusi and historian Michael Barrier. http://michaelbarrier.com/Feedback/feedback_johnk.htm
59 Vaughns interview.
60 Nolen-Weathington, 31.
61 Klein interview.
62 Michael Dougan, "People meters may doom shows for toddlers who can't 'sign in'," *San Francisco Examiner*, 24 September 1988.
63 Gomez interview, 2011.
64 John Kricfalusi, "Writing for Cartoons 4—Ideas: The Origin of Cecils," *John K Stuff*, http://johnkstuff.blogspot.com/2007/03/ writing-for-cartoons-4-ideas-origin-of.html (accessed 16 June 2011).
65 Ibid.
66 Chuck Lorre, "The First Time I Got Fired," from *The First Time I Got Paid For It: Writers' Tales From The Hollywood Trenches*, 124, 2002.
67 Dan Persons, "Spumco's Ren & Stimpy Revolution," *Cinefantastique*, Vol. 24, No. 1, June 1993, 30.
68 Lorre, 126.
69 Ibid, 127.
70 Paul Dini, phone interview with the author, 9 February 2012.
71 Ibid.
72 Nolen-Weathington, 31.
73 Cathleen Schine, "From Lassie to Pee-Wee," *The New York Times*, 30 October 1988.
74 Dini interview.
75 Persons, 1993, 30.
76 Nolen-Weathington, 36.

77 John Kricfalusi, "Maintaining Guts from Storyboard to Layout," *John K Stuff*, 9 October 2007, http://johnkstuff.blogspot.com/2007/10/maintaining-guts-from-storyboard-to.html (accessed 16 June 2011).
78 Bob Miller, e-mail interview with the author, 5 November 2009.
79 Gomez interview, 2011.
80 Chris Reccardi, e-mail interview with the author, 9 September 2009.
81 Dini interview.
82 Nolen-Weathington, 31.
83 John Kricfalusi, letter to Jennie Trias and Jeff Holder, 2 September 1988. Collection of the author, photocopy provided by Mark Kausler.
84 Bob Camp, phone interview with the author, 6 July 2006.

Chapter 2

1 "Hi Fructose Feature Interview with Chris Reccardi," *Hi Fructose Magazine*, 6 October 2008, http://www.hifructose.com/index.php?option=com_content&task=view&id=208
2 Butterworth interview.
3 Camp interview, 2006.
4 Beck interview.
5 Carl Macek, interview with the author, Anaheim, California, 13 March 2010.
6 Camp interview, 2006.
7 Gomez interview, 2009.
8 Vanessa Coffey, phone interview with the author, 2 December 2009.
9 Wheeler Winston Dixon, *Collected Interviews: Voices from Twentieth-Century Cinema* (Carbondale and Edwardsville: Southern Illinois University Press, 2001), 89.
10 Macek interview.
11 Persons, 1993, 30.
12 Macek interview.
13 Dixon, 89.
14 Coffey interview.
15 Macek interview.

16 Coffey interview.
17 John Kricfalusi, "In the Beginning," *The Ren & Stimpy Show: The First and Second Seasons* DVD, 2004.
18 Christian Gore, "Celling Out," *Film Threat*, Vol. 2, No. 7, October 1992, 24.
19 John Kricfalusi, "Ren & Stimpy History," *Comics Interview* #131, 1994, 13.
20 John Kricfalusi, Reddit.com chat, http://www.m.reddit.com/r/IAmA/comments/aocjg/iamajohnk_ren_and_stimpy_creator/
21 Jim Gomez, e-mail interview with the author, 15 January 2010.
22 Anders, "A Conversation with Ralph Bakshi."
23 Macek interview.
24 Persons, 1993, 31 and 34.
25 Macek interview.
26 Beck interview.
27 Camp interview, 2006.
28 Dixon, 92.
29 Jordan Reichek, e-mail interview with the author, 7 January 2010.
30 Don Shank, e-mail interview with the author, 3 March 2010.
31 Jason Anders, "The Ren & Stimpy Show: A Retrospective," *Hogan's Alley*, No. 18, December 2011, 49.
32 John Kricfalusi, "Big House Blues Spumco 2—Why Ren no longer Has a Tail," *John K Stuff*, 18 April 2009, http://johnkstuff.blogspot.com/2009/04/big-house-blues-spumco-2-why-ren- no.html (accessed 27 February 2012).
33 Anders, 47.
34 Camp interview, 2006.
35 Kelly Armstrong, e-mail interview with the author, 18 January 2012.
36 John Kricfalusi, "Carbunkle 2—Ren's Romantic Dream," *John K Stuff*, 12 April 2009, http://johnkstuff.blogspot.com/2009/04/ carbunkle-2-rens-romantic-dream.html (accessed 27 February 2012).
37 Billy West, interview with the author, with Jim Gomez, Hollywood, California, 18 March 2010.
38 Persons, 1993, 34 and 37.

39 Reccardi interview.
40 Ibid.
41 Beck interview.
42 Linda Simensky, phone interview with the author, 15 January 2010.
43 Coffey interview.

Chapter 3

1   John Kricfalusi, "Artists Finally Win Some Respect and Credit." *John K Stuff*, 19 October 2009, http://johnkstuff.blogspot. com/2009/10/artists-finally-win-some-respect-and.html (accessed 24 May 2010).
2   Chris Danzo, interview with the author, Malibu, California, 16 March 2010.
3   Camp interview, 2006.
4   Dixon, 94.
5   Gomez interview, 2009.
6   Anders, 46.
7   John Kricfalusi, "Writing for Cartoons—Stimpy's Invention—Outline Hierarchy." *John K Stuff*, 8 May 2007, http:// johnkstuff.blogspot.com/2007/05/writing-for-cartoons- stimpys-invention.html (accessed 24 May 2010).
8   Persons, 1993, 38.
9   Mitch Kriegman, phone interview with the author, 12 January 2010.
10 Persons, 1993, 47.
11 Danzo interview.
12 Outline: "Nurse Stimpy," 7 December 1990. Collection of the author, photocopy provided by Jerry Beck.
13 Gore, "Celling Out," 39.
14 Kriegman interview.
15 Smallbridge.
16 Danzo interview.
17 Roy Smith, interview with Bob Jaques, Hollywood, California, 2008.

18 Mark Langer, "Ren & Stimpy: Fan Culture and Corporate Strategy," in *Nickelodeon Nation: The History, Politics, and Economics of America's Only TV Channel for Kids*, ed. Heather Hendershot (New York: New York University Press, 2004), 174.
19 Anders, 45.
20 Coffey interview.
21 Kriegman interview.
22 Camp interview, 2006.
23 Persons, 1993, 55.
24 Richard Katz, "Not All Fun & Games," *Cablevision*, 24 May 1993, 40.
25 Bob Camp, e-mail message to the author, 19 October 2010.
26 Will McRobb, phone interview with the author, 5 November 2009.
27 Outline for "Stimpy's Invention", dated 21 January 1991, cites Will McRobb as story editor, not Mitchell Kriegman.
28 Kriegman interview.
29 Reichek interview.
30 Lawrence interview. Camp interview, 2006.
31 Richard Pursel, e-mail message to the author, 15 June 2011.
32 Gomez interview, 2009.
33 Bob Camp, interview published in *X Magazine* #10, 1992.
34 Bill Wray, interview with Greg Theakston, published in *Pure Images* #5, 1992.
35 Reichek interview.
36 Teale Wang, e-mail interview with the author, 26 November 2009.
37 Anders, 46.
38 "Hi Fructose Feature Interview with Chris Reccardi."
39 David Koenigsberg, phone interview with the author, 10 October 2010.
40 Pursel e-mail.
41 Nolen-Weathington, 40.
42 Persons, 1993, 27.
43 Matt Roush, "'Ren & Stimpy' eez it," *USA Today*, 11 August 1992.

44 Josh Ozersky, "Cat-eat-dog (and worse) world to animate TV," *The Washington Times*, 13 August 1992.
45 Andy Mesiler, "Ren and Stimpy's Triumphant Return," *The New York Times*, 16 August 1992.
46 Jamie Oliff, e-mail message to the author, 4 February 2010.
47 Ibid.
48 Bob Jaques, e-mail message to the author, 24 September 2009.
49 Chris Savino, interview with Jon Drukman, 8 February 1992. Published in *X Magazine* #10.
50 Howard Baker, e-mail interview with the author, 6 November 2009.
51 Ibid.
52 Koenigsberg interview, 2010.
53 Nolen-Weathington, 28.
54 John Kricfalusi, "BGs and Style 10 —use reference, get ideas and inspiration from different styles." *John K Stuff*, 22 February 2007, http://johnkstuff.blogspot.com/2007/02/bgs-and-style-10-use-reference-get.html (accessed 3 April 2012).
55 "Big Blown Bill Wray," 13.
56 Bob Camp and Bill Wray, interview with the author, 17 April 2016, at East Coast Coast Comicon in Secaucus, New Jersey. Published online at Jerry Beck's *Animation Scoop* as "Interview: 25 Years Later, Directors Bob Camp and Bill Wray Remember *The Ren & Stimpy Show*."
57 Persons, 1993, 30.
58 Persons, 1993, 29.
59 Beck interview.
60 Reccardi interview.
61 John Kricfalusi, "L.O. 1—Why Layout," *John K Stuff*, 17 March 2010, http://johnkstuff.blogspot.com/2010/03/lo-1-why-layout.html (accessed 24 May 2010).
62 Shank interview.
63 Stephen DeStefano, e-mail interview with the author, 11 August 2009.
64 Kim interview.

65 Gomez interview, 2010
66 Shank interview.
67 Smith interview.
68 John Kricfalusi, "BGs and Style 7—Inki and the Minah Bird (1943) Backgrounds." *John K Stuff*, 23 January 2007, http:// johnkstuff.blogspot.com/2006/11/inki-and-minah-bird- 1943-backgrounds.html (accessed 3 April 2012).
69 John Kricfalusi, "Big Layout Memo," 3 April 1991. Collection of the author, photocopy provided by Mark Kausler.
70 Eddie Fitzgerald, audio commentary for "A Cartoon" (a.k.a. "Untamed World"), *The Ren & Stimpy Show UNCUT: The Complete First and Second Seasons* DVD, 2004.
71 Reichek interview.
72 Bob Camp, interview with Greg Method, January 1994.
73 Persons, 1993, 38.
74 Ibid.
75 McRobb interview.
76 Anders, 46.
77 West interview.
78 "Ren Audition" Sign-In Sheet, 4 April 1991. Collection of the author, original provided by Jerry Beck.
79 Danzo interview.
80 Wray with Theakston.
81 Carbunkle Payment Log for *Space Madness*. First scenes were completed by Chris Sauve on 14 June 1991. Collection of the author, photocopy provided by Bob Jaques.
82 Bob Jaques, e-mail message to the author, 24 September 2009.
83 Persons, 1993, 49.
84 Kim interview.
85 Ron Zorman, e-mail interview with the author, 21 December 2009.
86 Scott Mansz, e-mail interview with the author, 21 January 2014.

87 Chris Sauve, interview with the author, with Bob Jaques, San Diego, California, 27 July 2007.
88 Armstrong interview.
89 Bob Jaques, e-mail message to the author, 4 June 2011.
90 Camp interview, 2006.
91 David Koenigsberg, phone interview with the author, 9 January 2011.
92 John Kricfalusi, "Space Madness Gets Extra Credits." *John K Stuff*, 20 October 2009, http:// http://johnkstuff.blogspot. com/2009/10/space-madness-gets-extra-credits.html (accessed 24 May 2010).
93 John Kricfalusi, "Artists Finally Win Some Respect and Credit." *John K Stuff*, 19 October 2009, http://johnkstuff. blogspot.com/2009/10/artists-finally-win-some-respect-and. html (accessed 24 May 2010).
94 Persons, 1993, 30.
95 Bob Jaques, e-mail message to the author, 4 January 2010.
96 John Kricfalusi, memo to Chris Danzo, 20 February 1991. Collection of the author, photocopy provided by Bob Jaques.
97 Danzo interview.
98 Kricfalusi to Danzo.
99 Kricfalusi, "Big Layout Memo."
100 "Artists Finally Win Some Respect and Credit."
101 Danzo interview.
102 Cheryl Chase, phone interview with the author, 11 June 2010.
103 Koenigsberg interview, 2010.
104 Camp interview, 2006.
105 Coffey interview.
106 Vanessa Coffey, e-mail message to the author, 11 January 2011.
107 Paula Parisi, "Nicktoons Gets $40 mil infusion," *The Hollywood Reporter*, 21 November 1991.

Chapter 4

1 Persons, 1993, 38.
2 Darrel L. Boatz, "John Kricfalusi," Comics Interview no. 131, 1994, 8.

3   Persons, 1993, 42.
4   Vincent Waller, comment on "Stimpy's Invention." *John K Stuff*, comment posted October 25, 2009, http://johnkstuff. blogspot.com/2009/10/stimpys-invention.html (accessed May 13, 2010).
5   Vincent Waller, John Kricfalusi, Audio Commentary for "Stimpy's Invention", *The Ren & Stimpy Show: The First and Second Seasons Uncut*, 2004.
6   Outline, "Stimpy's Invention."
7   Coffey interview.
8   Danzo interview.
9   Persons, 1993, 42.
10 Gomez interview, 2009.
11 Chris Savino, interview with Jon Drukman, 8 February 1992. Published in *X Magazine*, no. 10.
12 Reichek interview.
13 Wang interview.
14 Beck interview.
15 Wang interview.
16 Koenigsberg interview, 2010.
17 Payment Log for Animators, RS06B "Stimpy's Inventions," 1991. Collection of the author, photocopy provided by Bob Jaques.
18 Mark Kausler, e-mail messages to the author, 20 and 21 September 2009.
19 Danzo interview.
20 Koenigsberg interview, 9 January 2011.
21 Persons, 1993, 38.
22 Anders, 50.
23 Bob Jaques, phone call with the author, 3 June 2011; elaboration and clarification added via e-mail 6 January 2014.
24 Danzo interview.
25 Persons, 1993, 42.
26 Gomez interview, 2009.
27 Gore, "Celling Out," 30.
28 Kricfalusi, audio commentary for "Stimpy's Invention".

29 Armstrong interview.
30 Zorman interview.
31 Persons, 1993, 49.
32 Kricfalusi, "Writing for Cartoons—Stimpy's Invention—Outline Hierarchy."
33 Savino with Drukman.
34 Danzo interview.

Chapter 5

1 Parisi, "Nicktoons Gets $40 mil infusion."
2 "'The Ren & Stimpy Show' comes to MTV Dec. 28," *Business Wire*, 16 December 1991.
3 Bob Camp, interview appearing in *X Magazine* #10, 1992 (http://groups.google.com/group/alt.animation.spumco/msg/ baa4cab0e9ce5e2f ?hl=en).
4 Reichek interview.
5 Camp and Wray interview, 2016.
6 Tom Hay, interview with the author, Ottawa, Ontario, 21 November 2010.
7 Camp interview, 2006.
8 Diane Joy Moca, "Hot Dog and Gritty Kitty Make History as 'Ren and Stimpy,'" *The Seattle Post-Intelligencer* (originally from *The Los Angeles Daily News*), 15 August 1992.
9 John Armstrong, "Laughing at their own jokes," *The Vancouver Sun*, 17 August 1992.
10 Wang interview.
11 Elinor Blake, phone interview with the author, 7 June 2010.
12 Bell interview.
13 Ray Richmond, "Cartoonist injecting creativity into lifeless art form," *The Orange County Register*, 14 August 1992.
14 Stefan Kanfer, "Loonier toon tales," *Time*, 13 April 1992, 79.
15 Roush, "'Ren & Stimpy' eez it."
16 Daniel Cerone, "Toontown Terrors," *The Los Angeles Times*, 9 August 1992.
17 Ibid.

18 Andy Meisler, "Ren and Stimpy's Triumphant Return," *The New York Times*, 16 August 1992.
19 Ibid.
20 Coffey interview.
21 Matt Roush, "'Ren & Stimpy' stay off the wall," *USA Today*, 7 July 1992.
22 Andy Meisler, "While Team 2 Works to Reform 'Ren and Stimpy,'" *The New York Times*, 21 November 1993.
23 Koenigsberg interview, 9 January 2011.
24 Mathew Klickstein, *Slimed! An Oral History of Nickelodeon's Golden Age* (New York: Penguin, 2013), 181.
25 Moca, "Hot Dog and Gritty Kitty Make History as 'Ren and Stimpy.'"
26 *Comics Interview* #122, 1993, 11.
27 Cerone, "Toontown Terrors."
28 Simensky interview.
29 McRobb interview.
30 Bob Camp, e-mail message to the author, 26 October 2009.
31 Will McRobb, "Ren and Stimpy Notes: Sven Hoek and Visit to Anthony," 6 November 1991. Collection of the author, photocopy provided by Jerry Beck.
32 Will McRobb, "Ren and Stimpy Notes: Rubber Nipple Salesmen," 6 November 1991. Collection of the author, provided by Jerry Beck.
33 Ibid.
34 McRobb, "Ren and Stimpy Notes: Sven Hoek and Visit to Anthony."
35 Simensky interview.
36 McRobb, "Ren and Stimpy Notes: Rubber Nipple Salesmen."
37 "Ren & Stimpy Third Season Fact Sheet," dated 19 November 1993, as it appears in *Comics Interview* #131, 1994.
38 Gore, "Celling Out," 39.
39 Camp interview, 2006.
40 Coffey interview.
41 McRobb interview.
42 Coffey interview.

43 Donna Gable, "Will new 'Ren & Stimpy' be as purposely perverse?" *USA Today*, 30 October 1992.
44 Libby Simon, phone interview with the author, 20 October 2009.
45 Bob Camp, interview with Jason Anders, June 2010 http://fullecirclestuff.blogspot.com/2010/06/conversation-with-bob-camp-part-ii.html.
46 Cerone, "Toontown Terrors."
47 Jim Ballantine to Robert Farro, "Ren & Stimpy Budget Variance Notes Season II," 22 March 1993. Collection of the author.
48 Simensky interview.
49 Coffey interview.
50 Rod Granger, "'Ren and Stimpy' creator talks back to Nick," Multichannel News, 9 November 1992.
51 Danzo interview.
52 Smith interview.
53 McRobb interview.
54 Beck interview.
55 Koenigsberg interview.
56 Camp interview, *X Magazine* #10, 1992.
57 Dan Jeup, e-mail interview with the author, 21 September 2010.
58 Klickstein, 175.
59 Advertisement in *Comic Buyer's Guide*, 28 February 1992.
60 Camp interview, *X Magazine* #10.
61 Scott Wills, phone interview with the author, 28 January 2010.
62 Lawrence interview.
63 DeStefano interview.
64 Bell interview.
65 Lawrence interview.
66 Blake interview.
67 Jim Smith, interview with Greg Method, January 1994.
68 Ballantine to Farro.
69 Ted Loos, "Commuting the Pacific, Unseating 'The Simpsons,'" *The New York Times*, 10 November 2002.

70 John Kricfalusi, *The Ren & Stimpy Show: Seasons Three and a Half-ish*, Audio Commentary for "A Yard Too Far", 2005.
71 David Koenigsberg, e-mail message to the author, 28 June 2014.
72 Bob Camp, e-mail message to the author, 16 September 2009.
73 Persons, 1993, 51.
74 Kricfalusi with Boatz, 7.
75 Bob Camp, phone interview with the author, 10 February 2010.
76 Ballantine to Farro.
77 Camp e-mail, 16 September 2009.
78 Sauve interview.
79 Bob Jaques, e-mail message to the author, 30 December 2009.
80 Reccardi interview.
81 Ballantine to Farro.
82 Ron Hughart, e-mail interview with the author, 31 October 2009.
83 Ballantine to Farro.
84 Wills interview.
85 Ibid.
86 Hughart interview.
87 Bell interview.
88 Shank interview.
89 Beck interview.
90 Karen Mazurkewich, *Cartoon Capers: The History of Canadian Animators* (McArthur & Company, 1999), 267.
91 Richmond, "Cartoonist injecting creativity into lifeless art form."
92 John Kricfalusi to Vanessa Coffey, 9 June 1992.
93 Persons, 50.
94 Simensky interview.
95 Kricfalusi to Coffey.
96 Daniel Cerone, "'Ren & Stimpy' and Its Creator: A Parting of Ways Animation," *Los Angeles Times*, 28 September 1992.
97 Spumco Status Report, 24 July 1992. Collection of the author.
98 Kricfalusi to Coffey.

99 Jeup interview.
100 Hughart interview.
101 Kent Butterworth, comment on "The Tiny Toon That Got Rejected and Became a Ren & Stimpy," *What About Thad?*, comment posted 6 April 2010, http://www.whataboutthad. com/2010/04/the-tiny-toon-that-got-rejected-and-became- a-ren-stimpy/.
102 Richard Pursel, e-mail message to the author, 15 June 2011.
103 Persons, 1993, 56.
104 Ballantine to Farro.
105 Steve Loter, e-mail interview with the author, 15 December 2013.
106 DeStefano interview.

Chapter 6

1 Gomez interview, 2010.
2 McRobb interview.
3 Persons, 1993, 48.
4 Ballantine to Farro.
5 Persons, 1993, 43.
6 Wray with Novinskie, 16.
7 Will McRobb to John Kricfalusi, "Ren & Stimpy Comments: Firedogs II," 6 November 1991. Collection of the author, photocopy provided by Jerry Beck.
8 McRobb interview.
9 Bob Jaques, phone call with the author, 3 June 2011.
10 Kim interview.
11 Persons, 1993, 43.
12 West interview.
13 Sauve interview.
14 Shank interview.
15 Anders, 49.
16 Smith with Method.
17 Persons, 1993, 48.
18 Vanessa Coffey, phone call with the author, 6 January 2010.

19 Reccardi interview.
20 Coffey interview.
21 Spumco, "Season 2 Schedule, First Draft," 1992.
22 Persons, 1993, 50.
23 Original source unknown. Quote reprinted on *Information is Not Knowledge*, http://globalia.net/donlope/fz/videography/Ren_and_Stimpy.html (accessed 7 May 2012).
24 Simensky interview.
25 Paula Parisi, "Nick ticked by late 'Stimpy's,'" *The Hollywood Reporter*, 23 September 1992.
26 Roy Smith, e-mail message to the author, 19 January 2010.
27 Klickstein, 181.
28 Ibid, 167.
29 Simensky interview.
30 Spumco Status Report, 24 July 1992.
31 Smith interview.
32 Ballantine to Farro.
33 Lawrence interview.
34 Jim Ballantine, e-mail message to the author, 17 September 2009.
35 Coffey interview.
36 Josh Ozersky, "Cat-eat-dog (and worse) world to animate TV," *The Washington Times*, 13 August 1992.
37 Richard Gehr, "You Filthy Worms!," *The Village Voice*, 17 November 1992.
38 Persons, 1993, 51.
39 Coffey interview.
40 Simensky interview.
41 Ballantine to Farro.
42 Reichek interview.
43 Camp and Wray interview, 2016.
44 Camp interview, 2006.
45 Gore, "Celling Out," 39.
46 Smith interview.

47   Camp and Wray interview, 2016.
48   Camp interview, 2006.
49   Coffey interview.
50   Smith interview.
51   Bell interview.
52   Reichek interview.
53   Smallbridge.
54   Coffey, phone call.
55   Cerone, "'Ren & Stimpy' and Its Creator: A Parting of Ways Animation."
56   Beck interview.
57   Vincent Waller, comment on "Question To Mr. Vincent Waller!" *Spumboard*, comment posted 11April 2009, http:// www.spumboard.lyris-lite.net/index.php?topic=2002. msg29370 (accessed 22 September 2009).
58   Camp and Wray interview, 2016.
59   "Nickelodeon and John Kricfalusi reach agreement on production of 'The Ren & Stimpy Show,'" *Business Wire*, 28 September 1992.
60   Cerone.
61   Camp interview, 2006.
62   John Kricfalusi to Bob Jaques, September 1992 (exact date unknown).
63   Jim Smith, *The Ren & Stimpy Show: The First and Second Seasons Uncut*, Audio Commentary for "Svën Höek", 2004.
64   Will McRobb to John Kricfalusi, "Ren & Stimpy Comments: Sven Hoek," 6 November 1991.
65   John Kricfalusi, *The Ren & Stimpy Show: The First and Second Seasons Uncut*, Audio Commentary for "Svën Höek", 2004.
66   John Kricfalusi, *The Ren & Stimpy Show: The First and Second Seasons Uncut*, Audio Commentary for "Son of Stimpy", 2004.
67   Ballantine to Farro.
68   Bob Jaques, during Sauve interview.
69   John Kricfalusi, "Specific Acting—Sven Hoek." *John K Stuff*, 25 April 2010, http://johnkstuff.blogspot.com/2010/04/specific-acting-sven-hoek.html (accessed 24 May 2010).

70 Audio Commentary for "Son of Stimpy".
71 "An Exchange with John K."
72 Kricfalusi to Jaques, September 1992.
73 Persons, 1993, 48.
74 Wills interview.
75 Sauve interview.
76 Kricfalusi to Jaques, September 1992 (exact date unknown).
77 Mansz interview.
78 Jaques, during Sauve interview.
79 Persons, 1993, 52.
80 Shawn Patterson, interview with the author, 9 January 2014.
81 Irwin Chusid, "Raymond Scott: Accidental Music for Animated Mayhem," in *The Cartoon Music Book*, ed. Daniel Goldmark and Yuval Taylor (Chicago: A Cappella Books), 158. Porch's quote originally appeared in *SPIN* Magazine.
82 Ballantine to Farro.
83 Jeup interview.
84 Persons, 1993, 45.
85 John Evan Frook, "Kricfalusi: Final 'Ren' is gift to Nickelodeon," *Daily Variety*, 13 January 1993.
86 Ibid.
87 Persons, 1993, 57.
88 Coffey interview.
89 Bob Camp to John Kricfalusi, 16 August 1993. The fax included a copy of the original letter Todd Binkley, the Emmy Awards Administrator, sent to to Kricfalusi; Kricfalusi, in turn, annotated that letter with sarcastic jabs and a note to Camp. Camp also sent the fax to Vincent Waller, Richard Pursel, and Bob Jaques.
90 Parisi.
91 Traci Grant, "'Ren & Stimpy' fans worry about the show," *The Boston Globe*, 5 October 1992.
92 Michael Saunders, "'Ren & Stimpy' creator won't be heard on show," *The Boston Globe*, 9 October 1992.
93 Cerone.

94 John Kricfalusi and Chris Gore, "The Plot to Kill Cartoons," *Wild Cartoon Kingdom* #1, 1993, 31.
95 Eddie Fitzgerald, interview with Charles Brubaker, posted 16 December 2008, http://bakertoons.blogspot.com/2008/12/ interview-with-eddie-fitzgerald.html (accessed 22 September 2009).
96 Simon interview.
97 Camp and Wray interview, 2016.
98 Jim Schembri, "The Rise & Fall of Ren & Stimpy," *The Age*, 15 December 1994.
99 Camp and Wray interview, 2016.
100 Roy Smith, e-mail message to the author, 19 January 2010.
101 Klickstein, 180.
102 Pursel e-mail.
103 Shank interview.
104 Klickstein, 177-8.
105 Butterworth interview.
106 Wang interview.
107 Wray with Novinskie, 16.
108 Billy West, interview with Joel Keller, appeared on *AOL TV*, http://www.aoltv.com/2006/06/15/billy-west-the-tv-squad-interview/.
109 West interview.
110 Bell interview.
111 Jennifer Pendleton, "Cel-Shocked Kricfalusi Talks," *Daily Variety*, 2 October 1992; Gehr.
112 Gail Shister, "Ren & Stimpy Going Through Creative Changes," *Miami Herald*, 30 September 1992.
113 Schembri.
114 Cooper, Epstein, & Hurewitz Law Office to Lois Peel Eisenstein, 18 May 1993.
115 Coffey interview.
116 Jim Gomez, during West interview.
117 Richard Katz, "Not All Fun & Games," *Cablevision*, 24 May 1993, 34.

118 Vincent Waller to *Los Angeles Times*, printed 7 November 1993.
119 Jim Smith to David Anthony Kraft, printed in *Comics Interview* #125, 1993, 46.
120 Kricfalusi with Boatz, 5.
121 Camp interview, 2006.
122 Kricfalusi and Gore, "The Plot to Kill Cartoons," 31.
123 Bob Camp, e-mail message to the author, 20 February 2013.
124 John Kricfalusi, "The Plot to Kill Cartoons" draft, 16. Collection of the author, photocopy provided by Bob Jaques.
125 McRobb interview.
126 Koenigsberg interview, 9 January 2011.
127 Kricfalusi and Gore, "The Plot to Kill Cartoons," 34.
128 Saunders.
129 Smith interview.
130 Coffey interview.
131 Reichek interview.

Chapter 7

1 Saunders.
2 "New 'Ren' segment set for Nick schedule," *Daily Variety*, 30 October 1992, 26.
3 Katz, 42.
4 Coffey interview.
5 Gomez interview, 2009.
6 Kim interview.
7 "Games Rates As of 30 November 1993." Collection of the author.
8 Meisler, "While Team 2 Works to Reform 'Ren and Stimpy.'"
9 Gore, "Celling Out," 39.
10 Bob Camp, e-mail message to the author, 13 August 2006.
11 Jim Ballantine, phone call with the author, 29 September 2009.
12 Ballantine to Farro, 22 March 1993.
13 Bob Jaques, interview with the author, 11 October 2010.

14 Smith with Method.
15 Jim Smith, comment on "Model Sheet." *Jim Smith Cartoons*, comment posted 5 March 2010, http://jimsmithcartoons. blogspot.com/2010/03/model-sheet_03.html (accessed 24 May 2010).
16 Ballantine to Farro.
17 Persons, 1993, 51.
18 Klickstein, 179.
19 Bob Camp, e-mail message to the author, 18 September 2009.
20 Koenigsberg interview, 8 January 2011.
21 *The Ren & Stimpy Show Exposed*, 1992, 25.
22 Paula Parisi, "'Ren' fan: happy, happy, joy joy," *The Hollywood Reporter*, 7 May 1993.
23 Wray with Novinskie, 17.
24 John Kricfalusi, comment on "Happy Birthday Dad and my obsession with authority." *John K Stuff*, comment posted 28 October 2009, http://johnkstuff.blogspot.com/2009/10/ happy-birthday-dad.html (accessed 24 May 2010).
25 Persons, 1993, 52.
26 Ballantine to Farro.
27 Katz, 42.
28 Bob Jaques, e-mail message to the author, 31 December 2009.
29 McRobb interview.
30 Spumco Status Report, 24 July 1992.
31 Ballantine to Farro.
32 Reccardi interview.
33 Koenigsberg interview, 8 January 2011.
34 Reccardi interview.
35 Bob Jaques, e-mail message to the author, 24 September 2009.
36 Sauve interview.
37 Katz, 42.
38 Armstrong interview.
39 Cooper, Epstein, & Hurewitz to Lois Peel Eisenstein, 18 May 1993.
40 Jim Ballantine, e-mail message to the author, 29 December 2009.

41 Danzo interview.

Chapter 8

1 Jim Ballantine, "Producer's Report," 11 March 1993. Collection of the author, provided by Ballantine.
2 Wray with Novinskie, 17.
3 Jim Ballantine, e-mail message to the author, 4 April 2011.
4 Bob Camp, comment on "Short cartoon writing tips!" *Bob Camp Cartoonist*, comment posted 13 August 2009, http://bobcampcartoonist.blogspot.com/2009/08/short-cartoon- writing-tips.html (accessed 12 January 2011).
5 Kim interview.
6 Hughart interview.
7 Jim Ballantine to Nickelodeon, "Quality Budget Schedule," 29 October 1993.
8 Wang interview.
9 Camp and Wray interview, 2016.
10 Koenigsberg interview, 8 January 2011.
11 Wang interview.
12 Persons, 1993, 55.
13 Daniel Cerone, "New Kings of TV's Toon Town," *The Los Angeles Times*, 17 October 1993.
14 Camp interview, 2006.
15 Camp interview, 2010.
16 Jim Ballantine, "Producer's Report," 25 February 1993. Collection of the author, provided by Ballantine.
17 Spumco Status Report, 24 July 1992; "Yogi Bear 'Pie Pirates', 1958, Frank Tipper, Yard To [sic] Far, Bob Camp and friends, Story Structure." *John K Stuff*, 15 February 2007, http://johnkstuff.blogspot.com/2006/12/ yogi-bear-pie-pirates-1958-frank.html (accessed 12 January 2011).
18 Bob Jaques, e-mail message to the author, 18 December 2009.
19 Wray with Novinskie, 18.

20 John Kricfalusi (as "Tom Paine"), "'They come out when they come out.' Third Season of Ren & Stimpy Finally Arrives!" *Wild Cartoon Kingdom* #3, 1994, 6.
21 John Kricfalusi, *The Ren & Stimpy Show: Seasons Three-and-a- Halfish*, Audio Commentary for "Stimpy's Cartoon Show", 2005.
22 Camp interview, 2010.
23 Gomez interview, 2011.
24 Dan Persons, "An Epitaph for Ren & Stimpy," *Cinefantastique*, Vol. 26, no. 6, October 1995, 111.
25 Jim Ballantine, e-mail message to the author, 14 September 2010.
26 Games Animation, "Season Three Schedule—Three Teams," 12 December 1993. Collection of the author, provided by Jim Ballantine.
27 Gomez interview, 2011.
28 Kim interview.
29 Loter interview.
30 Games Animation, "Worker's Schedule: Steve L.," November-December 1993. Schedule establishes that Loter would have been supervising layout of "Lair of the Lummox" for five weeks by November 1993.
31 Kim interview.
32 Games Animation, "Games Rates," 30 November 1993.
33 Baker interview.
34 Bill Wray, *The Ren & Stimpy Show: Season Five and Some More of Four*, Audio Commentary for "The Last Temptation", 2005.
35 Games Animation, "Season Three Delivery Dates," 2 August 1993 and 11 July 1994. Collection of the author, provided by Jim Ballantine.
36 Wayne Walley, "Nick hopes to weather 'Ren' production lag," *Electronic Media*, 5 October 1992.
37 Granger.
38 Gomez interview, 2011.
39 Bob Camp, e-mail message to the author, 26 October 2009.
40 Hughart interview.
41 Persons, 1995, 106-107.

42 Koenigsberg interview, 8 January 2011.
43 Loter interview.
44 DeStefano interview.
45 Anders, 54.
46 Games Animation, "Production Report," 19 January 1995. Collection of the author, provided by Jim Ballantine.
47 Arthur Filloy, e-mail message to the author, 26 November 2009.
48 Games Animation, "Production Report," 19 January 1995.
49 Arthur Filloy, e-mail interview with the author, 25 November 2009.
50 Camp interview, 2010.
51 Loter interview.
52 Mark Colangelo, e-mail interview with the author, 2 August 2009.
53 Loter interview.
54 Gomez interview, 2011.
55 Jim Ballantine, e-mail message to the author, 4 April 2011.
56 Persons, 1995, 103.
57 Gomez interview, 2011.
58 Ibid.
59 Stephen DeStefano, e-mail message to the author, 8 February 2011.
60 Gomez, during West interview.
61 Andre L. Shapiro to Jim Ballantine, 11 July 1994.
62 Camp interview, 2010.
63 Loter interview.
64 Coffey interview.
65 Camp interview, 2010.
66 Loter interview.
67 West interview.
68 "A Chat with John Kricfalusi," *Lyris-Lite*, http://www.lyris-lite.net/johnk_chat.html (accessed 12 January 2011).
69 Craig Bartlett, e-mail interview with the author, 12 September 2010.
70 Gomez, during West interview.
71 Brian Mendelsohn, e-mail interview with the author, 25 November 2009.

72 Bartlett interview.

Chapter 9

1   Jennifer Pendleton, "Kricfalusi, WB Have Short Talk," *Daily Variety*, 16 December 1992.
2   Phil Gallo, "Q&A with Spumco's John Kricfalusi; Thinking Big for a Loveable Idiot," *Daily Variety*, 24 March 1994.
3   Ginny Holbert, "Nick Cartoon Finds Niche; 'Ren & Stimpy' Not Just Kid Stuff," *The Chicago Sun-Times*, 18 November 1993.
4   Kim interview.
5   Camp interview, 2010.
6   Reccardi interview.
7   Wills interview.
8   Scott Wills, *The Ren & Stimpy Show: Season Five and Some More of Four*, Audio Commentary for "Feud for Sale", 2005.
9   Bill Wray, *The Ren & Stimpy Show: Season Five and Some More of Four*, Audio Commentary for "The Last Temptation", 2005.
10 Wray with Novinskie, 11.
11 Jim Ballantine, "Producer's Report," 11 March 1993.
12 Paula Parisi,"'Ren & Stimpy': Primetime Redux," *The Hollywood Reporter*, 22 November 1993.
13 Richard Pursel, *The Ren & Stimpy Show: Seasons Three-and-a-Halfish*, Audio Commentary for "No Pants Today", 2005.
14 Gomez interview, 2011.
15 Wray with Novinskie, 27.
16 West interview.
17 Coffey interview.
18 Bill Wray, *The Ren & Stimpy Show: Season Five and Some More of Four*, Audio Commentary for "Aloha Höek", 2005.
19 Wray with Novinskie, 25.
20 Sherm Cohen, e-mail interview with the author 9 December 2009.

21 Bill Wray, *The Ren & Stimpy Show: Season Five and Some More of Four*, Audio Commentary for "Sammy and Me", 2005.
22 Gomez interview, 2011.
23 Camp and Wray interview, 2016.
24 West interview.
25 Camp and Wray interview, 2016.
26 Camp interview, 2010.
27 Shank interview.
28 Reccardi interview.
29 Kim interview.
30 Camp interview, 2010.
31 Kim interview.
32 Bob Camp, e-mail message to the author, 20 February 2013.
33 Hughart interview.
34 Kim interview.
35 Ibid.
36 Bob Jaques, e-mail message to the author, 25 October 2009.
37 Kim interview.
38 Ibid.
39 Colangelo interview.
40 Reccardi interview.
41 Games Animation, "Production Report," 19 January 1995.
42 Bill Wray, *The Ren & Stimpy Show: Season Five and Some More of Four*, Audio Commentary for "I Was a Teenage Stimpy", 2005.
43 Stephen DeStefano, e-mail message to the author, 16 August 2009.
44 Kim interview.
45 Ibid.
46 Loter interview.
47 Games Animation, "Season Three Schedule—Three Teams," 6 December 1993.
48 Reccardi interview.
49 Koenigsberg interview, 8 January 2011.

50 Reccardi interview.
51 Games Animation, "Season Three Schedule—Three Teams," 6 December 1993.
52 West interview.
53 Mendelsohn interview.
54 Reccardi interview.
55 Games Animation, "Games Rates," 30 November 1993.
56 Colangelo interview.
57 "Hi Fructose Feature Interview with Chris Reccardi."
58 Games Animation, "Production Report," 19 January 1995.
59 Shank interview.
60 Mark Colangelo, e-mail message to the author, 19 January 2010.
61 Games Animation, "Production Report," 19 January 1995.
62 Meisler, "…While Team 2 Works to Reform Ren & Stimpy."
63 Games Animation, "Season Three Schedule—Three Teams," 30 September 1993.
64 Reccardi interview.
65 Colangelo e-mail.
66 Colangelo interview.
67 Jason Anders, "A Conversation with Bob Camp," 22 October 2008, http://fullecirclestuff.blogspot.com/2008/10/conversation-with-bob-camp.html.
68 Sherm Cohen, e-mail message to the author, 18 September 2010.

Chapter 10

1 Billy West on *The Howard Stern Show*, 21 June 1995.
2 Lawrence interview.
3 Michael Barrier, "The Uses of Disgust," *Michael Barrier.com*, http://www.michaelbarrier.com/Commentary/Ren_and_Stimpy/RenStimpy.htm.
4 Michelle Klein-Hass, "Jim Smith: Rock and Roll Cartoonist," *Animato!* #28, Spring 1994.
5 Mazurkewich, 271.
6 Blake interview.

7   Simensky interview.
8   Libby Simon, e-mail message to the author, 22 October 2009.
9   Casey Davidson and Jessica Shaw, "Lawsuits," *Entertainment Weekly*, 27 October 1995.
10 David Robb, "'Ren & Stimpy' creator in Viacom settlement," *The Hollywood Reporter*, 10 May 1996.
11 Michael Barrier, "Master of the cult cartoon," *Nation's Business*, June 1998, 83.
12 Scott Goodings, "The Strange World of John K.," *T.V. Freak*, July 2006. http://www.abc.net.au/fly/tvfreak/feature/johnk_home.htm.
13 Klickstein, 235.
14 Goodings.
15 David Pietila, e-mail interview with the author, 22 June 2010.
16 Steve Stefanelli, interview with the author, Ottawa, Ontario, 22 November 2010.
17 Nellie Andreeva, "'Ren' resurrected at TNN; Kricfalusi unleashing new episodes," *The Hollywood Reporter*, 17 July 2002.
18 Ibid.
19 "Interview: John Kricfalusi," IGN.com, 18 July 2006, http://dvd.ign.com/articles/719/719569p1.html.
20 Andreeva.
21 John Kricfalusi, Audio Commentary for "My Shiny Friend", *The Ren & Stimpy Show: Season Five and Some More of Four*, 2005.
22 West interview.
23 Robertryan Cory, phone interview with the author, 15 December 2009.
24 Bob Jaques, "Recollections of Working on a Still-born Series," *Apatoons* #150, April 2008.
25 Armstrong interview.
26 Amid Amidi, "The John Kricfalusi Interview, Part 2," *Cartoon Brew*, 31 August 2004, http://www.cartoonbrew.com/old-brew/the-john-kricfalusi-interview-part-2.html.
27 Nick Cross, e-mail interview with the author, 27 September 2009.
28 Helder Mendonca, e-mail interview with the author, 8 January 2010.

ENDNOTES

29 Stefanelli interview.
30 Warren Leonhardt, *Apatoons* #154, January 2009.
31 Bob Jaques, "Recollections of Working on a Still-born Series Part 2," *Apatoons* #152, August 2008.
32 Greg Stainton, e-mail interview with the author, 13 November 2009.
33 Cross interview.
34 Nathan Affolter, phone interview with the author, 1 August 2006.
35 Armstrong interview.
36 Cory interview.
37 John Vincent, e-mail interview with the author, 29 August 2010.
38 Cross interview.
39 Bob Jaques, e-mail message to the author, relaying information from Mike Kerr, 17 April 2011.
40 Mike Kerr, e-mail interview with the author, 13 August 2010.
41 John Vincent, e-mail message to the author, 23 February 2010.
42 E-mail message from Kevin Kolde to John Kricfalusi, 24 July 2002. Carbon-copied to several in the production
43 Mendonca interview.
44 John Kricfalusi, Audio Commentary for "Aloha Höek", *The Ren & Stimpy Show: Season Five and Some More of Four*, 2005.
45 Jaques, "Recollections of Working on a Still-born Series."
46 Jamie Mason, e-mail interview with the author, 29 September 2009.
47 Jaques, "Recollections of Working on a Still-born Series."
48 Tom Provenzano, "Ren & Stimpy: Not not gay," *The Advocate*, 5 April 1994, 57.
49 Comment by John Kricfalusi, "George Liquor is a Good Salesman," *John K Stuff*, http://johnkstuff.blogspot. com/2006/07/george-liquor-is-good-salesman.html (accessed 11 January 2012).
50 Colin Giles, e-mail interview with the author, 9 August 2006.
51 Anders, 49.
52 Cory interview.
53 Ibid.

54 Bob Jaques, "Recollections of Working on a Still-born Series Part 3," *Apatoons* #155, March 2009.
55 Hay interview.
56 Affolter interview.
57 Mendonca interview.
58 John Vincent, e-mail message to the author, 24 February 2010.
59 Jaques, "Recollections of Working on a Still-born Series Part 3."
60 Will McRobb, "Ren and Stimpy Comments: Firedogs II," 6 November 1991.
61 John Kricfalusi, Introduction for *Firedogs 2, Ren & Stimpy: The Lost Episodes*, 2006.
62 Cory interview.
63 Ibid.
64 Ibid.
65 Chris Ross, e-mail interview with the author, 15 August 2006.
66 McRobb, "Ren and Stimpy Comments: Firedogs II."
67 Anders, "A Conversation with Ralph Bakshi."
68 John Kricfalusi, Introduction for *Naked Beach Frenzy, Ren & Stimpy: The Lost Episodes*, 2006.
69 Cory interview.
70 Leonhardt.
71 Stainton interview.
72 Jaques, "Recollections of Working on a Still-born Series Part 3."
73 Bob Jaques, e-mail message to the author, 22 September 2008.
74 WGN broadcast with Nick Digilio and John Kricfalusi, 19 August 2003.
75 Cross interview.
76 Greg Duffell, "The Ren and Stimpy Lost Episodes," *Apatoons* #142, September 2006.
77 Amidi, "The John Kricfalusi Interview, Part 2."
78 Cross interview.
79 James Hibberd, "Spike Retooling Its Toon Strategy," *Television Week*, 3 November 2003, http://www.tvweek.com/ topstorys/11303spike.html (accessed 13 January 2012, via archive.org).

80 Kerr interview.
81 Armstrong interview.
82 John Kricfalusi, *Ren & Stimpy: The Lost Episodes*, Disc One introduction.
83 Anders, 59.
84 John Kricfalusi, comment on "Lost Episodes are Out," on *John K Stuff*, 16 July 2006, http://johnkstuff.blogspot.com/2006/07/ lost-episodes-are-out_18.html. The records at the United States Patent and Trademark Office shows that the trademark for Spumco expired 19 May 2007.

INDEX

"An Abe Divided", 246, *247*, 385
The Adventures of Sonic the Hedgehog, 208, 300
Aerosmith, 272
Affolter, Nathan, 328
"Aloha Höek", 278, 279, 412-13
"Altruists", 321-22, 334-35, 337, 434
An American Tail, 29
Armstrong, Kelly, 59, 61-62, 67, 100, 101, 104, *107*, 108, 127, 128, *143*, 177-78, 197, 233, 235, 312, 315, 334, 338
Associated Production Music, 65, 322
Avery, Tex, 3, 139, 154

Baker, Howard, 91-92, 123, 248
Bakshi, Ralph, *11*, 31, 32, 51, 56, 76, 204, *333*; as independent filmmaker, 1-2; and *Mighty Mouse: The New Adventures*, 10-17, 21, 25-28; and "Fire Dogs 2", 329-332

Ballantine, Jim, 151, 152, 174, 185, 186, 189, 195, 207, 223, 226, 231, 235-36, 239, 245, 246, 253, 257, 264, 281, 322
Barr, Glenn, 164, 310
Bartlett, Craig, 263-65
"Bass Masters", 219, 249, 388-89
"Bat with a Golden Tongue", 28
Bauza, Eric, 328
Bay, Michael, 302
Bean, Charlie, *134*
Beauty and the Beast, 146
Beavis and Butt-Head, 301
Beck, Jerry, 7, 49, 50, 57, 66, 120, 154, 166
"Bellhops", 257, 423
Benedict, Ed, 59, 303
"Big Baby Scam", 159, 170, 171, 181, 191, 218, 223, 369-70
"Big Flakes", 426
Big House Blues, 57-67, 349-351
"The Big Shot!", 88, 352
Big Star (Korean animation studio), 315, 331, 335, 337
Bird, Brad, 29, 47, 342
Birdy and the Beast, 54
Björk, 302
"Black Hole", 99-100, 123, 357
Blake, Elinor, 145, *156*, 157, 205, 219, 242, 302
"Blazing Entrails", 253, 400-01
Bluth, Don, 29
Bobby's Girl, 10
Bon-Art (Korean animation studio), 90
"Boo Boo Runs Wild", 303
"The Boy Who Cried Rat!", 97, 101, 174, 354
Bruce, Ken, 227, 252-53
Butterworth, Kent, 13, 15, 16, 26, 27, 47, 59, 208

Calandra, Vince, 257
Camp, Bob, 42, 48, 76, 84, 88, 94, 95, 96, 97, 98, 105, *106*, 107, 112, *119*, 138, 140, *144*, 149, 150, 151, 154, 155, *156*, *163*, 171, 185, 188-89, 192, *196*, 201, 203, 207, 208, 210-12, 218, 219, 223, 227, 251, 254, 267, 321, 329, 338; as creative director at Games Animation, 228, 230, 238-44, 249, 255, 257-61, 263-64, 272, 281-82; as director at Spumco, 159-63; as writer/artist at Spumco, 57, 58, 61, 77, 78, 82, 99; and "Stimpy's Invention", 115-19, 123, 127; cofounds Spumco, 49-51
Captain Quantum Vs. the Ugly Druggies (board game), 51
Carbunkle Cartoons, 107, 157, 161, 194, 224, 231, 284, 310; and *Adult Party Cartoon*, 312, 314-16, 323-24, 328, 330, 331, 334-35; and *Big House Blues*, 59-64; and "Man's Best Friend", 176-78; and "Out West", 162-63; and "The Royal Canadian Kilted Yaksmen", 233-35; and "Space Madness", 101-05; and "Son

of Stimpy", 197-98; and "Stimpy's Invention", 121-23, 128; and "Svën Höek", 197-98
"A Cartoon", 91, 97-8, 356
Cartoon Cavalcade, 55
Cartoon Network, 303
"Catastrophe Cat", 17
"The Cat That Laid the Golden Hairball", 227-28, 375
Charren, Peggy, xxv, 41
Chase, Cheryl, 62, 111
"Cheese Rush Days", 414-15
"Chicken in a Drawer", 396
Christmas in Tattertown, 17, 28, 51
Cimino, Michael, 186
"Circus Midgets", 245-46, 382-83
"City Hicks", 253, 257, 421-22
Clampett, Bob, xxiv, 5, 8, 16, 17, 30-33, 51, 54, 63, 80, 138, 139, 146, 336
Clampett, Rob (Jr.), 35
Clampett, Sody, 34, 35, 36
Coal Black and De Sebben Dwarfs, 8
Coffey, Vanessa, 89, 112, 113, 116, 126, 147, 148, 150, 151-52, 174, 177, 192, 195, 198, 210, 246, 302; as executive producer, 75, 76, 81, 117-18, 179, 181, 186-87, 189, 190, 202, 222, 240, 257, 260, 276; as independent producer, 51-3, 56, 65, 67-8
Cohen, Sherm, 277, 297
Colangelo, Mark, 255, 286, 293, 294, 296
Coonskin, 2
Corliss, Richard, 41
Cory (as in Robertryan Cory), 311, 315, 324, 326, 330, 334
"The Courtship of Cecilia", 35
Cow & Chicken, 300
Cross, Nick, 313, 315, 316, 319, 335, 337
Cuckoo's Nest (see James Wang)

Danzo, Christine, 76, 79, 80, 100, 108, 109, 110, 118, 122, 126, 130, 152, 153, 236,
Daum, Glen, 65
Deja, Andreas, 29
Deputy Droopy, 154
DeStefano, Stephen, 96, 156, 252, 258, 264, 287
DIC, 26, 49, 50, 186, 208, and *The New Adventures of Beany & Cecil*, 31-43
Dini, Paul, 35, 36, 40
"Dinner Party", 426
"Dog Show", 164, 179-81, *180*, 185, 223, 288, 370-71
"Dog Tags", 257, 423-24
"Dog Water", 396
"Dog Water #2", 431
"Don't Touch That Dial", 27
Dorman, John, 307

"Double Header", *285*, 285-86, 288, 409-10
Doug, 53, 67, 68, 78, 109, 112, 113, 137, 153, 154, 299
Douglas, Kirk, 20, 28, 89, 100
Duckett, Harold, 54
DuckTales, 47
Duffell, Greg, 335-36
Dumbo, 146
"D.J. Goes Ape", 41
Dr. Seuss' Butter Battle Book, 28

"Eat My Cookies", 251, 393-94
"Eggyölkeo", 258-60, *259*, 408-09

Fajnor, Joel, 54
"Fake Dad", 164, 168, 185, 191, 224-26, *225*, *226*, 373-74
"Family Dog", 29
"Farm Hands", 403
Feiss, David, 5, 58, *60*, 300
"Feud for Sale", 263, 294, 420-21
"Field Guide", 419
Fil-Cartoons (Filipino studio), 91-2, 102, 104, 107, 123-24, 130
Filloy, Arthur, 253-54
Film Threat (magazine), 211
Fine, Larry, 63-4, 120
"Fire Dogs", 94, 107, 113, 123, 158, 227, 355-56
"Fire Dogs 2", 315, 329-32, *333*, 433
Fitzgerald, Eddie, 15-17, *17*, 37, 40, 48, 56, 84, 98, 187, 204, 205, 206, 310, 330
The Flintstones, xxiv
"Flod", 396
Fontanelli, Mike, 97, *143*, 156, *182*, 197, 204, 205, 207, 232
Forte, Felix, 55
"A Friend in Your Face!", 399-400
Fritz the Cat, 2
Funbag Animation, 307-08

"Galoot Wranglers", 257, 416
Games Animation, 189, 191, 206, 207, 209, 300, 305 313, 319, 320, 321, 329, 332, 338; and production of *Ren & Stimpy*, 221-36, 237-266, 271-297; and transition from Spumco, 200-13, 221-24
George Liquor, 173-80, 199, 224, 246, 258, 289, 317, 318, 331, 344
Gomez, Jim, 3, 5, 12, 14, 18, 19, 33, 38, 40, 51, 55, 76, 77, 84, 96, 118, 127, 149, 173, 210, 222, 251, 253, 260, 275, 279, 284, 287, 294; as director, 245-47; as writer, 256-58, 263-64; and "Reverend Jack Cheese", 267-69
The Goddamn George Liquor Show, 306
Gordon, Steven, 15, 16, 18
Gore, Chris, 211-12
The Great Mouse Detective, 29

"The Great Outdoors", 191, 227, 374-75
Groening, Matt, 47, 204, 301
A Gruesome Twosome, 54

"Hair of the Cat", 253, 421
Hanna-Barbera, xxiv, xxvi, 3, 4, 5, 8, 33, 36, 49, 59, 88, 91, 92, 93, 95, 96, 139, 186, 256, 303, 306
"A Hard Day's Luck", 293, 404-05
"Hard Times for Haggis", 289-90, 392-93
The Harlem Shuffle, 8, *9*, 20, 267,
Harrington, Mary, 78, 110, 126, 207, 227, 295
Hartt, Reg, 2
Hauge, 244, 246, 257
"Haunted House", 157, 169-70, 223, 224, 368-69
Hay, Tom, 140, 328
Heavy Traffic, 2
Hecht, Albie, 309
"Hermit Ren", 290-92, 295, 397-98
He-Hog the Atomic Pig, 52
Hillenburg, Stephen, 299
Holder, Jeff, 32, 34, 41
Hound Town, 28
"House of Next Tuesday", 398-99
Hubley, John, xxvi
Hughart, Ron, 164, 165, 169, 170, 171, 200, 238-39, 241, 251, 252, 253, 254, 255, 263, 282, 286
Huml, Scott, 66, 198

"I Love Chicken", 263, 406
"The Ice Goose Cometh", 20-21, *23*
The Incredibles, 342
"Insomniac Ren", 255, 413
"In the Army", 158, 160, 161, 362
"It's a Dog's Life", 258, 408
"I Was a Teenage Stimpy", 287, 296, 424

Jaques, Bob, 5, 8, 15, 18, 91, 140, *144*, 175, 194, 268-69, 284; as animation director on *Ren & Stimpy*, 101-06, 162-63, 196-98; as animation director on *Ren & Stimpy: Adult Party Cartoon*, 311, 314, 321-23, 329, 333, 334-36; and *Big House Blues*, 59, 61-62; and "Mighty's Benefit Plan", 20; and "The Royal Canadian Kilted Yaksmen", 224, 231, 232-35; and "Stimpy's Invention", 123-24, *125*, 127-28
"Jerry the Bellybutton Elf", 251, 391
The Jetsons, 5-6, 15
"Jimminy Lummox", 387-88
Jimmy's Clubhouse, 52, 53, 56
Jinkins, Jim, 53

Jenson, Victoria, 8, 93
Jeup, Dan, 154, 169, 200
Jones, Chuck, 104, 335

Kausler, Mark, 121, *122*
Kay, Kevin, 310, 333, 337
Kazaleh, Mike, 27, 148
Keane, Glen, 25
Kerr, Michael, 318, 338
Kim, Michael, 96, 102, 144, 175-76, 183, *194*, 222, 230, 238, 241, 246, 247, 248, 272, 281, 282-88, 291, 294
Klasky-Csupo, 52, 53
Klein, Tom, 8, 10, 12, 19, 26, 27, 32
Koenigsberg, David, 87, 92, 105, 111, 120, 124, *125*, 148, 154, 159, 212, 228, 232, 233, 239, 252, 290
Kolde, Kevin, 306, 311, 313, 318, 319, 330
Kricfalusi, John, *11, 22, 23, 24, 30, 55, 58, 79, 116, 122, 143, 144, 202*, 221, 223, 225, 226, 235-36, 238-40, 243, 247, 250, 260, 263-65, 267-69, 271, 272, 273, 274, 281, 282; after *Ren & Stimpy*, 301-08, 343-44; arrives in Hollywood, 2-7; and Ralph Bakshi, 7-11, 18-26; and *Big House Blues*, 57-68; creates Ren and Stimpy, 53-56; as director for DIC, 31-43; is fired by Nickelodeon, 184-92, 203-13; cofounds Spumco, 49-51; influence of, 299-301; and "Man's Best Friend", 173-84; and popularity of *Ren & Stimpy*, 139-45, 147-48; as producer/director during the first season of *Ren & Stimpy*, 75-113; as producer/director during the second season of *Ren & Stimpy*, 149-71, 192-203; and *Ren & Stimpy: Adult Party Cartoon*, 309-339
and *The Ripping Friends*, 306-08; sells *Ren & Stimpy* to Nickelodeon, 52-57; sues Viacom/MTV, 305; and "Stimpy's Invention", 115-30; and "A Visit to Anthony", 229-32
Kriegman, Mitchell, 78-83, 149
Kurtzman, Harvey, 84, 139

Lacewood (Ottawa animation studio), 90-91, 107
"Lair of the Lummox", 150, 168, 395
Lantz, Walter, xxii-xxiii, 269
"The Last Temptation", 249, 265, 430
Lawrence, Doug, 29, 155, 156, 186, 301
Laybourne, Geraldine, 51-53, 137, 148, 184
"The League of Super-Rodents", 19
Leonhardt, Warren, 314
The Little Mermaid, 46, 146
"The Littlest Giant", 94, 355
"The Littlest Tramp", 20, 22, 27-28
"Log", 108
Lorre, Chuck, 34-35
Lorre, Peter, 54, 101, 223

INDEX

Loter, Steve, 170, 246, 248, 252, 254, 255, 260, 261, 277, 289
"Lumber-Jerks", 401

MacCurdy, Jean, 48
McCracken, Craig, 300
McGrath, Tom, 246, 248, 252, 283, *285*, 286, 287
McRobb, Will, 82, 83, 100, 117, 148-51, 154, 174, 175, 193, 195, 212, 232, 329, 331
Macek, Carl, 50, 52, 53, 56, 57, 76, 84
"Mad Dog Höek", 160, 161, 369
"Magical Golden Singing Cheeses", 284, 403-04
"Man's Best Friend", 174-81, 183-85, 199, 224, 258, 331, 364-65
"Marooned", 99, 113, 356
Marren, Mark (a.k.a. "Kirk Field"), 253
Marvin Digs, 1
Mason, Jamie, 321-22
Mendelsohn, Brian, 264-65, 292
Mendonca, Helder, 313-14, 320, 328
Method, Greg, 179
MetroCel Animation Studios, 157, 224
"Me-Yowwww!", 19
Mighty Mouse: The New Adventures, 10-28
"Mighty's Benefit Plan", 20
"Mighty's Wedlock Whimsy", 28
Mildman, 55
Miller, Bob, 38
Minton, Tom, 6, 7, 12, 13, 14, 16, 27
Miyazaki, Hayao, 50, 118
"Monkey See, Monkey Don't!", 160, 185, 227, 372-73
Moore, Rich, 12
Muddy Mudskipper, 88, 102
Murray, Joe, 300
"My Shiny Friend", 277-79, *320*, 413-14
Mr. Big (animation studio), 253-54, 277
Mr. Horse, 89, 107, 158, 170, 326, 328
Mr. and Mrs. Pipe, 249

Naylor, Lynne, 3, 5, *6*, 7, 8, 10, 18, 38, *39*, 157, 174, 188, 235, 338; and cofounding Spumco, 49-50
and creating Ren and Stimpy, 54-55; at Games Animation, 281, 282, 291, 293-94; at Spumco, 57-58, 61, 85-87
The New Adventures of Beany & Cecil, 31-43
Nickelodeon, 137, 138, 238, 240, 242, 265, 299, 301, 302, 305, 310, 339; as network, 63-68, 76-83, 99, 108-13, 116-30, 147-54, 167-68, 201-05, 221, 224, 250-51, 260-61, 275-77, 295-96; buys *Ren & Stimpy*, 56-57; early days of, 51-53; fires John Kricfalusi, 184-92, 209-13
Nickelodeon's Thanksgiving Fest, 51
"Night of the Bat-Bat", 19-20

"Night on Bald Pate", 20
"No Pants Today", 274-75, 383-84
"Nurse Stimpy", 80, 94-95, 353

"Ol' Blue Nose", 255, 417
Oliff, Jamie, 90-91, 177
"Onward and Upward", 150, 310, 311, 312, 315, 316, 318-20, *319*, *323*, 325, 432
"Out West", 151, 160, 161, 162-63, *163*, 365-66
Owens, Gary, 208

"Pen Pals", 426-27
Pietila, David, 307
Pixar, 342-43
"Pixie King", 252, 411-12
Popular Animation, 6
Porch, Henry, 62, 65, 199-200
Powdered Toast Man (character), *107*, 108, 150, 208
"Powdered Toast Man" (episode), 145, 158, 181, *182*, 183, 362-63
"Powdered Toast Man Vs. Waffle Woman", 293-94, 406-07
The Predator, 52
"Prehistoric Stimpy", 249, 402-03
Price, Judy, 10, 28
A Pup Named Scooby Doo, 36
Pursel, Richard, 81, 83-84, 87, 157, 169-70, 205, 206, 207-08, 274-75, 294, 310, 312,
A Pup Named Scooby Doo, 31
Pursel, Richard, 144, 156, 186, 247, 264, 280, 281, 296, 329

Raimi, Sam, 302
Ratatouille, 342
Raynis, Richard, 33
Reardon, Jim, 12, 27, 28
Reccardi, 38, 46, 86, 207; at Games, 230, *231*, 232-35, *234*, 241, 243, *244*, *262*, 272-73, 281-82, 286, 288-95, *291*, *296*; at Spumco, 65-66, 76, 84, 94, 95, 101, 120, 155, 159, 164, 180, *180*, 188, 198-99

Red Rover (Toronto studio), 307
Reichek, Jordan, 59, 83, 85, 98, 119-20, 139, 188, 213
Ren Höek; origins of, 53-55
"Ren Needs Help!", 262, *262*, 294, 416
"Ren Seeks Help", 311, 315, 326-29, *327*, 432-33
"Ren's Bitter Half", 282-84, 286, 288, 394-95
"Ren's Brain", 294-95, 422-23
"Ren's Pecs", 384-85
"Ren's Retirement", 249, 275-76, 390-91
"Ren's Toothache", 363-64
"Reverend Jack", 263-65, 267-69, 427-28
The Ripping Friends, 50, 306-08, 311, 312, 318

"Road Apples", 248-49, 389-90
"Robin Höek", 94, 113, 174, 353
Rocko's Modern Life, 300
Rocky & Bullwinkle, 78, 108
Ross, Chris, 331
Roth, Ed, 126
Rough Draft, 158-59, 170, 180, 191, 224, 227, 229, 231, 241, 243, 246, 259, 274, 284, 303
"The Royal Canadian Kilted Yaksmen", 168, 224, 228, 231, 232-34, *234*, 288, 324, 377-78
"Rubber Nipple Salesmen", 149-50, 158, 164, 170, 366-67
Ruegger, Tom, 48
Rugrats, 53, 67, 68, 78, 91, 112, 113, 137, 206, 299

"Sammy and Me", 278, 279, 280, 429-30
Sauve, Chris, 103-04, 162, 176-77, 197, 234
Scannell, Herb, 147, 250, 260
"School Mates", 253, 257, 425
"A Scooter for Yaksmas", 296, 428-29
"The Scotsman in Space", 410-11
"Scrap Happy", 16
"Scrappy's Field Day", 17
Der Screamin' Lederhosen, 66, 198-99
Scribner, Rod, 336
The Secret of NIMH, 29
Seibert, Fred, 309
Shank, Don, 59, 95, 96, *143*, 166, 177, *178*, 207, 246, *247*, *278*, 281, 283, 293, 294
Shnookums & Meat Funny Cartoon Show, 300
Silver, Joel, 302
Simensky, Linda, 67, 81, 148, 149, 152, 167, 183, 185, 187, 303
Simon, Libby, 130, 151, 153, 205, 305, 306, 312-13
The Simpsons, 47, 49, 85, 139, 145, 146, 147, 204, 206, 301, 344
Smith, Jim, 8, 10, 18, 37, 39, 40, *98*, 162, 198-99, 211, 261, 301; and *Big House Blues*, 57-58, 61, 66; and "A Cartoon", 98; and "Fake Dad", 191, 224-26, *225*; and "Space Madness", 99, 101; and "A Visit to Anthony", *229*, 230; at Spumco, 77, 93, 94, 96, 98, 127, 157, 159, 164, 168, 179, 184, 185, 192-93, 200, 205, 206, 307, 310, 311, 312, 313, 330; cofounds Spumco, 49-50
Smith, Roy, 81, 97, 152-53, 183-84, 185, 186, 189, 206, 213
Snow White and the Seven Dwarfs, 146
Solomon, Charles, 25
"Son of Stimpy", 192-98, 201-03, 371-72
South Park, 301, 324
"Space Dogged", 255, 420
"Space Madness", 96, 100-107, *106*, 113, 179, 199, 294, 353-54
Spielberg, Steven, 29, 46, 48, 169
Spike TV, 309, 310, 316, 318, 324, 325, 331, 332, 333, 334, 337, 338, 339
SpongeBob Squarepants, 299, 343

Spumco; and *Big House Blues*, 57-68; bankruptcy of, 339; formation of, 49-51; environment of, 83-87, 95-97, 109-13, 145, 153-57, 301-02, 313-17, 330-31; and Nickelodeon, 51-53, 66-68, 78-83, 109-13, 147-53, 166-68, 178-92, 203-13; and production of *Ren & Stimpy*, 75-113, 115-30, 137-71, 173-213; and production of *Ren & Stimpy: Adult Party Cartoon*, 309-39; and transition to Games Animation, 184-92, 203-13
Stainton, Greg, 315, 334
Stanton, Andrew, 12
Stefanelli, Steve, 307-08, 314
Stimpson J. Cat; origins of, 53-55
"Stimpy's Big Day", 85-92, 352
"Stimpy's Cartoon Show", 150, 241, 242-44, *244*, 386-87
"Stimpy's Fan Club", 228-29, 375-76
"Stimpy's First Fart" (see "Son of Stimpy")
"Stimpy's Invention", 113, *116*, *119*, *122*, *125*, 175, 184, 283, 284, 294, 329, 358-59; making of, 115-130
"Stimpy's Pet", 255, 422
"Stimpy's Pregnant", 322, 326, 334-37, 435
Streamline Pictures, 50, 57, 62
"Stupid Sidekick Union", 286, 287, 417-18
"Superstitious Stimpy", 261-62, 418
"Svën Höek", 149, 161, 164, 165, 185, 191, 192-201, *194*, *196*, 223, 225, 283, 321, 329, 367-68

Tartakovsky, Genndy, 300
Ted Bakes One, *4*, 5, 344
"Terminal Stimpy", 254, 427
Terrytoons, 1, 12, 20, 26, 316
"This Island Mouseville", 17
The Three Stooges, 63, 321
Timm, Bruce, 18, 19, 35-36, 37, 39, 40, 41, 87, 93
Tin Pan Alley Cats, 8
Tiny Toon Adventures, 48, 50, 88, 91, 146, 169
TNN (see Spike TV)
Tortoise Wins By a Hare, 337
"To Salve and Salve Not!", 241, 242, 381
"Travelogue", 254, 419
Twisted Tales of Felix the Cat, 300
Trias, Jennie, 32, 34, 36, 41
Tyer, Jim, 316

"Untamed World" (see "A Cartoon")
United Productions of America (UPA), xxvi, 139, 292

Vaughns, Byron, 13, 20, 31
Ventura, Pat, 8

Vincent, John, 316
"A Visit to Anthony", 149, 168, 228, 229-31, *229*, *231*, 376-77

Waller, Vincent, 76, 77, 84, 97, 117, 150, *156*, 159, 164, 170, 171, 191, 205, 206, 210-11, 212, *214-16*, 223, 227, 310, 311, 312, 313, 318, *323*
Wang, James, 15, 39, 259
Wang, Teale, 85, 120, 140, 208, 239, 240
Ward, Jay, xxiv, 12, 27, 108
Weekend Pussy Hunt, 306
West, Billy, 63-64, 100, 101, 145, 176, 207, 208, 227, 261, 275-76, 292, 299, 309, 310-11, 328
Who Framed Roger Rabbit?, 45-49
"Who's Stupid Now?", 287-88, 424-25
"Wiener Barons", 415
Wilbur Cobb, 242-43, 249, 276
Wild Cartoon Kingdom, 211-12
"The Wilderness Adventure", 76, 317-18
Williams, Richard, 46, 335
Williams, Robin, 145
Wills, Scott, 155, 165, 196-97, 273-74
Woodside, Bruce, 15-18
Wray, Bill, 4-5, 84, 101, 102, 140, *144*, 174, 188, 198, 200, 207, 211, 223, 230, 249, 254, *278*, *280*, 306; at Games Animation, 208, 222, 238, 241, 242, 273-80, 287; at Spumco, 93-95, 164-65, 184, 191, 205

"A Yard Too Far", 241-42, 381-82
Yogi Bear, xxiv, 88, 242, 303
"You Are What You Eat", 293, 396
Your Gang, 52-56

Zappa, Frank, 145
Zemeckis, Robert, 46
Zorman, Ron, 103, 128, 243